PostgreSQL 9 Administration Cookbook
Second Edition

Over 150 recipes to help you run an efficient PostgreSQL database in the cloud

Simon Riggs

Gianni Ciolli

Hannu Krosing

Gabriele Bartolini

[PACKT] open source*
PUBLISHING   community experience distilled

BIRMINGHAM - MUMBAI

PostgreSQL 9 Administration Cookbook
Second Edition

First published: October 2010

Second edition: April 2015

Production reference: 1280415

Published by Packt Publishing Ltd.
Livery Place
35 Livery Street
Birmingham B3 2PB, UK.

ISBN 978-1-84951-906-9

www.packtpub.com

Credits

Authors
Simon Riggs
Gianni Ciolli
Hannu Krosing
Gabriele Bartolini

Reviewers
Atdhe Buja MSc
Jérôme Étévé
Piotr Isajew
Dmitry Spikhalskiy
Enrique Vidal
Qingqing Zhou

Commissioning Editor
Sarah Cullington

Acquisition Editor
Rebecca Youé

Content Development Editor
Ruchita Bhansali

Technical Editor
Taabish Khan

Copy Editor
Vikrant Phadke

Project Coordinator
Kranti Berde

Proofreaders
Maria Gould
Linda Morris

Indexer
Tejal Soni

Production Coordinator
Nitesh Thakur

Cover Work
Nitesh Thakur

About the Authors

Simon Riggs is the CTO of 2ndQuadrant and an active PostgreSQL committer. He has contributed to PostgreSQL as a major developer for more than 10 years, having written and designed many new features in every release over that period. His feature credits include replication, performance, business intelligence, management, and security. Under his guidance, 2ndQuadrant is now a leading developer of open source PostgreSQL and a platinum sponsor of the PostgreSQL Project, serving hundreds of clients in USA, Europe, Asia-Pacific, the Middle East, and Africa.

Simon is a frequent speaker at many conferences and is well known for his speeches on PostgreSQL Futures and different aspects of replication. He has worked with many different databases as a developer, architect, data analyst, and designer with companies across USA and Europe for nearly 30 years.

Thanks to my clients for trusting me with hard problems, having faith, and giving me the energy to solve them; every one of you has helped me. Thanks to my friends and colleagues at 2ndQuadrant for such strong teamwork and the PostgreSQL Community for your belief in community. Lastly, thanks to my family for everything!

Gianni Ciolli is a principal consultant at 2ndQuadrant Italia, where he has been working since 2008 as a developer, consultant, and trainer. He has spoken at PostgreSQL conferences in Europe and abroad, and his other IT skills include functional languages and symbolic computing.

Gianni has a PhD in mathematics, and is the author of published research on Algebraic Geometry, Theoretical Physics, and Formal Proof Theory. He previously worked at the University of Florence as a researcher and teacher.

Gianni has been working on free and open source software for almost 20 years. From 2001 to 2004, he was a cofounder and the president of PLUG, short for Prato Linux User Group. He organized many sessions of the Italian PostgreSQL conference, and in 2013, he was elected to the board of ITPUG, the Italian PostgreSQL Users Group.

He currently lives in London with his son. His other interests include music, drama, poetry, and sport—athletics in particular, where he competes in combined events.

First, I wish to thank all the persons whose dedication and knowledge have helped me learn everything so far: my colleagues at 2ndQuadrant, the members of the PostgreSQL community, and also my former colleagues and teachers.

I am grateful for what was shared with me, and also for being given the opportunity to find useful applications.

Hannu Krosing is a principal consultant at 2ndQuadrant and a technical advisor at Ambient Sound Investments. As the original database architect at Skype Technologies, he was responsible for designing the SkyTools suite of replication and scalability technology. He has worked with and contributed to the PostgreSQL project for more than 12 years.

Gabriele Bartolini is a long-time open source programmer, a principal consultant with 2ndQuadrant, and an active member of the international PostgreSQL community.

Gabriele has a degree in statistics from the University of Florence. His areas of expertise are data mining and data warehousing, and he has worked on web traffic analysis in Australia and Italy.

He currently lives in Prato, a small but vibrant city located in the northern part of Tuscany, Italy. His second home is Melbourne, Australia, where he studied at Monash University and worked in the ICT sector. Gabriele's hobbies include playing his Fender Stratocaster electric guitar and "calcio" (football or soccer, depending on which part of the world you come from).

Thanks to my family, especially my wife, Cathy, who always encourages me to learn something new. Thanks to all the members of 2ndQuadrant, particularly the Italian team; all of you are fantastic people who share the same vision and passion for PostgreSQL, Linux, and open source software.

About the Reviewers

Atdhe Buja MSc is a certified ethical hacker, DBA (MCITP, OCA11g), and manager with good management skills. He is a DBA at the Ministry of Public Administration, Pristina, Republic of Kosovo, where he manages some e-governance projects. He has 10 years of experience in databases and SQL Server.

Atdhe is an active contributor to the Albanian ICT Awards (www.ictawards.com) and is a regular columnist for the newspaper of University for Business and Technology, Pristina. He holds an MSc in computer science and engineering and a bachelor's in management and information. He is pursuing a bachelor's in political science at the University of Pristina.

He specializes in, and is certified in, many technologies such as SQL Server 2000-2005-2008 R2, Oracle 11g, CEH, Windows Server, Microsoft Project, System Center, and BizTalk Server.

I would like to thank my wife, Donika, for encouraging me and my Buja family for their support.

Jérôme Étévé is a full stack web application developer with a wide range of technological interests. After getting a master's degree in bioinformatics from the University of Lille, France, in 2002, he began developing web applications for the corporate sector and the general public, which he has been doing until now. He currently works at Broadbean, a recruitment technology company in London. He regularly creates and shares open source software on his GitHub account (`jeteve`), and he has reviewed the last two Solr Enterprise Server books by Packt Publishing. As far as RDBMS systems are concerned, he is a keen advocate and enthusiastic user of PostgreSQL.

> I'd like to thank my wife, Joanna, for drip-feeding me with tea during the hours I spent reviewing this book.

Piotr Isajew is a mobile technology expert with several years of expertise in mobile and messaging projects. He gained his skills while working for media and mobile marketing companies, and now he runs his own IT consulting business.

Piotr's first encounter with PostgreSQL was in 1997, and after a short trial period, it became his RDBMS of choice. Since then, he has used PostgreSQL in every server-side project he has been responsible for and knows it well from both the administration and application development perspectives.

Piotr can be contacted by e-mail at `info@ex.com.pl`.

Dmitry Spikhalskiy is currently a software engineer at the Russian social network, Odnoklassniki, and is working on a search engine, video recommendation system, and movie content analysis.

Previously, Dmitry took part in developing Mind Labs' platform, infrastructure, and benchmarks for high-load videoconferencing and streaming services, which entered the Guinness Book of World Records as "The biggest online training in the world", with more than 12,000 participants. He launched a mobile social banking start-up, called Instabank, as a technical lead and architect. He has also reviewed *Learning Google Guice, Packt Publishing*.

Dmitry has graduated from Moscow State University with an MSc degree in computer science, where he first developed an interest in parallel data processing, high-load systems, and databases.

Enrique Vidal is a software engineer from Tijuana. He has worked on web development and system administration for many years, and he focuses on Ruby and CoffeeScript development these days.

Enrique feels fortunate to work alongside great developers such as this book's author and in different companies in the United States and México. He enjoys challenges such as coding payment systems, online invoicing, and social networking applications. He is fond of helping start-ups at an early stage and actively supporting open source projects.

I'd like to thank Packt Publishing and the author for allowing me to be part of this book's technical reviewing team.

Qingqing Zhou has worked on database engine implementation for more than 15 years. He has hands-on experience in academic prototypes, database startup, PostgreSQL, and Microsoft SQL Server's internals, particularly in terms of performance and scalability. He is currently leading an effort in Huawei to build a cloud-scale parallel database system, targeting a wide spectrum of interactive analytical applications. In his spare time, Qingqing enjoys arts, soccer, fishing, hiking, family time, and everything that has elegance.

Thanks to my family, particularly my wife, Hongyu, and my dear daughter, Hana, for supporting me in the nontechnical side of my life.

www.PacktPub.com

Support files, eBooks, discount offers, and more

For support files and downloads related to your book, please visit www.PacktPub.com.

Did you know that Packt offers eBook versions of every book published, with PDF and ePub files available? You can upgrade to the eBook version at www.PacktPub.com and as a print book customer, you are entitled to a discount on the eBook copy. Get in touch with us at service@packtpub.com for more details.

At www.PacktPub.com, you can also read a collection of free technical articles, sign up for a range of free newsletters and receive exclusive discounts and offers on Packt books and eBooks.

https://www2.packtpub.com/books/subscription/packtlib

Do you need instant solutions to your IT questions? PacktLib is Packt's online digital book library. Here, you can search, access, and read Packt's entire library of books.

Why Subscribe?

- ▸ Fully searchable across every book published by Packt
- ▸ Copy and paste, print, and bookmark content
- ▸ On demand and accessible via a web browser

Free Access for Packt account holders

If you have an account with Packt at www.PacktPub.com, you can use this to access PacktLib today and view 9 entirely free books. Simply use your login credentials for immediate access.

Table of Contents

Preface

PostgreSQL is an advanced SQL database server available on a wide range of platforms, and is fast becoming one of the world's most popular server databases, with an enviable reputation for performance, stability, and an enormous range of advanced features. PostgreSQL is one of the oldest open source projects, completely free to use, and developed by a very diverse worldwide community. Most of all, it just works!

One of the clearest benefits of PostgreSQL is that it is open source, meaning that you have a very permissive license to install, use, and distribute PostgreSQL without paying anyone any fees or royalties. On top of that, PostgreSQL is well-known as a database that stays up for long periods, and requires little or no maintenance in many cases. Overall, PostgreSQL provides a very low total cost of ownership.

PostgreSQL 9 Administration Cookbook Second Edition offers the information you need to manage your live production databases on PostgreSQL. The book contains insights straight from the main author of the PostgreSQL replication and recovery features, and the database architect of the most successful start-up that uses PostgreSQL: Skype. This hands-on guide will assist developers working on live databases, supporting web or enterprise software applications using Java, Python, Ruby, and .NET from any development framework. It's easy to manage your database when you've got *PostgreSQL 9 Administration Cookbook Second Edition* at hand.

This practical guide gives you quick answers to common questions and problems, building on the authors' experience as trainers, users, and core developers of the PostgreSQL database server.

Each technical aspect is broken down into short recipes that demonstrate solutions with working code, and then explain why and how they work. This book is intended to be a desk reference for both new users and technical experts.

The book covers all the latest features available in PostgreSQL 9. Soon, you will be running a smooth database with ease.

What this book covers

Chapter 1, First Steps, covers topics such as introduction to PostgreSQL 9, downloading and installing PostgreSQL 9, connecting to a PostgreSQL server, enabling server access to network/remote users, using graphical administration tools, using the psql query and scripting tools, changing your password securely, avoiding hardcoding your password, using a connection service file, and troubleshooting a failed connection.

Chapter 2, Exploring the Database, helps you identify the version of the database server you are using and also the server uptime. This chapter helps you locate the database server files, database server message log, and database's system identifier. It shows you how to list a database on the database server and contains recipes that let you know the number of tables in your database, how much disk space is used by the database and tables, which are the biggest tables, how many rows a table has, how to estimate rows in a table, and how to understand object dependencies.

Chapter 3, Configuration, covers topics such as reading the fine manual (RTFM), planning a new database, changing parameters in your programs, the current configuration settings, parameters that are at non-default settings, updating the parameter file, setting parameters for particular groups of users, the basic server configuration checklist, and adding an external module to the PostgreSQL server.

Chapter 4, Server Control, provides information about starting the database server manually, stopping the server quickly and safely, stopping the server in an emergency, reloading the server configuration files, restarting the server quickly, preventing new connections, restricting users to one session each, and pushing users off the system. It contains recipes that help you decide on a design for multitenancy. You can learn how to use multiple schemas, give users their own private database, run multiple database servers on one system, and set up a connection pool.

Chapter 5, Tables and Data, guides you through the process of choosing good names for database objects, handling objects with quoted names, enforcing the same name and the same definition for columns, identifying and removing duplicate rows, preventing duplicate rows, finding a unique key for a set of data, generating test data, randomly sampling data, loading data from a spreadsheet, and loading data from flat files.

Chapter 6, Security, provides recipes on revoking user access to a table, granting user access to a table, creating a new user, temporarily preventing a user from connecting, removing a user without dropping their data, checking whether all users have a secure password, giving limited superuser powers to specific users, auditing DDL changes, auditing data changes, integrating with LDAP, connecting using SSL, and encrypting sensitive data.

Chapter 7, Database Administration, covers useful topics such as writing a script wherein either all succeed or all fail, writing a psql script that exits immediately after the first error, performing actions on many tables, adding or removing columns from tables, changing the data type of a column, adding or removing schemas, moving objects between schemas, adding or removing tablespaces, moving objects between tablespaces, accessing objects in other PostgreSQL databases, and making views updatable.

Chapter 8, Monitoring and Diagnosis, provides recipes that answer questions such as, "Is the user connected? What are they running? Are they active or blocked? Who is blocking them? Is anybody using a specific table? When did anybody last use it? How much disk space is used by temporary data? And why are my queries slowing down?" It also helps you with investigating and reporting a bug, producing a daily summary report of log file errors, killing a specific session, and resolving an in-doubt prepared transaction.

Chapter 9, Regular Maintenance, includes useful recipes on controlling automatic database maintenance, avoiding auto-freezing and page corruptions, avoiding transaction wraparound, removing old prepared transactions, actions for heavy users of temporary tables, identifying and fixing bloated tables and indexes, maintaining indexes, finding unused indexes, carefully removing unwanted indexes, and planning maintenance.

Chapter 10, Performance and Concurrency, covers topics such as finding slow SQL statements, collecting regular statistics from pg_stat* views, finding out what makes SQL slow, reducing the number of rows returned, simplifying complex SQL code, speeding up queries without rewriting them, finding out why a query is not using an index, forcing a query to use an index, using optimistic locking, and reporting performance problems.

Chapter 11, Backup and Recovery, provides useful information about backup and recovery of your PostgreSQL database through recipes on understanding and controlling crash recovery, planning backups, hot logical backup of one database, hot logical backup of all databases, hot logical backup of all tables in a tablespace, backup of database object definitions, standalone hot physical database backup, and hot physical backup and continuous archiving. It also includes topics such as recovery of all databases; recovery to a point in time; recovery of a dropped or damaged table, database, or tablespace; improving performance of backup and recovery; and incremental/differential backup and restore.

Chapter 12, Replication and Upgrades, covers replication best practices; setting up file-based or streaming replication; setting up streaming replication security; Hot Standby and read scalability; managing Streaming Replication; using repmgr; using replication slots; monitoring replication; performance and synchronous replication; delaying, pausing, and synchronizing replication; Logical Replication; Bi-Directional Replication; archiving transaction log data, upgrading minor release upgrades, and major release upgrades, both in-place and online.

What you need for this book

You'll need the following pieces of software for this book:

- ▶ PostgreSQL 9.4 server software
- ▶ psql client utility (a part of 9.4)
- ▶ pgAdmin3 1.20

Who this book is for

This book is for system administrators, database administrators, architects, developers, and anyone with an interest in planning for, or running, live production databases. This book is most suited to those who have some technical experience.

Sections

In this book, you will find several headings that appear frequently (Getting ready, How to do it, How it works, There's more, and See also).

To give clear instructions on how to complete a recipe, we use the following sections.

Getting ready

This section tells you what to expect in the recipe, and describes how to set up any software or any preliminary settings required for the recipe.

How to do it...

This section contains the steps required to follow the recipe.

How it works...

This section usually consists of a detailed explanation of what happened in the previous section.

There's more...

This section consists of additional information about the recipe in order to make you more knowledgeable about the recipe.

See also

This section provides helpful links to other useful information for the recipe.

Conventions

In this book, you will find a number of text styles that distinguish between different kinds of information. Here are some examples of these styles and an explanation of their meaning.

Code words in text, database table names, folder names, filenames, file extensions, pathnames, dummy URLs, user input, and Twitter handles are shown as follows: "The service can also be set using an environment variable named `PGSERVICE`."

A block of code is set as follows:

```
[dbservice1]
host=postgres1
port=5432
dbname=postgres
```

When we wish to draw your attention to a particular part of a code block, the relevant lines or items are set in bold:

```
Database system identifier:         5805760367713220187
Database cluster state:             in production
```

Any command-line input or output is written as follows:

```
$ psql -c "SELECT current_time"
```

New terms and **important words** are shown in bold. Words that you see on the screen, for example, in menus or dialog boxes, appear in the text like this: "Keep the **Guru Hints** option on."

Warnings or important notes appear in a box like this.

Tips and tricks appear like this.

Reader feedback

Feedback from our readers is always welcome. Let us know what you think about this book—what you liked or disliked. Reader feedback is important for us as it helps us develop titles that you will really get the most out of.

To send us general feedback, simply e-mail `feedback@packtpub.com`, and mention the book's title in the subject of your message.

If there is a topic that you have expertise in and you are interested in either writing or contributing to a book, see our author guide at `www.packtpub.com/authors`.

Customer support

Now that you are the proud owner of a Packt book, we have a number of things to help you to get the most from your purchase.

Downloading the example code

You can download the example code files from your account at `http://www.packtpub.com` for all the Packt Publishing books you have purchased. If you purchased this book elsewhere, you can visit `http://www.packtpub.com/support` and register to have the files e-mailed directly to you.

Errata

Although we have taken every care to ensure the accuracy of our content, mistakes do happen. If you find a mistake in one of our books—maybe a mistake in the text or the code—we would be grateful if you could report this to us. By doing so, you can save other readers from frustration and help us improve subsequent versions of this book. If you find any errata, please report them by visiting `http://www.packtpub.com/submit-errata`, selecting your book, clicking on the **Errata Submission Form** link, and entering the details of your errata. Once your errata are verified, your submission will be accepted and the errata will be uploaded to our website or added to any list of existing errata under the Errata section of that title.

To view the previously submitted errata, go to `https://www.packtpub.com/books/content/support` and enter the name of the book in the search field. The required information will appear under the **Errata** section.

Piracy

Piracy of copyrighted material on the Internet is an ongoing problem across all media. At Packt, we take the protection of our copyright and licenses very seriously. If you come across any illegal copies of our works in any form on the Internet, please provide us with the location address or website name immediately so that we can pursue a remedy.

Please contact us at copyright@packtpub.com with a link to the suspected pirated material.

We appreciate your help in protecting our authors and our ability to bring you valuable content.

Questions

If you have a problem with any aspect of this book, you can contact us at questions@packtpub.com, and we will do our best to address the problem.

1
First Steps

In this chapter, we will cover the following recipes:

- Getting PostgreSQL
- Connecting to the PostgreSQL server
- Enabling access for network/remote users
- Using graphical administration tools
- Using the psql query and scripting tool
- Changing your password securely
- Avoiding hardcoding your password
- Using a connection service file
- Troubleshooting a failed connection

Introduction

PostgreSQL is a feature-rich, general-purpose database management system. It's a complex piece of software, but every journey begins with the first step.

We'll start with your first connection. Many people fall at the first hurdle, so we'll try not to skip that too swiftly. We'll quickly move on to enabling remote users, and from there, we will move to access through GUI administration tools.

We will also introduce the **psql** query tool, which is the tool used to load our sample database, as well as many other examples in the book.

For additional help, we've included a few useful recipes that you may need for reference.

Introducing PostgreSQL 9

PostgreSQL is an advanced SQL database server, available on a wide range of platforms. One of the clearest benefits of PostgreSQL is that it is open source, meaning that you have a very permissive license to install, use, and distribute PostgreSQL without paying anyone fees or royalties. On top of that, PostgreSQL is well-known as a database that stays up for long periods and requires little or no maintenance in most cases. Overall, PostgreSQL provides a very low total cost of ownership.

PostgreSQL is also noted for its huge range of advanced features, developed over the course of more than 20 years of continuous development and enhancement. Originally developed by the Database Research Group at the University of California, Berkeley, PostgreSQL is now developed and maintained by a huge army of developers and contributors. Many of those contributors have full-time jobs related to PostgreSQL, working as designers, developers, database administrators, and trainers. Some, but not many, of those contributors work for companies that specialize in support for PostgreSQL, like we (the authors) do. No single company owns PostgreSQL, nor are you required (or even encouraged) to register your usage.

PostgreSQL has the following main features:

- ▶ Excellent SQL standards compliance up to SQL:2011
- ▶ Client-server architecture
- ▶ Highly concurrent design where readers and writers don't block each other
- ▶ Highly configurable and extensible for many types of applications
- ▶ Excellent scalability and performance with extensive tuning features
- ▶ Support for many kinds of data models: relational, document (JSON and XML), and key/value

What makes PostgreSQL different?

The PostgreSQL project focuses on the following objectives:

- ▶ Robust, high-quality software with maintainable, well-commented code
- ▶ Low maintenance administration for both embedded and enterprise use
- ▶ Standards-compliant SQL, interoperability, and compatibility
- ▶ Performance, security, and high availability

What surprises many people is that PostgreSQL's feature set is more comparable with Oracle or SQL Server than it is with MySQL. The only connection between MySQL and PostgreSQL is that these two projects are open source; apart from that, the features and philosophies are almost totally different.

One of the key features of Oracle, since Oracle 7, has been **snapshot isolation**, where readers don't block writers and writers don't block readers. You may be surprised to learn that PostgreSQL was the first database to be designed with this feature, and it offers a complete implementation. In PostgreSQL, this feature is called **Multiversion Concurrency Control (MVCC)**, and we will discuss this in more detail later in this book.

PostgreSQL is a general-purpose database management system. You define the database that you would like to manage with it. PostgreSQL offers you many ways to work. You can use a *normalized database model*, augmented with features such as arrays and record subtypes, or use a fully dynamic schema with the help of JSONB and an extension named **hstore**. PostgreSQL also allows you to create your own server-side functions in any of a dozen different languages.

PostgreSQL is highly extensible, so you can add your own data types, operators, index types, and functional languages. You can even override different parts of the system using plugins to alter the execution of commands or add a new optimizer.

All of these features offer a huge range of implementation options to software architects. There are many ways out of trouble when building applications and maintaining them over long periods of time. Regrettably, we simply don't have space in this book for all the cool features for developers; this book is about administration, maintenance, and backup.

In the early days, when PostgreSQL was still a research database, the focus was solely on the cool new features. Over the last 15 years, enormous amounts of code have been rewritten and improved, giving us one of the most stable and largest software servers available for operational use.

You may have read that PostgreSQL was, or is, slower than My Favorite DBMS, whichever that is. It's been a personal mission of mine over the last ten years to improve server performance, and the team has been successful in making the server highly performant and very scalable. That gives PostgreSQL enormous headroom for growth.

Who is using PostgreSQL? Prominent users include Apple, BASF, Genentech, Heroku, IMDB. com, Skype, McAfee, NTT, The UK Met Office, and The U. S. National Weather Service. 5 years ago, PostgreSQL received well in excess of 1 million downloads per year, according to data submitted to the European Commission, which concluded, "PostgreSQL is considered by many database users to be a credible alternative."

We need to mention one last thing. When PostgreSQL was first developed, it was named Postgres, and therefore many aspects of the project still refer to the word "postgres"; for example, the default database is named `postgres`, and the software is frequently installed using the postgres user ID. As a result, people shorten the name PostgreSQL to simply Postgres, and in many cases use the two names interchangeably.

PostgreSQL is pronounced as "post-grez-q-l". Postgres is pronounced as "post-grez."

Some people get confused, and refer to "Postgre", which is hard to say, and likely to confuse people. Two names are enough, so please don't use a third name!

The following sections explain the key areas in more detail.

Robustness

PostgreSQL is robust, high-quality software, supported by automated testing for both features and concurrency. By default, the database provides strong disk-write guarantees, and the developers take the risk of data loss very seriously in everything they do. Options to trade robustness for performance exist, though they are not enabled by default.

All actions on the database are performed within transactions, protected by a transaction log that will perform automatic crash recovery in case of software failure.

Databases may be optionally created with data block checksums to help diagnose hardware faults. Multiple backup mechanisms exist, with full and detailed Point-In-Time Recovery, in case of the need for detailed recovery. A variety of diagnostic tools are available.

Database replication is supported natively. Synchronous Replication can provide greater than "5 Nines" (99.999 percent) availability and data protection, if properly configured and managed.

Security

Access to PostgreSQL is controllable via host-based access rules. Authentication is flexible and pluggable, allowing easy integration with any external security architecture.

Full SSL-encrypted access is supported natively. A full-featured cryptographic function library is available for database users.

PostgreSQL provides role-based access privileges to access data, by command type.

Functions may execute with the permissions of the definer, while views may be defined with security barriers to ensure that security is enforced ahead of other processing.

All aspects of PostgreSQL are assessed by an active security team, while known exploits are categorized and reported at `http://www.postgresql.org/support/security/`.

Ease of use

Clear, full, and accurate documentation exists as a result of a development process where doc changes are required. Hundreds of small changes occur with each release that smooth off any rough edges of usage, supplied directly by knowledgeable users.

PostgreSQL works in the same way on small or large systems and across operating systems.

Client access and drivers exist for every language and environment, so there is no restriction on what type of development environment is chosen now, or in the future.

SQL Standard is followed very closely; there is no weird behavior, such as silent truncation of data.

Text data is supported via a single data type that allows storage of anything from 1 byte to 1 gigabyte. This storage is optimized in multiple ways, so 1 byte is stored efficiently, and much larger values are automatically managed and compressed.

PostgreSQL has a clear policy to minimize the number of configuration parameters, and with each release, we work out ways to auto-tune settings.

Extensibility

PostgreSQL is designed to be highly extensible. Database extensions can be loaded simply and easily using CREATE EXTENSION, which automates version checks, dependencies, and other aspects of configuration.

PostgreSQL supports user-defined data types, operators, indexes, functions and languages.

Many extensions are available for PostgreSQL, including the PostGIS extension that provides world-class **Geographical Information System** (**GIS**) features.

Performance and concurrency

PostgreSQL 9.4 can achieve more than 300,000 reads per second on a 32-CPU server, and it benchmarks at more than 20,000 write transactions per second with full durability.

PostgreSQL has an advanced optimizer that considers a variety of join types, utilizing user data statistics to guide its choices.

PostgreSQL provides MVCC, which enables readers and writers to avoid blocking each other.

Taken together, the performance features of PostgreSQL allow a mixed workload of transactional systems and complex search and analytical tasks. This is important because it means we don't always need to unload our data from production systems and reload them into analytical data stores just to execute a few ad hoc queries. PostgreSQL's capabilities make it the database of choice for new systems, as well as the right long-term choice in almost every case.

Scalability

PostgreSQL 9.4 scales well on a single node up to 32 CPUs. PostgreSQL scales well up to hundreds of active sessions, and up to thousands of connected sessions when using a session pool. Further scalability is achieved in each annual release.

PostgreSQL provides multinode read scalability using the **Hot Standby** feature. Multinode write scalability is under active development. The starting point for this is Bi-Directional Replication (discussed in *Chapter 12, Replication and Upgrades*).

SQL and NoSQL

PostgreSQL follows SQL Standard very closely. SQL itself does not force any particular type of model to be used, so PostgreSQL can easily be used for many types of models at the same time, in the same database. PostgreSQL supports the more normal SQL language statement.

With PostgreSQL acting as a relational database, we can utilize any level of denormalization, from the full Third Normal Form, to the more normalized Star Schema models. PostgreSQL extends the relational model to provide arrays, row types, and range types.

A document-centric database is also possible using PostgreSQL's text, XML, and binary JSON (JSONB) data types, supported by indexes optimized for documents and by full text search capabilities.

Key/value stores are supported using the hstore extension.

Popularity

When MySQL was taken over some years back, it was agreed in the EU monopoly investigation that followed that PostgreSQL was a viable competitor. That's been certainly true, with the PostgreSQL user base expanding consistently for more than a decade.

Various polls have indicated that PostgreSQL is the favorite database for building new, enterprise-class applications. The PostgreSQL feature set attracts serious users who have serious applications. Financial services companies may be PostgreSQL's largest user group, though governments, telecommunication companies, and many other segments are strong users as well. This popularity extends across the world; Japan, Ecuador, Argentina, and Russia have very large user groups, and so do USA, Europe, and Australasia.

Amazon Web Services' chief technology officer Dr. Werner Vogels described PostgreSQL as "an amazing database", going on to say that "PostgreSQL has become the preferred open source relational database for many enterprise developers and start-ups, powering leading geospatial and mobile applications".

Commercial support

Many people have commented that strong commercial support is what enterprises need before they can invest in open source technology. Strong support is available worldwide from a number of companies.

2ndQuadrant provides commercial support for open source PostgreSQL, offering 24 x 7 support in English and Spanish with bug-fix resolution times.

EnterpriseDB provides commercial support for PostgreSQL as well as their main product, which is a variant of Postgres that offers enhanced Oracle compatibility.

Many other companies provide strong and knowledgeable support to specific geographic regions, vertical markets, and specialized technology stacks.

PostgreSQL is also available as hosted or cloud solutions from a variety of companies, since it runs very well in cloud environments.

A full list of companies is kept up to date at `http://www.postgresql.org/support/professional_support/`.

Research and development funding

PostgreSQL was originally developed as a research project at the University of California, Berkeley in the late 1980s and early 1990s. Further work was carried out by volunteers until the late 1990s. Then, the first professional developer became involved. Over time, more and more companies and research groups became involved, supporting many professional contributors. Further funding for research and development was provided by the NSF. The project also received funding from the EU FP7 Programme in the form of the 4CaaST project for cloud computing and the AXLE project for scalable data analytics. AXLE deserves a special mention because it is a 3-year project aimed at enhancing PostgreSQL's business intelligence capabilities, specifically for very large databases. The project covers security, privacy, integration with data mining, and visualization tools and interfaces for new hardware. Further details of it are available at `http://www.axleproject.eu`.

Other funding for PostgreSQL development comes from users who directly sponsor features and companies selling products and services based around PostgreSQL.

Getting PostgreSQL

PostgreSQL is 100 percent open source software.

PostgreSQL is freely available to use, alter, or redistribute in any way you choose. Its license is an approved open source license, very similar to the **Berkeley Distribution Software** (**BSD**) license, though only just different enough that it is now known as **The PostgreSQL License** (**TPL**).

How to do it...

PostgreSQL is already being used by many different application packages, so you may find it already installed on your servers. Many Linux distributions include PostgreSQL as part of the basic installation, or include it with the installation disk.

One thing to be wary of, is that the version of PostgreSQL included may not be the latest release. It will typically be the latest major release that was available when that operating system release was published. There is usually no good reason to stick to that level—there is no increased stability implied there—and later production versions are just as well supported by the various Linux distributions as the earlier versions.

If you don't have a copy yet, or you don't have the latest version, you can download the source code or binary packages for a wide variety of operating systems from `http://www.postgresql.org/download/`.

Installation details vary significantly from platform to platform, and there aren't any special tricks or recipes to mention. Just follow the installation guide, and away you go! We've consciously avoided describing the installation processes here to make sure we don't garble or override the information published to assist you.

If you would like to receive e-mail updates of the latest news, then you can subscribe to the PostgreSQL announce mailing list, which contains updates from all the vendors that support PostgreSQL. You'll get a few e-mails each month about new releases of core PostgreSQL, related software, conferences, and user group information. It's worth keeping in touch with these developments.

 For more information about the PostgreSQL announce mailing list, visit `http://archives.postgresql.org/pgsql-announce/`.

How it works...

Many people ask questions such as "how can this be free?", "are you sure I don't have to pay someone?", or "who gives this stuff away for nothing?"

Open source applications such as PostgreSQL work on a community basis, where many contributors perform tasks that make the whole process work. For many of those people, their involvement is professional, rather a hobby, and they can do this because there is generally a great value for both contributors and their employers alike.

You might not believe it. You don't have to, because It Just Works!

There's more...

Remember that PostgreSQL is more than just the core software. There is a huge range of websites offering add-ons, extensions, and tools for PostgreSQL. You'll also find an army of bloggers describing useful tricks and discoveries that will help you in your work.

Besides, there is a range of professional companies that are able to offer you help when you need it.

Connecting to the PostgreSQL server

How do we access PostgreSQL?

Connecting to the database is most people's first experience of PostgreSQL, so we want to make it a good one. Let's do it now and fix any problems we have along the way. Remember that a connection needs to be made securely, so there may be some hoops for us to jump through to ensure that the data we wish to access is secure.

Before we can execute commands against the database, we need to connect to the database server, giving us a session.

Sessions are designed to be long-lived, so you connect once, perform many requests, and eventually disconnect. There is a small overhead during connection. It may become noticeable if you connect and disconnect repeatedly, so you may wish to investigate the use of connection pools. Connection pools allow preconnected sessions to be served quickly to you when you wish to reconnect.

Getting ready

First, catch your database. If you don't know where it is, you'll probably have difficulty accessing it. There may be more than one database, and you'll need to know the right one to access and have the authority to connect to it.

How to do it...

You need to specify the following parameters to connect to PostgreSQL:

- Host or host address
- Port
- Database name
- User
- Password (or other means of authentication, if any)

To connect, there must be a PostgreSQL server running on host, listening to port number `port`. On that server, a database named `dbname` and a user named `user` must also exist. The host must explicitly allow connections from your client (this is explained in the next recipe), and you must also pass authentication using the method the server specifies; for example, specifying a password won't work if the server has requested a different form of authentication.

Almost all PostgreSQL interfaces use the `libpq` interface library. When using `libpq`, most of the connection parameter handling is identical, so we can discuss that just once.

If you don't specify the preceding parameters, PostgreSQL looks for values set through environment variables, which are as follows:

- ▶ PGHOST or PGHOSTADDR
- ▶ PGPORT (set this to `5432` if it is not set already)
- ▶ PGDATABASE
- ▶ PGUSER
- ▶ PGPASSWORD (this is definitely not recommended)

If you specify the first four parameters somehow but not the password, then PostgreSQL looks for a password file, discussed in the *Avoiding hardcoding your password* recipe.

Some PostgreSQL interfaces use the client-server protocol directly, so the way defaults are handled may differ. The information we need to supply won't vary significantly, so check the exact syntax for that interface.

Starting from PostgreSQL 9.2, connection details can also be specified using a URI format, as follows:

```
psql postgresql://myuser:mypasswd@myhost:5432/mydb
```

This specifies that we will connect to PostgreSQL using the `myhost` host, `5432` port, `mydb` database name, `myuser` user, and `mypasswd` password.

How it works...

PostgreSQL is a client-server database. The system it runs on is known as the host. We can access the PostgreSQL server remotely through the network. However, we must specify `host`, which is a hostname, or `hostaddr`, which is an IP address. We can specify a host as `localhost` if we wish to make a TCP/IP connection to the same system. It is often better to use a Unix socket connection, which is attempted if the host begins with a slash (/) and the name is presumed to be a directory name (default is `/tmp`).

On any system, there can be more than one database server. Each database server listens to exactly one "well-known" network port, which cannot be shared between servers on the same system. The default port number for PostgreSQL is `5432`, which has been registered with IANA and is uniquely assigned to PostgreSQL (you can see it used in the `/etc/services` file on most *nix servers). The port number can be used to uniquely identify a specific database server if many exist. IANA is the acronym for Internet Assigned Numbers Authority (http://www.iana.org), the organization that coordinates the allocation of available numbers for various Internet protocols.

A database server is also sometimes known as a "database cluster", because the PostgreSQL server allows you to define one or more databases on each server. Each connection request must identify exactly one database identified by its dbname. When you connect, you will be able to see only the database objects created within that database.

A database user is used to identify the connection. By default, there is no limit on the number of connections for a particular user; in a later recipe, we will cover how to restrict that. In the more recent versions of PostgreSQL, users are referred to as login roles, though many clues remind us of the earlier nomenclature, and that still makes sense in many ways. A login role is a role that has been assigned the CONNECT privilege.

Each connection will typically be authenticated in some way. This is defined at server level: client authentication will not be optional at connection time, if the administrator has configured the server to require it.

Once you've connected, each connection can have one active transaction at a time and one fully active statement at any time.

The server will have a defined limit on the number of connections it can serve, so a connection request can be refused if the server is oversubscribed.

There's more...

If you are already connected to a database server with psql and you want to confirm that you've connected to the right place and in the right way, you can execute some, or all, of the following commands. Here is the command that shows the current database:

```
SELECT current_database();
```

The following command shows the current user ID:

```
SELECT current_user;
```

The next command shows the IP address and port of the current connection, unless you are using Unix sockets, in which case both values are NULL:

```
SELECT inet_server_addr(), inet_server_port();
```

A user's password is not accessible using general SQL for obvious reasons.

You may also need the following:

```
SELECT version();
```

From PostgreSQL version 9.1 onwards, you can also use psql's new meta-command, \conninfo. It displays most of the preceding information in a single line:

```
postgres=# \conninfo
```

```
You are connected to database "postgres" as user "postgres" via socket in
"/var/run/postgresql" at port "5432".
```

See also

There are many other snippets of information required to understand connections. Some of them are mentioned in this chapter, and others are discussed in *Chapter 6*, *Security*. For further details, refer to the PostgreSQL server documentation.

Enabling access for network/remote users

PostgreSQL comes in a variety of distributions. In many of these, you will notice that remote access is initially disabled as a security measure.

How to do it...

By default, PostgreSQL gives access to clients who connect using Unix sockets, provided the database user is the same as the system's username. Here, we'll show you how to enable other connections.

 In this recipe, we mention configuration files, which can be located as shown in the *Finding the current configuration settings* recipe in *Chapter 3*, *Configuration*.

The steps are as follows:

1. Add or edit this line in your postgresql.conf file:

   ```
   listen_addresses = '*'
   ```

2. Add the following line as the first line of pg_hba.conf to allow access to all databases for all users with an encrypted password:

   ```
   # TYPE    DATABASE    USER         CIDR-ADDRESS    METHOD
   Host      all         all          0.0.0.0/0       md5
   ```

3. After changing listen_addresses, we restart the PostgreSQL server, as explained in the *Updating the parameter file* recipe from *Chapter 3*, *Configuration*.

 This recipe assumes that `postgresql.conf` does not include any other configuration file, which is the case in a default installation. If changing `listen_addresses` in `postgresql.conf` does not seem to work, perhaps that setting is overridden by another configuration file. Check out the *Updating the parameter file* recipe in *Chapter 3, Configuration*, for more details.

How it works...

The `listen_addresses` parameter specifies which IP addresses to listen to. This allows you to flexibly enable and disable listening on interfaces of multiple network cards (NICs) or virtual networks on the same system. In most cases, we want to accept connections on all NICs, so we use *, meaning "all IP addresses."

The `pg_hba.conf` file contains a set of host-based authentication rules. Each rule is considered in a sequence until one rule fires or the attempt is specifically rejected with a `reject` method.

The preceding rule means that a remote connection that specifies any user or database on any IP address will be asked to authenticate using an MD5-encrypted password. Precisely, the following:

- **Type**: For this, `host` means a remote connection.
- **Database**: For this, `all` means "for all databases". Other names match exactly, except when prefixed with a plus (+) symbol, in which case we mean a group role rather than a single user. You can also specify a comma-separated list of users, or use the @ symbol to include a file with a list of users. You can even specify `sameuser`, so that the rule matches when you specify the same name for the user and database.
- **User**: For this, `all` means "for all users". Other names match exactly, except when prefixed with a plus (+) symbol, in which case we mean a group role rather than a single user. You can also specify a comma-separated list of users or use the @ symbol to include a file with a list of users.
- **CIDR-ADDRESS**: This consists of two parts, IP address and subnet mask. The subnet mask is specified as the number of leading bits of the IP address that make up the mask. Thus, `/0` means 0 bits of the IP address, so that all IP addresses will be matched. For example, `192.168.0.0/24` would mean match the first 24 bits, so any IP address of the form 192.168.0.x would match. You can also use `samenet` or `samehost`.

> ► **Method**: For this, md5 means that PostgreSQL will ask the client to provide a
> password encrypted with MD5. Another common setting is trust, which effectively
> means no authentication. Other authentication methods include GSSAPI, SSPI, LDAP,
> RADIUS, and PAM. PostgreSQL connections can also be made using SSL, in which
> case client SSL certificates provide authentication. See the *Using SSL certificates to
> authenticate the client* recipe in *Chapter 6, Security*, for more details about this.

Don't use the password setting, as this sends the password in plain text. This is not a real
security issue if your connection is encrypted with SSL, and there are normally no downsides
with MD5 anyway, and you have extra security for non-SSL connections.

There's more...

In earlier versions of PostgreSQL, accessing through the network was enabled by adding the
-i command-line switch when you started the server. This is still a valid option, but now it
means the following:

```
listen_addresses = '*'
```

So, if you're reading some notes about how to set things up and this is mentioned, then
be warned that those notes are probably long out of date. They are not necessarily wrong,
but it's worth looking further to see whether anything else has changed.

See also

Look at installer- and/or operating-system-specific documentation to find the standard
location of the files.

Using graphical administration tools

Graphical administration tools are often requested by system administrators.

PostgreSQL has a range of tool options. The two most popular options are as follows:

- ► pgAdmin3
- ► phpPgAdmin

We're going to describe pgAdmin3 in more detail here because it is installed by default with
the PostgreSQL Windows installer. That most likely makes it the most popular interface, even
though many people choose to use server software running on Linux or variants.

How to do it...

pgAdmin3 is a client application that sends and receives SQL to PostgreSQL, displaying the results for you to browse. One pgAdmin client can access many PostgreSQL servers, and a PostgreSQL server can be accessed by many pgAdmin clients.

pgAdmin3 is usually named just pgAdmin. The "3" at the end has a long history, but isn't that important. It is not the release level; the release level at the time of writing this book is 1.20.

When you start pgAdmin, you will be prompted to register a new server, as shown in the following screenshot:

Note the five basic connection parameters encircled in the preceding screenshot, as well as other information.

The port number prompted is **2345**, but this is deliberately not the default PostgreSQL port of 5432. Presumably, this is done to force you to think about the setting that should be used.

You should uncheck the **Store password** box.

If you have many database servers, you can group them together. Personally, I would avoid giving each server a color, as green, yellow, and red are usually taken to mean status, which can easily be misinterpreted. Just give each server a sensible name.

You will then get access to the main browser screen, with the object tree view on the left and properties on the right, as shown in the following screenshot:

pgAdmin easily displays much of the data that is available from PostgreSQL. The information is context sensitive, allowing you to navigate and see everything quickly and easily. The information is not dynamically updated; this will occur only when you click to refresh, so keep *F5* in mind when using the application.

You'll also notice that pgAdmin provides a **Tip of the Day**, though I would turn those off. Keep the **Guru Hints** option on. Luckily, there are no chirpy paperclips offering suggestions.

pgAdmin also provides an **Object Report** generator and a **Grant Wizard**. These are useful for DBAs for review and immediate maintenance.

The pgAdmin Query tool allows you to have multiple active sessions. The Query tool has a good-looking Visual Explain feature, which displays the best execution plan found for a given query, as well as **Graphical Query Builder**, as shown in the following screenshot:

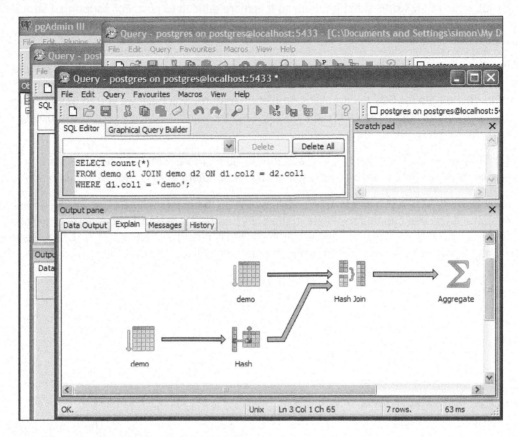

How it works...

pgAdmin provides a wide range of features, many of which are provided by other tools as well. This gives us the opportunity to choose which of those tools we want. For many reasons, it is best to use the right tool for the right job, and that is always a matter of expertise, experience, and personal taste.

pgAdmin submits SQL to the PostgreSQL server, and displays the results quickly and easily. As a browser, it is fantastic. For performing small DBA tasks, it is ideal. As you might've guessed from these comments, I don't recommend pgAdmin for every task.

Scripting is an important technique for DBAs. You keep a copy of the task executed, and you can edit and resubmit if problems occur. It's also easy to put all the tasks in a script into a single transaction, which isn't possible using the current GUI tools. pgAdmin provides pgScript, which only works with pgAdmin, so it is more difficult to port. For scripting, I strongly recommend the psql utility, which has many additional features that you'll increasingly appreciate over time.

Although I use psql as a scripting tool, I also find it convenient as a query tool. Some people may find this strange, and assume it is a choice for experts only. Two great features of psql are the online help for SQL and the tab completion feature, which allows you to build up SQL quickly without having to remember the syntax. See the *Using the psql query and scripting tool* recipe for more information.

pgAdmin also provides pgAgent, a task scheduler. Again, more portable schedulers are available, and you may wish to use those instead. Schedulers aren't covered in this book.

A quick warning—when you create an object in pgAdmin, the object will be created with a mixed case name if you use capitals anywhere in the object name. If I ask for a table named `MyTable`, then the only way to access that table is by referring to it in double quotes—`"MyTable"`. See the *Handling objects with quoted names* recipe in *Chapter 5, Tables and Data*.

There's more...

phpPgAdmin is available at `http://phppgadmin.sourceforge.net/`. There is an online demonstration of the software, so you can try it out yourself and see whether it does the job you want done. The following screenshot shows phpPgAdmin 4 displayed on the Windows Internet Explorer browser. Version 5.1 works with PostgreSQL 9:

One of the big contrasts with pgAdmin is that phpPgAdmin is browser-based, so it may be easier to provide secure access to administrators this way.

phpPgAdmin provides the familiar left-hand-side tree view of the database, and also provides a simple SQL query tool. These are the basics that you should be looking for. Many additional features in pgAdmin3 aren't available, but if you follow my advice you will be doing much of your work using scripts, so this may not be a problem.

For more details on the meaning of the output of the **Auto Explain** option, refer to the *Finding out what makes SQL slow* recipe from *Chapter 10, Performance and Concurrency*.

See also

You may also be interested in commercial tools of various kinds for PostgreSQL. A full listing is given in the PostgreSQL software catalogue at `http://www.postgresql.org/download/products/1`.

Using the psql query and scripting tool

psql is the query tool supplied as a part of the core distribution of PostgreSQL, so it is available and works similarly in all environments. This makes it an ideal choice for developing portable applications and techniques.

psql provides features for use as both an interactive query tool and a scripting tool.

Getting ready

From here on, we will assume that `psql` is a sufficient command to allow you access to the PostgreSQL server. This assumes that all of your connection parameters are defaults, which may not be true.

Written in full, the connection parameters would be as follows:

```
psql -h hostname -p 5432 -d dbname -U username
```

The default value for the port (`-p`) is `5432`. By default, `dbname` and `username` are both identical to the operating system's username. The default `hostname` on Windows is localhost, while on Unix, we use the default directory for Unix socket connections. The location of such directories varies across distributions and is set at compile time. However, note that you don't actually need to know its value because on local connections, both the server and the client are normally compiled together, so they use the same default.

How to do it...

The command that executes a single SQL command and prints the output is the easiest, as shown here:

```
$ psql -c "SELECT current_time"
     timetz
----------------
 18:48:32.484+01
(1 row)
```

The `-c` command is noninteractive. If we want to execute multiple commands, we can write those commands in a text file and then execute them using the `-f` option. This command loads a very small and simple set of examples:

```
$ psql -f examples.sql
```

It produces the following output when successful:

```
SET
SET
SET
SET
SET
SET
DROP SCHEMA
CREATE SCHEMA
SET
SET
SET
CREATE TABLE
CREATE TABLE
COPY 5
COPY 3
```

The `examples.sql` script is very similar to a dump file produced by PostgreSQL backup tools, so this type of file and the output it produces are very common. When a command is executed successfully, PostgreSQL outputs a "command tag" equal to the name of that command; this is how the preceding output was produced.

psql can also be used in interactive mode, which is the default, so it requires no option:

```
$ psql
postgres=#
```

The first interactive command you'll need is the following:

```
postgres=# help
```

You can then type in SQL or other commands. The last interactive command you'll need is this:

```
postgres=# \quit
```

Unfortunately, you cannot type `quit` on its own, nor can you type `\exit` or other options. Sorry, just `\quit` or `\q` for short!

How it works...

In psql, you can enter the following two types of commands:

- psql meta-commands
- SQL

A meta-command is a command for the psql client, whereas SQL is sent to the database server. An example of a meta-command is \q, which tells the client to disconnect. All lines that begin with \ (backslash) as the first nonblank character are presumed to be meta-commands of some kind.

If it isn't a meta-command, then it's SQL. We keep reading SQL until we find a semicolon, so we can spread SQL across many lines and format it any way we find convenient.

The `help` command is the only exception. We provide this for people who are completely lost, which is a good thought; so let's start from there ourselves.

There are two types of `help` commands, which are as follows:

- \?: This provides help on psql meta-commands
- \h: This provides help on specific SQL commands

Consider the following snippet as an example:

```
postgres=# \h DELETE
Command:     DELETE
Description: delete rows of a table
Syntax:
DELETE FROM [ ONLY ] table [ [ AS ] alias ]
```

```
[ USING usinglist ]
[ WHERE condition | WHERE CURRENT OF cursor_name ]
[ RETURNING * | output_expression [ AS output_name ] [,]]
```

I find this a great way to discover or remember options and syntax. You'll also like the ability to scroll back through the previous command history.

You'll get a lot of benefit from tab completion, which will fill in the next part of the syntax, just by pressing the *Tab* key. This also works for object names, so you can type in just the first few letters and then press *Tab*; all the options will be displayed. Thus, you can type in just enough letters to make the object name unique and then hit *Tab* to get the rest of the name.

One-line comments are used with two dashes, as follows:

```
-- This is a single-line comment
```

Multiline comments here are similar to those in C and Java:

```
/*
 * Multi-line comment
 */
```

You'll probably agree that psql looks a little daunting at first, with strange backslash commands. I do hope you'll take a few moments to understand the interface and keep digging for more information. psql is one of the most surprising parts of PostgreSQL, and it is incredibly useful for database administration tasks when used alongside other tools.

There's more...

psql works across releases, though in older versions you may see a message like the following, if you do so:

psql on Windows can be a little problematic, but things are constantly improving. I recommend using a terminal emulator to connect to your server and accessing psql from there.

See also

Check out some other useful features of psql, which are as follows:

- Information functions
- Output formatting
- Execution timing using the `\timing` command
- Input/output and editing commands
- Automatic startup files, such as `.psqlrc`
- Substitutable parameters (variables)
- Access to the OS command line

Changing your password securely

If you are using password authentication, then you may wish to change your password from time to time.

How to do it...

The most basic method is to use psql. The `\password` command will prompt you once for a new password and again to confirm. Connect to psql and type the following:

```
\password
```

Enter a new password. This causes psql to send a SQL statement to the PostgreSQL server, which contains an already encrypted password string. An example of the SQL statement sent, is as follows:

```
ALTER USER postgres PASSWORD ' md53175bce1d3201d16594cebf9d7eb3f9d';
```

Whatever you do, don't use `postgres` as your password. This will make you vulnerable to idle hackers, so make it a little more difficult than that, please!

Make sure you don't forget your password either. It may prove difficult to maintain your database if you can't get access to it later.

How it works...

As changing the password is just a SQL statement, any interface can do this. Other tools also allow this, such as the following:

- pgAdmin3
- phpPgAdmin

If you don't use one of the main routes to change the password, you can still do this yourself using SQL from any interface. Note that you need to encrypt your password because if you do submit a password in plain text, like the following, then it will be shipped to the server in plain text:

```
ALTER USER myuser PASSWORD 'secret'
```

Luckily the password in this case will still be stored in an encrypted form. It will also be recorded in plain text in psql's history file, as well as in any server and application logs, depending on the actual log-level settings.

PostgreSQL doesn't enforce a password change cycle, so you may wish to use more advanced authentication mechanisms such as GSSAPI, SSPI, LDAP, RADIUS, and so on.

Avoiding hardcoding your password

We all agree that hardcoding your password is a bad idea. This recipe shows you how to keep your password in a secure password file.

Getting ready

Not all database users need passwords; some databases use other means of authentication. Don't do this step unless you know you will be using password authentication and you know your password.

First, remove the hardcoded password from where you had set it previously. Completely remove the password = xxxx text from the connection string in a program. Otherwise, when you test the password file, the hardcoded setting will override the details you are just about to place in the file. Keeping the password hardcoded and in the password file is not any better. Using PGPASSWORD is not recommended either, so remove that also.

If you think someone may have seen the password, then change your password before placing it in the secure password file.

How to do it...

A password file contains the usual five fields that we require when connecting, as shown here:

```
host:port:dbname:user:password
```

Change this to the following:

```
myhost:5432:postgres:sriggs:moresecure
```

The password file is located using an environment variable named PGPASSFILE. If PGPASSFILE is not set, then a default filename and location must be searched for, as follows:

▸ On *nix systems, look for ~/.pgpass.

▸ On Windows systems, look for %APPDATA%\postgresql\pgpass.conf, where %APPDATA% is the application data subdirectory in the path (for me, that would be C:\).

> Don't forget to set the file permissions on the file, so that security is maintained. File permissions are not enforced on Windows, though the default location is secure. On *nix systems, you must issue the following:
>
> **chmod 0600 ~/.pgpass**
>
> If you forget to do this, the PostgreSQL client will ignore the .pgpass file. While psql will issue a clear warning, many other clients will just fail silently, so don't forget!

How it works...

Many people name the password file .pgpass, whether or not they are on Windows, so don't get confused if they do this.

The password file can contain multiple lines. Each line is matched against the requested host:port:dbname:user combination until we find a line that matches. Then, we use that password.

Each item can be a literal value or *, a wildcard that matches anything. There is no support for partial matching. With appropriate permissions, a user can potentially connect to any database. Using the wildcard in the dbname and port fields makes sense, but it is less useful in other fields. Here are a few examples:

▸ myhost:5432:*:sriggs:moresecurepw

▸ myhost:5432:perf:hannu:okpw

▸ myhost:*:perf:gianni:sicurissimo

There's more...

This looks like a good improvement if you have a small number of database servers. If you have many different database servers, you may want to think about using a connection service file instead (see the next recipe), or perhaps even storing details on an LDAP server.

Using a connection service file

As the number of connection options grows, you may want to consider using a **connection service** file.

The connection service file allows you to give a single name to a set of connection parameters. This can be accessed centrally to avoid the need for individual users to know the host and port of the database, and it is more resistant to future change.

You can set up a system-wide file as well as individual per-user files. The default file paths for these files are `/etc/pg_service.conf` and `~/.pg_service.conf` respectively.

A system-wide connection file controls service names for all users from a single place, while a per-user file applies only to that particular user. Keep in mind that the per-user file overrides the system-wide file: if a service is defined in both files, then the definition in the per-user file will prevail.

How to do it...

First, create a file named `pg_service.conf` with the following content:

```
[dbservice1]
host=postgres1
port=5432
dbname=postgres
```

You can then copy it either to `/etc/pg_service.conf` or another agreed central location. You can then set the `PGSYSCONFDIR` environment variable to that directory location.

Alternatively, you can copy it to `~/.pg_service.conf`. If you want to use a different name, set `PGSERVICEFILE`. Either way, you can then specify a connection string like the following:

```
service=dbservice1 user=sriggs
```

The service can also be set using an environment variable named `PGSERVICE`.

How it works...

This feature applies to libpq connections only, so it does not apply to JDBC.

The connection service file can also be used to specify the user, though that would mean that the username would be shared.

The `pg_service.conf` and `.pgpass` files can work together, or you can use just one of the two as you choose. Note that the `pg_service.conf` file is shared, so it is not a suitable place for passwords. The per-user connection service file is not shared, but in any cases, it seems best to keep things separate and confine passwords to `.pgpass`.

Troubleshooting a failed connection

This recipe is all about what you should do when things go wrong.

Bear in mind that 90 percent of the problems are just misunderstandings, and you'll quickly be on track again.

How to do it...

Here we've made a checklist to be followed in case a connection attempt fails:

- ▸ Check whether the database name and username are accurate. You may be requesting a service on one system while the database you require is on another system. Recheck your credentials. Especially ensure that you haven't mixed things up, so that you are using the database name as the username or vice versa. If you receive "too many connections," then you may need to disconnect another session before you can connect, or wait for the administrator to re-enable the connections.

- ▸ Check for explicit rejections. If you receive the **pg_hba.conf rejects connection for host** error message, it means your connection attempt has been explicitly rejected by the database administrator for that server. You will not be able to connect from the current client system using those credentials. There is little point attempting to contact the administrator, as you are violating an explicit security policy in what you are attempting to do.

- ▸ Check for implicit rejections. If the error message you receive is **no pg_hba.conf entry for**, it means there is no explicit rule that matches your credentials. This is likely an oversight on the part of the administrator and is common in very complex networks. Contact the administrator and request a ruling on whether your connection should be allowed (hopefully) or explicitly rejected in the future.

- ▸ Check whether the connection works with psql. If you're trying to connect to PostgreSQL from anything other than the psql command-line utility, switch to that now. If you can make psql connect successfully but cannot make your main connection work correctly, then the problem may be in the local interface you are using.

- PostgreSQL 9.3 and later versions ship the `pg_isready` utility, which checks the status of a database server, either local or remote, by establishing a minimal connection. Only the hostname and port are mandatory, which is great if you don't know the database name, username, or password. The following outcomes are possible:
    - The server is running and accepting connections
    - The server is running but not accepting connections (because it is starting up, shutting down, or in recovery)
    - A connection attempt was made, but it failed
    - No connection attempt was made because of a client problem (invalid parameters, out of memory, and so on)
- Check whether the server is up. If a server is shut down, then you cannot connect. The typical problem here is simply mixing up the server to which you are connecting. You need to specify the hostname and port, so it's possible that you are mixing up those details.
- Check whether the server is up and accepting new connections. A server that is shutting down will not accept new connections, apart from superusers. Also, a standby server may not have the `hot_standby` parameter enabled, preventing you from connecting.
- Check whether the server is listening correctly, and check the port to which the server is actually listening. Confirm that the incoming request is arriving on the interface listed in the `listen_addresses` parameter. Check whether it is set to * for remote connections and `localhost` for local connections.
- Check whether the database name and username exist. It's possible the database or user no longer exists.
- Check the connection request, that is, check whether the connection request was successful and was somehow dropped after connection. You can confirm this by looking at the server log when the following parameters are enabled:

```
log_connections = on
log_disconnections = on
```

- Check for other reasons for disconnection. If you are connecting to a standby server, it is possible that you have been disconnected because of Hot Standby conflicts. See *Chapter 12, Replication and Upgrades* for more information.

There's more...

Client authentication and security are the rapidly changing areas over over subsequent major PostgreSQL releases. You will also find differences between maintenance release levels. The PostgreSQL documents on this topic can be viewed at `http://www.postgresql.org/docs/current/interactive/client-authentication.html`.

Always check which release levels you are using before consulting the manual or asking for support. Many problems are caused simply by confusing the capabilities between release levels.

2
Exploring the Database

This chapter covers the following recipes:

- ▶ What version is the server?
- ▶ What is the server uptime?
- ▶ Locating the database server files
- ▶ Locating the database server's message log
- ▶ Locating the database's system identifier
- ▶ Listing databases on this database server
- ▶ How many tables in a database?
- ▶ How much disk space does a database use?
- ▶ How much disk space does a table use?
- ▶ Which are my biggest tables?
- ▶ How many rows in a table?
- ▶ Quickly estimating the number of rows in a table
- ▶ Listing extensions in this database
- ▶ Understanding object dependencies

Introduction

To understand PostgreSQL, you need to see it in use. An empty database is like a ghost town without houses.

For now, we're going to assume that you've already got a database. There are already more than 1,000 books on how to design your own database from nothing. So here, we aim to help people who already have access to a PostgreSQL database but are still learning to use the PostgreSQL database management system.

The best way to start is by asking some simple questions to orient yourself and begin the process of understanding. Incidentally, these are also questions you'll need to answer if you ask someone else for help.

What version is the server?

If you experience problems, then you'll need to double-check which version of the server you have. This will help you report a fault or to consult the correct version of the manual.

How to do it...

We will find out the version by directly querying the database server.

Connect to the database and issue the following command:

```
postgres # SELECT version();
```

You'll get a response that looks something like this:

```
PostgreSQL 9.4.0 on i686-pc-linux-gnu,
compiled by gcc (Debian 4.7.2-5) 4.7.2, 32-bit
```

That's probably too much information all at once!

How it works...

The PostgreSQL server version's format is `Major.Minor.Maintenance`.

In some other software products, the `Major` release number is all you need to know, but with PostgreSQL, the feature set and compatibility relate to the `Major.Minor` release level. What this means is that version 9.4 contains more additional features and compatibility changes than version 9.3. There is also a separate version of the manual, so if something doesn't work exactly the way you think it should, you must consult the *correct* version of the manual.

Maintenance software releases are identified by the full three-part numbering scheme. 9.4.0 was the initial release of 9.4, and 9.4.1 is a later maintenance release.

The release support policy for PostgreSQL is available at `http://www.postgresql.org/support/versioning/`. This article explains that each release will be supported for a period of 5 years.

All releases, up to and including 8.4, were de-supported in July 2014. So, by the time you're reading this book, only PostgreSQL 9.0 and higher versions will be supported. Those early versions are still robust, though many performance and enterprise features will be missing from those releases. The later de-support dates are as follows:

Version	Last supported date
PostgreSQL 9.0	September 2015
PostgreSQL 9.1	September 2016
PostgreSQL 9.2	September 2017
PostgreSQL 9.3	September 2018
PostgreSQL 9.4	December 2019

There's more...

Some other ways of checking the version number are as follows:

```
bash # psql --version
psql (PostgreSQL) 9.4.0
```

However, be wary that this shows the client software version number, which may differ from the server software version number. You should check the server version directly using the following command:

```
bash # cat $PGDATADIRECTORY/PG_VERSION
```

Here, you must set PGDATADIRECTORY to the actual data directory. See the *Locating the database server files* recipe for more information.

Notice that the preceding command does not show the maintenance release number.

Why is the database version important?

PostgreSQL has internal version numbers for the data file format, database catalog layout, and crash recovery format. Each of these is checked as the server runs to ensure that the data isn't corrupted. PostgreSQL doesn't change these internal formats for a single release; they only change across releases.

From a user's perspective, each release differs in terms of the way the server behaves. If you know your application well, then it should be possible to assess the differences simply by reading the release notes for each version. In many cases, a retest of the application is the safest thing to do.

What is the server uptime?

You may wonder, "How long is it since the server started?"

As in the previous recipe, we will find this out by asking the database server.

How to do it...

Issue the following SQL from any interface:

```
postgres=# SELECT date_trunc('second',
current_timestamp - pg_postmaster_start_time()) as uptime;
```

You should get an output like the following:

```
     uptime
_____

 2 days 02:48:04
```

How it works...

Postgres stores the server start time, so we can access it directly, as follows:

```
postgres=# SELECT pg_postmaster_start_time();
   pg_postmaster_start_time
_____

2013-03-27 14:31:51.382106+00
```

Then, we can do a SQL query to get the uptime, like this:

```
postgres=# SELECT current_timestamp - pg_postmaster_start_time();
        ?column?
```

```
2 days 02:50:02.23939
```

Finally, we apply some formatting:

```
postgres=# SELECT date_trunc('second',
current_timestamp - pg_postmaster_start_time()) as uptime;
        uptime
```

```
2 days 02:51:18
```

See also

This is simple stuff. Further monitoring and statistics are covered in *Chapter 8, Monitoring and Diagnosis*.

Locating the database server files

Database server files are initially stored in a location referred to as the `data` directory. Additional data files may also be stored in tablespaces, if any exist.

In this recipe, you will learn how to find the location of these directories on a given database server.

Getting ready

You'll need to get an operating system access to the database system, which is what we call the platform on which the database runs.

How to do it...

On Debian or Ubuntu systems, the default `data` directory location is `/var/lib/postgresql/R.r/main`.

Here, `R.r` represents the major and minor release numbers of the database server software respectively, for example, `9.4`. The configuration files are located at `/etc/postgresql/R.r/main/`.

In both cases, `main` is just the name of a database server. Other names are also possible. For the sake of simplicity, we assume that you have only a single installation, although the point of including the release number and database server name as components of the directory path is to allow multiple database servers to coexist on the same host.

The `pg_lsclusters` utility is specific to Debian/Ubuntu, and displays a list of all the available database servers, including information such as the following for each server:

- ▸ Major release number
- ▸ Port
- ▸ Status (for example, online, down, and so on)
- ▸ Data directory
- ▸ Log file

The `pg_lsclusters` utility is part of the `postgresql-common` Debian/Ubuntu package, which provides *a structure under which multiple versions of PostgreSQL can be installed and multiple clusters can be maintained at one time.*

On Red Hat RHEL, CentOS, and Fedora, the default `data` directory location is `/var/lib/pgsql/data/`. This also contains, by default, the configuration files (`*.conf`).

Again, `data` is just the default location. You can create additional data directories using the `initdb` utility.

On Windows and OS X, the default `data` directory location is `C:\Program Files\PostgreSQL\R.r\data`.

The `initdb` utility populates a given `data` directory with the initial content. The directory will be created for convenience in case it is missing, but for safety the utility will stop in case the `data` directory is not empty. The `initdb` utility will read the `data` directory name from the `PGDATA` environment variable, unless the `-d` command line option is used.

How it works...

Even though the Debian/Ubuntu and Red Hat file layouts are different, they both follow the Linux **Filesystem Hierarchy Standard** (**FHS**), so neither layout is *wrong*.

The Red Hat layout is simpler and easier to understand. The Debian/Ubuntu layout is more complex, but it has different and more adventurous goals. The Debian/Ubuntu layout is similar to the **Optimal Flexible Architecture** (**OFA**) of other database systems. As pointed out earlier, the goals are to provide a file layout that will allow you to have multiple PostgreSQL database servers on one system, and to allow many versions of the software to exist at once in the filesystem.

Again, the layout for the Windows and OS X installers is different. Multiple database clusters are possible, but are also more complex than on Debian/Ubuntu.

I recommend that you follow the Debian/Ubuntu layout on whichever platform you are using. It doesn't really have a name, so I call it the **PostgreSQL Flexible Architecture** (**PFA**). Clearly, if you are using Debian or Ubuntu, then the Debian/Ubuntu layout is already being used. If you do this on other platforms, you'll need to lay things out yourself, but it does pay off on the long run. To implement PFA, you can set the following environment variables to name parts of the file layout:

```
export PGROOT=/var/lib/pgsql/
export PGRELEASE=9.4
export PGSERVERNAME=mamba
export PGDATA=$PGROOT/$PGRELEASE/$PGSERVERNAME
```

In this example, PGDATA is /var/lib/pgsql/9.4/mamba.

Finally, you must run initdb to actually initialize the data directory, as noted earlier, and custom administration scripts should be prepared to automate actions such as starting or stopping the database server when the system undergoes similar procedures.

Note that server applications such as initdb can only work with one major PostgreSQL version. On distributions that allow several major versions, such as Debian or Ubuntu, these applications are placed in dedicated directories, which are not put in the default command path. This means that if you just type initdb, then the system will not find the executable, and you will get an error message.

This may look like a bug, but in fact it is the desired behavior. Instead of directly accessing `initdb`, you are supposed to use the `pg_createcluster` utility from `postgresql-common`, which will select the right `initdb` depending on the major version you specify.

 If you plan to run more than one database server on the same host, you must set the preceding variables differently for each server, as they mandate the name of the `data` directory. For instance, you can set them in the script that you use to start or stop the database server, which would be enough because `PGDATA` is mostly used only by the database server process.

There's more...

Once you've located the `data` directory, you can look for the files that comprise the PostgreSQL database server. The layout is as follows:

Subdirectory	Purpose
base	This is the main data directory. Beneath this directory, each database has its own directory, within which are the files for each database table or index.
global	Here are the database server catalog tables that are shared across all databases.
pg_clog	Here are the transaction status files.
pg_dynshmem	This includes dynamic shared memory information (from 9.4 onwards).
pg_multixact	This includes the row-level lock status files.
pg_notify	This includes the LISTEN/NOTIFY status files.
pg_replslot	This includes information about Replication Slots (from 9.4 onwards).
pg_serial	This includes information on committed serializable transactions (from 9.1).
pg_snapshot	This includes the exported snapshot files (from 9.2 onwards).
pg_stat	This includes the server activity statistics and permanent files (from 9.3 onwards).
pg_stat_tmp	This includes the server activity statistics and temporary files.
pg_subtrans	This includes the subtransaction status files.
pg_tblspc	This includes the links to external tablespaces.

Subdirectory	Purpose
pg_twophase	This includes the 2-phase commit or prepared transaction status.
pg_xlog	This includes the transaction log, or **Write-Ahead log** (**WAL**)).

None of the aforementioned directories contain user-modifiable files, nor should any of the files be manually deleted, to save space or for any reason. *Don't touch it, because you'll break it*, and you may not be able to fix it! It's not even sensible to copy files in those directories without carefully following the procedures described in *Chapter 11, Backup and Recovery*. Keep off the grass!

We'll talk about tablespaces later in this Cookbook. We'll also discuss a performance enhancement that involves putting the transaction log on its own set of disk drives in *Chapter 10, Performance and Concurrency*.

The only things you are allowed to touch are configuration files, which are all `*.conf` files, and server message log files. Server message log files may or may not be in the `data` directory. For more details on this, see the next recipe *Locating the database server's message log*.

Locating the database server's message log

The database server's message log is a record of all messages recorded by the database server. This is the first place to look if you have server problems, and a good place to check regularly.

This log will have messages in it that look something like the following:

```
2013-01-29 23:15:41 CET LOG:   database system was not properly shut
down; automatic recovery in progress
2013-01-29 23:15:41 CET LOG:   record with zero length at A/A3478F08
2013-01-29 23:15:41 CET LOG:   redo is not required
2013-01-29 23:15:42 CET LOG:   database system is ready to accept
connections
2013-01-29 23:15:42 CET LOG:   autovacuum launcher started
```

We'll explain some more about these logs once we've located the files.

Getting ready

You'll need to get operating system access to the database system, which is what we call the platform on which the database runs.

How to do it...

The server log can be in a few different places, so first let's list all of those so that we can locate the log or decide where we want it to be placed:

- ▶ The server log may be in a directory beneath the `data` directory.
- ▶ It may be in a directory elsewhere on the filesystem.
- ▶ It may be redirected to `syslog`.
- ▶ There may be no server log at all. Then it's time to add a log soon!

If not redirected to `syslog`, the server log consists of one or more files. You can change the names of these files, so it may not always be the same on every system.

On Debian or Ubuntu systems, the default server log location is `/var/log/postgresql`.

The current server log file is named `postgresql-R.r-main.log`, where `R.r` represents the major and minor release number of the server, for example `9.4`. Older log files are numbered as `postgresql-9.4-main.log.1`. The higher the final number, the older the file, since they are being rotated by the `logrotate` utility.

On Red Hat, RHEL, CentOS, and Fedora, the default server log location is a subdirectory of the `data` directory, that is `/var/lib/pgsql/data/pg_log`.

On Windows systems, the messages are sent to the Windows Event Log by default.

How it works...

The server log is just a file that records messages from the server. Each message has a severity level, the most typical of them being `LOG`, though there are others, as shown in the following table:

PostgreSQL severity	Meaning	Syslog severity	Windows Event Log
DEBUG 1 to DEBUG 5	Internal diagnostics	DEBUG	INFORMATION
INFO	Command output for user	INFO	INFORMATION
NOTICE	Helpful information	NOTICE	INFORMATION
WARNING	Warns of likely problems	NOTICE	WARNING

PostgreSQL severity	Meaning	Syslog severity	Windows Event Log
ERROR	Current command aborted	WARNING	ERROR
LOG	For sysadmins	INFO	INFORMATION
FATAL	Event that disconnects one session only	ERR	ERROR
PANIC	Event that crashes the server	CRIT	ERROR

Watch out for FATAL and PANIC. They shouldn't happen in most cases during normal server operation, apart from certain cases related to replication; so check out *Chapter 12, Replication and Upgrades*, also.

You can adjust the number of messages that appear in the log by changing the log_min_messages server parameter. You can also change the amount of information that is displayed for each event by changing the log_error_verbosity parameter. If the messages are sent to a standard log file, then each line in the log will have a prefix of useful information that can also be controlled by the system administrator, with a parameter named log_line_prefix.

You can also alter the "what" and the "how much" that goes into the logs by changing other settings such as log_statements, log_checkpoints, log_connections/log_disconnections, log_verbosity, log_lock_waits, and so on.

There's more...

The log_destination parameter controls where log messages are stored. Valid values are stderr, csvlog, syslog, and eventlog (the latter only on Windows).

The logging collector is a background process that writes to a log file everything that the PostgreSQL server outputs to stderr. This is probably the most reliable way to log messages in case of problems, since it depends on fewer services.

Log rotation can be controlled with settings such as log_rotation_age and log_rotation_size if you are using the logging collector. Alternatively, it is possible to configure the logrotate utility to perform log rotation, which is the default on Debian and Ubuntu systems.

In general, monitoring activities are covered in *Chapter 8, Monitoring and Diagnosis*, and examining the message log is just one part of it. See the *Producing a daily summary of log file errors* recipe in that chapter for more details.

Locating the database's system identifier

Each database server has a system identifier assigned when the database is initialized (created). The server identifier remains the same if the server is backed up, cloned, and so on.

Many actions on the server are keyed to the system identifier, and you may be asked to provide this information when you report a fault.

In this recipe, you will learn how to display the system identifier.

Getting ready

Connect as the `postgres` OS user, or another user with execute privileges on the server software.

How to do it...

We just have to launch the following command:

```
pg_controldata <data-directory> | grep "system identifier"
Database system identifier:            5558338346489861223
```

Note that the preceding syntax will not work on Debian or Ubuntu systems, for the same reasons explained for `initdb` in the *Locating the database server files* recipe. However, in this case, there is no `postgresql-common` alternative, so if you must run `pg_controldata`, you have to specify the full path to the executable.

> Don't use `-D` in front of the data directory name. This is the only PostgreSQL server application where you don't need to do that.

How it works...

`pg_controldata` is a PostgreSQL server application that shows the content of a server's control file. The control file is located within the `data` directory of a server and is created at database initialization time. Some of the information within it is updated regularly, or when certain major events occur.

The full output of `pg_controldata` looks like the following (the bold values are those that may change over time as the server runs):

```
pg_control version number:            922
Catalog version number:               201204301
Database system identifier:           5805760367713220187
Database cluster state:               in production
pg_control last modified:             Thu Mar 28 21:23:23 2013
Latest checkpoint location:           12/64BD95C0
Prior checkpoint location:            12/64BD9450
Latest checkpoint's REDO location:    12/64BD95C0
Latest checkpoint's TimeLineID:       1
Latest checkpoint's full_page_writes: on
Latest checkpoint's NextXID:          0/1885903
Latest checkpoint's NextOID:          1380618
Latest checkpoint's NextMultiXactId:  3
Latest checkpoint's NextMultiOffset:  5
Latest checkpoint's oldestXID:        673
Latest checkpoint's oldestXID's DB:   1
Latest checkpoint's oldestActiveXID:  0
Time of latest checkpoint:            Thu Mar 28 21:23:22 2013
Minimum recovery ending location:     0/0
Backup start location:                0/0
Backup end location:                  0/0
End-of-backup record required:        no
Current wal_level setting:            minimal
Current max_connections setting:      100
Current max_prepared_xacts setting:   0
Current max_locks_per_xact setting:   64
Maximum data alignment:               8
Database block size:                  8192
Blocks per segment of large relation: 131072
WAL block size:                       8192
Bytes per WAL segment:                16777216
Maximum length of identifiers:        64
Maximum columns in an index:          32
Maximum size of a TOAST chunk:        1996
Date/time type storage:               64-bit integers
Float4 argument passing:              by value
Float8 argument passing:              by value
```

 Never edit the PostgreSQL control file. If you do, the server probably won't start correctly, or you may mask other errors. And if you do that, people will be able to tell, so fess up as soon as possible!

Listing databases on this database server

When we connect to PostgreSQL, we always connect to just one specific database on any database server. If there are many databases on a single server, it can get confusing, so sometimes you may just want to find out which databases are parts of the database server.

This is also confusing because we can use the word "database" in two different but related contexts. Initially, we start off by thinking that PostgreSQL is a "database" in which we put data, referring to the whole database server by just the word "database". In PostgreSQL, a database server is potentially split into multiple individual databases, so as you get more used to working with PostgreSQL, you'll start to separate the two concepts.

How to do it...

If you have access to psql, you can type the following command:

```
bash $ psql -l
                          List of databases
    Name     | Owner  | Encoding |   Collate    |    Ctype     | Access
privileges
-----------+--------+----------+--------------+--------------+-------------
------
 postgres   | sriggs | UTF8     | en_GB.UTF-8  | en_GB.UTF-8  |
 template0  | sriggs | UTF8     | en_GB.UTF-8  | en_GB.UTF-8  | =c/sriggs
+
            |        |          |              |              | sriggs=CTc/
sriggs
 template1  | sriggs | UTF8     | en_GB.UTF-8  | en_GB.UTF-8  | =c/sriggs
+
            |        |          |              |              | sriggs=CTc/
sriggs
(3 rows)
```

You can also get the same information while running psql by simply typing \l.

The information that we just looked at is stored in a PostgreSQL catalog table named pg_database. We can issue a SQL query directly against that table from any connection to get a simpler result, as follows:

```
postgres=# select datname from pg_database;
  datname
```

```
- - - - - - - - - - -
template1
template0
postgres
(3 rows)
```

How it works...

PostgreSQL starts with three databases, namely `template0`, `template1`, and `postgres`. The main user database is `postgres`.

You can create your own databases as well, like this:

```
CREATE DATABASE my_database;
```

You can do the same from the command line, using the following expression:

```
bash $ createdb my_database
```

After you've created your databases, make sure you secure them properly, as discussed in *Chapter 6, Security*.

When you create another database, it actually takes a copy of an existing database. Once it is created, there is no further link between the two databases.

The `template0` and `template1` databases are known as template databases. The `template1` database can be changed to allow you to create a localized template for any new databases that you create. The `templatc0` database exists so that when you alter `template1`, you still have a pristine copy on which to fall back on. In other words, if you break `template1`, then you can drop it and recreate it from `template0`.

You can drop the database named `postgres`. But don't, okay? Similarly, don't try to touch `template0` because you won't be allowed to do anything with it except using it as a template. On the other hand, the `template1` database exists to be modified, so feel free to change that.

There's more...

The information that we just saw is stored in a PostgreSQL catalog table named `pg_database`. We can look at this directly to get some more information. In some ways, the output is less useful as well, as we need to look up some of the code in other tables:

```
postgres=# \x
postgres=# select * from pg_database;
```

```
-[ RECORD 1 ]-+------------------------------
datname       | template1
datdba        | 10
encoding      | 6
datcollate    | en_GB.UTF-8
datctype      | en_GB.UTF-8
datistemplate | t
datallowconn  | t
datconnlimit  | -1
datlastsysoid | 11620
datfrozenxid  | 644
dattablespace | 1663
datacl        | {=c/sriggs,sriggs=CTc/sriggs}
-[ RECORD 2 ]-+------------------------------
datname       | template0
datdba        | 10
encoding      | 6
datcollate    | en_GB.UTF-8
datctype      | en_GB.UTF-8
datistemplate | t
datallowconn  | f
datconnlimit  | -1
datlastsysoid | 11620
datfrozenxid  | 644
dattablespace | 1663
datacl        | {=c/sriggs,sriggs=CTc/sriggs}
-[ RECORD 3 ]-+------------------------------
datname       | postgres
datdba        | 10
encoding      | 6
datcollate    | en_GB.UTF-8
datctype      | en_GB.UTF-8
datistemplate | f
datallowconn  | t
datconnlimit  | -1
datlastsysoid | 11620
```

```
datfrozenxid  | 644
dattablespace | 1663
datacl        |
```

First of all, look at the use of the \x command. It makes the output in psql appear as one column per line, rather than one row per line.

This output raises many questions, I know. We've already discussed templates. Other interesting things are that we can turn connections on and off for a database, and we can set connection limits for them as well.

Also, you can see that each database has a default tablespace. Therefore, data tables get created inside one specific database, and the data files for that table get placed in one tablespace.

You can also see that each database has a collation sequence, which is the way various language features are defined. We'll cover more on that in the *Choosing good names for database objects* recipe in *Chapter 5, Tables and Data*.

How many tables in a database?

The number of tables in a relational database is a good measure of the complexity of a database, so it is a simple way to get to know any database.

In this recipe, we will show you how to compute the number of tables.

How to do it...

From any interface, type the following SQL command:

```
SELECT count(*) FROM information_schema.tables
WHERE table_schema NOT IN ('information_schema',
                           'pg_catalog');
```

You can also look at the list of tables directly and judge whether the list is a small or large number.

In psql, you can see your own tables using the following command:

```
postgres@ebony:~/8.3/main$ psql -c "\d"
        List of relations
 Schema |   Name    | Type  |  Owner
--------+-----------+-------+----------
 public | accounts  | table | postgres
 public | branches  | table | postgres
```

In pgAdmin3, you can see the tables in the tree view on the left-hand side, as shown in the following screenshot:

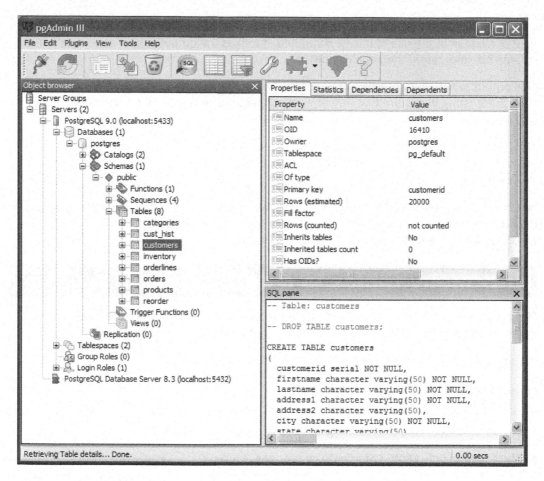

How it works...

PostgreSQL stores information about the database in catalog tables. They describe every aspect of the way the database has been defined. There is a main set of catalog tables stored in a schema, named pg_catalog. There is a second set of catalog objects named the Information Schema, which is the SQL standard way of accessing information in a relational database. We want to exclude both of these schemas from our query. Otherwise, we'll get too much information. We excluded them in the preceding query using the NOT IN phrase in the WHERE clause.

Note that this query shows only the number of tables in one of the databases on the PostgreSQL server. You can only see the tables in the database to which you are currently connected, so you'll need to run the same query on each database in turn.

There's more...

As I said, the number of tables in a relational database is a good measure of the complexity. But complexity of what? Well, a complex database may have been designed to be deliberately flexible in order to cover a variety of business situations, or a complex business process may have a limited portion of its details covered in the database. So, a large number of tables might likely reveal a complex business process or just a complex piece of software.

The highest number of distinct, major tables I've ever seen in a database is 20,000, not counting partitions, views, and work tables. That clearly rates as a very complex system.

Number of distinct tables (entities)	Complexity rating
20,000	Incredibly complex. You're either counting wrong or you have a big team to manage this.
2,000	Complex business database. Usually, not many of these are seen.
200	Typical modern business database.
20	Simple business database.
2	Database with a single clear purpose, tightly designed for performance or some other goal.
0	You haven't loaded any data yet!

Of course, you can't always tell easily which tables are entities, so we just need to count the tables. Some databases use a lot of partitions or similar tables, so the numbers can grow dramatically. I've seen databases with up to 200,000 tables (of any kind). That's not recommended, however, as the database catalog tables then begin to be awfully large.

How much disk space does a database use?

For planning or space monitoring, we often need to know how big the database is.

How to do it...

We can do this in the following ways:

- ▶ Look at the size of the files that make up the database server
- ▶ Run a SQL request to confirm the database size

If you look at the size of the actual files, you'll need to make sure that you include the data directory and all subdirectories, as well as all other directories that contain tablespaces. That can be tricky, and it is also difficult to break out all the different pieces.

The easiest way is to just ask the database a simple query, like this:

```
SELECT pg_database_size(current_database());
```

However, this is limited to only the current database. If you want to know the size of all the databases together, then you'll need a query such as the following:

```
SELECT sum(pg_database_size(datname)) from pg_database;
```

How it works...

The database server knows which tables it has loaded. It also knows how to calculate the size of each table, so the pg_database_size() function just goes and looks at the file sizes.

How much disk space does a table use?

How big is a table? What is the total size of all the parts of a table?

How to do it...

We can see the size of a table using this command:

```
postgres=# select pg_relation_size('pgbench_accounts');
```

The output of this command is the following:

```
pg_relation_size
------------------
        13582336
(1 row)
```

We can also see the total size of a table including indexes and other related spaces, as follows:

```
postgres=# select pg_total_relation_size('pgbench_accounts');
```

The output is as follows:

```
pg_total_relation_size
------------------------
        15425536
(1 row)
```

We can also use a psql command, like this:

```
postgres=# \dt+ pgbench_accounts
                      List of relations
 Schema  |       Name        | Type  | Owner  | Size  | Description
---------+-------------------+-------+--------+-------+-------------
 gianni  | pgbench_accounts  | table | gianni | 13 MB |
(1 row)
```

How it works...

In PostgreSQL, a table is made up of many "relations". The main relation is the data table. In addition, there are a variety of additional data files. Each index created on a table is also a relation. Long data values are placed in a secondary table named TOAST, so in most cases, each table also has a TOAST table and a TOAST index.

Each relation consists of multiple data files. The main data files are broken into 1 GB pieces. The first file has no suffix; others have a numbered suffix (such as .2). There are also files marked .vm and .fsm, which represent the Visibility Map and Free Space Map respectively. They are used as part of maintenance operations. They stay fairly small, even for very large tables.

There's more...

The preceding functions that measure the size of a relation output the number of bytes, which is normally too large to be immediately clear. You can apply the `pg_size_pretty()` function to format that number nicely, as shown in the following example:

```
SELECT pg_size_pretty(pg_relation_size('pgbench_accounts'));
```

This yields the following output:

```
pg_size_pretty
----------------
13 MB

(1 row)
```

TOAST stands for **The Outsized Attribute Storage Technique**. As the name implies, this is a mechanism used to store long column values. PostgreSQL allows many data types to store values up to 1 GB in size. It transparently stores large data items in many smaller pieces, so the same data type can be used for data ranging from 1 byte to 1 GB.

Which are my biggest tables?

We've looked at getting the size of a specific table, so now it's time to widen the problem to related areas. Rather than an absolute value for a specific table, let's look at the relative sizes.

How to do it...

The following basic query will tell us the 10 biggest tables:

```
SELECT table_name
,pg_relation_size(table_schema || '.' || table_name) as size
FROM information_schema.tables
WHERE table_schema NOT IN ('information_schema', 'pg_catalog')
ORDER BY size DESC
LIMIT 10;
```

The tables are shown in descending order of size, with at most 10 rows displayed. In this case, we look at all tables in all schemas, apart from tables in the `information_schema` or in `pg_catalog`, like we did in the *How many tables in a database?* recipe.

How it works...

PostgreSQL provides a dedicated function, `pg_relation_size`, to compute the actual disk space used by a specific table or index. We just have to provide the table name. In addition to the main data files, there are other files (called **forks**) that can be measured by specifying an optional second argument. These include the Visibility Map, the Free Space Map, and the Initialization Fork for unlogged objects.

How many rows in a table?

Counting is one of the easiest SQL statements, so it is also many people's first experience of a PostgreSQL query.

How to do it...

From any interface, the SQL command used to count rows is as follows:

```
SELECT count(*) FROM table;
```

This will return a single integer value as the result.

In psql, the command looks like the following:

```
postgres=# select count(*) from orders;
count

-------

    345
(1 row)
```

How it works...

PostgreSQL can choose between two techniques available to compute the SQL `count(*)` function.

The first is called Sequential Scan, and it is available in all currently supported versions. We access every data block in the table one after the other, reading the number of rows in each block. If the table is on disk, it will cause a beneficial disk access pattern, and the statement will be fairly fast.

The other technique is known as Index-Only Scans, and it was introduced in PostgreSQL 9.2. It requires an index on the table, and it covers a more general case than optimizing SQL queries with `count(*)`, so we will cover it in more detail in *Chapter 10, Performance and Concurrency*.

Some people think that the count SQL statement is a good test of the performance of a DBMS. Some DBMSes have specific tuning features for the count SQL statement, and Postgres optimizes this from 9.2. The PostgreSQL project has talked about this many times, but few people thought we should try to optimize this. Yes, the count function is frequently used within applications, but without any WHERE clause it is not that useful. Therefore, the capability added in version 9.2 is more complex and applies to a wider set of problems, including this recipe.

We scan every block of the table because of a major feature of Postgres named MVCC, which stands for **Multi-Version Concurrency Control**. MVCC allows us to run the count SQL statement at the same time that we are inserting, updating, or deleting data from the table. That's a very cool feature, and we got into a lot of trouble in Postgres to provide it for you.

MVCC requires us to record information on each row of a table, stating when that change was made. If the changes were made after the SQL statement begins to execute, then we just ignore those changes. This means that we need to carry out "visibility checks" on each row in the table, to allow us to work out the result of the count SQL statement. The optimization provided by Index-Only Scans is the ability to skip such checks on the table blocks that are already known to be visible to all sessions. Rows in these blocks can be counted directly on the index, which is normally smaller than the table, and hence faster.

If you think a little deeper about this, you'll see that the result of the count SQL statement is just the value at a moment in time. Depending on what happens to the table, that value could change a little or a lot while the count SQL statement is executing. So, once you've executed this, all you really know is that at a particular point in the past, there were exactly x rows in the table.

Quickly estimating the number of rows in a table

We don't always need an accurate count of rows, especially on a large table—that may take a long time to execute. Administrators often need to estimate how big a table is so that they can estimate how long other operations may take.

How to do it...

We can get a quick estimate of the number of rows in a table using roughly the same calculation that the Postgres optimizer uses:

```
SELECT (CASE WHEN reltuples > 0 THEN
        pg_relation_size('mytable')*reltuples/(8192*relpages)
        ELSE 0
        END)::bigint AS estimated_row_count
FROM pg_class
WHERE oid = 'mytable'::regclass;
```

This gives us the following output:

```
estimated_count
```
_____

293

```
(1 row)
```

It returns a row count very quickly, no matter how large the table that we are examining is.

How it works...

We saw the `pg_relation_size()` function earlier, so we know it brings back an accurate value for the current size of the table.

When we vacuum a table in Postgres, we record two pieces of information in the `pg_class` catalog entry for the table. These two items are the number of data blocks in the table (`relpages`) and the number of rows in the table (`reltuples`). Some people think they can use the value of `reltuples` in `pg_class` as an estimate, but it could be severely out of date. You will also be fooled if you use information in another table named `pg_stat_user_tables`, which is discussed in more detail in *Chapter 10, Performance and Concurrency*.

The Postgres optimizer uses the `relpages` and the `reltuples` values to calculate the average rows per block, which is also known as the average tuple density.

If we assume that the average tuple density remains constant over time, then we can calculate the number of rows using this formula: *Row estimate = number of data blocks * rows per block*.

We include some code to handle the cases where the `reltuples` or `relpages` fields are zero. The Postgres optimizer actually works a little harder than we do in that case, so our estimate isn't very good.

The `WHERE oid = 'mytable'::regclass;` syntax introduces the concept of **object identifier types**. They are just a short-hand trick used to convert the name of an object to the object identifier number for that object. The best way to understand this is to think of that syntax as meaning the same as a function named `relname2relid()`.

There's more...

The good thing about the aforementioned recipe is that it returns a value in about the same time, no matter how big the table is. The bad thing about it is that `pg_relation_size()` requests a lock on the table, so if any other user has an `AccessExclusiveLock` lock on the table, then the table size estimate will wait for the lock to be released before returning a value.

Err... so what is an `AccessExclusiveLock` lock? While performing a SQL maintenance action, such as changing the data type of a column, PostgreSQL will lock out all other actions on that table, including `pg_relation_size`, which takes a lock in the `AccessShareLock` mode. The typical case for me is where I issue some form of SQL maintenance action, such as `ALTER TABLE` and then, the statement takes much longer than I thought it would. At that point, I think, "Oh, was that table bigger than I thought? How long will I be waiting?" Yes, it's better to calculate that beforehand, but hindsight doesn't get you out of the hole you are in right now. So, we need a way to calculate the size of a table without needing the lock.

My solution is to look at the operating system files that Postgres uses to store data, and figure out how large they are.

Now, this can get somewhat difficult. If the table is locked, PostgreSQL is probably doing something to the table, and so trying to look at the files might well be fruitless or give wrong answers. Anyway, here goes:

1. First, get some details on the table from `pg_class`:

   ```
   SELECT reltablespace, relfilenode FROM pg_class
   WHERE oid = 'mytable'::regclass;
   ```

2. Then, confirm the `databaseid` in which the table resides:

   ```
   SELECT oid as databaseid FROM pg_database
   WHERE datname = current_database();
   ```

Together, `reltablespace`, `databaseid`, and `relfilenode` are the three things we need to locate the underlying data files within the `data` directory.

If `reltablespace` is zero, then the files will be in the following location:

   ```
   $PGDATADIR/base/{databaseid}/{relfilenode}*
   ```

The bigger the table, the more files you see. If `reltablespace` is not zero, then the files will be in the following location:

   ```
   $PGDATADIR/pg_tblspc/{reltablespace}/
   {databaseid}/{relfilenode}*
   ```

Every file should be 1 GB in size, apart from the last file.

The preceding discussion glossed over a few other points, as follows:

   ▸ Postgres uses the terms **data blocks** and **pages** to refer to the same concept. Postgres also does that with the terms **tuple** and **row**.

   ▸ A data block is 8,192 bytes in size, by default. You can change that if you recompile the server yourself, and create a new database.

You may want to create SQL functions for the preceding calculations, so you won't need to retype the SQL code every now and then.

Function 1 – estimating the number of rows

The following function estimates the total number of rows using a mathematical procedure called **extrapolation**. In other words, we take the average number of bytes per row resulting from the last statistics collection, and we apply it to the current table size:

```
CREATE OR REPLACE FUNCTION estimated_row_count(text)
RETURNS bigint
LANGUAGE sql
AS $$
SELECT (CASE WHEN reltuples > 0 THEN
            pg_relation_size($1)*reltuples/(8192*relpages)
        ELSE 0
        END)::bigint
FROM pg_class
WHERE oid = $1::regclass;
$$;
```

Function 2 – computing the size of a table without locks

Here is a function that does what `pg_relation_size` does more or less, without taking any locks. Because of this, it is always fast, but it may give an incorrect result if the table is being heavily altered at the same time:

```
CREATE OR REPLACE FUNCTION     pg_relation_size_nolock(tablename
regclass)
RETURNS BIGINT
LANGUAGE plpgsql
AS $$
DECLARE    classoutput    RECORD;    tsid        INTEGER;    rid
INTEGER;    dbid            INTEGER;    filepath    TEXT;    filename
TEXT;    datadir    TEXT;    i        INTEGER := 0;    tablesize
BIGINT;
BEGIN    --    -- get data directory    --    EXECUTE 'SHOW data_
directory' INTO datadir;    --    -- get relfilenode and reltablespace
--    SELECT    reltablespace as tsid    ,relfilenode as rid
INTO classoutput    FROM pg_class    WHERE oid = tablename    AND
relkind = 'r';    --    -- Throw an error if we can't find the
tablename specified    --    IF NOT FOUND THEN        RAISE EXCEPTION
'tablename % not found', tablename;    END IF;    tsid := classoutput.
tsid;    rid := classoutput.rid;    --    -- get the database
object identifier (oid)    --    SELECT oid INTO dbid    FROM pg_
database    WHERE datname = current_database();    --    -- Use some
internals knowledge to set the filepath    --    IF tsid = 0 THEN
filepath := datadir || '/base/' || dbid || '/' || rid;    ELSE
filepath := datadir || '/pg_tblspc/'                || tsid || '/'
|| dbid || '/'                    || rid;    END IF;    --    --
Look for the first file. Report if missing    --    SELECT (pg_stat_
file(filepath)).size    INTO tablesize;    --    -- Sum the sizes of
```

```
additional files, if any    --    WHILE FOUND LOOP        i := i +
1;      filename := filepath || '.' || i;      --         -- pg_
stat_file returns ERROR if it cannot see file      -- so we must
trap the error and exit loop        --        BEGIN          SELECT
tablesize + (pg_stat_file(filename)).size           INTO tablesize;
EXCEPTION            WHEN OTHERS THEN            EXIT;
END;     END LOOP;     RETURN tablesize;
END;
$$;
```

This function can also work on Windows with a few minor changes, which are left as an exercise for you.

Listing extensions in this database

Every PostgreSQL database contains some objects that are brought in automatically when the database is created. Every user will find a `pg_database` system catalog that lists databases, as shown in the *Listing databases on this database server* recipe. There is little point in checking whether these objects exist, because even superusers are not allowed to drop them.

On the other hand, PostgreSQL comes with tens of collections of optional objects, called **modules**, or equivalently **extensions**. The database administrator can install or uninstall these objects depending on the requirements. They are not automatically included in a newly created database, because they might not be required by every use case. Users will install only the extensions they actually need, and when they need them; an extension can be installed while a database is up and running.

In this recipe, we will explain how to list extensions that have been installed on the current database. This is important to get to know the database better, and also because certain extensions affect the behavior of the database.

Getting ready

A significant change happened in version 9.1, when the infrastructure that manages extensions was introduced, and all the optional objects were repackaged accordingly. The extensions infrastructure is a radical change in how optional objects are managed, so you should check beforehand whether your PostgreSQL version is prior to 9.1 or not.

How to do it...

In PostgreSQL 9.1 and later versions, there is a catalog table recording the list of installed extensions, so this recipe is quite simple. Issue the following command:

```
cookbook=> SELECT * FROM pg_extension;
```

This results in the following output (note that the format is expanded, as if the \x meta-command has been previously issued):

```
-[ RECORD 1 ]--+--------
extname        | plpgsql
extowner       | 10
extnamespace   | 11
extrelocatable | f
extversion     | 1.0
extconfig      |
extcondition   |
```

To get the same list with fewer technical details, you can use the meta-command \dx, like when listing databases.

If you are using an earlier version of PostgreSQL, the situation is fairly different. There is no list of installed extensions in the catalog, and installing an extension is essentially the same as manually creating all its objects. So, you need to check the list of existing tables, views, types, functions, and so on to see whether you spot anything that reminds you of one of the extensions. If you don't find any unexpected objects, then everything should be fine.

How it works...

A PostgreSQL extension is represented by a control file, `<extension name>.control`, located in the `SHAREDIR/extension` directory, plus one or more files containing the actual extension objects. The control file specifies the extension name, version, and other information that is useful for the extension infrastructure. Each time an extension is installed, uninstalled, or upgraded to a new version, the corresponding row in the `pg_extension` catalog table is inserted, deleted, or updated respectively.

There's more...

In this recipe, we only mentioned extensions distributed with PostgreSQL, solely for the purpose of listing which ones are being used in the current database. The infrastructure for extensions will be described in greater detail in *Chapter 3*, *Configuration*. We will talk about the version number of an extension, and we will show you how to install, uninstall, and upgrade extensions, including those distributed independently of PostgreSQL.

Understanding object dependencies

In most databases, there will be dependencies between objects in the database. Sometimes, we need to understand those dependencies to figure out how to perform certain actions. Let's look at this in detail.

Getting ready

We'll use the following simple database to understand the issues and investigate them. There are two tables, as follows:

```
CREATE TABLE orders (
orderid integer PRIMARY KEY
);
CREATE TABLE orderlines (
 orderid integer
,lineid smallint
,PRIMARY KEY (orderid, lineid)
);
```

Now, we add a link between them to enforce what is known as **Referential Integrity**, as follows:

```
ALTER TABLE orderlines ADD FOREIGN KEY (orderid)
REFERENCES orders (orderid);
```

If we try to drop the referenced table, we get the following message:

```
DROP TABLE orders;
```

```
ERROR: cannot drop table orders because other objects depend on it
```

```
DETAIL: constraint orderlines_orderid_fkey on table orderlines depends on
table orders
```

```
HINT: Use DROP ... CASCADE to drop the dependent objects too.
```

Be very careful! If you follow the hint, you may accidentally remove all the objects that have any dependency on the `orders` table. You might think that this would be a great idea, but to me it seems lazy and foolish. It might work, but we need to ensure that it will work.

Therefore, you need to know what dependencies are present on the `orders` table, and then review them. Then, you can decide whether it is okay to issue the `CASCADE` version of the command, or whether you should reconcile the situation manually.

How to do it...

You can use the following command from psql to display full information about a table, the constraints that are defined upon it, and the constraints that reference it:

```
\d+ orders
```

You can also get specific details of the constraints using the following query:

```
SELECT * FROM pg_constraint
WHERE confrelid = 'orders'::regclass;
```

Unfortunately, this is not the end of the story, so read the *There's more...* section.

How it works...

When we create a foreign key, we add a constraint to the catalog table known as `pg_constraint`. Therefore, the query shows us how to find all the constraints that depend upon the `orders` table.

There's more...

With Postgres, there's always a little more when you look beneath the surface. In this case, there's a lot more, and it's important.

The aforementioned queries only covered constraints between tables. We didn't discuss dependencies with other kinds of objects. Two important types of objects that might have dependencies to tables are views and functions.

Consider the following command:

```
DROP TABLE orders;
```

If you issue this, the dependency on any of the views will prevent the table from being dropped. Thus, you need to remove those views, and then drop the table.

The story with function dependencies is not as useful. Relationships between functions and tables are not recorded in the catalog, nor is the dependency information between functions and functions. This is partly due to the fact that most functional languages allow dynamic query execution, so you wouldn't be able to tell which tables or functions a function would access until it executes. That's only partly the reason, because most functions clearly reference other tables and functions, so it should be possible to identify and store those dependencies. However, right now, we don't do that. So, make a note that you need to record the dependency information for your functions manually, so that you'll know if and when it's okay to remove or alter a table or other objects that the functions depend on.

3
Configuration

In this chapter, we will cover the following recipes:

- ▶ Reading The Fine Manual (RTFM)
- ▶ Planning a new database
- ▶ Changing parameters in your programs
- ▶ Finding the current configuration settings
- ▶ Which parameters are at nondefault settings?
- ▶ Updating the parameter file
- ▶ Setting parameters for particular groups of users
- ▶ The basic server configuration checklist
- ▶ Adding an external module to PostgreSQL
- ▶ Using an installed module
- ▶ Managing installed extensions

Introduction

I get asked many questions about parameter settings in PostgreSQL. Everybody's busy and most people want a 5-minute tour of how things work. That's exactly what a Cookbook does, so we'll do our best.

Some people believe that there are some magical parameter settings that will improve their performance, spending hours combing the pages of books to glean insights. Others feel comfortable because they have found some website somewhere that "explains everything", and they "know" they have their database configured OK.

For the most part, the settings are easy to understand. Finding the best setting can be difficult, and the optimal setting may change over time in some cases. This chapter is mostly about knowing how, when, and where to change parameter settings.

Reading The Fine Manual (RTFM)

RTFM is often used rudely to mean "don't bother me, I'm busy", or it is used as a stronger form of abuse. The strange thing is that asking you to read a manual is most often very good advice. Don't flame the advisors back; take the advice! The most important point to remember is that you should refer to a manual whose release version matches that of the server on which you are operating.

The PostgreSQL manual is very well-written and comprehensive in its coverage of specific topics. However, one of its main failings is that the "documents" aren't organized in a way that helps somebody who is trying to learn PostgreSQL. They are organized from the perspective of people checking specific technical points so that they can decide whether their difficulty is a user error or not. It sometimes answers "What?" but seldom "Why?" or "How?"

I've helped write sections of the PostgreSQL documents, so I'm not embarrassed to steer you towards reading them. There are, nonetheless, many things to read here that are useful.

How to do it...

The main documents for each PostgreSQL release are available at `http://www.postgresql.org/docs/manuals/`.

The most frequently accessed parts of the documents are as follows:

▶ SQL command reference, as well as client and server tools reference: `http://www.postgresql.org/docs/current/interactive/reference.html`

▶ Configuration: `http://www.postgresql.org/docs/current/interactive/runtime-config.html`

▶ Functions: `http://www.postgresql.org/docs/current/interactive/functions.html`

You can also grab yourself a PDF version of the manual, which can allow easier searching in some cases. Don't print it! The documents are more than 2000 pages of A4-sized sheets.

How it works...

The PostgreSQL documents are written in SGML, which is similar to, but not the same as, XML. These files are then processed to generate HTML files, PDF, and so on. This ensures that all the formats have exactly the same content. Then, you can choose the format you prefer, and you can even compile it in other formats such as EPUB, INFO, and so on.

Moreover, the PostgreSQL manual is actually a subset of the PostgreSQL source code, so it evolves together with the software. It is written by the same people who make PostgreSQL. Even more reasons to read it!

There's more...

More information is also available at `http://wiki.postgresql.org`.

Many distributions offer packages that install static versions of the HTML documentation. For example, on Debian and Ubuntu, the docs for the most recent stable PostgreSQL version are named `postgresql-9.4-docs` (unsurprisingly).

Planning a new database

Planning a new database can be a daunting task. It's easy to get overwhelmed by it, so here, we present some planning ideas. It's also easy to charge headlong at the task as well, thinking that whatever you know is all you'll ever need to consider.

Getting ready

You are ready. Don't wait to be told what to do. If you haven't been told what the requirements are, then write down what you think they are, clearly labeling them as "assumptions" rather than "requirements"—we mustn't confuse the two things.

Iterate until you get some agreement, and then build a prototype.

How to do it...

Write a document that covers the following items:

- Database design—plan your database design
    - Calculate the initial database sizing

- Transaction analysis—how will we access the database?
    - Look at the most frequent access paths
    - What are the requirements for response times?

- Hardware configuration
    - Initial performance thoughts—will all of the data fit into RAM?
    - Choose the operating system and filesystem type
    - How do we partition the disk?

- Localization plan
    - Decide server encoding, locale, and time zone

- ▸ Access and security plan
  - ❏ Identify client systems and specify required drivers
  - ❏ Create roles according to a plan for access control
  - ❏ Specify `pg_hba.conf`
- ▸ Maintenance plan—who will keep it working? How?
- ▸ Availability plan—consider the availability requirements
  - ❏ `checkpoint_timeout` (for more details on this parameter, see the *Understanding and controlling crash recovery* recipe in *Chapter 11, Backup and Recovery*)
  - ❏ Plan your backup mechanism and test it
- ▸ High-availability plan
  - ❏ Decide which form of replication you'll need, if any

How it works...

One of the most important reasons for planning your database ahead of time is that retrofitting some things is difficult. This is especially true of server encoding and locale, which can cause much downtime and exertion if we need to change them later. Security is also much more difficult to set up after the system is live.

There's more...

Planning always helps. You may know what you're doing, but others may not. Tell everybody what you're going to do before you do it to avoid wasting time. If you're not sure yet, then build a prototype to help you decide. Approach the administration framework as if it were a development task. Make a list of things you don't know yet, and work through them one by one.

This is deliberately a very short recipe. Everybody has their own way of doing things, and it's very important not to be too prescriptive about how to do things. If you already have a plan, great! If you don't, think about what you need to do, make a checklist, and then do it.

Changing parameters in your programs

PostgreSQL allows you to set some parameter settings for each session or transaction.

How to do it...

You can change the value of a setting during your session, like this:

```
SET work_mem = '16MB';
```

This value will then be used for every future transaction. You can also change it only for the duration of the "current transaction":

```
SET LOCAL work_mem = '16MB';
```

The setting will last until you issue this command:

```
RESET work_mem;
```

Alternatively, you can issue the following command:

```
RESET ALL;
```

SET and RESET commands are SQL commands that can be issued from any interface. They apply only to PostgreSQL server parameters, but this does not mean that they affect the entire server. In fact, the parameters you can change with SET and RESET apply only to the current session. Also, note that there may be other parameters, such as JDBC driver parameters, that cannot be set in this way. Refer to the *Connecting to the PostgreSQL server* recipe in *Chapter 1, First Steps*, for help with those parameters.

How it works...

Suppose you change the value of a setting during your session, for example, by issuing this command:

```
SET work_mem = '16MB';
```

Then, the following will show up in the pg_settings catalog view:

```
postgres=# SELECT name, setting, reset_val, source
                  FROM pg_settings WHERE source = 'session';
   name    | setting | reset_val | source
----------+---------+-----------+---------
 work_mem | 16384   | 1024      | session
```

Until you issue this command:

```
RESET work_mem;
```

After issuing it, the setting returns to `reset_val` and the source returns to default:

```
 name    | setting | reset_val | source
---------+---------+-----------+---------
work_mem | 1024    | 1024      | default
```

There's more...

You can change the value of a setting during your transaction as well, like this:

```
SET LOCAL work_mem = '16MB';
```

Then, this will show up in the `pg_settings` catalog view:

```
postgres=# SELECT name, setting, reset_val, source
                  FROM pg_settings WHERE source = 'session';
 name    | setting | reset_val | source
---------+---------+-----------+---------
work_mem | 1024    | 1024      | session
```

Huh? What happened to your parameter setting? The `SET LOCAL` command takes effect only for the transaction in which it was executed, which was just the `SET LOCAL` command in our case. We need to execute it inside a transaction block to be able to see the setting take hold, as follows:

```
BEGIN;
SET LOCAL work_mem = '16MB';
```

Here is what shows up in the `pg_settings` catalog view:

```
postgres=# SELECT name, setting, reset_val, source
                  FROM pg_settings WHERE source = 'session';
 name    | setting | reset_val | source
---------+---------+-----------+---------
work_mem | 16384   | 1024      | session
```

You should also note that the value of `source` is `session` rather than `transaction`, as you might have been expecting.

Finding the current configuration settings

At some point, it will occur to you to ask, "What are the current configuration settings?"

Most settings can be changed in more than one way, and some ways do not affect all users or all sessions, so it is quite possible to get confused.

How to do it...

Your first thought is probably to look in `postgresql.conf`, which is the configuration file, described in detail in the *Updating the parameter file* recipe. That works, but only as long as there is only one parameter file. If there are two, then maybe you're reading the wrong file! (How do you know?) So, the cautious and accurate way is not to trust a text file, but to trust the server itself.

Moreover, you learned in the previous recipe, *Changing parameters in your programs*, that each parameter has a scope that determines when it can be set. Some parameters can be set through `postgresql.conf`, but others can be changed afterwards. So, the current value of configuration settings may have been subsequently changed.

We can use the `SHOW` command like this:

```
postgres=# SHOW work_mem;
```

Its output is as follows:

```
work_mem
----------

1MB

(1 row)
```

However, remember that it reports the current setting at the time it is run, and that can be changed in many places.

Another way of finding the current settings is to access a PostgreSQL catalog view named `pg_settings`:

```
postgres=# \x
Expanded display is on.
postgres=# SELECT * FROM pg_settings WHERE name = 'work_mem';
[ RECORD 1 ] -------------------------------------------------------
name       | work_mem
```

```
setting     | 1024
unit        | kB
category    | Resource Usage / Memory
short_desc  | Sets the maximum memory to be used for query workspaces.
extra_desc  | This much memory can be used by each internal sort operation
and hash table before switching to temporary disk files.
context     | user
vartype     | integer
source      | default
min_val     | 64
max_val     | 2147483647
enumvals    |
boot_val    | 1024
reset_val   | 1024
sourcefile  |
sourceline  |
```

Thus, you can use the SHOW command to retrieve the value for a setting, or you can access the full details via the catalog table.

There's more...

The actual location of each configuration file can be asked directly to the PostgreSQL server, as shown in this example:

```
postgres=# SHOW config_file;
```

This returns the following output:

```
            config_file
-----------------------------------------
 /etc/postgresql/9.4/main/postgresql.conf
(1 row)
```

The other configuration files can be located by querying similar variables, hba_file and ident_file.

How it works...

Each parameter setting is cached within each session so that we can get fast access to the parameter settings. This allows us to access the parameter settings with ease.

Remember that the values displayed are not necessarily settings for the server as a whole. Many of those parameters will be specific to the current session. That's different from what you experience with many other database software, and is also very useful.

Which parameters are at nondefault settings?

Often, we need to check which parameters have been changed or whether our changes have correctly taken effect.

In the previous two recipes, we have seen that parameters can be changed in several ways, and with different scope. You learned how to inspect the value of one parameter or get the full list of parameters.

In this recipe, we will show you how to use SQL capabilities to list only those parameters whose value in the current session differs from the system-wide default value.

This list is valuable for several reasons. First, it includes only a few of the 200-plus available parameters, so it is more immediate. Also, it is difficult to remember all our past actions, especially in the middle of a long or complicated session.

Version 9.4 introduces the ALTER SYSTEM syntax, which we will describe in the next recipe, *Updating the parameter file*. From the viewpoint of this recipe, its behavior is quite different from all other setting-related commands; you run it from within your session and it changes the default value, but not the value in your session.

How to do it...

We write a SQL query that lists all parameter values, excluding those whose current value is either the default or set from a configuration file:

```
postgres=# SELECT name, source, setting
                FROM pg_settings
                WHERE source != 'default'
                AND source != 'override'
                ORDER by 2, 1;
```

The output is as follows:

```
            name            |         source        |      setting
----------------------------+-----------------------+-------------------
 application_name           | client                | psql
 client_encoding            | client                | UTF8
 DateStyle                  | configuration file    | ISO, DMY
 default_text_search_config | configuration file    | pg_catalog.english
 dynamic_shared_memory_type | configuration file    | posix
 lc_messages                | configuration file    | en_GB.UTF-8
 lc_monetary                | configuration file    | en_GB.UTF-8
 lc_numeric                 | configuration file    | en_GB.UTF-8
 lc_time                    | configuration file    | en_GB.UTF-8
 log_timezone               | configuration file    | Europe/Rome
 max_connections            | configuration file    | 100
 port                       | configuration file    | 5460
 shared_buffers             | configuration file    | 16384
 TimeZone                   | configuration file    | Europe/Rome
 max_stack_depth            | environment variable  | 2048
```

How it works...

You can see from `pg_settings` which parameters have nondefault values and what the source of the current value is.

The `SHOW` command doesn't tell you whether a parameter is set at a nondefault value. It just tells you the value, which isn't of much help if you're trying to understand what is set and why.

If the source is a configuration file, then the `sourcefile` and `sourceline` columns are also set. These can be useful in understanding where the configuration came from.

There's more...

The `setting` column of `pg_settings` shows the current value, but you can also look at `boot_val` and `reset_val`. The `boot_val` parameter shows the value assigned when the PostgreSQL database cluster was initialized (`initdb`), while `reset_val` shows the value that the parameter will return to if you issue the `RESET` command.

The `max_stack_depth` parameter is an exception because `pg_settings` says it is set by the environment variable, though it is actually set by `ulimit -s` on Linux and Unix systems. The `max_stack_depth` parameter just needs to be set directly on Windows.

The time zone settings are also picked up from the OS environment, so you shouldn't need to set those directly. In older releases, `pg_settings` showed them as command-line settings. From version 9.1 onwards, they are written to `postgresql.conf` when the `data` directory is initialized, so they show up as configuration files.

Updating the parameter file

The parameter file is the main location for defining parameter values for the PostgreSQL server. All the parameters can be set in the parameter file, which is known as `postgresql.conf`.

There are also two other parameter files: `pg_hba.conf` and `pg_ident.conf`. Both of these relate to connections and security, so we'll cover them in the appropriate chapters that follow.

Getting ready

First, locate `postgresql.conf`, as described earlier.

How to do it...

Some of the parameters take effect only when the server is first started. A typical example might be `shared_buffers`, which defines the size of the shared memory cache.

Many of the parameters can be changed while the server is still running. After changing the required parameters, we issue a `reload` operation to the server, forcing PostgreSQL to reread the `postgresql.conf` file (and all other configuration files):

pg_ctl reload

As noted earlier, Debian and Ubuntu have different multiversion architecture, so you should issue the following command instead:

pg_ctlcluster 9.4 main reload

Some other parameters require a restart of the server for changes to take effect, for instance, `max_connections`, `listen_addresses`, and so on. The syntax is very similar to a `reload` operation, as shown here:

pg_ctl restart

For Debian and Ubuntu, use this command:

pg_ctlcluster 9.4 main restart

Of course, a restart also has some impact on existing connections. See the *Restarting the server quickly* recipe in *Chapter 4, Server Control*, for further details.

The `postgresql.conf` file is a normal text file that can be simply edited. Most of the parameters are listed in the file, so you can just search for them and then insert the desired value in the right place.

How it works...

If you set the same parameter twice in different parts of the file, the last setting is what applies. This can cause lots of confusion if you add settings to the bottom of the file, so you are advised against doing that.

The best practice is to either leave the file as it is and edit the values, or to start with a blank file and include only the values that you wish to change. I personally prefer a file with only the nondefault values. That makes it easier to see what's happening.

Whichever method you use, you are strongly advised to keep all the previous versions of your `.conf` files. You can do this by copying, or you can use a version control system such as Git or SVN.

There's more...

The `postgresql.conf` file also supports an `include` directive. This allows the `postgresql.conf` file to reference other files, which can then reference other files, and so on. That may help you organize your parameter settings better, if you don't make it too complicated.

For more on reloading, see the *Reloading the server configuration files* recipe in *Chapter 4, Server Control*.

If you are working with PostgreSQL version 9.4 or later, you can change the values stored in the parameter files directly from your session, with syntax such as the following:

```
ALTER SYSTEM SET shared_buffers = '1GB';
```

This command will not actually edit `postgresql.conf`. Instead, it writes the new setting to another file named `postgresql.auto.conf`. The effect is equivalent, albeit in a safer way. The original configuration is never written, so it cannot be damaged in the event of a crash. If you mess up with too many `ALTER SYSTEM` commands, you can always delete `postgresql.auto.conf` manually and reload the configuration, or restart PostgreSQL, depending on what parameters you had changed.

Setting parameters for particular groups of users

PostgreSQL supports a variety of ways of defining parameter settings for various user groups. This is very convenient, especially to manage user groups that have different requirements.

How to do it...

For all users in the `saas` database, use the following commands:

```
ALTER DATABASE saas
SET configuration_parameter = value1;
```

For a user named `simon` connected to any database, use this:

```
ALTER ROLE Simon
SET configuration_parameter = value2;
```

Alternatively, you can set a parameter for a user only when connected to a specific database, as follows:

```
ALTER ROLE Simon
IN DATABASE saas
SET configuration_parameter = value3;
```

The user won't know that these have been executed specifically for them. These are default settings, and in most cases, they can be overridden if the user requires nondefault values.

How it works...

You can set parameters for each of the following:

- Database
- User (which is named **role** by PostgreSQL)
- Database/user combination

Each of the parameter defaults is overridden by the one below it.

In the preceding three SQL statements:

- ▸ If user `hannu` connects to the `saas` database, then `value1` will apply
- ▸ If user `simon` connects to a database other than `saas`, then `value2` will apply
- ▸ If user `simon` connects to the `saas` database, then `value3` will apply

PostgreSQL implements this in exactly the same way as if the user had manually issued the equivalent `SET` statements immediately after connecting.

The basic server configuration checklist

PostgreSQL arrives configured for use on a shared system, though many people want to run dedicated database systems. The PostgreSQL project wishes to ensure that PostgreSQL will play nicely with other server software, and will not assume that it has access to the full server resources. If you, as the system administrator, know that there is no other important server software running on this system, then you can crank up the values much higher.

Getting ready

Before we start, we need to know two sets of information:

- ▸ We need to know the size of the physical RAM that will be dedicated to PostgreSQL
- ▸ We need to know something about the types of applications for which we will use PostgreSQL

How to do it...

If your database is larger than 32 MB, then you'll probably benefit from increasing `shared_buffers`. You can increase this to much larger values, but remember that running out of memory induces many problems.

For instance, PostgreSQL is able to store information to the disk when the available memory is too small, and it employs sophisticated algorithms to treat each case differently and to place each piece of data either in the disk or in the memory, depending on each use case.

On the other hand, overstating the amount of available memory confuses such abilities and results in suboptimal behavior. For instance, if the memory is swapped to disk, then PostgreSQL will inefficiently treat all data as if it were the RAM. Another unfortunate circumstance is when the Linux **Out-Of-Memory** (**OOM**) killer terminates one of the various processes spawned by the PostgreSQL server. So, it's better to be conservative. It is good practice to set a low value in your `postgresql.conf` and increment slowly to ensure that you get the benefits from each change.

If you increase `shared_buffers` and you're running on a non-Windows server, you will almost certainly need to increase the value of the SHMMAX OS parameter (and on some platforms, other parameters as well).

On Linux, Mac OS, and FreeBSD, you will need to either edit the `/etc/sysctl.conf` file or use `sysctl -w` with the following values:

- For Linux, use `kernel.shmmax=value`
- For Mac OS, use `kern.sysv.shmmax=value`
- For FreeBSD, use `kern.ipc.shmmax=value`

There's more...

For more information, you can refer to `http://www.postgresql.org/docs/9.4/static/kernel-resources.html#SYSVIPC`.

For example, on Linux, add the following line to `/etc/sysctl.conf`:

```
kernel.shmmax=value
```

Don't worry about setting `effective_cache_size`. It is much less important a parameter than you might think. There is no need for too much fuss selecting the value.

If you're doing heavy write activity, then you may want to set `wal_buffers` to a much higher value than the default. If you are using PostgreSQL 9.1 or later, then `wal_buffers` is set automatically from the value of `shared_buffers`, following a rule that fits most cases. Anyway, it is always possible to specify an explicit value that overrides the computation for the very few cases where the rule is not good enough.

If you're doing heavy write activity and/or large data loads, you may want to set `checkpoint_segments` higher than the default to avoid wasting I/O in excessively frequent checkpoints.

If your database has many large queries, you may wish to set `work_mem` to a value higher than the default. However, remember that such a limit applies separately to *each* node in the query plan, so there is a real risk of overallocating memory, with all the problems discussed earlier.

Ensure that autovacuum is turned on, unless you have a very good reason to turn it off—most people don't. See later chapters for more information on autovacuum, in particular *Chapter 9, Regular Maintenance*.

Leave the settings as they are for now. Don't fuss too much about getting the settings right. You can change most of them later, so you can take an iterative approach to improving things.

Get the basics right, and keep it simple and solid. Then, buy Greg Smith's book, *PostgreSQL 9.0 High Performance, Packt Publishing*, which goes beyond the basics.

Especially, don't touch the `fsync` parameter. It's keeping you safe.

Adding an external module to PostgreSQL

Another strength of PostgreSQL is its extensibility. Extensibility was one of the original design goals, going back to the late 1980s. Now, in PostgreSQL 9.4, there are many additional modules that plug into the core PostgreSQL server.

There are many kinds of additional module offerings, such as the following:

- Additional functions
- Additional data types
- Additional operators
- Additional indexes

Note that many tools and client interfaces work with PostgreSQL without any special installation. Here, we are discussing modules that extend and alter the behavior of the server beyond its normal range of SQL Standard syntax, functions, and behavior.

The procedure that makes a module usable is actually a two-step process. First, you install the module's files on your system so that they become available to the database server. Next, you connect to the database (or databases) where you want to use the module, and create the required objects. The first step is discussed in this recipe. For the second step, refer to the next recipe, *Using an installed module*.

In this book, we will use the words "extension" and "module" as synonyms, like in the PostgreSQL documentation. Note, however, that the SQL commands that manage extensions, which we'll describe in the next recipe, are spelt as follows:

```
CREATE EXTENSION myext;
ALTER EXTENSION myext UPDATE;
```

In particular, commands such as CREATE MODULE won't work at all!

Getting ready

First, you'll need to select an appropriate module to install.

The walk towards a complete, automated package management system for PostgreSQL is not over yet, so you need to look in more than one place for the available modules, such as the following:

- **Contrib**: The PostgreSQL "core" includes many functions. There is also an official section for add-in modules, known as "contrib" modules. They are always available for your database server, but are not automatically enabled in every database because not all users might need them. On PostgreSQL version 9.4, we will have more than 40 such modules. These are documented at `http://www.postgresql.org/docs/9.4/static/contrib.html`.

- **pgFoundry**: This is an open source development website created specifically to allow PostgreSQL modules and tools to be shared. pgFoundry uses the same software as SourceForge. For more details, take a look at `http://pgFoundry.org/`.

- **PGXN**: This is the PostgreSQL Extension Network, a central distribution system dedicated to sharing PostgreSQL extensions. The website started in 2010, as a repository dedicated to the sharing of extension files. At the time of writing this book, it contains about 140 extensions from 160 different authors. You can learn more about it at `http://pgxn.org/`.

- **Separate projects**: These are large external projects, such as PostGIS, offering extensive and complex PostgreSQL modules. For more information, take a look at `http://www.postgis.org/`.

How to do it...

There are several ways to make additional modules available for your database server, as follows:

- Using a software installer
- Installing from PGXN
- Installing from a manually downloaded package
- Installing from source code

Often, a particular module will be available in more than one way, and users are free to choose their favorite, exactly like PostgreSQL itself, which can be downloaded and installed through many different procedures.

Installing modules using a software installer

Certain modules are available exactly like any other software packages that you may want to install in your server. All main Linux distributions provide packages for the most popular modules, such as PostGIS, SkyTools, procedural languages other than those distributed with core, and so on.

In some cases, modules can be added during installation if you're using a standalone installer application, for example, the OneClick installer, or tools such as rpm, apt-get, and YaST on Linux distributions. The same procedure can also be followed after the PostgreSQL installation, when the need for a certain module arrives. We will actually describe this case, which is way more common.

For example, let's say that you need to manage a collection of Debian package files, and that one of your tasks is to be able to pick the latest version of one of them. You start by building a database that records all the package files. Clearly, you need to store the version number of each package. However, Debian version numbers are much more complex than what we usually call "numbers". For instance, on my Debian laptop, I currently have version `9.2.4-1.pgdg70` of the PostgreSQL client package. Despite being complicated, that string follows a clearly defined specification, which includes many bits of information, including how to compare two versions to establish which of them is older.

Since this recipe discussed extending PostgreSQL with custom data types and operators, you might have already guessed that I will now consider a custom data type for Debian version numbers that is capable of tasks such as understanding the Debian version number format, sorting version numbers, choosing the latest version number in a given group, and so on. It turns out that somebody else already did all the work of creating the required PostgreSQL data type, endowed with all the useful accessories: comparison operators, input/output functions, support for indexes, and maximum/minimum aggregates. All of this has been packaged as a PostgreSQL extension, as well as a Debian package (not a big surprise), so it is just a matter of installing the `postgresql-9.2-debversion` package with a Debian tool such as apt-get, aptitude, or synaptic. On my laptop, that boils down to the command line:

```
apt-get install postgresql-9.2-debversion
```

This will download the required package and unpack all the files in the right locations, making them available to my PostgreSQL server.

Installing modules from PGXN

The PostgreSQL Extension Network, PGXN for short, is a website (`http://pgxn.org`) launched in late 2010 with the purpose of providing "a central distribution system for open source PostgreSQL extension libraries". Anybody can register and upload their own module, packaged as an extension archive. The website allows browsing available extensions and their versions, either via a search interface or from a directory of package and user names.

The simple way is to use a command-line utility, called **pgxnclient**. It can be easily installed in most systems; see the PGXN website on how to do so. Its purpose is to interact with PGXN and take care of administrative tasks, such as browsing available extensions, downloading the package, compiling the source code, installing files in the proper place, and removing installed package files. Alternatively, you can download the extension files from the website and place them in the right place by following the installation instructions.

PGXN is different from official repositories because it serves another purpose. Official repositories usually contain only seasoned extensions because they accept new software only after a certain amount of evaluation and testing. On the other hand, anybody can ask for a PGXN account and upload their own extensions, so there is no filter except requiring that the extension has an open source license and a few files that any extension must have.

Installing modules from a manually downloaded package

You might have to install a module that is correctly packaged for your system but is not available from the official package archives. For instance, it could be the case that the module has not been accepted in the official repository yet, or you could have repackaged a bespoke version of that module with some custom tweaks, which are so specific that they will never become official. Whatever the case, you will have to follow the installation procedure for standalone packages specific to your system.

Here is an example with the Oracle compatibility module, described at `http://postgres.cz/wiki/Oracle_functionality_(en)`:

1. First, we get the package, say for PostgreSQL 8.4 on a 64-bit architecture, from `http://pgfoundry.org/frs/download.php/2414/orafce-3.0.1-1.pg84.rhel5.x86_64.rpm`.

2. Then, we install the package in the standard way:

   ```
   rpm -ivh orafce-3.0.1-1.pg84.rhel5.x86_64.rpm
   ```

If all the dependencies are met, we are done.

> I mentioned dependencies because that's one more potential problem in installing packages that are not officially part of the installed distribution—you can no longer assume that all software version numbers have been tested, all requirements are available, and there are no conflicts. If you get error messages that indicate problems in these areas, you may have to solve them yourself, by manually installing missing packages and/or uninstalling conflicting packages.

Installing modules from source code

In many cases, useful modules may not have full packaging. In these cases, you may need to install the module manually. This isn't very hard and it's a useful exercise that helps you understand what happens.

Each module will have different installation requirements. There are generally two aspects of installing a module. They are as follows:

- ▶ Building the libraries (only for modules that have libraries)
- ▶ Installing the module files in the appropriate locations

You need to follow the instructions for the specific module in order to build the libraries, if any are required. Installation will then be straightforward, and usually there will be a suitably prepared configuration file for the make utility so that you just need to type the following command:

```
make install
```

Each file will be copied to the right directory. Remember that you normally need to be a system superuser in order to install files on system directories.

Once a library file is in the directory expected by the PostgreSQL server, it will be loaded automatically as soon as requested by a function. Modules such as auto_explain do not provide any additional user-defined function, so they won't be auto-loaded; that needs to be done manually by a superuser with a LOAD statement.

How it works...

PostgreSQL can dynamically load libraries in the following ways:

- ▶ Using the explicit LOAD command in a session
- ▶ Using the shared_preload_libraries parameter in postgresql.conf at server start
- ▶ At session start, using the local_preload_libraries parameter for a specific user, as set using ALTER ROLE

PostgreSQL functions and objects can reference code in these libraries, allowing extensions to be bound tightly to the running server process. The tight binding makes this method suitable for use even in very high-performance applications, and there's no significant difference between additionally supplied features and native features.

Using an installed module

In this recipe, we will explain how to enable an installed module so that it can be used in a particular database. The additional types, functions, and so on will exist only in those databases where we have carried out this step.

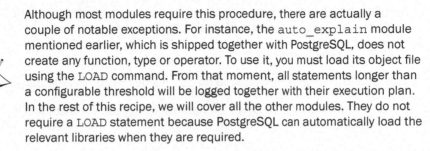

> Although most modules require this procedure, there are actually a couple of notable exceptions. For instance, the auto_explain module mentioned earlier, which is shipped together with PostgreSQL, does not create any function, type or operator. To use it, you must load its object file using the LOAD command. From that moment, all statements longer than a configurable threshold will be logged together with their execution plan. In the rest of this recipe, we will cover all the other modules. They do not require a LOAD statement because PostgreSQL can automatically load the relevant libraries when they are required.

This recipe describes a procedure that has been greatly simplified in version 9.1 of PostgreSQL with the introduction of the infrastructure to install, uninstall, and upgrade the available modules. As mentioned in the previous recipe, *Adding an external module to PostgreSQL*, specially packaged modules are called extensions in PostgreSQL. They can be managed with dedicated SQL commands.

Extension support is a great step towards an automated package management system for PostgreSQL, but it happened quite recently. We must wait a few more months (probably September 2015) before assuming that *all* PostgreSQL servers support extensions. Therefore, we will also cover operations such as the following:

- How to install modules without using the extension infrastructure
- How to upgrade an existing module, previously installed without using the extension infrastructure, to a PostgreSQL extension

Getting ready

Suppose you have chosen to install a certain module among those available for your system (see the previous recipe, *Adding an external module to PostgreSQL*). Next, you must ask yourself two questions:

- Am I running PostgreSQL version 9.1 or later?
- Is the chosen module available as a PostgreSQL extension?

If the answer to both questions is "yes", then you can benefit from the infrastructure for extensions, which we will describe in this recipe and the next one.

How to do it...

There are two different variants, depending on whether your server supports the extension infrastructure.

Using the extension infrastructure

We will now explain how to install a module using the extension infrastructure. Each extension has a unique name, so it is just a matter of issuing the following command:

```
CREATE EXTENSION myextname;
```

This will automatically create all the required objects inside the current database.

For security reasons, you need to do so as a database superuser. For instance, if you want to install the dblink extension, type this:

```
CREATE EXTENSION dblink;
```

Without the extension infrastructure

Normally, each module should have two SQL scripts, one of each to create and drop all the database objects belonging to the module. For contrib modules, they are named MODULENAME.sql and uninstall_MODULENAME.sql, and can be found in the SHAREDIR/contrib directory. The exact value of SHAREDIR varies, depending on the installation, and can be displayed using the following command:

```
pg_config --sharedir
```

To install the dblink contrib module on PostgreSQL 9.0, we must load SHAREDIR/contrib/dblink.sql as a database superuser. On my Debian system, SHAREDIR is /usr/share/postgresql/9.0, so I can do it by connecting as a database superuser and issuing these commands:

```
BEGIN;
\i /usr/share/postgresql/9.0/contrib/dblink.sql
COMMIT;
```

Note that the installation script is wrapped into a single transaction by the BEGIN / COMMIT commands. This is best practice, because it avoids leaving partial changes in case something fails (for example, if there is a name collision with a previously created object).

How it works...

When you issue a `CREATE EXTENSION` command, the database server looks for a file named `EXTNAME.control` in the `SHAREDIR/extension` directory. That file tells PostgreSQL some properties of the extension, including a description, some installation information, and the default version number of the extension (which is unrelated to the PostgreSQL version number). Then, a creation script is executed in a single transaction, so if it fails, the database is unchanged. The database server also notes in a catalog table the extension name and all the objects that belong to it.

If you install a module without using the extension infrastructure, you only execute a creation script; the database will not remember which objects belong to modules. You should also remember to wrap the creation script in a transaction.

There's more...

At this point, you are more likely to welcome extension support than not. In any case, you will appreciate it even more when it comes to maintenance work directly related to extensions.

In particular, we refer to activities such as listing installed extensions, uninstalling unwanted extensions, upgrading extensions that have a newer version, and also other maintenance work (which seems unrelated at first), such as taking and restoring database backups.

When using PostgreSQL version 9.1 or later, there is no reason to add a module without using the extension infrastructure, except in the case when the module has not been packaged as an extension.

As time goes by, this will keep getting less likely; all the contrib modules were packaged as extensions as soon as version 9.1 was released. Maintainers of the other modules are rapidly catching up, since extensions simplify things for them too.

Managing installed extensions

In the last two recipes, we showed you how to install external modules in PostgreSQL to augment its capabilities. Actually, the last recipe came in two variants, depending on whether we can use the newly introduced extension infrastructure.

In this recipe, we will show you some more capabilities offered by the extension infrastructure. Everything here applies only to PostgreSQL version 9.1 and later.

Getting ready

You only need to ensure that your PostgreSQL version is 9.1 or later.

How to do it...

First, we list all available extensions:

```
postgres=# \x on
Expanded display is on.
postgres=# SELECT *
postgres-# FROM pg_available_extensions
postgres-# ORDER BY name;
-[ RECORD 1 ]-----+--------------------------------------------------
name              | adminpack
default_version   | 1.0
installed_version |
comment           | administrative functions for PostgreSQL
-[ RECORD 2 ]-----+--------------------------------------------------
name              | autoinc
default_version   | 1.0
installed_version |
comment           | functions for autoincrementing fields
(...)
```

In particular, if the dblink extension is installed, then we see a record like this:

```
-[ RECORD 10 ]----+--------------------------------------------------
name              | dblink
default_version   | 1.0
installed_version | 1.0
comment           | connect to other PostgreSQL databases from within a
database
```

Now, we can list all the objects in the dblink extension, as follows:

```
postgres=# \x off
Expanded display is off.
postgres=# \dx+ dblink
```

```
                    Objects in extension "dblink"
                       Object Description
-------------------------------------------------------------------
 function dblink_build_sql_delete(text,int2vector,integer,text[])
 function dblink_build_sql_insert(text,int2vector,integer,text[],text[])
 function dblink_build_sql_update(text,int2vector,integer,text[],text[])
 function dblink_cancel_query(text)
 function dblink_close(text)
 function dblink_close(text,boolean)
 function dblink_close(text,text)
(...)
```

Objects created as parts of extensions are not special in any way, except that you can't drop them individually. This is done to protect you from mistakes:

```
postgres=# DROP FUNCTION dblink_close(text);
ERROR:  cannot drop function dblink_close(text) because extension dblink
requires it
HINT:  You can drop extension dblink instead.
```

Extensions might have dependencies too. The cube and earthdistance contrib extensions provide a good example, since the latter depends on the former:

```
postgres=# CREATE EXTENSION earthdistance;
ERROR:  required extension "cube" is not installed
postgres=# CREATE EXTENSION cube;
CREATE EXTENSION
postgres=# CREATE EXTENSION earthdistance;
CREATE EXTENSION
```

As you can reasonably expect, dependencies are taken into account when dropping objects, just like for other objects:

```
postgres=# DROP EXTENSION cube;
ERROR:  cannot drop extension cube because other objects depend on it
DETAIL:  extension earthdistance depends on extension cube
HINT:  Use DROP ... CASCADE to drop the dependent objects too.
postgres=# DROP EXTENSION cube CASCADE;
NOTICE:  drop cascades to extension earthdistance
DROP EXTENSION
```

How it works...

The `pg_available_extensions` system view shows one row for each extension control file in the `SHAREDIR/extension` directory (see the *Using an installed module* recipe). The `pg_extension` catalog table records only the extensions that have actually been created.

The psql command-line utility provides the `\dx` meta-command to examine e"x"tensions. It supports an optional plus sign (+) to control verbosity and an optional pattern for the extension name to restrict its range. Consider the following command:

```
\dx+ db*
```

This will list all extensions whose name starts with `db`, together with all their objects.

The `CREATE EXTENSION` command creates all objects belonging to a given extension, and then records the dependency of each object on the extension in `pg_depend`. That's how PostgreSQL can ensure that you cannot drop one such object without dropping its extension.

The extension control file admits an optional line, `requires`, that names one or more extensions on which the current one depends. The implementation of dependencies is still quite simple. For instance, there is no way to specify a dependency on a specific version number of other extensions, and there is no command that installs one extension and all its prerequisites.

As a general PostgreSQL rule, the `CASCADE` keyword tells the `DROP` command to delete all the objects that depend on `cube`, the `earthdistance` extension in this example.

There's more...

Another system view, `pg_available_extension_versions`, shows all the versions available for each extension. It can be valuable when there are multiple versions of the same extension available at the same time, for example, when making preparations for an extension upgrade.

When a more recent version of an already installed extension becomes available to the database server, for instance because of a distribution upgrade that installs updated package files, the superuser can perform an upgrade by issuing the following command:

```
ALTER EXTENSION myext UPDATE TO '1.1';
```

This assumes that the author of the extension taught it how to perform the upgrade.

Extensions interact nicely with logical backup and restore, a topic that will be fully discussed in *Chapter 11, Backup and Recovery*. As an example, if your database contains the `cube` extension, then you would surely want a single line (`CREATE EXTENSION cube;`) in the dump file instead of lots of lines recreating each object individually, which is inefficient and also dangerous.

4
Server Control

In this chapter, we will cover the following recipes:

- ▸ Starting the database server manually
- ▸ Stopping the server safely and quickly
- ▸ Stopping the server in an emergency
- ▸ Reloading the server configuration files
- ▸ Restarting the server quickly
- ▸ Preventing new connections
- ▸ Restricting users to only one session each
- ▸ Pushing users off the system
- ▸ Deciding on a design for multitenancy
- ▸ Using multiple schemas
- ▸ Giving users their own private database
- ▸ Running multiple servers on one system
- ▸ Setting up a connection pool
- ▸ Accessing multiple servers using the same host and port

Introduction

PostgreSQL consists of a set of server processes, the group leader of which is named the **postmaster**. Starting the server is the act of creating these processes, and stopping the server means to terminate those processes.

Each postmaster listens for client connection requests on a defined port number. Multiple concurrently running postmasters cannot share that port number. The port number is often used to uniquely identify a particular postmaster and hence also the database server that it leads.

When we start a database server, we refer to a **data directory**, which contains the heart and soul—or at least the data—of our database. Subsidiary tablespaces may contain some data outside the main data directory, so the data directory is just the main central location, and not the only place where data for that database server is held. Each running server has one data directory, and one data directory can have at the most one running server (or instance).

To perform any action for a database server, we must know the data directory for that server. The basic actions we can perform on the database server are starting and stopping. We can also perform a restart, though that is just a stop followed by a start. In addition, we can reload the server, which means we can reread the server's configuration files.

We should also mention a few other points.

The default port number for PostgreSQL is 5432. That has been registered with the **Internet Assigned Numbers Authority** (**IANA**), and so it should already be reserved for PostgreSQL's use in most places. Because each PostgreSQL server requires a distinct port number, the normal convention is to use subsequent numbers for any additional server, for example, 5433, 5434, and so on. Subsequent port numbers might not be as easily recognized by the network infrastructure, which might, in some cases, make life more difficult for you in large enterprises, especially in more security-conscious ones.

Port number 6432 has been registered with IANA for PgBouncer, the connection pooler that we will describe in the *Setting up a connection pool* recipe. This happened only recently, and many installations are using nonstandard port numbers such as 6543 only because they were deployed earlier.

A database server is also sometimes referred to as a database cluster. I don't recommend that term for normal usage because it makes people think about multiple nodes, not one database server on one system.

Starting the database server manually

Typically, the PostgreSQL server will start automatically when the system boots. You may have opted to stop and start the server manually, or you may need to start up or shut down for various operational reasons.

Getting ready

First, you need to understand the difference between the service and the server. The word "server" refers to the database server and its processes. The word "service" refers to the operating system wrapper by which the server gets called. The server works in essentially the same way on every platform, whereas each operating system and distribution has its own concept of a service.

How to do it...

On all platforms, there is a specific command to start the server:

▶ Here is the command for Ubuntu and Debian:

```
pg_ctlcluster 9.4 main start
```

▶ For Red Hat/Fedora, the command is as follows:

```
pg_ctl -D /var/lib/pgsql/data start
```

▶ For Solaris, this is the command:

```
pg_ctl -D /var/lib/pgsql/data start
```

▶ For Mac OS, the command is as follows:

```
pg_ctl -D /var/lib/pgsql/data start
```

▶ For FreeBSD, the following is the command:

```
pg_ctl -D /var/lib/pgsql/data start
```

On some platforms, the service can be started in various ways, such as these:

▶ For Red Hat/Fedora, you can use this command:

```
service postgresql start
```

▶ For Windows, the command is as follows:

```
net start postgres
```

How it works...

On Ubuntu/Debian, the `pg_ctlcluster` wrapper is a convenient utility that allows multiple servers to coexist more easily, which is especially good when you have servers with different versions. This is very useful.

Another feature specific to Ubuntu and Debian is the `start.conf` file, located next to the other configuration files (that is, in the same directory). Apart from the informational comments, it contains only a single word, with the following meaning:

▶ `auto`: The server will be started automatically on booting. This is the default when creating a new server. It is suitable for frequently used servers, such as those powering live services or being used for everyday development activities.

▶ `manual`: The server will not be started automatically on boot, but can be started with `pg_ctlcluster`. This is suitable for custom servers that are seldom used.

▶ `disabled`: The server is not supposed to be started. This setting is only a protection from starting the server accidentally. The `pg_ctlcluster` wrapper won't let you start it, but a skilled user can easily bypass the protection.

 If you need to reserve a port for a server not managed by `pg_ctlcluster`, for example, when compiling directly from the source code, then you can create a cluster with `start.conf` set to `disabled`, and then use its port. Any new servers will be allocated different ports.

Stopping the server safely and quickly

There are several modes to stop the server, depending on the level of urgency. We'll do a comparison in view of the effects in each mode.

How to do it...

You can issue a database server `stop` command using fast mode, as follows:

```
pg_ctl -D datadir -m fast stop
```

You must use `-m fast` if you wish to shut down as soon as possible. Normal shutdown means "wait for all users to finish before we exit". That can take a very long time, though all the while new connections are refused.

On Debian/Ubuntu systems, this command can be as follows:

```
pg_ctlcluster 9.0 main stop --force
```

How it works...

When you do a fast stop, all users have their transactions aborted and all connections are disconnected. This is not very polite to users, but it still treats the server and its data with care, which is good.

PostgreSQL is similar to other database systems in that it does do a shutdown checkpoint before it closes. This means that the startup that follows will be quick and clean. The more work the checkpoint has to do, the longer it will take to shut down.

One difference between PostgreSQL and some other RDBMSes such as Oracle, DB2, or SQL Server is that the transaction rollback is very fast. On those other systems, if you shut down the server in a mode that rolls back transactions, it can cause the shutdown to take a while, possibly a very long time. This difference is for internal reasons, and isn't in any way unsafe. Some distributions (for example, Debian and Ubuntu) support the ``--force`` option, which is rather nice because it first attempts a fast shutdown, and if that fails, it performs an immediate shutdown. After that, it kills the postmaster.

See also

The technology that provides immediate rollback for PostgreSQL is called MVCC. More information on this is provided in the *Identifying and fixing bloated tables and indexes* recipe in *Chapter 9*, *Regular Maintenance*.

Stopping the server in an emergency

If nothing else is working, we may need to stop the server quickly, without caring about disconnecting the clients gently.

"Break the glass in case of emergency!"

How to do it...

The basic command to perform an emergency restart on the server is the following:

```
pg_ctl -D datadir stop -m immediate
```

We must use an immediate stop mode.

How it works...

When you do an immediate stop, all users have their transactions aborted and all connections are disconnected. There is no clean shutdown, nor is there politeness of any kind.

An immediate mode stop is similar to a database crash. Some cached files will need to be rebuilt, and the database itself needs to undergo crash recovery when it comes back up.

 Note that for DBAs with Oracle experience, immediate mode is the same thing as a **shutdown abort**. The PostgreSQL immediate mode stop is *not* the same thing as *shutdown immediate* on Oracle.

Reloading the server configuration files

Some PostgreSQL configuration parameters can only be changed by reloading the entire configuration file.

How to do it...

On all platforms, there is a specific command to reload the server. All of these are listed as follows:

- Here is the command for Ubuntu and Debian:

  ```
  pg_ctlcluster 9.4 main reload
  ```

- For Red Hat/Fedora, the command is as follows:

  ```
  service postgresql reload
  ```

  You can also use the following command:

  ```
  pg_ctl -D /var/lib/pgsql/data reload
  ```

- For Solaris, this is the command:

  ```
  pg_ctl -D /var/lib/pgsql/data reload
  ```

- For Mac OS, the command is as follows:

  ```
  pg_ctl -D /var/lib/pgsql/data reload
  ```

- Here is the command for FreeBSD:

  ```
  pg_ctl -D /var/lib/pgsql/data reload
  ```

You can reload the configuration files while still connected to PostgreSQL. This can be done from the command line as follows, if you are a superuser:

```
postgres=# select pg_reload_conf();
```

The output is rather short:

```
 pg_reload_conf
----------------
 t
```

This function is also often executed from an admin tool, such as pgAdmin3.

If you do this, you should realize that it's possible to implement a new authentication rule that is violated by the current session. It won't force you to disconnect, but when you do disconnect, you may not be able to reconnect.

> Any error in a configuration file will be reported in the message log, so we recommend to look there immediately after reloading. You will quickly notice (and fix!) syntax errors, because they prevent any login even before reloading. Other errors, such as typos in parameter names, or wrong units, will only be reported in the log; moreover, only some non-syntax errors will prevent reloading the whole file, so it's best to check the log in any case.

How it works...

To reload the configuration files, we send the SIGHUP signal to the postmaster, which then passes that to all connected backends. That's why some people call reloading the server "sigh-up-ing".

If you look at the pg_settings catalog table, you'll see that there is a column named context. Each setting has a time and a place where it can be changed. Some parameters can only be reset by a server reload, and so the value of context for those parameters will be a sighup. Here are a few of the parameters you'd want to change sometimes during server operation (there are others, however):

```
postgres=#  SELECT name, setting, unit
                        ,(source = 'default') as is_default
            FROM pg_settings
            WHERE context = 'sighup'
            AND (name like '%delay' or name like '%timeout')
            AND setting != '0';
```

```
           name              | setting | unit | is_default
-----------------------------+---------+------+------------
 authentication_timeout      | 60      | s    | t
 autovacuum_vacuum_cost_delay| 20      | ms   | t
 bgwriter_delay              | 10      | ms   | f
 checkpoint_timeout          | 32      | s    | f
 deadlock_timeout            | 1000    | ms   | t
 max_standby_delay           | 30      |      | t
 wal_sender_delay            | 200     | ms   | t
 wal_writer_delay            | 200     | ms   | t
(8 rows)
```

There's more...

As reloading the configuration file is achieved by sending the SIGHUP signal, we can reload the configuration file only for a single backend using the kill command. As you might expect, you may get some strange results from doing this, so don't try it at home.

First, find the PID of the backend using pg_stat_activity. Then, from the OS prompt, issue the following:

```
kill -SIGHUP    pid
```

Alternatively, we can do both at once, as shown in this command:

```
kill -SIGHUP \
`psql -t -c "select procpid from pg_stat_activity limit 1"`
```

This is only useful with a sensible WHERE clause.

Restarting the server quickly

Some of the database server parameters require you to stop and start the server again fully. Doing this as quickly as possible can be very important in some cases. The best time to do this is usually a quiet time, with lots of planning, testing, and forethought. Sometimes, not everything goes according to plan.

How to do it...

The basic command to restart the server is the following:

```
pg_ctl -D datadir restart -m fast
```

A restart is just a stop followed by a start, so it sounds very simple. In many cases, it will be simple, but there are times when you'll need to restart the server while it is fairly busy. That's when we need to start pulling some tricks to make that restart happen faster.

First, the stop performed needs to be a fast stop. If we do a default or "smart" stop, then the server will just wait for everyone to finish. If we do an immediate stop, then the server will crash, and we will need to crash-recover the data, which will be slower overall.

The running database server has a cache full of data blocks, many of them dirty. PostgreSQL is similar to other database systems in that it does a shutdown checkpoint before it closes. This means that the startup that follows will be quick and clean. The more work the checkpoint has to do, the longer it will take to shut down.

The actual shutdown will happen much faster if we issue a normal checkpoint first, as the shutdown checkpoint will have much less work to do. So, flush all the dirty shared buffers to disk with the following command, issued by a database superuser:

```
psql -c "CHECKPOINT"
```

The next consideration is that once we restart, the database cache will be empty again and will need to refresh itself. The larger the database cache, the longer it takes for the cache to get warm again, and 30 to 60 minutes is not uncommon before returning to full speed. So, what was a simple restart can actually have a large business impact if handled badly.

There's more...

There is an extension called **pgfincore** that implements a set of functions to manage PostgreSQL data pages in the operating system's file cache. One possible use is to preload some tables so that PostgreSQL will load them faster when requested. The general idea is that you can provide more detailed information for the operating system cache, which can therefore behave more efficiently.

The pgfincore extension is a stable project started in 2009. More details about it are available at http://pgfoundry.org/projects/pgfincore, including the source code. However, it should be noted that most distributions include a prebuilt pgfincore package, which makes installation easier.

Preventing new connections

In certain emergencies, you may need to lock down the server completely, or just prevent specific users from accessing the database. It's hard to foresee all the situations in which you might need to do this, so we present a range of options.

How to do it...

Connections can be prevented in a number of ways, as follows:

- Pause and resume the session pool. See the *Setting up a connection pool* recipe later in this chapter on controlling connection pools.

- Stop the server! See the *Stopping the server safely and quickly* and *Stopping the server in an emergency* recipes, but this is not recommended.

- Restrict the connections for a specific database to zero, by setting the connection limit to zero:

   `ALTER DATABASE foo_db CONNECTION LIMIT 0;`

   This will limit normal users from connecting to that database, though it will still allow superuser connections.

- Restrict the connections for a specific user to zero by setting the connection limit to zero (see the *Restricting users to only one session each* recipe):

   `ALTER USER foo CONNECTION LIMIT 0;`

   This will limit normal users from connecting to that database, but it will still allow connections if the user is a superuser, so luckily you cannot shut yourself out accidentally.

- Change the **host-based authentication** (**HBA**) file to refuse all incoming connections, and then reload the server:

   - Create a new file named `pg_hba_lockdown.conf`, and add the following two lines to the file. This puts in place rules that will completely lock down the server, including superusers. You should have no doubt that this is a serious and drastic action:

```
# TYPE   DATABASE   USER         CIDR-ADDRESS    METHOD
  local  all        all          reject
  host   all        all          0.0.0.0/0  reject
```

If you still want superuser access, then try something like the following:

```
# TYPE    DATABASE    USER        CIDR-ADDRESS    METHOD
  local   all         postgres                    peer
  local   all         all                         reject
  host    all         all         0.0.0.0/0       reject
```

This will prevent connections to the database by any user except the `postgres` operating system user ID, which connects locally to any database. Be careful not to confuse the second and third columns—the second column is the database and the third column is the username. It's worth keeping the header line just for that reason. The `peer` method should be replaced by other authentication methods if a more complex configuration is in use.

 In versions prior to 9.1, you need to use the `ident` method to obtain this behavior for local connections.

❏ Copy the existing `pg_hba.conf` file to `pg_hba_access.conf` so that it can be replaced later, if required.

❏ Copy `pg_hba_lockdown.conf` to `pg_hba.conf`.

❏ Reload the server following the recipe earlier in this chapter.

How it works...

The `pg_hba.conf` file is where we specify the host-based authentication rules. We do not specify the authentications themselves, but just specify which authentication mechanisms will be used. This is the top-level set of rules for PostgreSQL authentication. The rules are specified in a file and applied by the postmaster process when connections are attempted. To prevent denial-of-service attacks, the HBA rules never involve database access, so we do not know whether a user is a superuser or not. As a result, you can lock out all users, but note that you can always re-enable access by editing the file and reloading.

Restricting users to only one session each

If resources need to be closely controlled, you may wish to restrict users so that they can only connect at most once to the server. The same technique can be used to prevent connections entirely for that user.

How to do it...

We can restrict users to only one connection using the following command:

```
postgres=# ALTER ROLE fred CONNECTION LIMIT 1;
ALTER ROLE
```

This will then cause any additional connections to receive the error message:

```
FATAL: too many connections for role "fred".
```

You can eliminate this restriction by setting the value to -1.

It's possible to set the limit to zero or any positive integer. You can set this to a number other than max_connections, though it is up to you to make sense of that if you do.

Setting the value to zero will completely restrict normal connections. Note that even if you set the connection limit to zero for superusers, they will still be able to connect.

How it works...

The connection limit is applied during session connection. Raising this limit will never affect any connected users. Lowering the limit doesn't have any effect either, unless they try to disconnect and reconnect.

So, if you lower the limit, you should immediately check to see whether there are more sessions connected than the new limit you just set. Otherwise, there may be some surprises in case there is a crash:

```
postgres=> SELECT rolconnlimit
           FROM pg_roles
           WHERE rolname = 'fred';
 rolconnlimit
--------------
            1
(1 row)

postgres=> SELECT count(*)
           FROM pg_stat_activity
           WHERE usename = 'fred';
 count
-------
     2
(1 row)
```

If you have more connected sessions than the new limit, you can ask users politely to disconnect, or apply the next recipe, *Pushing users off the system*.

Users can't raise or lower their own connection limit, just in case you are worried that they might be able to override this somehow.

Pushing users off the system

Sometimes, we may need to remove groups of users from the database server for various operational reasons. Here's how.

How to do it...

You can terminate a user's session with the `pg_terminate_backend()` function included with PostgreSQL. That function takes the **PID**, or the process ID, of the user's session on the server. This process is known as the backend, and it is a different system process from the program that runs the client.

> Some of the columns used in this recipe had a different name in version 9.1 and before:
>
> ► pid was called `procpid`
> ► query was called `current_query`
>
> The queries in this recipe are written for PostgreSQL 9.4, the most recent stable version at the time of writing this book. They work without changes on versions 9.3 and 9.2. To run them on prior versions, you only have to replace each occurrence of pid with `procpid` and query with `current_query`.

To find the PID of a user, we can look at the `pg_stat_activity` view. We can use it in a query, like this:

```
SELECT pg_terminate_backend(pid)
FROM pg_stat_activity
WHERE ...
```

There are a couple of things to note if you run this query. If the WHERE clause doesn't match any sessions, then you won't get any output from the query. Similarly, if it matches multiple rows, you will get a fairly useless result, that is, a list of boolean `true` values. Unless you are careful enough to exclude your own session from the query, you will disconnect yourself! What's even funnier is that you'll disconnect yourself halfway through disconnecting the other users, as the query will run `pg_terminate_backend()` in the order in which sessions are returned from the outer query.

Therefore, I suggest a safer and more useful query that gives a useful response in all cases, which is as follows:

```
postgres=# SELECT count(pg_terminate_backend(pid))
FROM pg_stat_activity
WHERE usename NOT IN
(SELECT usename
 FROM pg_user
WHERE usesuper);
 count
-------
     1
```

This is assuming that superusers are performing administrative tasks.

Other good filters might be the following:

▸ `WHERE application_name = 'myappname'`

▸ `WHERE waiting`

▸ `WHERE query = '<IDLE> in transaction'`

▸ `WHERE query = '<IDLE>'`

How it works...

The `pg_terminate_backend()` function sends a signal directly to the operating system process for that session.

It's possible that the session may have closed by the time `pg_terminate_backend()` is named. As PID numbers are assigned by the operating system, it could even happen that you try to terminate a given session (call it "session A"), but you actually terminate another session (call it "session B").

Here is how it could happen. Suppose you take note of the PID of session A and decide to disconnect it. Before you actually issue `pg_terminate_backend()`, session A disconnects, and right after, a new session B is given exactly the same PID. So, when you terminate that PID, you hit session B instead.

On one hand, you need to be careful. On the other hand, this case is really unlikely, and is only mentioned for completeness. For it to happen, *all* the following events must happen as well:

- One of the sessions you are trying to close must terminate independently in the very *short* interval between the moment `pg_stat_activity` is read and the moment `pg_terminate_backend()` is executed

- Another session on the same database server must be started in the *even shorter* interval between the old session closing and the execution of `pg_terminate_backend()`

- The new session must get *exactly* the same PID value as the old session, which is less than 1 chance in 32,000 on a 32-bit Linux machine

Nonetheless, Probability Theory is tricky, even for experts. Therefore, it's better to be aware that there is a tiny risk, especially if you use the query many times per day over a long period of time, in which case the probability of getting caught at least once builds up.

It's also possible that new sessions could start after we get the list of active sessions. There's no way to prevent that other than by following the *Preventing new connections* recipe.

Finally, you should note that starting with version 9.3 any user can terminate a session, unless it belongs to a different user. In older PostgreSQL versions, only superusers were able to terminate sessions.

Deciding on a design for multitenancy

There are many reasons why we might want to split groups of tables or applications: security, resource control, convenience, and so on. Whatever the reason, we often need to separate groups of tables (I avoid saying the word "database", just to avoid various kinds of confusion).

This topic is frequently referred to as **multitenancy**, though it is not a fully accepted term as yet.

The purpose of this recipe is to discuss the options and lead to other, more detailed recipes.

How to do it...

If you want to run multiple physical databases on one server, then you have four main options, which are as follows:

- Option 1: Run multiple sets of tables in different schemas in one database of a PostgreSQL instance (covered in the *Using multiple schemas* recipe)

- Option 2: Run multiple databases in the same PostgreSQL instance (covered in the *Giving users their own private database* recipe)

- ▸ Option 3: Run multiple PostgreSQL instances on the same virtual/physical system (covered in the *Running multiple servers on one system* recipe)
- ▸ Option 4: Run separate PostgreSQL instances in separate virtual machines on the same physical server

Which is best? Well, that's certainly a question many people ask, and something on which many views exist. The answer lies in looking at the specific requirements, which are as follows:

- ▸ If our goal is the separation of physical resources, then options 3 or 4 work best. Separate database servers can easily be assigned different disks, individual memory allocations can be assigned, and we can take the servers up or down without impacting the others.
- ▸ If our goal is security, then option 2 is sufficient.
- ▸ If our goal is merely the separation of tables for administrative clarity, then options 1 or 2 can be useful.

Option 2 allows complete separation for security purposes. This, however, does prevent someone with privileges on both groups of tables from performing a join between those tables. So, if there is a possibility of future cross-analytics, it might be worth considering option 1. However, it might also be argued that such analytics should be carried out on a separate data warehouse, not by co-locating production systems.

Option 3 has a difficulty in many of the PostgreSQL distributions: the default installation uses a single location for the database, making it a little harder to configure that option. Ubuntu/ Debian handles that aspect particularly well, making it more attractive in that environment.

Option 4 can be applied using virtualization technology, but that is outside the scope of this book.

How it works...

I've seen people who use PostgreSQL with thousands of databases, but it is my opinion that the majority of people use only one database, such as `postgres` (or at least, only a few databases). I've also seen people with a great many schemas.

One thing you will find is that almost all admin GUI tools become significantly less useful if there are hundreds or thousands of items to display. In most cases, administration tools use a tree view, which doesn't cope gracefully with a large number of items.

Using multiple schemas

We can separate groups of tables into their own "namespaces", referred to as "schemas" by PostgreSQL. In many ways, they can be thought of as being similar to directories, though that is not a precise description.

Getting ready

Make sure you've read the *Deciding on a design for multitenancy* recipe so that you're certain that this is the route you wish to take. Other options exist, and they may be preferable in some cases.

How to do it...

1. Schemas can be easily created using the following commands:

    ```
    CREATE SCHEMA finance;

    CREATE SCHEMA sales;
    ```

2. We can then create objects directly within those schemas using "fully qualified" names, like this:

    ```
    CREATE TABLE finance.month_end_snapshot (.....)
    ```

    The default schema in which an object is created is known as the current schema. We can find out which is our current schema using the following query:

    ```
    postgres=# select current_schema;
    ```

    This returns an output like the following:

    ```
     current_schema
    ----------------
     public
    (1 row)
    ```

3. When we access database objects, we use the user-settable `search_path` parameter to identify the schemas to search. The current schema is the first schema in the `search_path` parameter. There is no separate parameter for the current schema.

So, if we want to let only a specific user look at certain sets of tables, we can modify their `search_path` parameter. This parameter can be set for each user so that the value will be set when they connect. The SQL queries for this would be something like the following:

```
ALTER ROLE fiona SET search_path = 'finance';
ALTER ROLE sally SET search_path = 'sales';
```

 The public schema is not mentioned on `search_path`, so it will not be searched. All tables created by `fiona` will go into the `finance` schema by default, whereas all tables created by `sally` will go into the `sales` schema by default.

4. The users for `finance` and `sales` will be able to see that the other schema exists and change `search_path` to use it, but we will be able to grant or revoke privileges such that they can neither create objects nor read data in others' schemas:

```
REVOKE ALL ON SCHEMA finance FROM public;
GRANT ALL ON SCHEMA finance TO fiona;
REVOKE ALL ON SCHEMA sales FROM public;
GRANT ALL ON SCHEMA sales TO sally;
```

An alternate technique is to allow one user to create privileges on only one schema, but grant usage rights on all other schemas. We can set up that arrangement like this:

```
REVOKE ALL ON SCHEMA finance FROM public;
GRANT USAGE ON SCHEMA finance TO fiona;
GRANT CREATE ON SCHEMA finance TO fiona;
REVOKE ALL ON SCHEMA sales FROM public;
GRANT USAGE ON SCHEMA sales TO sally;
GRANT CREATE ON SCHEMA sales TO sally;
```

5. Note that you need to grant the privileges for usage on the schema, as well as specific rights on the objects in the schema. So, you will also need to issue specific grants for objects, as shown here:

```
GRANT SELECT ON month_end_snapshot TO public;
```

You can also set default privileges so that they are picked up when objects are created, using the following command:

```
ALTER DEFAULT PRIVILEGES FOR USER fiona IN SCHEMA finance
GRANT SELECT ON TABLES TO PUBLIC;
```

How it works...

Earlier, I said that schemas work like directories—a little at least.

The PostgreSQL concept of `search_path` is similar to the concept of a `PATH` environment variable.

The PostgreSQL concept of the current schema is similar to the concept of the current working directory. There is no `cd` command to change the directory. The current working directory is changed by altering `search_path`.

A few other differences exist; for example, PostgreSQL schemas are not arranged in a hierarchy like filesystem directories.

Many people create a user of the same name as the schema to make this work in a way similar to other RDBMSes, such as Oracle.

 Both the `finance` and `sales` schemas exist within the same PostgreSQL database, and run on the same database server. They use a common buffer pool, and there are many global settings that tie the two schemas fairly closely together.

Giving users their own private database

Separating data and users is a key part of administration. There will always be a need to give users a private, secure, or simply risk-free area ("sandpit") to use the database. Here's how.

Getting ready

Again, make sure you've read the *Deciding on a design for multitenancy* recipe so that you're certain this is the route you wish to take. Other options exist, and they may be preferable in some cases.

How to do it...

1. We can create a database for a specific user with some ease. From the command line, as a superuser, these actions would be as follows:

```
postgres=# create user fred;
CREATE ROLE
postgres=# create database fred owner = fred;
CREATE DATABASE
```

2. As the database owners, users have login privileges, so they can connect to any database by default. There is a command named `ALTER DEFAULT PRIVILEGES`, however, that does not currently apply to databases, tablespaces, or languages. The `ALTER DEFAULT PRIVILEGES` command also currently applies only to roles (that is, users) that already exist.

So, we need to revoke the privilege to connect to our new database from everybody except the designated user. There isn't a `REVOKE ... FROM PUBLIC EXCEPT` command. Therefore, we need to revoke everything and then just regrant everything we need, all in one transaction, such as the following:

```
postgres=# BEGIN;

BEGIN

postgres=# REVOKE connect ON DATABASE  fred FROM public;

REVOKE

postgres=# GRANT connect ON DATABASE fred TO fred;

GRANT

postgres=# COMMIT;

COMMIT

postgres=# create user bob;

CREATE ROLE
```

3. Then, try to connect as `bob` to the `fred` database:

```
os $ psql -U bob fred

psql: FATAL:  permission denied for database "fred"

DETAIL:  User does not have CONNECT privilege.
```

This is exactly what we wanted.

How it works...

If you didn't catch it before, PostgreSQL allows transactional DDL in most places, so either both of the `REVOKE` and `GRANT` commands in the preceding section work or neither works. This means that the `fred` user never loses the ability to connect to the database. Note that `CREATE DATABASE` cannot be performed as part of a transaction, though nothing serious happens as a result.

There's more...

Superusers can still connect to the new database, and there is no way to prevent them from doing so.

No other users can see the tables created in the new database, nor can they know the names of any of the objects.

The new database can be seen to exist by other users, and they can also see the name of the user who owns the database.

See also

See *Chapter 6, Security*, for more details on these issues.

Running multiple servers on one system

Running multiple PostgreSQL servers on one physical system is possible if it is convenient for your needs.

Getting ready

Once again, make sure you've read the *Deciding on a design for multitenancy* recipe so that you're certain this is the route you wish to take. Other options exist, and they may be preferable in some cases.

How to do it...

Core PostgreSQL easily allows multiple servers to run on the same system, but there are a few wrinkles to be aware of.

Some installer versions create a PostgreSQL data directory named `data`. It then gets a little difficult to have more than one `data` directory without using different directory structures and names.

Debian/Ubuntu packagers chose a layout specifically designed to allow multiple servers, potentially running with different software release levels. You might remember this from the *Locating the database server files* recipe in *Chapter 2, Exploring the Database*.

Starting from `/var/lib/postgresql`, which is the home directory of the Postgres user, there is a subdirectory for each major version, for example, `8.4` or `9.3`, inside which the individual data directories are placed. When installing PostgreSQL server packages, a data directory is created with the default name of `main`. Configuration files are separately placed in `/etc/postgresql/<version>/<name>`, and log files are created in `/var/log/postgresql/postgresql-<version>-<name>.log`.

Thus, not all files will be found in the `data` directory. As an example, let's create an additional `data` directory:

1. We start by running this command:

   ```
   sudo -u postgres pg_createcluster 9.4 main2
   ```

2. The new database server can then be started using the following command:

   ```
   sudo -u postgres pg_ctlcluster 9.4 main2 start
   ```

   This is sufficient to create and start an additional database cluster in version 9.4, named `main2`. The data and configuration files are stored inside the `/var/lib/postgresql/9.4/main2/` and `/etc/postgresql/9.4/main2/` directories respectively, giving the new database the next unused port number, for example `5433` if this is the second PostgreSQL server on that machine.

Local access to multiple PostgreSQL servers has been simplified as well. PostgreSQL client programs, such as psql, are wrapped by a special script that takes the cluster name as an additional parameter and automatically uses the corresponding port number. Hence, you don't really need the following command:

```
psql --port 5433 -h /var/run/postgresql ...
```

Instead, you can refer to the database server by name, as shown here:

```
psql --cluster 9.4/main2 ...
```

This has its advantages, especially if you wish (or need) to change the port in the future. I find this extremely convenient, and another reason is that it works with other utilities such as `pg_dump`, `pg_restore`, and so on.

With Red Hat systems, you will need to run `initdb` directly, selecting your directories carefully:

1. First, initialize your `data` directory with something like the following:

   ```
   sudo -u postgres initdb -D /var/lib/pgsql/datadir2
   ```

2. Then, modify the `port` parameter in the `postgresql.conf` file and start using the following command:

```
sudo -u postgres pg_ctl -D /var/lib/pgsql/datadir2 start
```

This will create an additional database server at the default server version, with files stored in `/var/lib/pgsql/datadir2`.

You can set up the server with `chkconfig` also, if your distribution supports it.

How it works...

PostgreSQL servers are controlled using `pg_ctl`. Everything else is a wrapper of some kind around this utility. The only constraints on running multiple versions of PostgreSQL come from file locations and naming conventions, assuming (of course) that you have enough resources such as disk space, memory, and so on. Everything else is straightforward. Having said that, the Debian/Ubuntu design is currently the only design that makes it actually easy to run multiple servers.

Setting up a connection pool

A connection pool is a term used for a collection of already connected sessions that can be used to reduce the overhead of connection and reconnection.

There are various ways by which connection pools can be provided, depending on the software stack in use. Probably, the best option is to look at the server-side connection pool software because that works for all connection types, not just within a single software stack.

Here, we're going to look at **PgBouncer**, which is designed as a very lightweight connection pool. The name comes from the idea that the pool can be paused and resumed to allow the server to be restarted, or "bounced".

Getting ready

First of all, decide where you're going to store the PgBouncer parameter files, log files, and PID files. PgBouncer can manage more than one database server's connections at the same time, though that probably isn't wise. If you keep PgBouncer files associated with the database server, then it should be easy to manage.

How to do it...

Carry out the following steps to configure PgBouncer:

1. Create a `pgbouncer.ini` file, as follows:

```
;
; pgbouncer configuration example
;
[databases]
postgres = port=5432 dbname=postgres
[pgbouncer]
listen_port = 6432
listen_addr = 127.0.0.1
admin_users = postgres
;stats_users = monitoring userid
auth_type = trust
; put these files somewhere sensible
auth_file = users.txt
logfile = pgbouncer.log
pidfile = pgbouncer.pid
; required for 9.0
ignore_startup_parameters = application_name
server_reset_query = DISCARD ALL;
; default values
pool_mode = session
default_pool_size = 20
log_pooler_errors = 0
```

2. Create a `users.txt` file. This must contain the minimum users mentioned in `admin_users` and `stats_users`. Its format is very simple: a collection of lines with a username and a password. Consider the following as an example:

```
"postgres"     ""
```

3. PgBouncer also supports MD5 authentication. To use that effectively, you need to copy the encrypted passwords from the database server.

4. You may wish to create the `users.txt` file by directly copying the details from the server. That can be done using the following psql script:

```
postgres=> \o users.txt

postgres=> \t

postgres=> SELECT '"'||rolname||'" "'||rolpassword||'"'
postgres-> FROM pg_authid;

postgres=> \q
```

5. Launch PgBouncer:

    ```
    pgbouncer -d pgbouncer.ini
    ```

6. Test the connection; it should respond to `reload`:

    ```
    psql -p 6432 -h 127.0.0.1 -U postgres pgbouncer -c "reload"
    ```

7. Finally, verify that PgBouncer's `max_client_conn` parameter does not exceed the `max_connections` parameter on PostgreSQL.

How it works...

PgBouncer is a great piece of software. Its feature set is very carefully defined to ensure that it is simple, robust, and very fast. PgBouncer is not multithreaded, so it runs in a single process, and thus, on a single CPU. It is very efficient, but very large data transfers will take more time and reduce concurrency, so create those data dumps using a direct connection. PgBouncer doesn't support SSL connections. If it did, then all of the encryption/decryption would need to take place in a single process, which would make that solution perform poorly. If you need secure communications, then you should use stunnel.

PgBouncer provides connection pooling. If you set `pool_mode = transaction`, then PgBouncer will also provide connection concentration. This allows hundreds or even thousands of incoming connections to be managed, while only a few server connections are made.

As new connections, transactions, or statements arrive, the pool will increase in size up to the user-defined maximum values. Those connections will stay around for at most the `server_idle_timeout` value before the pool releases them.

PgBouncer also releases sessions every `server_lifetime`. This allows the server to free backends in rotation to avoid issues with very long-lived session connections.

The earlier query that creates `users.txt` includes only database users that have a password. All other users will have a null `rolpassword` field, so the whole string evaluates to `NULL`, and the line is omitted from the password file. This is intentional; users without a password represent a security risk, unless they are closely guarded. An example of this is the `postgres` system user connecting from the same machine, which bypasses PgBouncer, and is used only for maintenance by responsible and trusted people.

There's more...

It's possible to connect to PgBouncer itself to issue commands. This can be done interactively, as if you were entering psql, or it can be done using single commands or scripts.

To shut down the server, we can just type SHUTDOWN or enter a single command, as follows:

```
psql -p 6432 pgbouncer -c "SHUTDOWN"
```

You can also use the RELOAD command to make the server reload (which means reread) the parameter files, like we did to test that all is working.

If you are using pool_mode = transaction or pool_mode = statement, then you can use the PAUSE command. This waits for the current transaction to complete before holding further work on that session. Thus, it allows you to perform DDL more easily or restart the server.

PgBouncer also allows you to use the SUSPEND mode, which waits for all server-side buffers to flush.

The PAUSE or SUSPEND modes should eventually be followed by RESUME when the work is done.

In addition to the PgBouncer control commands, there are many varieties of SHOW commands, as listed here:

SHOW **command**	**Result set**
SHOW STATS	Traffic stats, total and average requests, query duration, bytes sent/received, and so on
SHOW SERVERS	One row per connection to the database server
SHOW CLIENTS	One row per connection from the client
SHOW POOLS	One row per pool of users
SHOW LISTS	Gives a good summary of resource totals
SHOW USERS	Lists users in users.txt
SHOW DATABASES	Lists databases in pgbouncer.ini
SHOW CONFIG	Lists configuration parameters
SHOW FDS	Show file descriptors
SHOW SOCKETS	Show file sockets
SHOW VERSION	Shows the PgBouncer version

Accessing multiple servers using the same host and port

We will now show you one simple, yet important, application of the previous recipe, *Setting up a connection pool*. In that recipe, you saw how to reuse connections with PgBouncer, and thus reduce the cost of disconnecting and reconnecting.

Here, we will demonstrate another way to use PgBouncer—one instance can connect to databases hosted by different database servers at the same time. The databases can be on separate hosts, and can even have different major versions of PostgreSQL!

Getting ready

Suppose we have three database servers, each one hosting one database. All you need to know beforehand is the connection string for each database server.

More complex arrangements are possible, but those are left to you as an exercise.

Before you try this recipe, you should have already gone through the previous recipe. These two recipes have many steps in common, but we've kept them separate because they have clearly different goals.

How to do it...

Each database is completely identified by its connection string. PgBouncer will read this information from its configuration file. The steps to be done are as follows:

1. All you need to do is to set up PgBouncer as was done in the previous recipe, replacing the databases section of pgbouncer.ini with the following:

    ```
    [databases]
    myfirstdb = port=5432 host=localhost
    anotherdb = port=5437 host=localhost
    sparedb = port=5435 host=localhost
    ```

2. Once you have started PgBouncer, you can connect to the first database:

    ```
    $ psql -p 6432 -h 127.0.0.1 -U postgres myfirstdb
    psql (9.4.0)
    Type "help" for help.

    myfirstdb=# show port;
     port
    ------
     5432
    (1 row)


    myfirstdb=# show server_version;
     server_version
    ----------------
     9.4.0
    (1 row)
    ```

3. Now, you can connect to the `anotherdb` database as if it were on the same server:

    ```
    myfirstdb=# \c anotherdb
    psql (9.4.0, server 9.1.14)
    You are now connected to database "anotherdb" as user "postgres".
    ```

4. The server's greeting message suggests that we have landed on a different server, so we check the port and version:

    ```
    anotherdb=# show port;
     port
    ------
     5437
    (1 row)

    anotherdb=# show server_version;
     server_version
    ----------------
     9.1.14
    (1 row)
    ```

There's more...

The *Listing databases on this database server* recipe in *Chapter 2, Exploring the Database*, shows you how to list the available databases on the current database server, using either the \l meta-command or a couple of equivalent variations. Unfortunately, that doesn't work when using PgBouncer, for the very good reason that the current database server cannot know the answer.

We need to ask PgBouncer instead, and we do so using the SHOW command when connected to the pgbouncer special administrative database:

```
myfirstdb=# \c pgbouncer
psql (9.2.4, server 1.5.4/bouncer)
You are now connected to database "pgbouncer" as user "postgres".
pgbouncer=# show databases;
    name     |    host    | port |  database  | force_user | pool_size |
reserve_pool
-----------+------------+------+------------+------------+------------+------
---------
 anotherdb | localhost  | 5437 | anotherdb  |            |        20 |
0
 myfirstdb | localhost  | 5432 | myfirstdb  |            |        20 |
0
 pgbouncer |            | 6432 | pgbouncer  | pgbouncer  |         2 |
0
 sparedb   | localhost  | 5435 | sparedb    |            |        20 |
0
(4 rows)
```

5
Tables and Data

In this chapter, we will cover the following recipes:

- ▶ Choosing good names for database objects
- ▶ Handling objects with quoted names
- ▶ Enforcing the same name and definition for columns
- ▶ Identifying and removing duplicates
- ▶ Preventing duplicate rows
- ▶ Finding a unique key for a set of data
- ▶ Generating test data
- ▶ Randomly sampling data
- ▶ Loading data from a spreadsheet
- ▶ Loading data from flat files

Introduction

This chapter covers a range of general recipes for your tables and working with the data they contain. Many of the recipes contain general advice, though with specific PostgreSQL examples.

Some system administrators I've met work only on the external aspects of the database server. What's actually in the database is someone else's problem.

Look after your data, and your database will look after you. Keep your data clean, and your queries will run faster and cause less application errors. You'll also gain many friends in the business. Getting called in the middle of the night to fix data problems just isn't cool.

Choosing good names for database objects

The easiest way to help other people understand a database is to ensure that all the objects have a meaningful name.

What makes a name meaningful?

Getting ready

Take some time to reflect on your database to make sure you have a clear view of its purpose and main use cases. This is because all the items in this recipe describe certain naming choices, which you need to consider carefully in view of your specific circumstances.

How to do it...

Here are the points you should consider when naming your database objects:

- The name follows the existing standards and practices in place. Inventing new standards isn't helpful; enforcing existing standards is.

- The name clearly describes the role or table contents.

- For major tables, use short, powerful names.

- Name lookup tables after the table to which they are linked, such as `account_status`.

- For associative or linked tables, use all the names of the major tables to which they relate, such as `customer_account`.

- Make sure that the name is clearly distinct from other similar names.

- Use consistent abbreviations.

- Use underscores. Case is not preserved by default, so using CamelCase names, such as `customerAccount`, as used in Java will just leave them unreadable. See the *Handling objects with quoted names* recipe.

- Use consistent plurals, or don't use them at all.

- Use suffixes to identify the content type or domain of an object. PostgreSQL already uses suffixes for automatically generated objects.

- Think ahead. Don't pick names that refer to the current role or location of an object. So, don't name a table `London` because it exists on a server in London. That server might get moved to Los Angeles.

- Think ahead. Don't pick names that imply that an entity is the only one of its kind, such as a table named `TEST`, or a table named `BACKUP_DATA`. On the other hand, such information can be put in the database name, which is not normally used from within the database.

- Avoid using acronyms in place of long table names. For example, `money_allocation_decision` is much better than `MAD`. This is especially important when PostgreSQL translates the names into lower case, so the fact that it is an acronym may not be clear.

- The table name is commonly used as the root for other objects that are created, so don't add the `table` suffix or similar ideas.

There's more...

The standard names for indexes in PostgreSQL are as follows:

```
{tablename}_{columnname(s)}_{suffix}
```

Here, the suffix is one of the following:

- `pkey`: This is used for a primary key constraint

- `key`: This is used for a unique constraint

- `excl`: This is used for an exclusion constraint

- `idx`: This is used for any other kind of index

The standard suffix for all sequences is `seq`.

Tables can have multiple triggers fired on each event. Triggers are executed in alphabetical order, so trigger names should have some kind of action name to differentiate them and to allow the order to be specified. It might seem a good idea to put `INSERT`, `UPDATE`, or `DELETE` in the trigger name, but that can get confusing if you have triggers that work on both `UPDATE` and `DELETE`, and all of this may end up as a mess.

> The alphabetical order for trigger names always follows the C locale, regardless of your actual locale settings. If your trigger names use non-ASCII characters, then the actual ordering might not be what you expect.
>
> The following example shows how the characters è and é are ordered in the C locale. You can change the locale and/or the list of strings to explore how different locales affect ordering:
>
> ```
> WITH a(x) AS (
>   VALUES ('è'),('é')
> ) SELECT *
> FROM a
> ORDER BY x
> COLLATE "C";
> ```

A useful naming convention for triggers is as follows:

```
{tablename}_{actionname}_{after|before}_trig
```

If you do find yourself with strange or irregular object names, it will be a good idea to use the RENAME subcommands to get things tidy again. Here is an example of this:

```
ALTER INDEX badly_named_index RENAME TO tablename_status_idx;
```

Handling objects with quoted names

PostgreSQL object names can contain spaces and mixed case characters if we enclose the table names in double quotes. This can cause some difficulties, so this recipe is designed to help you if you get stuck with this kind of problem.

Case sensitivity issues can often be a problem for people more used to working with other database systems, such as MySQL, or for people who are facing the challenge of migrating code away from MySQL.

Getting ready

First, let's create a table that uses a quoted name with mixed case, such as the following:

```
CREATE TABLE "MyCust"
AS
SELECT * FROM cust;
```

How to do it...

If we try to access these tables without the proper case, we get this error:

```
postgres=# SELECT count(*) FROM mycust;
ERROR:  relation "mycust" does not exist
LINE 1: SELECT * FROM mycust;
```

So, we write it in the correct case:

```
postgres=# SELECT count(*) FROM MyCust;
ERROR:  relation "mycust" does not exist
LINE 1: SELECT * FROM mycust;
```

This still fails, and in fact gives the same error.

If you want to access a table that was created with quoted names, then you must use quoted names, such as the following:

```
postgres=# SELECT count(*) FROM "MyCust";
```

The output is as follows:

```
 count
-------
     5
(1 row)
```

The usage rule is that if you create your tables using quoted names, then you need to write your SQL using quoted names. Alternatively, if your SQL uses quoted names, then you will probably have to create the tables using quoted names as well.

How it works...

PostgreSQL folds all names to lowercase when used within a SQL statement.
Consider this command:

```
SELECT * FROM mycust;
```

This is exactly the same as the following command:

```
SELECT * FROM MYCUST;
```

It is also exactly the same as this command:

```
SELECT * FROM MyCust;
```

However, it is not the same thing as the following command:

```
SELECT * FROM "MyCust";
```

There's more...

If you are extracting values from a table that is being used to create object names, then you may need to use a handy function named quote_ident(). This function puts double quotes around a value if PostgreSQL requires that for an object name, as shown here:

```
postgres=# select quote_ident('MyCust');
 quote_ident
```

```
- - - - - - - - - - - - -
 "MyCust"
(1 row)
postgres=# select quote_ident('mycust');
 quote_ident
- - - - - - - - - - - - -
 mycust
(1 row)
```

The `quote_ident()` function may be especially useful if you are creating a table based on a variable name in a PL/pgSQL function, as follows:

```
EXECUTE 'CREATE TEMP TABLE ' || quote_ident(tablename) ||
            '(col1             INTEGER);'
```

Enforcing the same name and definition for columns

Sensibly designed databases have smooth, easy-to-understand definitions. This allows all users to understand the meaning of data in each table. It is an important way of removing data quality issues.

Getting ready

If you want to run the queries in this recipe as a test, then use the following examples. Alternatively, you can just check for problems in your own database:

```
CREATE SCHEMA s1;
CREATE SCHEMA s2;
CREATE TABLE s1.X
(col1 smalliER
,col2 TEXT);
CREATE TABLE s2.X
(col1 smallint
,col3 NUMERIC);
```

How to do it...

First, we will show you how to identify columns that are defined in different ways in different tables, using a query against the catalog. We use an Information Schema query, as follows:

```
SELECT
 table_schema
,table_name
,column_name
,data_type
  ||coalesce(' ' || text(character_maximum_length), '')
  ||coalesce(' ' || text(numeric_precision), '')
  ||coalesce(',' || text(numeric_scale), '')
  as data_type
FROM information_schema.columns
WHERE column_name IN
(SELECT
 column_name
FROM
(SELECT
  column_name
 ,data_type
 ,character_maximum_length
 ,numeric_precision
 ,numeric_scale
 FROM information_schema.columns
 WHERE table_schema NOT IN ('information_schema', 'pg_catalog')
 GROUP BY
  column_name
 ,data_type
 ,character_maximum_length
 ,numeric_precision
 ,numeric_scale
) derived
```

```
GROUP BY column_name
HAVING count(*) > 1
)
AND table_schema NOT IN ('information_schema', 'pg_catalog')
ORDER BY column_name
;
```

The query gives an output such as the following:

```
 table_schema | table_name | column_name |   data_type
--------------+------------+-------------+---------------
 s2           | x          | col1        | integer 32,0
 s1           | x          | col1        | smallint 16,0
(2 rows)
```

Comparing two given tables is more complex, as there are so many ways that the tables might be similar and yet a little different. The following query looks for all tables of the same name (and hence, in different schemas) that have different definitions:

```
SELECT
 table_schema
,table_name
,column_name
,data_type
FROM information_schema.columns
WHERE table_name IN
(SELECT
  table_name
 FROM
 (SELECT DISTINCT
   table_name
  ,def
   FROM
   (SELECT
    table_schema
   ,table_name
   ,string_agg(column_name||' '||data_type, ',' ORDER BY column_name) AS
def
    FROM information_schema.columns
```

```
       WHERE table_schema NOT IN ('information_schema','pg_catalog')
       GROUP BY
        table_schema
        ,table_name
        ) t
  ) def
  GROUP BY
   table_name
  HAVING
   count(*) > 1
  )
  ORDER BY
   table_name
  ,table_schema
  ,column_name;
```

Here is its output:

```
 table_schema | table_name | column_name | data_type
--------------+------------+-------------+----------
 s1           | x          | col1        | smallint
 s1           | x          | col2        | text
 s2           | x          | col1        | integer
 s2           | x          | col3        | numeric
(4 rows)
```

How it works...

The definitions of tables are held within PostgreSQL, and can be accessed using the Information Schema catalog views.

There might be valid reasons why the definitions differ. We've excluded PostgreSQL's own internal tables because there are similar names between the two catalogs: PostgreSQL's implementation of the SQL Standard Information Schema and PostgreSQL's own internal `pg_catalog` schema.

Those queries are fairly complex. In fact, there is even more complexity we could add to those queries to compare all sorts of things such as default values or constraints. The basic idea can be extended in various directions from here.

There's more...

We can compare the definitions of any two tables using the following function:

```
CREATE OR REPLACE FUNCTION diff_table_definition
(t1_schemaname text
,t1_tablename text
,t2_schemaname text
,t2_tablename text)
RETURNS TABLE
(t1_column_name text
,t1_data_type text
,t2_column_name text
,t2_data_type text
)
LANGUAGE SQL
as
$$
SELECT
 t1.column_name
,t1.data_type
,t2.column_name
,t2.data_type
FROM
 (SELECT column_name, data_type
  FROM information_schema.columns
  WHERE table_schema = $1
     AND table_name = $2
 ) t1
 FULL OUTER JOIN
 (SELECT column_name, data_type
  FROM information_schema.columns
  WHERE table_schema = $3
     AND table_name = $4
 ) t2
 ON t1.column_name = t2.column_name
 AND t1.data_type = t2.data_type
WHERE t1.column_name IS NULL OR t2.column_name IS NULL
;
$$;
```

Identifying and removing duplicates

Relational databases work on the idea that items of data can be uniquely identified. However hard we try, there will always be bad data arriving from somewhere. This recipe shows you how to diagnose that and clean up the mess.

Getting ready

Let's start by looking at our example table, `cust`. It has a duplicate value in `customerid`:

```
postgres=# SELECT * FROM cust;
 customerid | firstname | lastname | age
------------+-----------+----------+-----
          1 | Philip    | Marlowe  |  38
          2 | Richard   | Hannay   |  42
          3 | Holly     | Martins  |  25
          4 | Harry     | Palmer   |  36
          4 | Mark      | Hall     |  47
(5 rows)
```

Before you delete duplicate data, remember that sometimes, it isn't the data that is wrong; it is your understanding of it. In those cases, it may be that you haven't properly normalized your database model, and that you need to include additional tables to account for the shape of the data. You might also find that duplicate rows are caused because of you deciding to exclude a column somewhere earlier in a data load process. Check twice, and delete once.

How to do it...

First, identify the duplicates using a query such as the following:

```
CREATE UNLOGGED TABLE dup_cust AS
SELECT *
FROM cust
WHERE customerid IN
  (SELECT customerid
   FROM cust
   GROUP BY customerid
   HAVING count(*) > 1);
```

We save the list of duplicates in a separate table because the query can be very slow if the table is big, so we don't want to run it more than once.

An UNLOGGED table can be created with less I/O because it does not write WAL. It is better than a temporary table, because it doesn't disappear if you disconnect and then reconnect. The other side of the coin is that you lose it after a crash, but this is not too bad, as you can recreate it in that unlikely event.

The results can be used to identify the bad data manually, and you can resolve the problem by carrying out the following steps:

1. Merge the two rows to give the best picture of the data, if required. This might use values from one row to update the row you decide to keep, as shown here:

    ```
    UPDATE cust
    SET age = 47
    WHERE customerid = 4
    AND lastname = 'Palmer';
    ```

2. Delete the remaining undesirable rows:

    ```
    DELETE FROM cust
    WHERE customerid = 4
    AND lastname = 'Hall';
    ```

In some cases, the data rows might be completely identical, as in the `new_cust` table, which looks like the following:

```
postgres=# SELECT * FROM new_cust;
 customerid
------------
          1
          2
          3
          4
          4
(5 rows)
```

Unlike the preceding case, we can't tell the data apart at all, so we cannot remove duplicate rows without any manual process. SQL is a set-based language, so picking only one row out of a set is slightly harder than most people want it to be.

In these circumstances, we should use a slightly different procedure to detect duplicates. We will use a hidden column named ctid. It denotes the physical location of the row you are observing; for example, duplicate rows will all have different ctid values. The steps are as follows:

1. First, we start a transaction:

    ```
    BEGIN;
    ```

2. Then, we lock the table in order to prevent any INSERT, UPDATE or DELETE operations, which would alter the list of duplicates and/or change their ctid values:

    ```
    LOCK TABLE new_cust IN SHARE ROW EXCLUSIVE MODE;
    ```

3. Now, we locate all duplicates, keeping track of the minimum ctid value so that we don't delete that value:

    ```
    CREATE TEMPORARY TABLE dups_cust AS
    SELECT customerid, min(ctid) AS min_ctid
    FROM new_cust
    GROUP BY customerid
    HAVING count(*) > 1;
    ```

4. Then, we can delete each duplicate, with the exception of the duplicate with the minimum ctid value:

    ```
    DELETE FROM new_cust
    USING dups_cust
    WHERE new_cust.customerid = dups_cust.customerid
    AND new_cust.ctid != dups_cust.min_ctid;
    ```

5. We commit the transaction, which also releases the lock we previously took:

    ```
    COMMIT;
    ```

6. Finally, we clean up the table after the deletions:

    ```
    VACUUM new_cust;
    ```

How it works...

The first query works by grouping together the rows on the unique column and counting rows. Anything with more than one row must be caused by duplicate values. If we're looking for duplicates of more than one column (or even all columns), then we have to use a SQL of the following form:

```
SELECT *
FROM mytable
WHERE  (col1, col2, … ,colN) IN
(SELECT col1, col2, … ,colN
 FROM mytable
 GROUP BY  col1, col2, … ,colN
 HAVING count(*) > 1);
```

Here, `col1`, `col2`, and so on until `colN` are the columns of the key.

Note that this type of query may need to sort the complete table on all the key columns. That will require sort space equal to the size of the table, so you'd better think first before running that SQL on very large tables. You'll probably benefit from a large `work_mem` setting for this query, probably 128 MB or more.

The `DELETE FROM` … `USING` query that we showed only works with PostgreSQL, because it uses the `ctid` value, which is the internal identifier of each row in the table. If you wanted to run that query against more than one column, as we did earlier in the chapter, you'd need to extend the queries in step 3, as follows:

```
SELECT customerid, customer_name, …, min(ctid) AS min_ctid

FROM …

GROUP BY customerid, customer_name, …

…;
```

Then, extend the query in step 4, like this:

```
DELETE FROM new_cust

…

WHERE new_cust.customerid = dups_cust.customerid

AND new_cust.customer_name = dups_cust.customer_name

AND …

AND new_cust.ctid != dups_cust.min_ctid;
```

The preceding query works by grouping together all the rows with similar values and then finding the row with the lowest ctid value. The lowest will mean closer to the start of the table, so duplicates will be removed from the far end of the table. When we run VACUUM, we may find that the table gets smaller, because we have removed rows from the far end.

The BEGIN and COMMIT commands wrap the LOCK and DELETE commands into a single transaction, which is required. Otherwise, the lock will be released immediately after being taken.

Another reason to use a single transaction is that we can always **roll back** if anything goes wrong, which is a good thing when we are removing data from a live table.

There's more...

Locking the table against changes for long periods may not be possible while we remove duplicate rows. That gives some fairly hard problems with large tables. In that case, we need to do things slightly differently:

1. Identify the rows to be deleted, and save them in a side table.
2. Build an index on the main table to speed up access to rows (maybe using the CONCURRENTLY keyword, as explained in the *Maintaining indexes* recipe in *Chapter 9, Regular Maintenance*).
3. Write a program that reads the rows from the side table in a loop, performing a series of smaller transactions.
4. Start a new transaction.
5. From the side table, read a set of rows that match.
6. Select those rows from the main table for updates, relying on the index to make those accesses happen quickly.
7. Delete the appropriate rows.
8. Commit, and then loop again.

The aforementioned program can't be written as a database function, as we can't have multiple transactions in a function. We need multiple transactions to ensure that we hold locks on each row for the shortest possible duration.

Preventing duplicate rows

Preventing duplicate rows is one of the most important aspects of data quality for any database. PostgreSQL offers some useful features in this area, extending beyond most relational databases.

Getting ready

Identify the set of columns that you wish to make unique. Does this apply to all rows, or just a subset of rows?

Let's start with our example table:

```
postgres=# SELECT * FROM newcust;
 customerid
------------
          1
          2
          3
          4
(4 rows)
```

How to do it...

To prevent duplicate rows, we need to create a unique index that the database server can use to enforce uniqueness of a particular set of columns. We can do this in the following three similar ways for basic data types:

- ▶ Create a primary key constraint on the set of columns. We are allowed only one of these per table. The values of the data rows must not be NULL, as we force the columns to be NOT NULL if they aren't already:

  ```
  ALTER TABLE newcust ADD PRIMARY KEY(customerid);
  ```

  This creates a new index named `newcust_pkey`.

- ▶ Create a unique constraint on the set of columns. We can use these instead of—or with—a primary key. There is no limit on the number of these per table. NULL values are allowed in the columns:

  ```
  ALTER TABLE newcust ADD UNIQUE(customerid);
  ```

  This creates a new index named `newcust_customerid_key`.

- Create a unique index on the set of columns:

```
CREATE UNIQUE INDEX ON newcust (customerid);
```

This creates a new index named `newcust_customerid_idx`.

All of these techniques exclude duplicates, just with slightly different syntaxes. All of them create an index, but only the first two create a formal "constraint". Each of these techniques can be used when we have a primary key or unique constraint that uses multiple columns.

The last method is important because it allows you to specify a `WHERE` clause on the index. This can be useful if you know that the column values are unique only in certain circumstances. The resulting index is then known as a partial index.

Suppose our data looked like this:

```
postgres=# select * from partial_unique;
```

This gives the following output:

```
 customerid | status | close_date
------------+--------+------------
          1 | OPEN   |
          2 | OPEN   |
          3 | OPEN   |
          3 | CLOSED | 2010-03-22
(4 rows)
```

Then, we can put a partial index on the table to enforce uniqueness of `customerid` only for `status = 'OPEN'`, like this:

```
CREATE UNIQUE INDEX ON partial_unique (customerid)
  WHERE status = 'OPEN';
```

If your uniqueness constraint needs to be enforced across more complex data types, then you may need to use a more advanced syntax. A few examples will help here.

Let's start with the simplest example: create a table of boxes and put sample data in it. This may be the first time you're seeing PostgreSQL's data type syntax, so bear with me:

```
postgres=# CREATE TABLE boxes (name text, position box);
CREATE TABLE
postgres=# INSERT INTO boxes VALUES
                        ('First', box '((0,0), (1,1))');
INSERT 0 1
```

```
postgres=# INSERT INTO boxes VALUES
                        ('Second', box '((2,0), (2,1))');
INSERT 0 1
postgres=# SELECT * FROM boxes;
  name  |   position
--------+-------------
 First  | (1,1),(0,0)
 Second | (2,1),(2,0)
(2 rows)
```

We can see two boxes that neither touch nor overlap, based on their x and y coordinates.

To enforce uniqueness here, we want to create a constraint that will throw out any attempt to add a position that overlaps with any existing box. The overlap operator for the box data type is defined to be &&, so we use the following syntax to add the constraint:

```
postgres=# ALTER TABLE boxes ADD EXCLUDE USING gist
                        (position WITH &&);
NOTICE:  ALTER TABLE / ADD EXCLUDE will create implicit index "boxes_
position_excl" for table "boxes"
ALTER TABLE
```

This creates a new index named boxes_position_excl.

We can use the same syntax even with the basic data types. So, a fourth way of performing our first example would be as follows:

```
ALTER TABLE newcust ADD EXCLUDE (customerid WITH =);
```

This creates a new index named newcust_customerid_excl.

How it works...

Uniqueness is always enforced by an index.

Each index is defined with a data type operator. When a new row is inserted or the set of column values is updated, we use the operator to search for existing values that conflict with the new data.

So, to enforce uniqueness, we need an index and a search operator defined on the data types of the columns. When we define normal UNIQUE constraints, we simply assume that we mean the equality operator (=) for the data type. The EXCLUDE syntax offers a richer syntax to allow us to express the same problem with different data types and operators.

There's more...

Unique and exclusion constraints can be marked as "deferrable", meaning that the user can choose to postpone the check to the end of the transaction—a nice way to "relax" constraints without reducing data integrity. However, as of PostgreSQL 9.4, there are a few limitations that you should be aware of; the restrictions are as follows:

> ▸ You must define a constraint as DEFERRABLE when creating it, either in the CREATE TABLE statement or in the ALTER TABLE statement. You cannot change an existing constraint from NOT DEFERRABLE to DEFERRABLE, nor can you make it INITIALLY DEFERRED or INITIALLY IMMEDIATE. If you need to apply such a change on an existing constraint, you need to create a new constraint and then drop the old constraint. Optionally, you can rename the new constraint in the end.

> ▸ You cannot mix deferrable unique constraints with foreign keys. You will get an error message if you try to add a foreign key that refers to a unique constraint that is deferrable.

It's likely that these restrictions will be lifted in later releases.

Duplicate indexes

Note that PostgreSQL allows you to have multiple indexes with exactly the same definition. This is useful in some contexts, but can also be annoying if you accidentally create multiple indexes, as each index has its own cost in terms of writes. You can also have constraints defined using each of the aforementioned different ways. Each of these ways enforces essentially the same constraint, so take care.

Uniqueness without indexes

It's possible to have uniqueness in a set of columns without creating an index. That might be useful if all we want is to ensure uniqueness rather than allow index lookups.

To do that, you can do either of the following:

> ▸ Use a serial data type

> ▸ Manually alter the default to be the nextval() function of a sequence

Each of these will provide a unique value for use as a row's key. The uniqueness is not enforced, nor will there be a unique constraint defined. So, there is still a possibility that someone might reset the sequence to an earlier value, which will eventually cause duplicate values.

Consider also that this method provides the unique value as a default, which is not used when the user specifies an explicit value. An example of this is as follows:

```
CREATE TABLE t(id serial, descr text);
INSERT INTO t(descr) VALUES ('First value');
INSERT INTO t(id,descr) VALUES (1,'Cheating!');
```

Finally, you might also wish to have mostly unique data, such as using the `clock_timestamp()` function to provide ascending times to microsecond resolution.

Real-world example – IP address range allocation

The problem is about assigning ranges of IP addresses, while at the same time ensuring that we don't allocate (or potentially allocate) the same addresses to different people or purposes. This is easy to do if we keep track of each individual IP address, and much harder to do if we want to deal solely with ranges of IP addresses.

Initially, you may think of designing the database as follows:

```
CREATE TABLE iprange
(iprange_start inet
,iprange_stop inet
,owner text);
INSERT INTO iprange VALUES
        ('192.168.0.1','192.168.0.16', 'Simon');
INSERT INTO iprange VALUES
        ('192.168.0.17','192.168.0.24', 'Gianni');
INSERT INTO iprange VALUES
        ('192.168.0.32','192.168.0.64', 'Hannu');
```

However, you'll realize that there is no way to create a unique constraint that enforces the constraint. You could create an after trigger that checks existing values, but it's going to be messy.

Download and install the **ip4r** data type module for PostgreSQL so that we can get access to a good data type for solving this type of problem; you can follow the *Adding an external module to PostgreSQL* and *Using an installed module* recipes from *Chapter 3, Configuration*. If it's not already available in your package manager, you can download it from `http://pgfoundry.org/projects/ip4r/`. Then, create a table like the following, and populate it with the same data in a slightly different form:

```
CREATE TABLE iprange2
(iprange ip4r
,owner text);
```

```
INSERT INTO iprange2 VALUES
       ('192.168.0.1-192.168.0.16', 'Simon');

INSERT INTO iprange2 VALUES
       ('192.168.0.17-192.168.0.24', 'Gianni');

INSERT INTO iprange2 VALUES
       ('192.168.0.32-192.168.0.64', 'Hannu');
```

You can now create a unique exclusion constraint on the table, using the following command:

```
ALTER TABLE iprange2
ADD EXCLUDE USING GIST (iprange WITH &&);
```

> From PostgreSQL 9.2 onwards, you can create a range type on any type that supports a `btree` operator class, that is, a way of ordering any couple of values. Here's an alternate solution to the same exercise using a range type on the built-in **inet** data type:
>
> ```
> CREATE TYPE inetrange AS RANGE (SUBTYPE = inet);
>
> CREATE TABLE iprange3
> (iprange inetrange
> ,owner text);
>
> INSERT INTO iprange3 VALUES
>        ('[192.168.0.1,192.168.0.16]', 'Simon');
>
> INSERT INTO iprange3 VALUES
>        ('[192.168.0.17,192.168.0.24]', 'Gianni');
>
> INSERT INTO iprange3 VALUES
>        ('[192.168.0.32,192.168.0.64]', 'Hannu');
>
> ALTER TABLE iprange3
> ADD EXCLUDE USING GIST (iprange WITH &&);
> ```

Real-world example – range of time

In many databases, there will be historical data tables with data that has a START_DATE and an END_DATE value, or something similar. As in the previous example, we can solve this example elegantly with a range type. Actually, this example is even shorter—we don't need to create the range type, since the most common cases are already built-in, and precisely: integers, decimal values, dates, and timestamps with and without a time zone.

On versions of PostgreSQL older than 9.2, you can install the `temporal` module, which defines a data type named a **period**. This is essentially a range type on timestamps with a time zone. Take a look at `http://temporal.projects.postgresql.org/`.

Real-world example – prefix ranges

Another common problem involves assigning credit card numbers or telephone numbers. For example, with credit card numbers, we may need to perform additional checking for certain financial institutions, assuming that each institution is assigned a given range, for example, 123[0-4], meaning "strings starting with 123 followed by a character between 0 and 4".

The **prefix range** data type has been specifically designed to address this class of problems. Again, this is available as a PostgreSQL plugin at `http://github.com/dimitri/prefix`.

A warning—despite the similar name, prefix ranges cannot be implemented as range types.

Finding a unique key for a set of data

Sometimes, it can be difficult to find a unique set of key columns that describe the data.

Getting ready

Let's start with a small table, where the answer is fairly obvious:

```
postgres=# select * from ord;
```

We assume that the output is as follows:

```
 orderid | customerid |   amt
---------+------------+--------
   10677 |          2 |   5.50
    5019 |          3 | 277.44
    9748 |          3 |  77.17
(3 rows)
```

How to do it...

First of all, there's no need to do this through a brute-force approach. Checking all the permutations of columns to see which is unique might take you a long time.

Let's start by using PostgreSQL's own optimizer statistics. Run the following command on our table to get a fresh sample of statistics:

```
postgres=# analyze ord;
ANALYZE
```

This runs quickly, so we don't have to wait too much. Now, we can examine the relevant columns of the statistics:

```
postgres=# SELECT attname, n_distinct
                    FROM pg_stats
                    WHERE schemaname = 'public'
                    AND tablename = 'ord';
```

attname	n_distinct
orderid	-1
customerid	-0.666667
amt	-1

(3 rows)

The preceding example was chosen because we have two potential answers. If the value of n_distinct is -1, then the column is thought to be unique within the sample of rows examined.

We would then need to use our judgment to decide whether one or both of those columns are unique by chance, or as part of the design of the database that created them.

It's possible that there is no single column that uniquely identifies the rows. Multiple-column keys are fairly common. If none of the columns were unique, then we should start looking for unique keys that are combinations of the most unique columns. The following query shows a frequency distribution for the table such that a value occurs twice in one case, and another value occurs only once:

```
postgres=# SELECT num_of_values, count(*)
            FROM (SELECT customerid, count(*) AS num_of_values
                    FROM ord
                    GROUP BY customerid) s


        GROUP BY num_of_values
        ORDER BY count(*);
```

num_of_values	count
2	1
1	1

(2 rows)

We can change the query to include multiple columns, like this:

```
SELECT num_of_values, count(*)
FROM (SELECT    customerid, orderid, …

               ,count(*) AS num_of_values
                FROM ord
                GROUP BY customerid, orderid, …

                ) s

GROUP BY num_of_values
ORDER BY count(*);
```

This query will result in only one row once we find a set of columns that is unique.
As we get closer to finding the key, we will see that the distribution gets tighter and tighter.
So, the procedure is as follows:

1. Choose one column to start with.

2. Compute the corresponding frequency distribution.

3. If the outcome is multiple rows, then add one more column and repeat from step 2. Otherwise, it means you have found a set of columns satisfying a uniqueness constraint.

   Now, you must verify that the set of columns is minimal; for example, check whether it is possible to remove one or more columns without violating the unique constraint. This can be done using the frequency distribution as a test. Precisely, do the following.

4. Test each column by computing the frequency distribution on all the other columns.

5. If the frequency distribution has one row, then the column is not needed in the uniqueness constraint. Remove it from the set of columns and repeat from step 4.

   Otherwise, you have found a minimal set of columns, which is also called a key for that table.

How it works...

Finding a unique key is possible for a program, but in most cases, a human can do this much faster by looking at things such as column names, foreign keys, or business understanding to reduce the number of searches required by the brute-force approach.

The ANALYZE command works by taking a sample of the table data, and then performing a statistical analysis of the results. The n_distinct value has two different meanings, depending on its sign: if positive, it is the estimate of the number of distinct values for the column; if negative, it is the estimate of the density of such distinct values, with the sign changed. For example, n_distinct = -0.2 means that a table of 1 million rows is expected to have 200,000 distinct values, while n_distinct = 5 means that we expect just 5 distinct values.

Generating test data

DBAs frequently need to generate test data for a variety of reasons, whether it's for setting up a test database or just for generating a test case for a SQL performance issue.

How to do it...

To create a table of test data, we need the following:

- Some rows
- Some columns
- Some order

The steps are as follows:

1. First, generate a lot of rows of data. We use something named a "set-returning function". You can write your own, though PostgreSQL includes a couple of very useful ones.

   You can generate a sequence of rows using a query like the following:

   ```
   postgres=# SELECT * FROM generate_series(1,5);
    generate_series
   -----------------
                  1
                  2
                  3
                  4
                  5
   (5 rows)
   ```

   Alternatively, you can generate a list of dates, like this:

   ```
   postgres=# SELECT date(generate_series(now(), now() + '1 week', '1 day'));
       date
   ------------
    2010-03-30
    2010-03-31
    2010-04-01
    2010-04-02
   ```

```
2010-04-03
2010-04-04
2010-04-05
2010-04-06
(8 rows)
```

Either of those functions can be used to generate both rows and reasonable primary key values for them.

2. Then, we want to generate a value for each column in the `test` table. We can break that down into a series of functions, using the following examples as a guide:

   ❑ For a random `integer` value, this is the function:

   ```
   (random()*(2*10^9))::integer
   ```

   ❑ For a random `bigint` value, the function is as follows:

   ```
   (random()*(9*10^18))::bigint
   ```

   ❑ For random `numeric` data, the function is the following:

   ```
   (random()*100.)::numeric(4,2);
   ```

   ❑ For a random-length string, up to a maximum length, this is the function:

   ```
   repeat('1',(random()*40)::integer)
   ```

   ❑ For a random-length substring, the function is as follows:

   ```
   substr('abcdefghijklmnopqrstuvwxyz',1, (random()*25)::integer)
   ```

   ❑ Here is the function for a random string from a list of strings:

   ```
   (ARRAY['one','two','three'])[0.5+random()*3].
   ```

3. Finally, we can put both techniques together to generate our table:

   ```
   postgres=# SELECT generate_series(1,10) as key
                     ,(random()*100.)::numeric(4,2)
                     ,repeat('1',(random()*25)::integer);
   key | numeric |          repeat
   ----+---------+------------------------------
     1 |   83.05 | 1111
     2 |    5.28 | 11111111111111
     3 |   41.85 | 111111111111111111111
     4 |   41.70 | 1111111111111111
     5 |   53.31 | 1
     6 |   10.09 | 111111111111111
   ```

```
 7 |   68.08 | 111
 8 |   19.42 | 111111111111111
 9 |   87.03 | 111111111111111111111
10 |   70.64 | 1111111111111
```
(10 rows)

Alternatively, we can use random ordering:

```
postgres=# SELECT generate_series(1,10) as key
                ,(random()*100.)::numeric(4,2)
                ,repeat('1',(random()*25)::integer)
                ORDER BY random();
```

```
key | numeric |        repeat
----+---------+------------------------
  6 |   70.31 | 111111111111111111111111
  4 |    2.37 | 111111111111111111
  1 |   76.99 | 1111111111111
  8 |   35.90 | 111111111111
  3 |   59.21 | 111111111
  2 |   88.86 | 11111111
  7 |   67.32 | 111111
  9 |   15.66 | 111111
  5 |   79.90 | 11111
 10 |   25.09 | 1
```
(10 rows)

How it works...

Set returning functions literally return a set of rows. That allows them to be used in either the FROM clause, as if they were a table, or the SELECT clause. The generate_series() set of functions returns either dates or integers, depending on the data types of the input parameters you use.

The :: operator is used to cast between data types. The "random string from a list of strings" example uses PostgreSQL arrays. You can create an array using the ARRAY constructor syntax, and then use an integer to reference one element in the array. In our case, we used a random subscript.

There's more...

There are also some commercial tools used to generate application-specific test data for PostgreSQL. They are available at `http://www.sqlmanager.net/products/postgresql/datagenerator` and `http://www.datanamic.com/datagenerator/index.html`.

The key features for any data generator are as follows:

► The ability to generate data in the right format for custom data types

► The ability to add data to multiple tables, while respecting foreign key constraints between tables

► The ability to add data to non-uniform distributions

The tools and tricks shown here are cool and clever, though there are some problems hiding here as well. Real data has so many strange things in it that it can be very hard to simulate. One of the most difficult things is generating data that follows realistic distributions. For example, if we had to generate data for people's heights, then we'd want to generate data to follow a normal distribution. If we were generating customer bank balances, we'd want to use a Zipf distribution, or for the number of reported insurance claims, perhaps a Poisson distribution (or perhaps not). Replicating the real quirks in data can take some time.

Finally, notice that casting a float into an integer rounds it to the nearest integer, so the distribution of integers is not uniform on each extreme. For instance, the probability of `(random()*10)::int` being 0 is just 5 percent, as is its probability of being 10, while each integer between 1 and 9 occurs with a probability of 10 percent. This is why we put 0.5 in the last example, which is simpler than using the `floor()` function.

See also

You can use existing data to generate test databases using sampling. That's the subject of our next recipe, *Randomly sampling data*.

Randomly sampling data

DBAs may be asked to set up a test server and populate it with test data. Often, that server will be old hardware, possibly with smaller disk sizes. So, the subject of data sampling raises its head.

The purpose of sampling is to reduce the size of the data set and improve the speed of later analysis. Some statisticians are so used to the idea of sampling that they may not even question whether its use is valid or it can cause further complications.

How to do it...

In this section, we will take a random sample of a given collection of data (for example, a given table). First, you should realize that there isn't a simple tool to slice off a sample of your database. It would be neat if there were, but there isn't. You'll need to read all of this to understand why:

1. We first consider using SQL to derive a sample. Random sampling is actually very simple because we can use the `random()` SQL function within the `WHERE` clause. Consider the following example:

   ```
   postgres=# SELECT count(*) FROM mybigtable;
    count
   -------
    10000
   (1 row)
   postgres=# SELECT count(*) FROM mybigtable
                       WHERE random() < 0.01;
    count
   -------
       95
   (1 row)
   postgres=# SELECT count(*) FROM mybigtable
                       WHERE random() < 0.01;
    count
   -------
      106
   (1 row)
   ```

   The `WHERE random() < 0.01` clause will generate a random number between 0.0 and 1.0 for each row, and then see if the number is less than 0.01. In other words, this `WHERE` clause will generate a 1 percent random sample of rows in the table. You can use a similar clause to vary the percentage to be anything you choose. Easy!

2. Now, we need to get the sampled data out of the database, which is tricky for a few reasons. Firstly, there is no option to specify a `WHERE` clause for `pg_dump`. Secondly, if you create a view that contains the `WHERE` clause, `pg_dump` dumps only the view definition, not the view itself.

3. You can use pg_dump to dump all databases, apart from a set of tables, so you can produce a sampled dump like this:

```
pg_dump --exclude-table=MyBigTable > db.dmp

pg_dump --table=MyBigTable -schema-only > mybigtable.schema

psql -c '\copy (SELECT * FROM MyBigTable
                    WHERE random() < 0.01) to mybigtable.dat'
```

4. Then, reload onto a separate database using the following commands:

```
psql -f db.dmp

psql -f mybigtable.schema

psql -c '\copy mybigtable from mybigtable.dat'
```

Overall, my advice is to avoid sampling if you can. Otherwise, at least minimize it to a few very large tables. This avoids both the mathematical issues surrounding sample design and the difficulty of extracting the data.

How it works...

The extract mechanism shows off the capabilities of the PostgreSQL command-line tools, psql and pg_dump, as pg_dump allows you to include or exclude files and dump the entire table (or only its schema), whereas psql allows you to dump out the result of an arbitrary query into a file.

We haven't discussed how random the random() function is. This isn't the right place for such details; if you prefer another mechanism, you can find an external random number generator, and call out to it from SQL using a C language function.

The sampling method shown earlier is a simple random sampling technique that has an **equal probability of selection** (**EPS**) design.

EPS samples are considered useful because the variance of the sample attributes is similar to the variance of the original dataset. However, bear in mind that this is useful only if you are considering variances.

Simple random sampling can make the eventual sample biased towards more frequently occurring data. For example, if you have a 1 percent sample of data on which some kinds of data occur only 0.001 percent of the time, you may end up with a dataset that doesn't have any of that outlying data.

What you might wish to do is to precluster your data and take different samples from each group to ensure that you have a sampled data set that includes many more outlying attributes. A simple method might be to do the following:

- Include 1 percent of all normal data
- Include 25 percent of outlying data

Note that if you do this, then it is no longer an EPS sample design.

Undoubtedly, there are statisticians who will be in apoplexy after reading this. You're welcome to use the facilities of the SQL language to create a more accurate sample. Just make sure that you know what you're doing and/or check out some good statistical literature, websites, or textbooks.

Loading data from a spreadsheet

Spreadsheets are the most obvious starting place for most data stores. Studies within a range of businesses consistently show that more than 50 percent of the smaller data stores are held in spreadsheets or small desktop databases. Loading data from these sources is a frequent and important task for many DBAs.

Getting ready

Spreadsheets combine data, presentation, and programs all into one file. That's perfect for power users wanting to work quickly. Like other relational databases, PostgreSQL is mainly concerned with the lowest level of data, so extracting just the data can present some challenges.

We can easily handle spreadsheet data if that spreadsheet's layout follows a very specific form, as follows:

- Each spreadsheet column becomes one column in one table
- Each row of the spreadsheet becomes one row in one table
- Data is only in one worksheet of the spreadsheet
- Optionally, the first row is a list of column descriptions/titles

This is a very simple layout, and more often there will be other things in the spreadsheet, such as titles, comments, constants for use in formulas, summary lines, macros, images, and so on. If you're in this position, the best thing to do is to create a new worksheet within the spreadsheet in the pristine form described earlier, and then set up cross-worksheet references to bring in the data. An example of a cross-worksheet reference would be =Sheet2.A1. You'll need a separate worksheet for each set of data that will become one table on PostgreSQL. You can load multiple worksheets into one table, however.

Some spreadsheet users will say that all of this is unnecessary, and is evidence of the problems of databases. The real spreadsheet gurus do actually advocate this type of layout: data in one worksheet and calculation and presentation in other worksheets. So, it is actually best practice to design spreadsheets in this way; however, we must work with the world the way it is.

How to do it...

Here, we will show you an example where data in a spreadsheet is loaded into a database:

1. If your spreadsheet data is neatly laid out in a single worksheet, as shown in the following screenshot, then you can go to **File** | **Save As** and then select CSV as the file type to be saved:

This will export the current worksheet to a file, like the following:

```
"Key","Value"
1,"c"
2,"d"
```

2. We can then load it into an existing PostgreSQL table, using the following psql command:

```
postgres=# \COPY sample FROM sample.csv CSV HEADER

postgres=# SELECT * FROM sample;

 key | value
-----+-------
   1 | c
   2 | d
```

Alternatively, from the command line, this would be as follows:

```
psql -c '\COPY sample FROM sample.csv CSV HEADER'
```

Note that the file can include a full file path if the data is in a different directory. The psql \COPY command transfers data from the client system where you run the command through to the database server, so the file is on the client.

3. If you are submitting SQL through another type of connection, then you should use the following SQL statement:

```
COPY sample FROM '/mydatafiledirectory/sample.csv' CSV HEADER;
```

Note that the preceding SQL statement runs on the database server and can only be executed by a superuser. So, you need to ensure that the server process is allowed to read that file, then transfer the data yourself to the server, and finally load the file. The COPY statement shown in the preceding SQL statement uses an absolute path to identify data files, which is required.

The COPY (or \COPY) command does not create the table for you; that must be done beforehand. Note also that the HEADER option does nothing but ignores the first line of the input file, so the names of the columns from the .csv file don't need to match those of the Postgres table. If it hasn't occurred to you yet, this is also a problem. If you say HEADER and the file does not have a header line, then all it does is ignore the first data row. Unfortunately, there's no way for PostgreSQL to tell whether the first line of the file is truly a header or not. Be careful!

There isn't a standard tool to load data directly from the spreadsheet to the database. It's fairly simple to write a spreadsheet macro to automate the aforementioned tasks, but that's not a topic for this book.

How it works...

The \COPY command executes a COPY SQL statement, so the two methods described earlier are very similar. There's more to be said about COPY, so we'll cover that in the next recipe.

There's more...

There are many data extract and loading tools available out there, some cheap and some expensive. Remember that the hardest part of loading data from any spreadsheet is separating the data from all the other things it contains. I've not yet seen a tool that can help with that.

Loading data from flat files

Loading data into your database is one of the most important tasks. You need to do this accurately and quickly. Here's how.

Getting ready

You'll need a copy of pgloader, which is available at `http://github.com/dimitri/pgloader`.

At the time of writing this book, the current stable version is 3.1.0. The 3.x series is a major rewrite, with many additional features, and the 2.x series is now considered obsolete.

How to do it...

PostgreSQL includes a command named `COPY` that provides the basic data load/unload mechanism. The `COPY` command doesn't do enough when loading data, so let's skip the basic command and go straight to pgloader.

To load data, we need to understand our requirements, so let's break this down into a step-by-step process, as follows:

1. Identify the data files and where they are located. Make sure that pgloader is installed at the location of the files.

2. Identify the table into which you are loading, ensure that you have the permissions to load, and check the available space.

3. Work out the file type (fixed, text, or CSV) and check the encoding.

4. Specify the mapping between columns in the file and columns on the table being loaded. Make sure you know which columns in the file are not needed—pgloader allows you to include only the columns you want. Identify any columns in the table for which you don't have data. Do you need them to have a default value on the table, or does pgloader need to generate values for those columns through functions or constants?

5. Specify any transformations that need to take place. The most common issue is date formats, though possibly there may be other issues.

6. Write the pgloader script.

7. pgloader will create a log file to record whether the load has succeeded or failed, and another file to store rejected rows. You need a directory with sufficient disk space if you expect them to be large. Their size is roughly proportional to the number of failing rows.

8. Finally, consider what settings you need for performance options. This is definitely last, as fiddling with things earlier can lead to confusion when you're still making the load work correctly.

9. You must use a script to execute pgloader. This is not a restriction; actually it is more like best practice, because it makes it much easier to iterate towards something that works. Loads never work the first time, except in the movies!

Let's look at a typical example from pgloader's documentation—the `example.load` file:

```
LOAD CSV
    FROM 'GeoLiteCity-Blocks.csv' WITH ENCODING iso-646-us
        HAVING FIELDS
        (
            startIpNum, endIpNum, locId
        )
    INTO postgresql://user@localhost:54393/dbname?geolite.blocks
        TARGET COLUMNS
        (
            iprange ip4r using (ip-range startIpNum endIpNum),
            locId
        )
    WITH truncate,
        skip header = 2,
        fields optionally enclosed by '"',
        fields escaped by backslash-quote,
        fields terminated by '\t'

    SET work_mem to '32 MB', maintenance_work_mem to '64 MB';
```

We can use the load script like this:

```
pgloader --summary summary.log example.load
```

How it works...

pgloader copes gracefully with errors. The COPY command loads all rows in a single transaction, so only a single error is enough to abort the load. pgloader breaks down an input file into reasonably sized chunks, and loads them piece by piece. If some rows in a chunk cause errors, then pgloader will split it iteratively until it loads all the good rows and skips all the bad rows, which are then saved in a separate "rejects" file for later inspection. This behavior is very convenient if you have large data files with a small percentage of bad rows; for instance, you can edit the rejects, fix them, and finally, load them with another pgloader run.

Versions 2.x of pgloader were written in Python and connected to PostgreSQL through the standard Python client interface. Version 3.x is written in Common Lisp. Yes, pgloader is less efficient than loading data files using a COPY command, but running a COPY command has many more restrictions: the file has to be in the right place on the server, has to be in the right format, and must be unlikely to throw errors on loading. pgloader has additional overhead, but it also has the ability to load data using multiple parallel threads, so it can be faster to use as well. pgloader's ability to call out to reformat functions is often essential in most cases; straight COPY is just too simple.

pgloader also allows loading from fixed-width files, which COPY does not.

There's more...

If you need to reload the table completely from scratch, then specify the –WITH TRUNCATE clause in the pgloader script.

There are also options to specify SQL to be executed before and after loading the data. For instance, you may have a script that creates the empty tables before, or you can add constraints after, or both.

After loading, if we have load errors, then there will be some junk loaded into the PostgreSQL tables. It is not junk that you can see, or that gives any semantic errors, but think of it more like fragmentation. You should think about whether you need to add a VACUUM command after the data load, though this will make the load take possibly much longer.

We need to be careful to avoid loading data twice. The only easy way of doing that is to make sure that there is at least one unique index defined on every table that you load. The load should then fail very quickly.

String handling can often be difficult, because of the presence of formatting or nonprintable characters. The default setting for PostgreSQL is to have a parameter named standard_ conforming_strings set to off, which means that backslashes will be assumed to be escape characters. Put another way, by default, the \n string means line feed, which can cause data to appear truncated. You'll need to turn standard_conforming_strings to on, or you'll need to specify an escape character in the load-parameter file.

If you are reloading data that has been unloaded from PostgreSQL, then you may want to use the pg_restore utility instead. The pg_restore utility has an option to reload data in parallel, -j number_of_threads, though this is only possible if the dump was produced using the custom pg_dump format. Refer to the recipes in *Chapter 11, Backup and Recovery*, for more details. This can be useful for reloading dumps, though it lacks almost all of the other pgloader features discussed here.

If you need to use rows from a read-only text file that does not have errors, and you are using version 9.1 or later of PostgreSQL, then you may consider using the `file_fdw` contrib module. The short story is that it lets you create a "virtual" table that will parse the text file every time it is scanned. This is different from filling a table once and for all, either with `COPY` or pgloader; therefore, it covers a different use case. For example, think about an external data source that is maintained by a third party and needs to be shared across different databases.

You may wish to send an e-mail to Dimitri Fontaine, the current author and maintainer of most of pgloader. He always loves to receive e-mails from users.

6
Security

In this chapter, we will cover the following recipes:

- The PostgreSQL superuser
- Revoking user access to a table
- Granting user access to a table
- Creating a new user
- Temporarily preventing a user from connecting
- Removing a user without dropping their data
- Checking whether all users have a secure password
- Giving limited superuser powers to specific users
- Auditing DDL changes
- Auditing data changes
- Always knowing which user is logged in
- Integrating with LDAP
- Connecting using SSL
- Using SSL certificates to authenticate the client
- Mapping external usernames to database roles
- Encrypting sensitive data

Introduction

Databases are mostly used to keep data with several restrictions on how it can be used. Some records or tables can only be seen by certain users, and even for those tables that are visible to everyone, there can be restrictions on who can insert new data or change the existing data. All of this is managed by a privilege system, where users are granted different privileges for different tables or other database objects, such as schemas or functions.

It is good practice not to grant these privileges directly to users, but to use an intermediate **role** to collect a set of privileges. Then, instead of granting all the same privileges to the actual user, this entire role is granted to users needing these privileges. For example, a "clerk" role may have rights to both insert data and update existing data in the user_account table, but may have rights to only insert data in the audit_log table.

Another aspect of database security is making sure that only the right people can access the database, and that one user can't see what other users are doing (unless you are an administrator or auditor), and whether users can or cannot grant forward the roles granted to them.

Yet another important part of security is to make sure that database servers are in physically secure locations, and that the procedures to access these servers are secure.

However, this is not a general guide to securing your database, server machine, or network, which is too large a topic to be covered here.

If you are serious about security, then read some of the available books and articles on security, or hire a security consultant. Database security is just a small piece in the overall security puzzle.

Typical user role

The minimal production database setup contains at least two types of users, namely administrators and end users, where administrators can do everything (they are superusers), and end users can only do very little, usually just modify the data in only a few tables and read from a few more.

It is not a good idea to let ordinary users create or change database object definitions, meaning that they should not have the CREATE privilege on any schema, including PUBLIC.

There can be more roles for different types of end users, such as analysts, who can only select from a single table or view, or some maintenance script "users" who see no data at all and just have the ability to execute a few functions.

Alternatively, there can also be a manager role, which can grant and revoke roles for other users but is not supposed to do anything else.

The PostgreSQL superuser

In this recipe, you will learn how to turn a user into an all-powerful **superuser** and back to an ordinary user.

A PostgreSQL superuser is a user that can do anything in the database regardless of what privileges it has been granted.

How to do it...

A user becomes a superuser when it is created with the SUPERUSER attribute set:

```
CREATE USER username SUPERUSER;
```

A user can be deprived of its superuser status by removing the SUPERUSER attribute, using this command:

```
ALTER USER username NOSUPERUSER;
```

A user can be restored to superuser status later, using the following command:

```
ALTER USER username SUPERUSER;
```

When neither SUPERUSER nor NOSUPERUSER is given in the CREATE USER command, then the default is to create a user who is not a superuser.

How it works...

Rights to some operations in PostgreSQL cannot be granted. They must be performed by a special user who has this special attribute set. The preceding commands set or reset this attribute for the user.

There's more...

The PostgreSQL system comes set up with at least one superuser. Most commonly, this superuser is named postgres, but it is actually named the same as the system user who owns the database directory and with whose rights the PostgreSQL server runs.

Other superuser-like attributes

In addition to SUPERUSER, there are two lesser attributes—CREATEDB and CREATEUSER—that give the user only some of the power reserved to superusers, namely creating new databases and users. See the *Giving limited superuser powers to specific users* recipe for more information on this.

Attributes are never inherited

Later, you will learn about granting one role to another, role inheritance, and how privileges can be granted through these intermediate "group roles". None of this applies to attributes—to perform superuser-only operations, you must be that user.

See also

Also check out the *Always knowing which user is logged in* recipe in this chapter.

 All of the following recipes assume a non-superuser unless explicitly mentioned that they apply to or need a superuser.

Revoking user access to a table

This recipe answers the question, "How do I make sure that user X cannot access table Y?"

Getting ready

The current user must either be a superuser, the owner of the table, or a user with a GRANT option for the table.

Also, you can't revoke rights from a user who is a superuser.

How to do it...

To revoke all rights on the table1 table from the user2 user, you must run the following SQL command:

```
REVOKE ALL ON table1 FROM user2;
```

However, if user2 had been granted another role that gives them some rights on table1, say role3, this command is not enough; you must also choose one of the following options:

▶ "Fix" the user; that is, revoke role3 from user2

▶ "Fix" the role; that is, revoke privileges on table1 from role3

Both choices are imperfect, because of their side effects: the former will revoke all the privileges associated to role3, not only the privileges concerning table1; the latter will revoke the privileges on table1 from all the other users that have been granted role3, not only from user2.

It is normally better to avoid damaging other legitimate users, so we opt for the first solution. Here is a worked example:

1. Using psql, display the list of roles that have been granted at least one privilege on `table1`, by issuing `\z table1`. For instance, you can obtain the following output (an extra column about column privileges has been removed from the right-hand side because it was not relevant here):

```
                                   Access privileges
  Schema |  Name  | Type  |     Access privileges      | ...
 --------+--------+-------+----------------------------+ ...
  public | table1 | table | postgres=arwdDxt/postgres+ | ...
         |        |       | role3=r/postgres          +| ...
         |        |       | role5=a/postgres           | ...
 (1 row)
```

2. Then, we check whether `user2` is a member of any of those roles by typing `\du user2`:

```
            List of roles
  Role name | Attributes |   Member of
 -----------+------------+---------------
  user2     |            | {role3, role4}
```

3. From the previous step, we notice that `role3` had been granted the SELECT privilege ("r" for "read") by the `postgres` user, so we must revoke it, as follows:

   REVOKE role3 FROM user2;

4. We must also inspect `role4`. Even if it doesn't have privileges on `table1`, in theory it could be a member of one of the three roles that have privileges on that table. We issue `\du role4` and get the following output:

```
             List of roles
  Role name |  Attributes  | Member of
 -----------+--------------+-----------
  role4     | Cannot login | {role5}
```

   Our suspicion was founded: `user2` can get the INSERT privilege ("a" for "append") on `table1`, first via `role4` and then via `role5`. So, we must break this two-step chain, as follows:

   REVOKE role4 FROM user2;

This example may seem too unlikely to be true. We unexpectedly gain access to the table via a chain of two different role memberships, which was made possible by the fact that a non-login role such as role4 was made a member of another non-login role, that is, role5. In most real-world cases, superusers will know very well whether such cases exist at all, so there will be no surprise; however, the goal of this recipe is to make sure that the user cannot access the table, meaning we cannot exclude less likely options.

How it works...

The \z command, as well as its synonym, \dp, displays all privileges granted on tables, views, and sequences. If the Access privileges column is empty, it means "default privileges"; that is, all privileges are given to the owner (and the superusers, as always).

The \du command shows attributes and roles that have been granted to roles.

Both commands accept an optional name or pattern to restrict the display.

There's more...

Here we'll cover some good practices on user and role management.

Database creation scripts

For production systems, it is usually a good idea to always include GRANT and REVOKE statements in the database creation script so that you can be sure that only the right set of users has access to the table. If this is done manually, it is easy to forget. Also, in this way, we are sure that the same roles are used on development and testing environments, so there are no surprises at deployment time.

The following is a sample extract from the database creation script:

```
CREATE TABLE table1(
...
);
GRANT SELECT ON table1 TO webreaders;
GRANT SELECT, INSERT, UPDATE, DELETE ON table1 TO editors;
GRANT ALL ON table1 TO admins;
```

Default search path

It is always good practice to use a fully qualified name when revoking or granting rights; otherwise, you may be working with the wrong table inadvertently.

To see the effective search path for the current database, run the following:

```
pguser=# show search_path ;
  search_path
----------------
 "$user",public
(1 row)
```

To see which table will be affected if you omit the schema name, run the following in psql:

```
pguser=# \d x
        Table "public.x"
 Column | Type | Modifiers
--------+------+-----------
```

The `public.x` table name in the response contains the full name, including the schema.

Securing views

It is a common technique to use a view to disclose only some parts of a secret table; however, a clever attacker can use access to the view to display the rest of the table using log messages. For instance, consider the following example:

```
CREATE VIEW for_the_public AS
  SELECT * FROM reserved_data WHERE importance < 10;
GRANT SELECT ON for_the_public TO PUBLIC;
```

A malicious user could define this function, as follows:

```
CREATE FUNCTION f(text)
RETURNS boolean
COST 0.00000001
LANGUAGE plpgsql AS $$
BEGIN
  RAISE INFO '$1: %', $1;
  RETURN true;
END;
$$;
```

Then, they could use it to filter rows from the view:

```
SELECT * FROM for_the_public x WHERE f(x :: text);
```

The PostgreSQL optimizer will then internally rearrange the query, expanding the definition of the view and then combining the two filter conditions into a single WHERE clause. The trick here is that the function has been "told" to be very cheap using the COST keyword, so the optimizer will choose to evaluate that condition first. In other words, the function will access all the rows in the table, as you will realize when you see the corresponding INFO lines on the console if you run the code yourself.

This security leak has been fixed in PostgreSQL version 9.2 with the introduction of the security_barrier attribute:

```
ALTER VIEW for_the_public SET (security_barrier = on);
```

This means that the conditions that define the view will always be computed first, irrespective of cost considerations.

The performance impact of this fix has been mitigated by introducing the LEAKPROOF attribute for functions. In short, a function that cannot "leak" information other than its output value can be marked as LEAKPROOF by a superuser, so the planner will know that it's secure to compute the function before the other view conditions.

Granting user access to a table

A user needs to have access to a table in order to perform any action on it.

Getting ready

Make sure that you have appropriate roles defined, and that privileges are revoked from the PUBLIC role.

How to do it...

Grant access to the schema containing the table, as follows:

```
GRANT USAGE ON someschema TO somerole;
GRANT SELECT, INSERT, UPDATE, DELETE ON someschema.sometable TO somerole;
GRANT somerole TO someuser, otheruser;
```

How it works...

This sequence of commands first grants full access to all objects in that schema to a role, gives viewing (SELECT) and modifying (INSERT, UPDATE, and DELETE) rights on that table to the role, and then grants membership in that role to two database users.

There's more...

There is no requirement in PostgreSQL to have some privileges in order to have others. This means that you may well have "write-only" tables, where you are allowed to insert but you can't select. This can be used to implement a mail-queue-like functionality, where several users post messages to one user, but they can't see what other users have posted.

Alternatively, you can write a record, but you can't change or delete it. This is useful for auditing log type tables, where all changes are recorded, and which are not tampered with.

Access to the schema

We had to grant access to the schema in order to allow access to the table. This suggests that access to a given schema can be used as a fast and extreme way to prevent any access to any object in that schema. Otherwise, if you want to allow some access, you must use specific GRANT and REVOKE statements as needed.

Granting access to a table through a group role

It is often desirable to give a group of users similar permissions to a group of database objects. To do this, you first assign all the permissions to a proxy role (also known as a permission group), and then assign the group to selected users, as follows:

```
CREATE GROUP webreaders;
GRANT SELECT ON pages TO webreaders;
GRANT INSERT ON viewlog TO webreaders;
GRANT webreaders TO tim, bob;
```

Now, both tim and bob have the SELECT privilege on the pages table and INSERT on the viewlog table. You can also add privileges to the group role after assigning it to users. Consider the following command:

```
GRANT INSERT, UPDATE, DELETE ON comments TO webreaders;
```

After running this command, both bob and tim have all of the aforementioned privileges on the comments table.

This assumes that both the bob and tim roles were created with the INHERIT default setting. Otherwise, they do not automatically "inherit" the rights of roles but need to explicitly set their role to the granted user to make use of the privileges granted to that role.

Granting access to all objects in a schema

Before version 9.0 of PostgreSQL, there was no easy way to manipulate privileges to more than one object at a time, except listing them all in the GRANT or REVOKE command.

Version 9.0 added a capability to grant or revoke privileges on all objects of a certain kind in a specific schema:

```
GRANT SELECT ON ALL TABLES IN SCHEMA staging TO bob;
```

You still need to grant the privileges on the schema itself in a separate GRANT statement.

Creating a new user

In this recipe, we will show you two ways of creating a new database user, one with a dedicated command-line utility, and one using SQL commands.

Getting ready

To create new users, you must either be a superuser or have the CREATEROLE or CREATEUSER privilege.

How to do it...

From the command line, you can run the createuser command:

```
pguser@hvost:~$ createuser bob
```

If you add the --interactive command-line option, you activate the interactive mode, which means you will be asked some questions, as follows:

```
pguser@hvost:~$ createuser --interactive alice
Shall the new role be a superuser? (y/n) n
Shall the new role be allowed to create databases? (y/n) y
Shall the new role be allowed to create more new roles? (y/n) n
```

Without --interactive, the preceding questions get "no" as the default answer; you can change that with the -, -d, and -r command-line options.

In interactive mode, questions are asked only if they make sense. One example is the case when the user will be a superuser; no other questions are asked because a superuser is not subject to privilege checks. Another example is when using one of the preceding options to specify a non-default setting; the corresponding question will not be asked.

The --interactive switch has been introduced in version 9.2; the interactive behavior is always active in prior versions.

How it works...

The `createuser` program is just a shallow wrapper around executing SQL against the database cluster. It connects to the `postgres` database and then executes SQL commands for user creation. To create the same users through SQL, you can issue the following commands:

```
CREATE USER bob;
CREATE USER alice CREATEDB;
```

There's more...

You can check the attributes of a given user in psql, as follows:

```
pguser=# \du alice
```

This gives the following output:

```
          List of roles
 Role name | Attributes  | Member of
-----------+-------------+-----------
 alice     | Create DB   | {}
```

The `CREATE USER` and `CREATE GROUP` commands are actually variations of `CREATE ROLE`. The `CREATE USER username;` statement is equivalent to `CREATE ROLE username LOGIN;`, and the `CREATE GROUP groupname;` statement is equivalent to `CREATE ROLE groupname NOLOGIN;`.

Temporarily preventing a user from connecting

Sometimes, you need to temporarily revoke a user's connection rights without actually deleting the user or changing the user's password. This recipe presents ways to do this.

Getting ready

To modify other users, you must either be a superuser or have the `CREATEROLE` privilege (in the latter case, only non-superuser roles can be altered).

How to do it...

To temporarily prevent the user from logging in, run this command:

```
pguser=# alter user bob nologin;
ALTER ROLE
```

To let the user connect again, run the following:

```
pguser=# alter user bob login;
ALTER ROLE
```

How it works...

This sets a flag in the system catalog, telling PostgreSQL not to let the user log in. It does not kick out already connected users.

There's more...

Here are some additional remarks.

Limiting the number of concurrent connections by a user

The same result can be achieved by setting a connection limit for that user to 0:

```
pguser=# alter user bob connection limit 0;
ALTER ROLE
```

To allow 10 concurrent connections for the bob user, run this command:

```
pguser=# alter user bob connection limit 10;
ALTER ROLE
```

To allow an unlimited number of connections for this user, run the following:

```
pguser=# alter user bob connection limit -1;
ALTER ROLE
```

Forcing NOLOGIN users to disconnect

In order to make sure that all users whose login privilege has been revoked are disconnected right away, run the following SQL statement as a superuser:

```
SELECT pg_terminate_backend(pid)
  FROM pg_stat_activity a
    JOIN pg_roles r ON a.usename = r.rolname AND not rolcanlogin;
```

This disconnects all users who no longer are allowed to connect by terminating the backends opened by these users.

 The preceding query works with PostgreSQL version 9.2 or above; on older releases, you must replace `pid` with `procpid` in the first line.

Removing a user without dropping their data

When trying to drop a user who owns some tables or other database objects, you get the following error, and the user is not dropped:

```
testdb=# drop user bob;
ERROR:  role "bob" cannot be dropped because some objects depend on it
DETAIL:  owner of table bobstable
owner of sequence bobstable_id_seq
```

This recipe presents two solutions to this problem.

Getting ready

To modify users, you must either be a superuser or have the CREATEROLE privilege.

How to do it...

The easiest solution to this problem is to refrain from dropping the user, and use the trick from a previous recipe to prevent the user from connecting:

```
pguser=# alter user bob nologin;
ALTER ROLE
```

This has the added benefit of the original owner of the table being available later, if needed, for auditing or debugging purposes ("Why is this table here? Who created it?").

Then, you can assign the rights of the "deleted" user to a new user, using the following code:

```
pguser=# grant bob bobs_replacement;
GRANT
```

How it works...

As noted previously, a user is implemented as a role with the login attribute set. This recipe works by removing that attribute from the user, which then is kept just as a role.

If you really need to get rid of a user, you have to assign all ownerships to another user. To do so, run the following query, which is a PostgreSQL extension to SQL standard:

```
REASSIGN OWNED BY bob TO bobs_replacement;
```

It does exactly what it says—assigns ownership of all database objects currently owned by the bob role to the `bobs_replacement` role.

However, you need to have privileges on both the old and the new roles to do that, and you need to do it in all databases where bob owns any objects, as the REASSIGN OWNED command works only on the current database.

After this, you can delete the original user, bob.

Checking whether all users have a secure password

PostgreSQL has no built-in facilities to make sure that you are using strong passwords.

The best you can do is make sure that all users' passwords are encrypted, and that your pg_hba.conf file does not allow logins with a plain password. That is, always use MD5 as the login method for users.

For client applications connecting from trusted private networks, either real or virtual (VPN), you may use host-based access, that is, if you know that the machine on which the application is running is not used by some non-trusted individuals. For remote access over public networks, it may be a better idea to use SSL client certificates.

How to do it...

To see which users have unencrypted passwords, use this query:

```
test2=# select usename,passwd from pg_shadow where passwd not like 'md5%'
or length(passwd) <> 35;
 usename   |    passwd
-----------+---------------
 tim       | weakpassword
 asterisk  | md5chicken
(2 rows)
```

To see users with encrypted passwords, use the following:

```
test2=# select usename,passwd from pg_shadow where passwd like 'md5%' and
length(passwd) = 35;
 usename  |                  passwd
----------+-------------------------------------
 bob2     | md518cf038878cd04fa207e7f5602013a36
(1 row)
```

How it works...

Having the passwords encrypted in the database is just half of the equation. The bigger problem is making sure that users actually use passwords that are hard to guess; that is, passwords such as password, secret, or test are out, and most common words are not good passwords either.

If you don't trust your users to select strong passwords, you can write a wrapper application that checks the password strength and make them use that when changing passwords. There exists a contrib module for doing so for a limited set of cases (password sent from client to server in plain text). Visit http://www.postgresql.org/docs/9.4/static/passwordcheck.html for more information on this.

Giving limited superuser powers to specific users

First, the superuser role has some privileges, which can also be granted to non-superuser roles separately.

To give the bob role the ability to create new databases, run this:

```
ALTER ROLE BOB WITH CREATEDB;
```

To give the bob role the ability to create new users, run the following:

```
ALTER ROLE BOB WITH CREATEUSER;
```

However, it is also possible to give ordinary users more fine-grained and controlled access to some action reserved for superusers, using **SECURITY DEFINER** functions. The same trick can also be used to pass partial privileges between different users.

Getting ready

First, you must have access to the database as a superuser in order to delegate some powers. Here, we assume the use of the default superuser named `postgres`.

We will demonstrate two cases of making some superuser-only functionality available to select an ordinary user.

The database must have support for the PL/pgSQL embedded language installed. Starting from PostgreSQL 9.0, the recommended default behavior is to have PL/pgSQL installed in a newly created database, but this can be changed by package creators or site administrators. If it is not, run the following as a PostgreSQL superuser:

```
test2=# CREATE LANGUAGE plpgsql;
CREATE LANGUAGE
```

How to do it...

One thing that a superuser can do and ordinary users cannot is telling PostgreSQL to copy table data from a file:

```
pguser@hvost:~$ psql -U postgres
 test2
...
test2=# create table lines(line text);
CREATE TABLE
test2=# copy lines from '/home/bob/names.txt';
COPY 37
test2=# SET ROLE to bob;
SET
test2=> copy lines from '/home/bob/names.txt';
ERROR:  must be superuser to COPY to or from a file
HINT:  Anyone can COPY to stdout or from stdin. psql's \copy command also
works for anyone.
```

To let bob copy directly from the file, the superuser can write a special wrapper function for bob, as follows:

```
create or replace function copy_from(tablename text, filepath text)
returns void
security definer
as
$$
 declare
 begin
      execute 'copy ' || quote_ident(tablename)
                 || ' from ' || quote_literal(filepath) ;
 end;
$$ language plpgsql;
```

It is usually a good idea to restrict usage of such a function to the intended user only:

```
revoke all on function copy_from( text,  text) from public;
grant execute on function copy_from( text,  text) to bob;
```

You may also want to verify that bob imports files only from his home directory.

Unfortunately, this solution is not completely secure against superuser privilege escalation by a malicious attacker. This is because the execution of the COPY command inside the function will also cause the execution, as the postgres user, of all side effects, such as the execution of any INSERT trigger, computation of any CHECK constraint, computation of any functional index, and more.

In other words, if the user wants to execute a given function as the superuser, it's enough to put that function inside any of the preceding functions.

There are a few workarounds for this security hole, none of which is optimal:

- Require that the table has no triggers, CHECK constraints, and functional indexes.
- Instead of running COPY on the given table, create a new table with the same structure using the CREATE newtable(LIKE oldtable) syntax. Run the COPY against the new table, drop the old table, and rename the new table like the old table.

How it works...

When a function defined with security definer is called, PostgreSQL changes the session's rights to those of the user who defined the function while that function is being executed.

So, when bob executes the `copy_from(tablename, filepath)` function, bob is effectively promoted to superuser for the time the function is running.

This behavior is similar to the `setuid` flag in Unix systems, where you can have a program to be run by anybody (with execute access) as the owner of that program. It also carries similar risks.

There's more...

There are other operations that are reserved for PostgreSQL superusers, such as setting certain parameters.

Writing a debugging_info function for developers

Several of the parameters controlling logging are reserved for superusers.

If you want to allow some of your developers to set logging on, you can write a function for them to do exactly that:

```
create or replace function debugging_info_on()
returns void
security definer
as
$$
  begin
    set client_min_messages to 'DEBUG1';
    set log_min_messages to 'DEBUG1';
    set log_error_verbosity to 'VERBOSE';
    set log_min_duration_statement to 0;
  end;
$$ language plpgsql;
revoke all on function debugging_info_on() from public;
grant execute on function debugging_info_on() to bob;
```

You may also want to have a function to go back to the default logging state by assigning `DEFAULT` to all the variables involved:

```
create or replace function debugging_info_reset()
returns void
security definer
as
$$
  begin
    set client_min_messages to DEFAULT;
    set log_min_messages to DEFAULT;
    set log_error_verbosity to DEFAULT;
    set log_min_duration_statement to DEFAULT;
  end;
$$ language plpgsql;
```

There's no need for `GRANT` and `REVOKE` statements here, as setting them back to default does not pose a security risk. Instead of `SET xxx to DEFAULT`, you can also use a shorter version of the same command, namely `RESET xxx`.

Alternatively, you can simply end your session, as the parameters are valid only for the current session.

Auditing DDL changes

This recipe shows you how you can collect **Data Definition Language** (**DDL**) from database logs in order to audit changes to the database structure.

Getting ready

Edit your `postgresql.conf` file to set the following:

```
log_statement = 'ddl'
```

Setting it to `mod` or `all` is also OK for this. Don't forget to reload the configuration:

/etc/init-d/postgresql reload

How to do it...

Now find all occurrences of the CREATE, ALTER, and DROP commands in the log:

```
postgres@hvost:~$ egrep -i "create|alter|drop" \ /var/log/postgresql/
postgresql-9.4-main.log
```

If log rotation is in effect, you may need to use grep on older logs as well.

If the available logs are too new, and you haven't saved the older logs in some other place, you are out of luck.

The default settings in the postgresql.conf file for log rotation are as follows:

```
log_filename = 'postgresql-%Y-%m-%d_%H%M%S.log'
log_rotation_age = 1d
log_rotation_size = 10MB
```

 Log rotation can also be implemented with third-party utilities. For instance, the default behavior on Debian and Ubuntu distributions is to use the logrotate utility to compress or delete old log files, according to the rules specified in the /etc/logrotate.d/postgresql-common file.

To make sure you have the full history of DDL commands, you may want to set up a cron job that saves the DDL statements extracted from the main PostgreSQL log to a separate DDL audit log. You would still want to verify that the logs are not rotating too fast for this to catch all DDL statements.

How it works...

The changes to postgresql.conf instruct PostgreSQL to log all DDL commands in PostgreSQL's main log.

The egrep... command extracts only the DDL queries from the log file.

There's more...

Some additional auditing information can be accessed as explained here.

Was the change committed?

It is possible to have some statements recorded in the log file but not visible in the database structure. Most DDL commands in PostgreSQL can be rolled back, so what is in the log is just a list of commands executed by PostgreSQL—not what was actually committed. The log file is not transactional, and it also keeps commands that were rolled back. It is possible to display the transaction identifier on each log line by including %x in the `log_line_prefix` setting.

Who made the change?

To be able to know the database user who made the DDL changes, you have to make sure that this information is logged as well.

In order to do so, you may have to change the `log_line_prefix` parameter to include the %u format string.

A recommended minimal `log_line_prefix` format string for auditing DDL is %t %u %d, which tells PostgreSQL to log the timestamp, database user, and database name at the start of every log line.

Can I find this information from the database?

If you don't have logging enabled, or don't have all the logs, then you can get only very limited information on who changed the database schema and when, from the system tables; and even that is not reliable.

What you can get is the owner of the database object (table, sequence, function, and so on), but this may have been changed by ALTER TABLE ... SET OWNER to yyyy, so you cannot be certain that the object was created by that user.

You may be able to guess the approximate time of object creation or the latest modification by looking up the transaction identifier in the xmin system column in the pg_class and pg_attribute system tables. Then, try to find a close xmin value from some other table that has automatic insert date logging, maybe having DEFAULT CURRENT_TIMESTAMP defined for some column.

This works only if the row has not been **frozen** yet, either by **autovacuum** or by an explicit VACUUM FREEZE command. After freezing, the xmin column will contain a special value, 2, that has no temporal relationship to the other rows with the same xmin value.

You may still miss some DDL...

The `log_statement = 'ddl'` statement will log only DDL statements explicitly given in top-level commands. It is still possible to perform DDL without it being logged by this setting if you use any of the PL languages, either through DO statements or by calling a function that includes DDL statements.

Starting from version 9.3, it is possible to capture and log DDL statements through the **EVENT TRIGGERS** mechanism. The basic idea is as follows; we define a special "event trigger" function, to be executed once after each DDL. The function will receive a string that describes the command tag (CREATE TABLE, ALTER VIEW, and so on) from PostgreSQL, and will log the desired information using the PostgreSQL logging infrastructure (for example, RAISE on PL/pgSQL).

Auditing data changes

This recipe provides different ways to collect changes to data contained in the tables for auditing purposes.

Getting ready

First, you must take the following decisions:

- ▸ Do you need to audit all changes or only some?
- ▸ What information about the changes do you need to collect? Only the fact that the data has changed?
- ▸ When recording the new value of a field or tuple, do you also need to record the old value?
- ▸ Is it enough to record what user did the change, or do you also need to record the IP address and other connection information?
- ▸ How secure (tamper-proof) must the auditing information be? For example, does it need to be kept separately, away from the database being audited?

Based on answers to these questions, you can select the right auditing method from the methods we present next.

How to do it...

Here, we'll describe several auditing techniques.

Collecting data changes from the server log

The following is the easiest way to do auditing, and requires the least amount of setup:

1. Set `log_statement` to `mod` or `all` in the server log.

2. Collect all `INSERT`, `UPDATE`, `DELETE`, and `TRUNCATE` commands from the log.

Alternatively, you can do one of the following: just set up a way to store the logs on the database server, copy them to another host, or collect them with a version of syslog that allows you to collect logs on a designated logging server from the start.

Collecting changes using triggers

Collecting changes using triggers requires more work, but it also allows much more flexibility:

1. Write a trigger function to collect new (and if needed, old) values from tuples, and save them to auditing table (s).

2. Add suitable triggers to those tables for which changes need to be tracked. The query sample is as follows (modified from the *A PL/pgSQL Trigger Procedure for Auditing* example in the PostgreSQL manual):

```
CREATE TABLE emp (
     empname            text NOT NULL,
     salary             integer
);
CREATE TABLE emp_audit(
     operation          text       NOT NULL,
     stamp              timestamp NOT NULL,
     userid             text       NOT NULL,
     empname            text       NOT NULL,
     salary integer
);
CREATE OR REPLACE FUNCTION process_emp_audit() RETURNS TRIGGER AS
$emp_audit$
     BEGIN
          IF (TG_OP = 'DELETE') THEN
               INSERT INTO emp_audit SELECT 'DEL', now(), user,
                  OLD.*;
          ELSIF (TG_OP = 'UPDATE') THEN
          -- save old and new values
```

```
                    INSERT INTO emp_audit SELECT 'OLD', now(), user,
                        OLD.*;
                    INSERT INTO emp_audit SELECT 'NEW', now(), user,
                        NEW.*;
                ELSIF (TG_OP = 'INSERT') THEN
                    INSERT INTO emp_audit SELECT 'INS', now(), user,
                        NEW.*;
                ELSEIF (TG_OP = 'TRUNCATE') THEN
                    INSERT INTO emp_audit SELECT 'TRUNCATE', now(),
                        user, '-', -1;
                END IF;
                RETURN NULL; -- result is ignored because this is an
                    AFTER trigger
            END;
    $emp_audit$ LANGUAGE plpgsql;
    CREATE TRIGGER emp_audit
    AFTER INSERT OR UPDATE OR DELETE ON emp
        FOR EACH ROW EXECUTE PROCEDURE process_emp_audit();
    CREATE TRIGGER emp_audit_truncate
    AFTER TRUNCATE ON emp
        FOR EACH STATEMENT EXECUTE PROCEDURE process_emp_audit();
```

Using a single audit trigger to collect changes from multiple tables

If you are using PostgreSQL version 9.1 or later, then you can use a new universal audit trigger; it logs both old and new values of rows in any table, serialized as JSON data type values. The latest version of the trigger and its documentation are available at https://github.com/2ndQuadrant/audit-trigger.

For earlier PostgreSQL versions, similar "one trigger functions for all tables" logging can be arranged using the hstore data type:

1. First, we must ensure that the hstore contrib module is installed; refer to the *Adding an external module to PostgreSQL* recipe from *Chapter 3, Configuration*.

2. Now we must create the tables for the data:
   ```
   CREATE TABLE people (id serial primary key
   , name text
   , age int);
   CREATE TABLE hats (id serial primary key
   ```

```
, owner int references people
, name text
, colour text);
```

3. Then, we create the table where the changes will be logged:

```
CREATE TABLE audit_log(
    ts timestamp,
    tablename text,
    op text,
    oldrow hstore,
    newrow hstore
);
```

4. Next, we create the trigger function that saves the changes:

```
CREATE OR REPLACE FUNCTION log_hstore() RETURNS TRIGGER AS $$
BEGIN

    INSERT INTO audit_log
    VALUES ( clock_timestamp(),
             TG_OP,
             TG_TABLE_SCHEMA || '.' || TG_TABLE_NAME,
             (CASE WHEN TG_OP IN ('UPDATE','DELETE')
              THEN hstore(OLD) END),
             (CASE WHEN TG_OP IN ('INSERT','UPDATE')
              THEN hstore(NEW) END)
           );
    RETURN NULL;
END;
$$ LANGUAGE plpgsql;
```

5. Then, we create triggers that fire this function:

```
CREATE TRIGGER audit_trigger
   AFTER INSERT OR UPDATE OR DELETE ON hats
   FOR EACH ROW EXECUTE PROCEDURE  log_hstore() ;
CREATE TRIGGER audit_trigger
   AFTER INSERT OR UPDATE OR DELETE ON people
   FOR EACH ROW EXECUTE PROCEDURE  log_hstore() ;
```

6. Finally, here are a few lines of SQL to test the logging functionality:

```
chap6=# insert into people (name, age) values('Mary',16),
('Jason',19) returning id, name;
 id | name
----+-------
  1 | Mary
  2 | Jason
(2 rows)


chap6=# INSERT INTO hats (owner, name, colour) VALUES(2,
'lacrosse','red') RETURNING *;
 id | owner |   name   | colour
----+-------+----------+--------
  1 |     2 | lacrosse | red
(1 row)


INSERT 0 1
chap6=# UPDATE hats SET owner = 1 WHERE id = 1;
UPDATE 1
```

7. Now, if you select the lines from the `audit_log` table, you will see the timestamps, operations, and new and old values for both the `people` and `hats` tables in the order in which they were done:

```
chap6=# select * from audit_log order by ts;
-[ RECORD 1 ]-----------------------------------------------
ts        | 2014-08-21 12:53:18.669467
tablename | INSERT
op        | public.people
oldrow    |
newrow    | "id"=>"1", "name"=>"Mary", "age"=>"16"}
… 4 rows removed here for brevity
-[ RECORD 6 ]-----------------------------------------------
ts        | 2014-08-21 12:56:49.776095
tablename | UPDATE
op        | public.hats
```

```
oldrow      | {"id"=>"1", "owner"=>"2", "name"=>"lacrosse",
"colour"=>"red"}
newrow      | {"id"=>"1", "owner"=>"1", "name"=>"lacrosse",
"colour"=>"red"}
```

 It is also possible to make this kind of universal trigger simply by converting the NEW and OLD values to text, but either this is complicated or the result is not very reader friendly.

Collecting changes using triggers and saving them in another database using dblink or plproxy

For security-critical systems, keeping the audit logs on the same machine as the rest of the data may not be enough. In that case, you may need to implement remote-change logging functionality. One way of doing this is by using PL/Proxy to send change logs to a remote database.

The following is a sample that shows how to log the preceding example to a remote database, named auditdb:

1. Create the emp_audit log table in the remote auditing database.

2. Create a function, log_emp_audit(), in the remote database, as follows:

```
CREATE FUNCTION log_emp_audit(
   operation text, userid text, empname text, salary integer
) RETURNS VOID AS
$$
INSERT INTO emp_audit VALUES($1, now(), $2, $3, $4)
$$ LANGUAGE SQL;
```

3. Create a proxy function for log_emp_audit() in the local audited database (you need to have the PL/Proxy language installed in the database for this):

```
CREATE OR REPLACE FUNCTION log_emp_audit(
   operation text, userid text, empname text, salary integer
) RETURNS VOID AS $$
  CONNECT 'dbname=auditdb';
$$ LANGUAGE plproxy;
```

4. Create trigger functions that use the proxy function to save the data in an external database:

```
CREATE OR REPLACE FUNCTION do_emp_audit() RETURNS TRIGGER AS
$$
    BEGIN
        IF (TG_OP = 'DELETE') THEN
            PERFORM log_emp_audit('DEL', user, OLD.empname,
                OLD.salary);
        ELSIF (TG_OP = 'UPDATE') THEN
            -- save old and new values
            PERFORM log_emp_audit('OLD', user, OLD.empname,
                OLD.salary);
            PERFORM log_emp_audit('NEW', user, NEW.empname,
                NEW.salary);
        ELSIF (TG_OP = 'INSERT') THEN
            PERFORM log_emp_audit('INS', user, NEW.empname,
                NEW.salary);
        END IF;
        RETURN NULL; -- result is ignored since this is an
            AFTER trigger
    END;
$$ LANGUAGE plpgsql;
```

5. Add the triggers to the emp table:

```
CREATE TRIGGER emp_remote_audit
AFTER INSERT OR UPDATE OR DELETE ON emp
    FOR EACH ROW EXECUTE PROCEDURE do_emp_audit();
```

Ensure that the audit database is secure. This includes verifying that the only thing the audit_logger user can do is call the log_emp_audit() function.

More information on PL/Proxy can be found at http://plproxy.projects.postgresql.org/doc/tutorial.html.

Always knowing which user is logged in

In the preceding recipes, we just logged the value of the `user` variable in the current PostgreSQL session to log the current user role.

This does not always mean that this particular user was the user that was actually authenticated at the start of session. For example, a superuser can execute the `SET ROLE TO …` command to set its current role to any other user or role in the system. As you might expect, non-superusers can assume only those roles that they own.

It is possible to differentiate between the logged-in role and the assumed role using the `current_user` and `session_user` session variables:

```
postgres=# select current_user, session_user;
 current_user | session_user
--------------+--------------
 postgres     | postgres
postgres=# set role to bob;
SET
postgres=> select current_user, session_user;
 current_user | session_user
--------------+--------------
 bob          | postgres
```

Sometimes, it is desirable to let each user log in with their own username and just assume the role needed on a case-by-case basis.

Getting ready

Prepare the required group roles for different tasks and access levels by granting the necessary privileges and options.

How to do it...

The steps are as follows:

1. Create user roles with no privileges and with the NOINHERIT option:

   ```
   postgres=# create user alice noinherit;
   CREATE ROLE
   postgres=# create user bob noinherit;
   CREATE ROLE
   ```

2. Then, create roles for each group of privileges that you need to assign:

   ```
   postgres=# create group sales;
   CREATE ROLE
   postgres=# create group superuser;
   CREATE ROLE
   postgres=# grant postgres to superuser;
   GRANT ROLE
   ```

3. Now, grant each user the roles it may need.

   ```
   postgres=# grant sales to alice;
   GRANT ROLE
   postgres=# grant superuser to alice;
   GRANT ROLE
   postgres=# grant sales to bob;
   GRANT ROLE
   ```

After you do this, the users alice and bob have no rights after login, but they can assume the sales role by executing SET ROLE TO sales;, and alice can additionally assume the superuser role.

How it works...

If a role or user is created with the NOINHERIT option, this user will not automatically get the rights that have been granted to the other roles that have been granted to itself. To claim these rights from a specific role, it has to set its role to one of those other roles.

In some sense, this works a bit like the su (set user) command in Unix and Linux systems. That is, you (may) have the right to become that user, but you do not automatically have the rights of the said user.

This setup can be used to get better audit information, as it lets you know who the actual user was. If you just allow each user to log in as the role needed for a task, there is no good way to know later which of the users was really logged in as `clerk1` when this $ 100000 transfer was made.

There's more...

The `SET ROLE` command works both ways; that is, you can both gain and lose privileges. A superuser can set its role to any user defined in the system. To get back to your original login role, just use `RESET ROLE`.

Not inheriting the user attributes

Not all rights come to users via `GRANT` commands. Some important rights are given via user attributes (`SUPERUSER`, `CREATEDB`, and `CREATEUSER`), and these are never inherited.

If your user has been granted a superuser role and you want to use the superuser powers of this granted role, you have to use `SET ROLE to mysuperuserrole;` before doing anything requiring the `superuser` attribute to be set.

In other words, the user **attributes** always behave as if the user had been a `NOINHERIT` user.

Integrating with LDAP

This recipe shows you how to set up your PostgreSQL system so that it uses the **Lightweight Directory Access Protocol** (**LDAP**) for authentication.

Getting ready

Ensure that the usernames in the database and your LDAP server match, as this method works for user authentication checks of users who are already defined in the database.

Unfortunately, as LDAP is used only to validate username/password pairs, this method cannot use the PostgreSQL **User Name Map** feature to allow a single LDAP user to connect as multiple database users.

How to do it...

In the PostgreSQL authentication file, `pg_hba.conf`, we define some address ranges to use LDAP as an authentication method, and we configure the LDAP server for this address range:

```
host    all         all         10.10.0.1/16            ldap \
ldapserver=ldap.our.net ldapprefix="cn=" ldapsuffix=",
    dc=our,dc=net"
```

How it works...

This setup makes the PostgreSQL server check passwords from the configured LDAP server.

User rights are not queried from the LDAP server, but have to be defined inside the database using the `ALTER USER`, `GRANT`, and `REVOKE` commands.

There's more...

We have shown how PostgreSQL can use an LDAP server for password authentication. It is also possible to use some more information from the LDAP server, as shown in the next two examples.

Setting up the client to use LDAP

If you are using the `pg_service.conf` file to define your database access parameters, you may define some of those to be queried from the LDAP server by including a line similar to the following in your `pg_service.conf` file:

```
ldap://ldap.mycompany.com/dc=mycompany,dc=com?uniqueMember?one?(cn=my
database)
```

Replacement for the User Name Map feature

Although we cannot use the User Name Map feature with LDAP, we can achieve a similar effect on the LDAP side. Use `ldapsearchattribute` and the **search+bind** mode to retrieve the PostgreSQL role name from the LDAP server.

See also

► For server setup, including the search+bind mode, visit `http://www.postgresql.org/docs/9.4/static/auth-methods.html#AUTH-LDAP`

► For client setup, visit `http://www.postgresql.org/docs/9.4/static/libpq-ldap.html`

Connecting using SSL

Here, we will demonstrate how to enable PostgreSQL to use SSL for protection of database connections by encrypting all of the data passed over that connection. Using SSL makes it much harder to sniff the database traffic, including usernames, passwords, and sensitive data that are passed between a client and the database by someone listening to a network somewhere between them. An alternative to using SSL is running the connection over a **Virtual Private Network** (**VPN**).

Using SSL makes the data transfer on the encrypted connection a little slower, so you may not want to use it if you are sure that your network is safe. The performance impact can be quite large if you are creating lots of short connections, as setting up an SSL connection is quite CPU-heavy. In this case, you may want to run a local connection pooling solution, such as PgBouncer, to which you connect without encryption, and make the SSL-protected connection using stunnel, as described in the PgBouncer FAQ at `http://pgbouncer.projects.postgresql.org/doc/faq.html`.

Getting ready

Get, or generate, an SSL server key and certificate pair for the server, and store these in the `data` directory of the current database instance as the `server.key` and `server.crt` files.

On some platforms, this is unnecessary; the key and certificate pair may be already generated by the packager. For example, on Ubuntu, PostgreSQL is set up to support SSL connections by default.

How to do it...

Set `ssl = on` in `postgresql.conf` and restart the database.

How it works...

If `ssl = on` is set, then PostgreSQL listens to both plain and SSL connections on the same port (`5432` by default), and determines the type of connection from the first byte of a new connection.

Then, it proceeds to set up an SSL connection if an incoming request asks for it.

There's more...

You can leave the choice of whether or not to use SSL to the client, or you can force SSL usage from the server's side.

To let the client choose, use a line of the following form in the `pg_hba.conf` file:

```
host database  user  IP-address  IP-mask  auth-method
```

If you want to allow only SSL clients, use the `hostssl` keyword instead of `host`.

The following fragment of `pg_hba.conf` enables both non-SSL and SSL connections from the `192.168.1.0/24` local subnet, but requires SSL from everybody accessing the database from other networks:

```
Host      all      all      192.168.1.0/24     md5
hostssl   all      all      0.0.0.0/0          md5
```

Getting the SSL key and certificate

For web servers, you must usually get your SSL certificate from a recognized **Certificate Authority** (**CA**), as most browsers complain if the certificate is not issued by a known CA. They warn the user of the most common security risks and require confirmation before connecting to a server with a certificate issued by an unknown CA.

For your database server, it is usually sufficient to generate the certificate yourself, using OpenSSL. The following commands generate a self-signed certificate for your server:

```
openssl genrsa 2048 > server.key

openssl req -new -x509 -key server.key -out server.crt
```

 Read more on X.509 keys and certificates in OpenSSL's *HOWTO's* pages at `http://www.openssl.org/docs/HOWTO/`.

Setting up a client to use SSL

The behavior of the client application regarding SSL is controlled by an environment variable, `PGSSLMODE`. This can have the following values, as defined in the official PostgreSQL documentation:

SSL mode	Eavesdropping protection	MITM protection	Statement
`disabled`	No	No	I don't care about security, and I don't want to pay the overhead of encryption.
`allow`	Maybe	No	I don't care about security, but I will pay the overhead of encryption if the server insists on it.
`prefer`	Maybe	No	I don't care about encryption, but I wish to pay the overhead of encryption if the server supports it.

SSL mode	Eavesdropping protection	MITM protection	Statement
require	Yes	No	I want my data to be encrypted, and I accept the overhead. I trust that the network will ensure that I always connect to the server I want.
verify-ca	Yes	Depends on the CA policy	I want my data encrypted, and I accept the overhead. I want to be sure that I connect to a server that I trust.
verify-full	Yes	Yes	I want my data encrypted, and I accept the overhead. I want to be sure that I connect to a server I trust, and that the server is the one I specify.

MITM in the preceding table means **Man-In-The-Middle** attack, that is, someone posing as your server—perhaps by manipulating DNS records or IP routing tables—but actually just observing and forwarding the traffic.

For this to be possible with an SSL connection, this "someone" needs to have obtained a certificate that your client considers valid.

Checking server authenticity

The last two SSL modes allow you to be reasonably sure that you are actually talking to your server, by checking the SSL certificate presented by the server.

In order to enable this useful security feature, the following files must be available on the client side. On Unix systems, they are located in the client home directory, in a subdirectory named ~/.postgresql; on Windows, they are in %APPDATA%\postgresql\.

File	Contents	Effect
root.crt	Certificates of one or more trusted CAs	PostgreSQL verifies that the server certificate is signed by a trusted CA
root.crl	Certificates revoked by CAs	The server certificate must not be on this list

Only the root.crt file is required for the client to authenticate the server certificate. It can contain multiple root certificates against which the server certificate is compared.

Using SSL certificates to authenticate the client

This recipe shows you how to set up your PostgreSQL system so that it *requires* clients to present a valid X.509 certificate before allowing them to connect.

This can be used as an additional security layer to use double authentication, where the client must both have a valid certificate to set up the SSL connection and also know the database user's password. It can also be used as the sole authentication method, where the PostgreSQL server will first verify the client connection using the certificate presented by the client, and then retrieve the username from the same certificate.

Getting ready

Get, or generate, a root certificate and a client certificate to be used by the connecting client.

How to do it...

For testing purposes, or for just setting up a single trusted user, you can use a self-signed certificate:

```
openssl genrsa 2048 > client.key
openssl req -new -x509 -key server.key -out client.crt
```

On the **server**, set up a line in pg_hba.conf with the hostssl method and the clientcert option set to 1:

```
    ...
    hostssl  all     all     0.0.0.0/0          md5  clientcert=1
```

Put the client root certificate in the root.crt file in the server data directory ($PGDATA/root.crt). This file may contain multiple trusted root certificates.

If you are using a central certificate authority, you probably also have a certificate revocation list, which should be put in a root.crl file and regularly updated.

On the **client**, put the client's private key and certificate in ~/.postgresql/postgresql.key and ~/.postgresql/postgresql.crt. Make sure that the private key file is not world readable or group readable by running the following command:

```
chmod 0600 ~/.postgresql/postgresql.key
```

On the Windows client, the corresponding files are `%APPDATA%\postgresql\postgresql.key` and `%APPDATA%\postgresql\postgresql.crt`. No permission check is done, as the location is considered secure.

If the client certificate is not signed by the root CA but by an intermediate CA, then all the intermediate CA certificates up to the root certificate must be placed in the `postgresql.crt` file as well.

How it works...

If the `clientcert=1` option is set for a `hostssl` row in `pg_hba.conf`, then PostgreSQL accepts only connection requests accompanied by a valid certificate.

The validity of the certificate is checked against certificates present in the `root.crt` file in the server data directory.

If there is a `root.crl` file, then the presented certificate is looked for in this file and, if found, is rejected.

After the client certificate is validated and the SSL connection is established, the server proceeds to validate the actual connecting user using whatever authentication method is specified in corresponding `hostssl` line.

In the following example, clients from a special address can connect as any user when using an SSL certificate, and they must specify an MD5 password for non-SSL connections. Clients from all the other addresses must present a certificate and use MD5 password authentication:

```
...
host      all    all    10.10.10.10/32    md5
hostssl   all    all    10.10.10.10/32    trust    clientcert=1
hostssl   all    all    all               md5      clientcert=1
```

There's more...

In this section, we provide some additional content, describing an important optimization for an SSL-only database server, plus two extensions of the basic SSL configuration.

Avoiding duplicate SSL connection attempts

In the *Setting up a client to use SSL* section of the previous recipe, *Connecting using SSL*, we saw how the client's SSL behavior is affected by environment variables. Depending on how the `SSLMODE` environment variable is set on the client (either via compile-time settings, the `PGSSLMODE` environment variable, or the `sslmode` connection parameter) the client may attempt to connect without SSL first, and then attempt an SSL connection only after the server rejects the non-SSL connection.

This duplicates connection attempts every time a client accesses an SSL-only server.

To make sure that the client tries to establish an SSL connection on the first attempt, `SSLMODE` must to be set to `prefer` or higher.

Using multiple client certificates

You may sometimes need different certificates to connect to different PostgreSQL servers.

The location of the certificate and key files in `postgresql.crt` and `postgresql.key` in the table from the *Checking server authenticity* section is just the default, and can be overridden by specifying alternative file paths using the `sslcert` and `sslkey` connection parameters or the `PGSSLCERT` and `PGSSLKEY` environment variables.

Using the client certificate to select the database user

It is possible to use the client certificate for two purposes at once: proving that the connecting client is a valid one, and selecting the database user to be used for the connection.

For this, you set the authentication method to `cert` in the `hostssl` line:

```
...
hostssl    all    all    0.0.0.0/0          cert
```

As you can see, the `clientcert=1` option used with `hostssl` to require client certificates is no longer required, being implied by the `cert` method itself.

When using the `cert` authentication method, a valid client certificate is required, and the `cn` (common name) attribute of the certificate will be compared to the requested database user name. The login will be allowed only if they match.

It is possible to use a User Name Map to map the common names in the certificates to database usernames by specifying the `map` option:

```
...
hostssl    all    all    0.0.0.0/0          cert    map=x509cnmap
```

Here, `x509cnmap` is the name that we have arbitrarily chosen for our mapping; more details on User Name Maps are provided in the next recipe, *Mapping external usernames to database roles*.

See also

► To understand more about SSL in general, and the OpenSSL library used by PostgreSQL in particular, visit `http://www.openssl.org`, or get a good book about SSL.

► To get started with the generation of simple SSL keys and certificates, see `http://www.openssl.org/docs/HOWTO/certificates.txt`.

► There is also a nice presentation named *Encrypted PostgreSQL* explaining these issues at PGCon 2009. The slides are available at `http://www.pgcon.org/2009/schedule/events/120.en.html`.

Mapping external usernames to database roles

When using certificate authentication, as described in the previous recipe, or any other external or single sign-on system authentication method from `http://www.postgresql.org/docs/9.4/static/auth-methods.html` (GSSAPI, SSPI, Kerberos, Radius, or PAM), you often have different usernames in the external system and your database. Or, you may just need to enable some externally authenticated user to connect as multiple database users.

Getting ready

Prepare a list of usernames from the external authentication system and decide which database users they are allowed to connect as—that is, which external users map to which database users.

How to do it...

Create a `pg_ident.conf` file in the usual place (`PGDATA`), with lines in the following format:

```
map-name system-username database-username
```

Here, `map-name` is the value of the `map` option from the corresponding line in `pg_hba.conf`, `system-username` is the username that the external system authenticated the connection as, and `database-username` is the database user this system user is allowed to connect as. The same system user may be allowed to connect as multiple database users, so this is not a 1:1 mapping, but rather a list of allowed database users for each system user.

If `system-username` starts with a slash (/), then the rest of it is treated as a regular expression, rather than a directly matching string, and it is possible to use the `\1` string in `database-username` to refer to the part "captured" by the parentheses in the regular expression. For example, consider the following lines:

```
salesmap    /^(.*)@sales\.comp\.com$        \1
salesmap    /^(.*)@sales\.comp\.com$     sales
salesmap    manager@sales.comp.com      auditor
```

These will allow any user authenticated with a `@sales.comp.com` e-mail address to connect both as a database user equal to the name before the `@` sign in their e-mail address, and as the `sales` user. They will additionally allow `manager@sales.comp.com` to connect as the `auditor` user if the corresponding `pg_hba.conf` line specifies the `map=salesmap` option.

How it works...

After authenticating the connection using an external authentication system, PostgreSQL will usually proceed to check that the externally authenticated username matches the database username that the user wishes to connect as, and rejects the connection if these two do not match.

If there is a `map=` parameter specified for the current line in `pg_hba.conf`, then the system will scan the map line by line, and will let the client proceed to connect if a match is found.

There's more...

By default, the map file is called `pg_ident.conf` (because it was first used for the `ident` authentication method).

Nowadays, it is possible to change the name of this file via the `ident_file` configuration parameter in `postgresql.conf`. It can be also be located outside the `PGDATA` directory, by setting `ident_file` to a full path.

A relative path can also be used, but since it is relative to where the `postgres` process is started, this is usually not a good idea.

Encrypting sensitive data

This recipe shows you how to encrypt data using the `pgcrypto` contrib package.

Getting ready

Make sure you (and/or your database server) are in a country where encryption is not illegal—it still is in some countries.

In order to create and manage PGP keys, you also need the well-known **GnuPG** command-line utility, which is available on practically all distributions.

Make sure that `pgcrypto` is installed on your database host. On Debian and Ubuntu, it comes with the `postgresql-contrib-9.4` package (change `9.4` for other PostgreSQL versions).

Install it on the database in which you want to use it, following the *Adding an external module to PostgreSQL* recipe from *Chapter 3, Configuration*.

You also need to have PGP keys set up:

pguser@laptop:~$ gpg --gen-key

Answer some questions here (defaults are OK unless you are an expert), select the key type as `DSA and Elgamal`, and enter an empty password.

Now, export the keys:

pguser@laptop:~$ gpg -a --export "PostgreSQL User (test key for PG Cookbook) <pguser@somewhere.net>" > public.key

pguser@laptop:~$ gpg -a --export-secret-keys "PostgreSQL User (test key for PG Cookbook) <pguser@somewhere.net>" > secret.key

Make sure only you and the `postgres` database user have access to the secret key:

pguser@laptop:~$ sudo chgrp postgres secret.key

pguser@laptop:~$ chmod 440 secret.key

pguser@laptop:~$ ls -l *.key

-rw-r--r-- 1 pguser pguser   1718 2010-03-26 13:53 public.key

-r--r----- 1 pguser postgres 1818 2010-03-26 13:54 secret.key

Last, but not least, make a copy of the public and the secret key; if you lose them, you'll lose the ability to encrypt/decrypt.

How to do it...

To ensure that the secret keys are never visible in database logs, write a wrapper function to get the keys from the file. You need to do it in an untrusted embedded language, such as PL/PythonU, as only untrusted languages can access the filesystem. You need to be a PostgreSQL superuser in order to create functions in untrusted languages.

It's not difficult to write a PostgreSQL function that reads a text file. For convenience, we provide an example that requires PL/PythonU:

```
create or replace function get_my_public_key() returns text as $$
return open('/home/pguser/public.key').read()
$$
language plpythonu;
revoke all on function get_my_public_key() from public;
create or replace function get_my_secret_key() returns text as $$
return open('/home/pguser/secret.key').read()
$$
language plpythonu;
revoke all on function get_my_secret_key() from public;
```

Starting with version 9.1 of PostgreSQL it is also easy to do this fully in PL/pgSQL using the built-in PostgreSQL system function, `pg_read_file` (filename), and you don't have to bother with PL/PythonU at all. However, you must place the files in the `data` directory as required by that function for additional security. Before 9.1, this function needed extra arguments for offset and length, which made its use slightly more cumbersome for reading a full file (you must explicitly specify an offset of zero and a length sufficiently large for the entire file, for example, 100000).

If you don't want other database users to be able to see the keys, you also need to write wrapper functions for encryption and decryption, and then give access to these wrapper functions to end users.

The encryption function can be like this:

```
create or replace function encrypt_using_my_public_key(
    cleartext text,
    ciphertext out bytea
)
AS $$
```

```
DECLARE
    pubkey_bin bytea;
BEGIN
    -- text version of public key needs to be passed through function
dearmor() to get to raw key
    pubkey_bin := dearmor(get_my_public_key());
    -- on  pg9.1 dearmor(pg_read_file('public.key'));
    ciphertext := pgp_pub_encrypt(cleartext, pubkey_bin);
END;
$$ language plpgsql security definer;
revoke all on function encrypt_using_my_public_key(text) from public;
grant execute on function encrypt_using_my_public_key(text) to bob;
```

The decryption function can be as follows:

```
create or replace function decrypt_using_my_secret_key(
    ciphertext bytea,
    cleartext out text
)
AS $$
DECLARE
    secret_key_bin bytea;
BEGIN
    -- text version of secret key needs to be passed through function
dearmor() to get to raw binary key
    secret_key_bin := dearmor(get_my_secret_key());
    -- on  pg9.1 dearmor(pg_read_file('secret.key'));
    cleartext := pgp_pub_decrypt(ciphertext, secret_key_bin);
END;
$$ language plpgsql security definer;
revoke all on function decrypt_using_my_secret_key(bytea) from public;
grant execute on function decrypt_using_my_secret_key(bytea) to bob;
```

Finally, we test the encryption:

```
test2=# select encrypt_using_my_public_key('X marks the spot!');
```

This function returns a bytea (that is binary) result that looks something like the following:

```
encrypt_using_my_public_key | \301\301N\003\22
3o\215\2125\203\252;\020\007\376-z\233\211H...
```

To see that it actually works, you must go both ways:

```
test2=# select decrypt_using_my_secret_key(encrypt_using_my_public_key('X
marks the spot!'));
 decrypt_using_my_secret_key
-----------------------------
 X marks the spot!
(1 row)
```

Yes, we got back our initial string!

How it works...

What we have done here is the following:

- Hidden the keys from non-superuser database users
- Provided wrappers for authorized users to use encryption and decryption functionalities

To ensure that your sensitive data is not stolen while in transit between the client and database server, make sure you connect to PostgreSQL either using an SSL-encrypted connection or from localhost.

You also have to trust your server administrators and all the other users with superuser privileges to be sure that your encrypted data is safe. And, of course, you must trust the safety of the entire environment; PostgreSQL can decrypt the data, so any other user or software that has access to the same files can do the same.

There's more...

A higher level of security is possible with more complex procedures and architecture, as shown in the next sections. We also mention a limited pgcrypto version that does not use OpenSSL.

For really sensitive data

For some data, you wouldn't want to risk keeping the decryption password on the same machine as the encrypted data.

In those cases, you can use **public-key cryptography**, also known as **asymmetric cryptography**, and carry out only the encryption part on the database server. This also means that you only have the encryption key on the database host, and not the key needed for decryption. Alternatively, you can deploy a separate, extra secure encryption server in your server infrastructure that provides just the encrypting and decrypting functionality as a remote call.

> This solution is secure because in asymmetric cryptography, the private (that is, decryption) key cannot be derived from the corresponding public (that is, encryption) key, hence the names "public" and "private", which denote the appropriate dissemination policies.
>
> If you wish to prove the identity of the author of a file, the correct method is to use a digital signature, which is an entirely different application of cryptography. Note that this is not currently supported by pgcrypto, so you must implement your own methods as C functions or in a procedural language capable of using cryptographic libraries.

For really, really, really sensitive data!

For even more sensitive data, you may never want the data to leave the client computer unencrypted. Hence, you need to encrypt the data before sending it to the database. In that case, PostgreSQL receives already encrypted data, and never sees the unencrypted version. This also means that the only useful indexes you can have are for use in WHERE encrypted_ column = encrypted_data and for ensuring uniqueness. Even these forms can be used only if the encryption algorithm always produces the same ciphertext (output) for the same plaintext (input), which is true only for weaker encryption algorithms. For example, it would be easy to determine the age or sex of a person if the same value is always encrypted into the same ciphertext. To avoid this vulnerability, strong encryption algorithms are able to produce a different ciphertext for the same value.

Two versions of pgcrypto are usually compiled to use the OpenSSL library (http://www.openssl.org). If, for some reason, you don't have OpenSSL or just don't want to use it, it is possible to compile pgcrypto without it, with a smaller number of supported encryption algorithms, and a slightly reduced performance.

See also

- The page on `pgcrypto` in the PostgreSQL online documentation is available at `http://www.postgresql.org/docs/9.4/static/pgcrypto.html`

- The OpenSSL web page can be accessed at `http://www.openssl.org/`

- *GNU Privacy Handbook* can be read at `http://www.gnupg.org/gph/en/manual.html`

7
Database Administration

In this chapter, we will cover the following recipes:

- Writing a script that either succeeds entirely or fails entirely
- Writing a psql script that exits on the first error
- Performing actions on many tables
- Adding/removing columns on a table
- Changing the data type of a column
- Changing the definition of a data type
- Adding/removing schemas
- Moving objects between schemas
- Adding/removing tablespaces
- Moving objects between tablespaces
- Accessing objects in other PostgreSQL databases
- Accessing objects in other foreign databases
- Updatable views
- Using materialized views

Introduction

In *Chapter 5, Tables and Data*, we looked at the contents of tables and various complexities. Now, we'll turn our attention to larger administration tasks that we need to perform from time to time, such as creating things, moving things around, storing things neatly, and removing them when they're no longer required.

The most sensible way to perform major administrative tasks is to write a script to do what you think is required. If you're unsure, you can always run the script on a system test server, and then run it again on the production server once you're happy. Manically typing commands against production database servers isn't wise. Worse, using an admin tool can lead to serious issues if that tool doesn't show you the SQL you're about to execute. If you haven't dropped your first live table yet, don't worry; you will. Perhaps, you might want to read *Chapter 11, Backup and Recovery*, first, eh? Back it up using scripts.

Scripts are great because you can automate common tasks, and there's no need to sit there with a mouse, working your way through a hundred changes.

If you're drawn to the discussion about the Command line versus GUI, then my thoughts and reasons are completely orthogonal to that. I want to encourage you to avoid errors and save time by repetitive and automatic execution of small administration programs or scripts. If it were safe or easy to do the equivalent of mouse movements in a script, then that would be an option; but it's definitely not. The only viable way to write a repeatable script is by writing text SQL commands.

Which scripting tool to use is a more interesting debate. We consider psql here because if you've got PostgreSQL, then you've certainly got psql, without needing to install additional software. So, we're on solid ground to provide examples that way.

On to the recipes! First, we'll start by looking at some scripting techniques that are valuable in PostgreSQL. This will make you more accurate and repeatable and free up time for other cool things.

Writing a script that either succeeds entirely or fails entirely

Database administration often involves applying a coordinated set of changes to the database. One of PostgreSQL's great strengths is the transaction system, wherein almost all actions can be executed inside a transaction. This allows us to build a script with many actions that will either all succeed or all fail. This means that if any of these actions fail, then all the other actions in the script are rolled back and never become visible to any other user, which can be critically important on a production system. This property is referred to as "atomicity" in the sense that the script is intended as a single unit that cannot be split, and this is the meaning of the "A" in the "ACID" properties of database transactions.

Transactions definitely apply to **Data Definition Language** (**DDL**), which refers to the set of SQL commands used to define, modify, and delete database objects. The term "DDL" goes back many years, but it persists because that subset is a useful short name for the commands that most administrators need to execute: CREATE, ALTER, DROP, and so on.

Although most commands in PostgreSQL are transactional, there are a few that cannot be. The most common example is of commands that use sequences. They cannot be transactional because when a new sequence number is allocated, the effect of having "consumed" that number must become visible immediately, without waiting for that transaction to be committed. Otherwise, the same number will be given to another transaction, which is contrary to what sequences are supposed to do.

How to do it...

The basic way to ensure that we get all commands successful or none at all is to literally wrap our script into a transaction, like the following:

```
BEGIN;
command 1;
command 2;
command 3;
COMMIT;
```

Writing a transaction control command involves editing the script, which you may not want to do or even have access to do. There are, however, other ways as well.

From psql, you can do this simply using the -1 or --single-transaction command-line options, as follows:

```
bash $ psql -1 -f myscript.sql
bash $ psql --single-transaction -f myscript.sql
```

The -1 option is short, but I recommend using --single-transaction, as it's much clearer which option is being selected.

How it works...

The entire script will fail if, at any point, one of the commands gives an error (or higher) message. Almost all of the SQL used to define objects (DDL) allows a way to avoid throwing errors. More precisely, commands that begin with the DROP keyword have an IF EXISTS option. This allows you to execute the DROP keyword, whether or not the object already exists.

Thus, by the end of the command, that object will not exist:

```
DROP VIEW IF EXISTS cust_view;
```

Similarly, most commands that begin with the CREATE keyword have the optional OR REPLACE suffix. This allows the CREATE statement to overwrite the definition if one already exists, or add the new object if it didn't exist yet, like this:

```
CREATE OR REPLACE VIEW cust_view AS
SELECT * FROM cust;
```

In the cases where both the DROP IF EXISTS and CREATE OR REPLACE options exist, you might think that CREATE OR REPLACE is usually sufficient. However, if you change the output definition of a function or a view, then using OR REPLACE is not sufficient. In that case, you must use DROP and recreate, as shown in the following example:

```
postgres=# CREATE OR REPLACE VIEW cust_view AS
SELECT col as title1 FROM cust;
CREATE VIEW
postgres=# CREATE OR REPLACE VIEW cust_view
AS SELECT col as title2 FROM cust;
ERROR:  cannot change name of view column "title1" to "title2"
```

Note also that CREATE INDEX does not have an OR REPLACE option. If you run it twice, you'll get two indexes on your table, unless you specifically name the index. There is a DROP INDEX IF EXISTS option, but it may take a long time to drop and recreate an index. An index exists just for the purpose of optimization, and does not change the actual result of any query, so this different behavior is actually very convenient. This is also reflected in the fact that the SQL standard doesn't mention indexes at all, even though they exist in practically all database systems.

PostgreSQL does not support nested transaction control commands, which can lead to unexpected behavior. For instance, consider the following code, written in a "nested transaction" style:

```
postgres=# BEGIN;
BEGIN
postgres=# CREATE TABLE a(x int);
CREATE TABLE
postgres=# BEGIN;
WARNING:  there is already a transaction in progress
BEGIN
```

```
postgres=# CREATE TABLE b(x int);
CREATE TABLE
postgres=# COMMIT;
COMMIT
postgres=# ROLLBACK;
NOTICE:  there is no transaction in progress
ROLLBACK
```

A hypothetical author of such code probably meant to create table a first, and then create table b. Then, he changed his mind and rolled back both the "inner" transaction and the "outer" transaction. However, what PostgreSQL does is discard the second BEGIN statement so that the COMMIT statement is matched with the first BEGIN statement and the "inner" transaction becomes a top-level transaction. Hence, right after the COMMIT statement, we are outside a transaction block, so the next statement is assigned its own transaction. When ROLLBACK is issued as the next statement, PostgreSQL notices that the transaction is actually empty.

The danger in this particular example is that the user inadvertently committed a transaction, thus waiving the right to roll it back, although we should say that a careful user would have noticed the warning and paused for a thought before going ahead.

From this example, you learn a valuable lesson: if you have used transaction control commands in your script, then wrapping them again in a higher-level script or command can cause problems of the worst kind, such as committing stuff that you wanted to roll back. This is important enough to deserve a boxed warning.

 PostgreSQL accepts nested transactional control commands but does not act on them. After the first commit, the commands will be assumed to be transactions in their own right and will persist should the script fail. Be careful!

There's more...

The following commands cannot be included in a script that uses transactions in the way we just described:

- CREATE DATABASE / DROP DATABASE
- CREATE TABLESPACE / DROP TABLESPACE
- CREATE INDEX CONCURRENTLY
- VACUUM
- REINDEX DATABASE / REINDEX SYSTEM
- CLUSTER

None of these actions need to be run manually on a regular basis within complex programs, so this shouldn't be a problem for you.

Note also that these commands do not substantially alter the "logical" content of a database; that is, they don't create new user tables or alter any rows, so there's less need to use them inside complex transactions.

Writing a psql script that exits on the first error

The default mode for the psql script tool is to continue processing when it finds an error. This sounds dumb, but it exists for historical compatibility only. There are some easy—and mostly permanent—ways to avoid this, so let's look at them.

Getting ready

Let's start with a simple script, with a command we know will fail:

```
$ $EDITOR test.sql
mistake1;
mistake2;
mistake3;
```

Execute the following script using psql to see what the results look like:

```
$ psql -f test.sql
psql:test.sql:1: ERROR:  syntax error at or near "mistake1"
LINE 1: mistake1;
        ^

psql:test.sql:2: ERROR:  syntax error at or near "mistake2"
LINE 1: mistake2;
        ^

psql:test.sql:3: ERROR:  syntax error at or near "mistake3"
LINE 1: mistake3;
        ^
```

How to do it...

To exit the script on the first error, we can write the following command:

```
$ psql -f test.sql -v ON_ERROR_STOP=on
psql:test.sql:1: ERROR:  syntax error at or near "mistake1"

LINE 1: mistake1;
                ^
```

Alternatively, we can edit the `test.sql` file with the initial line shown here:

```
$ $EDITOR test.sql
\set ON_ERROR_STOP
mistake1;
mistake2;
mistake3;
```

Note that the following command will *not* work because we have missed the crucial on value:

```
$ psql -f test.sql -v ON_ERROR_STOP
```

How it works...

The `ON_ERROR_STOP` variable is a psql special variable that controls the behavior of psql as it executes in script mode. When this variable is set, a SQL error will generate an OS return code 3, whereas other OS-related errors will return code 1.

There's more...

You can place some psql commands in a profile that will get executed when you run psql. Adding `ON_ERROR_STOP` to your profile will ensure that this setting is applied to all psql sessions:

```
$ $EDITOR ~/.psqlrc
\set ON_ERROR_STOP
```

You can forcibly override this, and request psql to execute without a profile using `-X`. This is probably the safest thing to do for batch execution of scripts, so they always work in the same way, irrespective of the local settings.

Performing actions on many tables

As a database administrator, you will often need to apply multiple commands as part of the same overall task. That task could be one of the following:

- ▸ Many different actions on multiple tables
- ▸ The same action on multiple tables
- ▸ The same action on multiple tables in parallel
- ▸ Different actions—one on each table—in parallel

The first is a general case where you need to make a set of coordinated changes. The solution is "write a script", as we've already discussed. We can also call this static scripting because you write the script manually and then execute it.

The second type of task can be achieved very simply with dynamic scripts, where we write a script that writes another script. This technique is the main topic of this recipe.

Performing actions in parallel sounds really cool, and it would be useful if it was easy. In some ways it is, but trying to run multiple tasks concurrently and trap and understand all the errors is much harder. And if you're thinking it won't matter if you don't check for errors, think again. If you run tasks in parallel, then you cannot run them inside the same transaction; so you definitely need error checking.

Don't worry! Running in parallel is usually much easier than that, and we'll explain it after a few basics.

Getting ready

Let's just create a basic schema to run some examples:

```
postgres=# create schema test;
CREATE SCHEMA
postgres=# create table test.a (col1 INTEGER);
CREATE TABLE
postgres=# create table test.b (col1 INTEGER);
CREATE TABLE
postgres=# create table test.c (col1 INTEGER);
CREATE TABLE
```

How to do it...

Our task is to run a SQL statement using this form, with X as the table name, against each of our three test tables:

```
ALTER TABLE X
ADD COLUMN last_update_timestamp TIMESTAMP WITH TIME ZONE;
```

The steps are as follows:

1. Our starting point is a script that lists the tables we want to perform tasks against—something like the following:

```
postgres=# SELECT relname
        FROM pg_class c
        JOIN pg_namespace n
        ON c.relnamespace = n.oid
        WHERE n.nspname = 'test';
```

This displays the list of tables that we will act upon (so that you can check it):

```
 relname
---------
 a
 b
 c
(3 rows)
```

2. We then use the preceding SQL to generate the text for a SQL script, substituting the schema name and table name in the SQL text. We then output to a script file named `multi.sql`, as follows:

```
postgres=# \t on
postgres=# \o multi.sql
postgres=# SELECT 'ALTER TABLE '|| n.nspname
        || '.' || c.relname ||
' ADD COLUMN last_update_timestamp TIMESTAMP WITH TIME ZONE;'
FROM pg_class c
JOIN pg_namespace n
ON c.relnamespace = n.oid
WHERE n.nspname = 'test';
\o
```

3. Once we've generated the script, we can check whether all of it looks correct:

```
postgres=# \! cat multi.sql

 ALTER TABLE test.a ADD COLUMN last_update_timestamp TIMESTAMP
WITH TIME ZONE;

 ALTER TABLE test.b ADD COLUMN last_update_timestamp TIMESTAMP
WITH TIME ZONE;

 ALTER TABLE test.c ADD COLUMN last_update_timestamp TIMESTAMP
WITH TIME ZONE;
```

4. Finally, we run the script and watch the results (success!):

```
postgres=# \i multi.sql
ALTER TABLE
ALTER TABLE
ALTER TABLE
```

How it works...

Overall, this is just an example of dynamic scripting, and it has been used by DBAs for many decades, even before PostgreSQL was born.

This method can go wrong in various ways, especially if you generate SQL text with syntax errors. Just fix that and carry on.

The \t command means "tuples only", so keeping \t to on will ensure there are no headers, command tags, or row counts following the results.

The \o FILENAME command redirects the output to a file until the subsequent \o command reverts to no redirection.

The \! command runs operating system commands, so \! cat will show the file contents on *nix systems.

The \i command redirects the input from a file, or in simpler terms, executes the named file. Running the script in this way may ignore earlier recipes, so I still recommend following those earlier guidelines.

Dynamic scripting can also be called a "quick and dirty" approach. The previous scripts didn't filter out views and other objects in the test schema, so you'll need to add that yourself, or not, as required.

There is another way of doing this as well:

```
DO $$
DECLARE t record;
BEGIN
    FOR t IN SELECT c.*, n.nspname
            FROM pg_class c JOIN pg_namespace n
            ON c.relnamespace = n.oid
            WHERE n.nspname = 'test' /* ; not needed */
    LOOP
            EXECUTE 'ALTER TABLE '|| quote_ident(t.nspname) ||
              '.' || quote_ident(t.relname) ||
              ' ADD COLUMN last_update_timestamp ' ||
              'TIMESTAMP WITH TIME ZONE';
    END LOOP;
END $$;
```

I don't prefer using this method because it executes the SQL directly and doesn't allow you to keep the script afterwards.

The preceding syntax with DO is called "anonymous code block" because it's like a function without a name. It was introduced in version 9.0. If you are running an earlier release, you'll get an error message.

There's more...

Earlier, I said I'll explain how to run multiple tasks in parallel. Some practical approaches to this are possible, with a bit of discussion.

Making tasks run in parallel can be thought of as subdividing the main task so that we run x2, x4, x8, and other subscripts, rather than one large script.

First, you should note that error checking gets worse when you spawn more parallel tasks, whereas performance improves most for the first few subdivisions. Also, we're often constrained by CPU, RAM, or I/O resources for intensive tasks. This means that splitting a main task into two to four parallel subtasks isn't practical without some kind of tool to help us manage them.

There are two approaches here, depending on the two types of the tasks:

- ▶ A task consists of many smaller tasks, all roughly of the same size
- ▶ A task consists of many smaller tasks, and the execution times vary according to the size and complexity of the database object

If we have lots of smaller tasks, then we can simply run our scripts multiple times using a simple round-robin split of tasks so that each subscript runs a part of all subtasks. Here is how to do it: each row in `pg_class` has a hidden column called `oid`, whose value is a 32-bit number allocated from an internal counter on table creation. Therefore, about half of the tables will have even values of `oid`, and we can achieve an even split by adding the following clauses:

- ▶ **Script 1**: Add WHERE `c.oid % 2 = 0`
- ▶ **Script 2**: Add WHERE `c.oid % 2 = 1`

The task we were performing as an example was to add a column to many tables. In the previous example, we were adding the column with no specified default; so the new column will have a NULL value, and as a result, it will run very quickly with ALTER TABLE, even on large tables. If we change the ALTER TABLE statement so as to specify a default, then PostgreSQL will need to rewrite the entire table. So, the runtime will vary according to the table size (approximately, and also according to the number and type of indexes).

Now that our subtasks vary in runtime according to size, we need to be more careful when splitting the subtasks so that we can end up with multiple scripts that will run for about the same time.

If we already know that we have just a few big tables, it's easy to split those manually into their own scripts.

If the database has many large tables, then we can sort SQL statements by table size and then distribute them using round-robin distribution into multiple subscripts that will have approximately the same runtime. The following SQL script, which should be saved in a `make-script.sql` file, is an example of this technique:

```
\t on
\o script-:i.sql
SELECT sql FROM (
SELECT 'ALTER TABLE '|| n.nspname || '.' || c.relname ||
' ADD COLUMN last_update_timestamp TIMESTAMP WITH TIME ZONE  DEFAULT
now();' as sql
,row_number() OVER (ORDER BY pg_relation_size(c.oid))
FROM pg_class c
 JOIN pg_namespace n
 ON c.relnamespace = n.oid
WHERE n.nspname = 'test'
```

```
ORDER BY 2 DESC) as s
WHERE row_number % 2 = :i;
\o
```

Then, we generate the two scripts, as follows:

```
$ psql -v i=0 -f make-script.sql
$ psql -v i=1 -f make-script.sql
```

Finally, we execute the two jobs in parallel, like this:

```
$ psql -f script-0.sql &
$ psql -f script-1.sql &
```

Note how we used psql parameters—via the -v command-line option—to select different rows using the same script.

Also note how we used the `row_number()` window function to sort the data by size. Then, we split the data into pieces using the following line:

```
WHERE row_number % N = i;
```

Here, N is the total number of scripts we're producing, and i ranges between 0 and N minus 1 (we are using modular arithmetic to distribute the subtasks).

Using pg_batch to run tasks in parallel

There is a tool for running tasks in parallel, available at `http://reorg.projects.postgresql.org/pg_batch.html`.

The `pg_batch` tool runs tasks in the order it finds them, and splits them blindly across multiple parallel sessions. This means that you'll need to write a script to preorder the items that need to be executed so that the tasks are distributed evenly across sessions. Thus, you'll end up writing something that looks similar to the preceding scripts anyway.

Adding/removing columns on a table

As designs change, we may want to add or remove columns from our data tables. These are common operations in development, though they need more careful planning on a running production database server, as they take full locks and may run for long periods.

How to do it...

You can add a new column to a table using this command:

```
ALTER TABLE mytable
ADD COLUMN last_update_timestamp TIMESTAMP WITHOUT TIME ZONE;
```

You can drop the same column using the following command:

```
ALTER TABLE mytable
DROP COLUMN last_update_timestamp;
```

You can combine multiple operations when using `ALTER TABLE`, which then applies the changes in a sequence. This allows you to do a useful trick, which is to add a column unconditionally, using `IF EXISTS`, like this:

```
ALTER TABLE mytable
DROP COLUMN IF EXISTS last_update_timestamp,
ADD COLUMN last_update_timestamp TIMESTAMP WITHOUT TIME ZONE;
```

Note that this will have almost the same effect as the following command:

```
UPDATE mytable SET last_update_timestamp = NULL;
```

However, `ALTER TABLE` runs much faster. That's very cool if you want to perform an update, but not much fun if you want to keep the data in the existing column.

How it works...

The `ALTER TABLE` statement, which is used to add or drop a column, takes a full table lock (at the `AccessExclusiveLock` lock level) so that it can prevent all other actions on the table. So, we want it to be as fast as possible.

The `DROP COLUMN` command doesn't actually remove the column from each row of the table; it just marks the column as dropped. This makes `DROP COLUMN` a very fast operation.

The `ADD COLUMN` command is also very fast if we are adding a nullable column with a null default value. If we use a `NOT NULL` constraint or specify an explicit default value, then we'll need to rewrite every row of the table, which can be quite slow.

The `ALTER TABLE` command allows us to execute many column operations at once, as shown in the main recipe. The `ALTER TABLE` command is optimized so that we are able to include all column operations in a single pass of the table, greatly improving the speed for complex sets of changes:

```
ALTER TABLE mytable
ADD COLUMN last_update_userid INTEGER DEFAULT 0,
ADD COLUMN last_update_comment TEXT;
```

If we rewrite the table, then the dropped columns are removed. If not, they may stay there for some time. Subsequent `INSERT` and `UPDATE` operations will insert a null value for the dropped column (s). Updates will reduce the size of the stored rows if they were not null already. So, in theory, you just have to wait, and the database will eventually reclaim the space. In practice, this works only if all the rows in the table are updated within a given period of time. Many tables contain historical data, so space may not be reclaimed at all without additional actions.

The PostgreSQL manual used to recommend changing the data type of a column to the same type—which forces rewriting of every row—as a technique to reclaim the space taken by the dropped columns. I don't recommend this because it will completely lock the table for a long period, at least on larger databases. My recommendation is not to drop the column at all, if you can avoid it, when you're in production. Just keep a track of the changes you would make if you get time, if ever. If you're looking at alternatives, then VACUUM will not rewrite the table, though a VACUUM FULL or a CLUSTER statement will. Be careful in those cases as well, because they also hold a full table lock.

There's more...

Indexes that depend on a dropped column are automatically dropped as well. All other objects that depend on the column (s), such as foreign keys from other tables, will cause the ALTER TABLE statement to be rejected. You can override this and drop everything in sight using the CASCADE option, as follows:

```
ALTER TABLE x
DROP COLUMN  last_update_timestamp
CASCADE;
```

Changing the data type of a column

Thankfully, changing column data types is not an everyday task, but when we need to do it, we must know all the details so that we can perform the conversion on a production system without any errors.

Getting ready

Let's start with a simple example of a table, as follows:

```
postgres=# select * from birthday;
```

This gives the following output:

```
 name  |  dob
-------+--------
 simon | 690926


(1 row)
```

The preceding table was created using this command:

```
CREATE TABLE birthday
( name          TEXT
, dob           INTEGER);
```

How to do it...

Let's say we want to change the `dob` column to another data type. Let's try with a simple example first, as follows:

```
postgres=# ALTER TABLE birthday
postgres-# ALTER COLUMN dob SET DATA TYPE text;
ALTER TABLE
```

This works fine. Let's just change that back to the `integer` type so that we can try something more complex, such as a `date` data type:

```
postgres=# ALTER TABLE birthday
postgres-# ALTER COLUMN dob SET DATA TYPE integer;
ERROR:  column "dob" cannot be cast to type integer
```

Oh! What went wrong? Let's try using an explicit conversion with the `USING` clause, as follows:

```
postgres=# ALTER TABLE birthday
           ALTER COLUMN dob SET DATA TYPE integer
           USING dob::integer;
ALTER TABLE
```

This works as expected. Now, let's try moving to a `date` type:

```
postgres=# ALTER TABLE birthday
ALTER COLUMN dob SET DATA TYPE date
USING date(to_date(dob::text, 'YYMMDD') -
     (CASE WHEN dob/10000 BETWEEN 16 AND 69 THEN interval '100
       years'
      ELSE interval '0' END));
```

Now, it gives what we were hoping to see:

```
postgres=# select * from birthday;
 name  |    dob
-------+------------
 simon | 26/09/1969
(1 row)
```

With PostgreSQL, you can also set or drop default expressions, irrespective of whether or not the NOT NULL constraints are applied:

```
ALTER TABLE foo
ALTER COLUMN col DROP DEFAULT;

ALTER TABLE foo
ALTER COLUMN col SET DEFAULT 'expression';

ALTER TABLE foo
ALTER COLUMN col SET NOT NULL;

ALTER TABLE foo
ALTER COLUMN col DROP NOT NULL;
```

How it works...

Moving from the integer to the date type uses a complex USING expression. Let's break that down step by step so that we can see why, as follows:

```
postgres=# ALTER TABLE birthday
ALTER COLUMN dob SET DATA TYPE date
USING date(to_date(dob::text, 'YYMMDD') -
      (CASE WHEN dob/10000 BETWEEN 16 AND 69
      THEN interval '100 years'
      ELSE interval '0' END));
```

First, we can't move directly from integer to date. We need to convert it to text and then to date. The dob::text statement means "cast to text".

Once we have text, we use the to_date() function to move to a date type.

This is not enough; our starting data was 690926, which we presume is a date in the YYMMDD format. When PostgreSQL converts this data to a date, it assumes that the two-digit year, 69, is in the current century because it chooses the year nearest to 2020. So, it outputs 2069 rather than 1969. This is why a case statement is added to reduce any year between 16 and 69 to be a date in the previous century by explicitly subtracting an interval of 100 years. We do not need to take away one century for years after 69 because they are already placed in the 20th century.

It is very strongly recommended that you test this conversion by performing a SELECT first. Converting data types, especially to/from dates, always causes some problems, so don't try to do this quickly. Always take a backup of the data first.

There's more...

The USING clause can also be used to handle complex expressions involving other columns. This could be used for data transformations, which might be useful for DBAs in some circumstances, such as migrating to a new database design on a production database server. Let's put everything together in a full, working example. We start with this table that has to be transformed:

```
postgres=# select * from cust;
 customerid | firstname | lastname | age
------------+-----------+----------+-----
          1 | Philip    | Marlowe  |  38
          2 | Richard   | Hannay   |  42
          3 | Holly     | Martins  |  25
          4 | Harry     | Palmer   |  36
(4 rows)
```

We want to transform it into a table design like the following:

```
postgres=# select * from cust;
 customerid |     custname    | age
------------+-----------------+-----
          1 | Philip Marlowe  |  38
          2 | Richard Hannay  |  42
          3 | Holly Martins   |  25
          4 | Harry Palmer    |  36
(4 rows)
```

We can decide to do it using these simple steps:

```
ALTER TABLE cust ADD COLUMN custname text NOT NULL DEFAULT '';
UPDATE cust SET custname = firstname || ' ' || lastname;
ALTER TABLE cust DROP COLUMN firstname;
ALTER TABLE cust DROP COLUMN lastname;
```

We can also use the SQL commands directly or make them use a tool such as **pgAdmin3**. Following those steps may cause problems, as the changes aren't within a transaction, meaning that other users can see the changes when they are only half finished. Hence, it would be better to do this in a single transaction, using BEGIN and COMMIT. Also, those four changes require us to make two passes over the table.

However, we can perform the entire transformation in one pass using multiple clauses on the `ALTER TABLE` command. So instead, we do the following:

```
BEGIN;
ALTER TABLE cust
  ALTER COLUMN firstname SET DATA TYPE text
        USING firstname || ' ' || lastname,
  ALTER COLUMN firstname SET NOT NULL,
  ALTER COLUMN firstname SET DEFAULT '',
  DROP COLUMN lastname;
ALTER TABLE cust RENAME firstname TO custname;
COMMIT;
```

This is a great example of why I personally prefer using scripts to make such changes to large production databases rather than directly making the changes using a GUI.

Some type changes can be performed without actually rewriting rows, for example, if you are casting data from `varchar` to `text`, or from `NUMERIC(10,2)` to `NUMERIC(18,2)` or simply to `NUMERIC`. However, older versions of PostgreSQL were not able to treat such cases differently from the rest, and to be on the safer side a rewrite was always forced. Even the identical conversion from a type to the same type forced a rewrite (this operation was actually recommended as a trick to cause a rewrite of all rows without changing their logical content).

Thanks to improvements in versions 9.1 and 9.2, `ALTER TABLE` can now perform suitable type changes without rewriting any row, and the documentation has been updated to suggest `VACUUM FULL` or `CLUSTER` as ways to rewrite all rows. Thanks to a similar addition to PostgreSQL 9.2, foreign key constraints will recognize type changes of the kind we just covered on the source table, and will therefore skip the constraint check whenever it is safe.

Changing the definition of a data type

PostgreSQL comes with several data types, but users can create custom types to most faithfully represent any value. Data type management is mostly, but not exclusively, a developer's job, and data type design goes beyond the scope of this book. This is a quick recipe that covers only the simpler problem of the need to apply a specific change to an existing data type.

Getting ready

Enumerative data types are defined like this:

```
CREATE TYPE cookbook_author AS ENUM ('Hannu','Simon');
```

The other popular case is composite data types, which are created in this way:

```
CREATE TYPE node AS (
  node_name text,
  connstr text,
  standbys text[]);
```

How to do it...

Say you are upgrading your database to edition, or version, 2.0 and you need a new value for the enumerative type that we defined in the preceding code. You want to put the new value in a certain position to preserve the alphabetical ordering. For that, you can use an ALTER TYPE syntax, like this:

```
ALTER TYPE cookbook_author ADD VALUE 'Gianni' BEFORE 'Hannu';
```

Composite data types can be changed with a similar command, as follows:

```
ALTER TYPE node
  DROP ATTRIBUTE standbys,
  ADD ATTRIBUTE async_standbys text[],
  ADD ATTRIBUTE sync_standbys text[];
```

This form supports a list of changes, perhaps because composite types are more complex than a list of enumerative values, and can therefore require complicated modifications.

How it works...

Each time you create a table, a composite type is automatically created with the same attribute names, types, and positions. Each ALTER TABLE command that changes table column definitions will silently issue a corresponding ALTER TYPE statement to keep the type in agreement with "its" table definition.

There's more...

When an attribute is removed from a composite data type, the corresponding values will instantly disappear from all the values of that same type stored in any database table. What actually happens is that these values are still inside the tables but they have become invisible because their attribute is now marked as deleted, and the space they occupy will be reclaimed only when the contents of the composite type are parsed again. This can be forced with a query like the following:

```
UPDATE mytable SET mynode = mynode :: text :: node;
```

Here, `mytable` is a table that has a `mynode` column of the `node` type. This query converts the values to the `text` type, displaying only current attribute values, and then back to `node`. You may have noticed that this behavior is very similar to the example of the dropped column in the previous recipe.

Adding/removing schemas

Separating groups of objects is a good way of improving administration efficiency. You need to know how to create new schemas and remove schemas that are no longer required.

How to do it...

To add a new schema, issue this command:

`CREATE SCHEMA sharedschema;`

If you want that schema to be owned by a particular user, then you can add the following option:

`CREATE SCHEMA sharedschema AUTHORIZATION scarlett;`

If you want to create a new schema that has the same name as an existing user, so that the user becomes the owner, then try this:

`CREATE SCHEMA AUTHORIZATION scarlett;`

In many database systems, the schema name is the same as that of the owning user. PostgreSQL allows schemas owned by one user to have objects owned by another user within them. This can be especially confusing when you have a schema of the same name as that of the owning user. To avoid this, you should have two types of schema: schemas that are named the same as the owning user should be limited to only objects owned by that user. Other general schemas can have shared ownership.

To remove a schema named `str`, we can issue the following command:

`DROP SCHEMA str;`

If you want to ensure that the schema exists in all cases, you can issue this:

`CREATE SCHEMA IF NOT EXISTS str;`

This command has been added to version 9.3. Clearly, you need to be careful because the outcome of the command depends on the previous state of the database. As an example, try issuing the following:

`CREATE TABLE str.tb (x int);`

This can generate an error if the `str` schema contained that table before CREATE SCHEMA IF NOT EXISTS was run. Otherwise, there's no namespace error.

Irrespective of your PostgreSQL version, there isn't a CREATE OR REPLACE SCHEMA command, so when you want to create a schema, regardless of whether or not it already exists, you can do the following:

```
DROP SCHEMA IF EXISTS newschema;
```

```
CREATE SCHEMA newschema;
```

The DROP SCHEMA command won't work unless the schema is empty or unless you use the nuclear option:

```
DROP SCHEMA IF EXISTS newschema CASCADE;
```

The nuclear option kills all known germs and all your database objects ("even the good objects").

There's more...

In the SQL standard, you can also create a schema and the objects it contains in one SQL statement. PostgreSQL accepts this syntax if you need it:

```
CREATE SCHEMA foo
    CREATE TABLE account
    (id          INTEGER NOT NULL PRIMARY KEY
    ,balance     NUMERIC(50,2))
    CREATE VIEW accountsample AS
    SELECT *
    FROM account
    WHERE random() < 0.1;
```

Mostly, I find this limiting. This syntax exists to allow us to create two or more objects at the same time. That can be achieved more easily using PostgreSQL's ability to allow transactional DDL, which was discussed in the *Writing a script that either succeeds entirely or fails entirely* recipe.

Using schema-level privileges

Privileges can be granted for objects in a schema using the GRANT command, as follows:

```
GRANT SELECT ON ALL TABLES IN SCHEMA sharedschema TO PUBLIC;
```

However, this will only affect tables that already exist. Tables created in the future will inherit privileges defined by the ALTER DEFAULT PRIVILEGES command, like this:

```
ALTER DEFAULT PRIVILEGES IN SCHEMA sharedschema
GRANT SELECT ON TABLES TO PUBLIC;
```

Moving objects between schemas

Once you've created schemas for administration purposes, you'll want to move existing objects to keep things tidy.

How to do it...

To move one table from its current schema to a new schema, use the following:

```
ALTER TABLE cust
SET SCHEMA anotherschema;
```

If you want to move all objects, you can consider renaming the schema itself, using the following query:

```
ALTER SCHEMA existingschema RENAME TO anotherschema;
```

This only works if another schema with that name does not exist. Otherwise, you'll need to run `ALTER TABLE` for each table you want to move. You can use this recipe to perform the same action on many tables to achieve that.

Views, sequences, functions, aggregates, and domains can also be moved by `ALTER` commands with `SET SCHEMA` options.

How it works...

When you move tables to a new schema, all the indexes, triggers, and rules defined on those tables will also be moved to the new schema. If you've used a `SERIAL` data type and an implicit sequence has been created, then that also moves to the new schema. Schemas are purely an administrative concept and do not affect the location of the table's data files. Tablespaces don't work this way, as we will see in later recipes.

Databases, users/roles, languages, and conversions don't exist in a schema. Schemas exist in a particular database. Schemas don't exist within schemas; they are not arranged in a tree or hierarchy. More details can be found in the *Using multiple schemas* recipe in *Chapter 4, Server Control*.

There's more...

Not all objects that exist in a specific schema have commands to move them to a new schema; at least, this was the case before PostgreSQL 9.1, when gaps were filled by adding `ALTER ... SET SCHEMA ...` syntaxes for text search objects, operators, operator classes, operator families, and conversions.

Also, **casts** don't exist in a schema, though the data types and functions they reference do exist. These things are not typically something we want to move around anyway. This is just a note if you're wondering how things work.

Adding/removing tablespaces

Tablespaces allow us to store PostgreSQL data across different devices. We might want to do that for performance or administrative ease, or our database might just have run out of disk space.

Getting ready

Before we can create a useful tablespace, we need to prepare the underlying devices in a production-ready form.

Think carefully about the speed, volume, and robustness of the disks you are about to use. Make sure that they are configured correctly. Those decisions will affect your life for the next few months and years!

Disk performance is a subtle issue that most people think can be decided in a few seconds. We recommend reading *Chapter 10, Performance and Concurrency,* from this book, as well as additional books on the same topic.

Once you've done all of that, then you can create a directory for your tablespace. The directory must be:

- ► Empty
- ► Owned by the PostgreSQL-owning user ID
- ► Specified with an absolute path name

On Linux and Unix systems, you shouldn't use a mount point directly. Create a subdirectory and use that instead. That simplifies ownership and avoids some filesystem-specific issues, such as getting `lost+found` directories.

The directory also needs to follow sensible naming conventions so that we can clearly identify which tablespace goes with which server. Do not be tempted to use something simple, such as `data`, because it will make later administration more difficult. Be especially careful that test or development servers do not and cannot get confused with production systems.

How to do it...

Once you've created your directory, adding the tablespace is simple:

```
CREATE TABLESPACE new_tablespace
LOCATION '/usr/local/pgsql/new_tablespace';
```

The command to remove the tablespace is also simple and is as follows:

```
DROP TABLESPACE new_tablespace;
```

Every tablespace has a location assigned to it, with the exception of the pg_global and pg_default default tablespaces for shared system catalogs and all other objects respectively. They don't have a location because they live in a subdirectory of the data directory.

A tablespace can be dropped only when it is empty, so how do you know when a tablespace is empty?

Tablespaces can contain both permanent and temporary objects. Permanent data objects are tables, indexes, and TOAST objects. We don't need to worry too much about TOAST objects because they are created and always live in the same tablespace as their main table, and you cannot manipulate their privileges or ownership.

Indexes can exist in separate tablespaces as a performance option, though that requires explicit specification in the CREATE INDEX statement. The default is to create indexes in the same tablespace as the table to which they belong.

Temporary objects may also exist in a tablespace. These exist when users have explicitly created temporary tables or there may be implicitly created data files when large queries overflow their work_mem settings. These files are created according to the setting of the temp_tablespaces parameter. That might cause an issue because you can't tell for certain what the setting of temp_tablespaces is for each user. Users can change their setting of temp_tablespaces from the default value specified in the postgresql.conf file to something else.

We can identify the tablespace of each user object using the following query (for PostgreSQL 9.1 and later versions):

```
SELECT spcname
       ,relname
       ,CASE WHEN relpersistence = 't' THEN 'temp ' ELSE '' END ||
       CASE
```

```
                    WHEN relkind = 'r' THEN   'table'
                    WHEN relkind = 'f' THEN   'foreign table'
                    WHEN relkind = 't' THEN   'TOAST table'
                    WHEN relkind = 'v' THEN   'view'
                    WHEN relkind = 'm' THEN   'materialized view'
                    WHEN relkind = 'S' THEN   'sequence'
                    WHEN relkind = 'c' THEN   'type'
        ELSE 'index' END as objtype
FROM pg_class c join pg_tablespace ts
ON (CASE WHEN c.reltablespace = 0 THEN
        (SELECT dattablespace FROM pg_database
           WHERE datname = current_database())
   ELSE c.reltablespace END) = ts.oid
WHERE relname NOT LIKE 'pg_toast%'
AND relnamespace NOT IN (SELECT oid FROM pg_namespace WHERE nspname
  IN ('pg_catalog', 'information_schema'))
;
```

This displays an output like the following:

```
    spcname        |   relname   |  objtype
-------------------+-----------+------------
 new_tablespace    | x           | table
 new_tablespace    | y           | table
 new_tablespace    | z           | temp table
 new_tablespace    | y_val_idx   | index
```

If you are using PostgreSQL 9.0, just replace `relpersistence = 't'` with `relistemp`.

You may also want to look at the `spcowner`, `relowner`, `relacl`, and `spcacl` columns to determine who owns what and what they're allowed to do. The `relacl` and `spcacl` columns refer to the **access control list** that details the privileges available on those objects. The `spcowner` and `relowner` columns record the owners of the tablespace and tables/indexes, respectively.

How it works...

A tablespace is just a directory where we store PostgreSQL data files. We use symbolic links from the `data` directory to the tablespace.

We exclude TOAST tables because they are always in the same tablespace as their parent tables, but remember that TOAST tables are always in a separate schema. You can exclude TOAST tables using the `relkind` column, but that would still include the indexes on the TOAST tables. TOAST tables and TOAST indexes both start with `pg_toast`, so we can exclude those easily from our queries.

The preceding query needs to be complex because `pg_class` entry for an object will show `reltablespace = 0` when an object is created in the database's default tablespace. So, if you directly join `pg_class` and `pg_tablespace`, you end up losing rows.

Note that we can see that a temporary object exists, and we can see the tablespace in which it is created, even though we cannot refer to a temporary object in another user's session.

There's more...

Some more notes on best practices follow.

A tablespace can contain objects from multiple databases, so it's possible to be in a position where there are no objects visible in the current database. The tablespace just refuses to go away, giving the following error:

```
ERROR:  tablespace "old_tablespace" is not empty
```

You are strongly advised to make a separate tablespace for each database to avoid confusion. This can be especially confusing if you have the same schema names and table names in the separate databases.

How to avoid this? If you just created a new tablespace directory, you might want to create subdirectories within that for each database that needs space, and then change the subdirectories to tablespaces instead.

You may also wish to consider giving each tablespace a specific owner, using the following query:

```
ALTER TABLESPACE new_tablespace OWNER TO eliza;
```

This may help smooth administration.

You may also wish to set default tablespaces for a user so that tables are automatically created there by issuing the following query:

```
ALTER USER eliza SET default_tablespace = 'new_tablespace';
```

Putting pg_xlog on a separate device

You may seek advice about placing the pg_xlog directory on a separate device for performance reasons. This sounds very similar to tablespaces, though there is no explicit command to do this once you have a running database, and files in pg_xlog are frequently written. So, you must perform the steps outlined in the following example:

1. Stop the database server:

   ```
   [postgres@myhost ~]$ pg_ctl stop
   ```

2. Move pg_xlog to a location supported by a different disk device:

   ```
   [postgres@myhost ~]$ mv $PGDATA/pg_xlog /mnt/newdisk/
   ```

3. Create a symbolic link from the old location to the new location:

   ```
   [postgres@myhost ~]$ ln -s /mnt/newdisk/pg_xlog $PGDATA/pg_xlog
   ```

4. Restart the database server:

   ```
   [postgres@myhost ~]$ pg_ctl stop
   ```

5. Verify that everything is working by committing any transaction (preferably, a transaction that does not damage the existing workload):

   ```
   [postgres@myhost ~]$ psql -c 'CREATE TABLE pgxlogtest(x int)'
   ```

Tablespace-level tuning

As each tablespace has different I/O characteristics, we may wish to alter the planner cost parameters for each tablespace. These can be set with the following command:

```
ALTER TABLESPACE new_tablespace SET
(seq_page_cost = 0.05, random_page_cost = 0.1);
```

In this example, settings are roughly appropriate for an SSD drive, and it assumes that the drive is 40 times faster than an HDD for random reads, and 20 times faster for sequential reads.

The values given need more discussion than we have time for here. Also, tablespace-level tuning is not available in version 8.4 and earlier versions.

Moving objects between tablespaces

Moving data between tablespaces may sometimes be required.

Getting ready

First, create your tablespaces. Once the old and new tablespaces exist, we can issue the commands to move them.

How to do it...

Tablespaces can contain both permanent and temporary objects.

Permanent data objects are tables, indexes, and TOAST objects. We don't need to worry too much about TOAST objects because they are created in and always live in the same tablespace as their main table. So, if you alter the tablespace of a table, its TOAST objects will also move:

```
ALTER TABLE mytable SET TABLESPACE new_tablespace;
```

Indexes can exist in separate tablespaces, and moving a table leaves the indexes where they are. Don't forget to run ALTER INDEX commands as well, one for each index, as follows:

```
ALTER INDEX mytable_val_idx SET TABLESPACE new_tablespace;
```

Temporary objects cannot be explicitly moved to a new tablespace, so we take that to mean you want to "ensure they are created somewhere else in the future". To do that you need to do the following:

- Edit the temp_tablespaces parameter, as shown in the *Updating the parameter file* recipe in *Chapter 3, Configuration*
- Reload the server to allow new configuration settings to take effect

There is no single command to do this that will work for all users.

How it works...

If you want to move a table and its indexes all in one pass, you can issue all the commands in a single transaction, as follows:

```
BEGIN;
ALTER TABLE mytable SET TABLESPACE new_tablespace;
```

```
ALTER INDEX mytable_val1_idx SET TABLESPACE new_tablespace;
ALTER INDEX mytable_val2_idx SET TABLESPACE new_tablespace;
COMMIT;
```

Moving tablespaces means bulk copying of data. Copying happens sequentially, block by block. That works well, but there's no way to avoid the fact that the bigger the table, the longer it will take.

Performance will be optimized if archiving or streaming replication is not active, as no WAL will be written in that case.

You should be aware that the table is fully locked (`AccessExclusiveLock` lock) while the copy is taking place, so this can cause an effective outage for your application. Be very careful!

If you want to ensure that objects are created in the right place next time you create them, then you can use this query:

```
SET default_tablespace = 'new_tablespace';
```

You can run this automatically for all users that connect to a database using the following query:

```
ALTER DATABASE mydb SET default_tablespace = 'new_tablespace';
```

Take care that you do not run the following command by mistake, however:

```
ALTER DATABASE mydb SET TABLESPACE new_tablespace;
```

This literally moves all objects that do not have an explicitly defined tablespace into `new_tablespace`. For a large database, this will take a very long time, and your database will be completely locked while it runs; not cool, if you do it by accident!

There's more...

If you just discovered that indexes don't get moved when you move a table, then you may want to check whether any indexes are in tablespaces different from their parent tables. Run the following to check:

```
SELECT   i.relname    as index_name
,        tsi.spcname  as index_tbsp
,        t.relname    as table_name
,        tst.spcname  as table_tbsp
FROM (
```

```
  pg_class t   /* tables */
  JOIN pg_tablespace tst
    ON t.reltablespace = tst.oid OR
       (t.reltablespace = 0 AND tst.spcname = 'pg_default'))
JOIN pg_index pgi
  ON pgi.indrelid = t.oid
JOIN (
  pg_class i  /* indexes */
  JOIN pg_tablespace tsi
    ON i.reltablespace = tsi.oid OR
       (i.reltablespace = 0 AND tsi.spcname = 'pg_default'))
  ON pgi.indexrelid = i.oid
WHERE i.relname NOT LIKE 'pg_toast%'
  AND i.reltablespace != t.reltablespace
;
```

If we have one table with an index in a separate tablespace, we might see this as a psql definition:

```
postgres=# \d y
     Table "public.y"
 Column | Type | Modifiers
--------+------+-----------
 val    | text |
Indexes:
    "y_val_idx" btree (val), tablespace "new_tablespace"
Tablespace: "new_tablespace2"
```

Running the previously presented query gives the following:

```
  relname   |     spcname     | relname |    spcname
------------+-----------------+---------+---------------
 y_val_idx  | new_tablespace  | y       | new_tablespace2
(1 row)
```

Accessing objects in other PostgreSQL databases

Sometimes, you may want to access data in other PostgreSQL databases. The reasons may be as follows:

▶ You have more than one database server, and you need to extract data (such as reference) from one server and load it into the other.

▶ You want to access data that is in a different database on the same database server, which was split for administrative purposes.

▶ You want to perform some changes that you do not wish to rollback in the event of an error or transaction abort. These are known as **function side-effects** or **autonomous transactions**.

You might also be considering this because you are exploring the scale out, sharding, or load balancing approaches. If so, read the last part of this recipe, the *See also* section, and then skip to *Chapter 12, Replication and Upgrades*.

 Access to external PostgreSQL databases was considerably enhanced in PostgreSQL version 9.3 with the introduction of the PostgreSQL Foreign Data Wrapper, which complements dblink, the existing contrib module. This new mechanism is more efficient and implements a part of the SQL standard, but does not fully replace dblink, nor is available on all supported PostgreSQL versions. Therefore, we provide two variants of this recipe.

Getting ready

First of all, let's make a distinction to prevent confusion:

▶ The **Foreign Data Wrapper** infrastructure, a mechanism to manage the definition of remote connections, servers, and users, is available in all supported PostgreSQL versions. It was introduced in 8.4.

▶ The **PostgreSQL Foreign Data Wrapper** is a specific contrib extension that uses the Foreign Data Wrapper infrastructure to connect to remote PostgreSQL servers. It is only available from version 9.3 onwards.

In particular, the Foreign Data Wrapper infrastructure will be used to manage definitions in both cases, that is, when using the PostgreSQL Foreign Data Wrapper and when using the dblink module.

Foreign Data Wrapper extensions for other database systems will be discussed in the next recipe, *Accessing objects in other foreign databases*.

How to do it...

We describe first the variant that uses `dblink`, which applies to all supported PostgreSQL versions:

1. First, we need to install the `dblink` contrib module. The general procedure is explained in the *Adding an external module to PostgreSQL* recipe of *Chapter 3, Configuration*.

2. Then, we create some access definitions. The preferred way is to use the following commands, which are SQL standard (SQL/MED):

```
postgres=# CREATE FOREIGN DATA WRAPPER postgresql
VALIDATOR postgresql_fdw_validator;
```

```
CREATE FOREIGN DATA WRAPPER
```

```
postgres=# CREATE SERVER otherdb
FOREIGN DATA WRAPPER postgresql
OPTIONS (host 'foo', dbname 'otherdb', port '5432');
```

```
CREATE SERVER
```

```
postgres=# CREATE USER MAPPING FOR PUBLIC
```

```
SERVER otherdb;
```

```
CREATE USER MAPPING
```

You must create `FOREIGN DATA WRAPPER` only once, though you need one `SERVER` for each PostgreSQL destination database to which you may wish to connect. This is just the connection definition, not the connection itself.

Creating a public user mapping with no options seems strange, though it will mean that we use the `libpq` default behavior. It will also mean that we will connect the remote database using the value of `PGUSER`, or if it is not set, use the operating system user. Clearly, if we want to use different credentials, then we must specify them with suitable options, either while creating the mapping or afterwards (`ALTER USER MAPPING`).

> The `VALIDATOR` clause specifies a function whose purpose is to validate the parameters. That function is a part of the Foreign Data Wrapper and should have been provided by the author, so you need to create it only if you are developing a new type of Foreign Data Wrapper yourself.

3. Now, connect using an unnamed connection, as follows:

```
SELECT dblink_connect('otherdb');
```

This produces the following output:

```
dblink_connect
----------------
 OK
(1 row)
```

 We limit ourselves to unnamed connections for simplicity. It is also possible to create a named connection, that is, a connection that is assigned a string so that it can be referred directly later. This is obviously useful if we want to manage several connections, but it comes at the price of actually having to manage their life cycle (connection and disconnection).

4. Suppose you want to execute the following command:

```
postgres=# INSERT INTO audit_log VALUES (current_user, now());
```

To do so, run it on the unnamed remote connection like this:

```
postgres=# SELECT dblink_exec('INSERT INTO audit_log VALUES'||
    ' (current_user, now())', true);
```

This will give the following output:

```
 dblink_exec
-------------
 INSERT 0 1
(1 row)
```

Notice that the remote command returns the command tag and number of rows processed as the return value of the function. The second option means "fail on error". If you look closely, there's also a subtle error—when the INSERT command is executed locally, we use this server's value of current_user. But, when we execute remotely, we use the remote server's value of current_user, which might differ, depending on the user mapping defined previously.

5. Similarly, suppose you want to execute the following query on the unnamed remote connection:

```
SELECT generate_series(1,3)
```

We start by typing this:

```
SELECT *
FROM dblink('SELECT generate_series(1,3)')
```

This will result in the following error:

```
ERROR:   a column definition list is required for functions
returning
"record"
LINE 2: FROM dblink('SELECT generate_series(1,3)');
              ^
```

This error message is telling us that we need to specify the list of output columns and output types that we expect from the `dblink()` function, because PostgreSQL is unable to determine them automatically at parsing time (that is, without running the query).

We can add the missing information by providing an alias in the FROM clause, as in the following example:

```
SELECT *
FROM dblink('SELECT generate_series(1,3)')
  AS link(col1 integer);
```

This will succeed, and result in the following output:

```
col1
------
    1
    2
    3
(3 rows)
```

6. To disconnect from the unnamed connection, you can issue the following:

   ```
   SELECT dblink_disconnect();
   ```

   You get the following output:

   ```
    dblink_connect
   ----------------
    OK
   (1 row)
   ```

Now, we will describe the second variant of this recipe, which uses the PostgreSQL Foreign Data Wrapper instead of `dblink`. This variant is preferred, but it does not work with PostgreSQL versions older than 9.3:

1. The first step is to install the `postgres_fdw` contrib module, which—since we are on 9.3 and later versions—is as simple as this:

   ```
   postgres=# CREATE EXTENSION postgres_fdw;
   ```

   The result is as follows:

   ```
   CREATE EXTENSION
   ```

   This extension automatically creates the corresponding Foreign Data Wrapper, as you can check with psql's `\dew` meta-command:

   ```
   postgres=# \dew
                     List of foreign-data wrappers
        Name      |  Owner  |       Handler        |      Validator
   --------------+--------+---------------------+-------------------
   -----
    postgres_fdw | gianni | postgres_fdw_handler | postgres_fdw_
   validator
   (1 row)
   ```

2. We can now define a server:

   ```
   postgres=# CREATE SERVER otherdb
   FOREIGN DATA WRAPPER postgres_fdw
   OPTIONS (host 'foo', dbname 'otherdb', port '5432');
   ```

   This produces the following output:

   ```
   CREATE SERVER
   ```

3. Then, we can define the user mapping:

   ```
   postgres=# CREATE USER MAPPING FOR PUBLIC SERVER otherdb;
   ```

   The output is as follows:

   ```
   CREATE USER MAPPING
   ```

4. As an example, we will access a portion of a remote table containing (integer, text) pairs:

   ```
   postgres=# CREATE FOREIGN TABLE ft (
     num int ,
     word text )
   ```

```
SERVER otherdb
OPTIONS (
  schema_name 'public' ,
  table_name 't' );
```

The result is quite laconic:

CREATE FOREIGN TABLE

5. This table can now be operated almost like any other table. We check whether it is empty:

    ```
    postgres=# select * from ft;
    ```

    This is the output:

    ```
     num | word
    -----+------
    (0 rows)
    ```

6. We can insert rows as follows:

    ```
    postgres=# insert into ft(num,word) values (1,'One'),
    (2,'Two'),(3,'Three');
    ```

    This query produces the following output:

    INSERT 0 3

7. Then, we can verify that the aforementioned rows have been inserted:

    ```
    postgres=# select * from ft;
    ```

    This is confirmed by the output:

    ```
     num | word
    -----+--------
       1 | One
       2 | Two
       3 | Three
    (3 rows)
    ```

 Note that you don't have to manage connections or format text strings to assemble your queries. Most of the complexity is handled automatically by the Foreign Data Wrapper.

How it works...

The `dblink` module establishes a persistent connection with the other database. The `dblink` functions track the details of that connection, so you don't need to worry about doing so yourself. You should be aware that this is an external "resource", and so the generic programming problem of "resource leaks" becomes possible. If you forget about your connection and forget to disconnect it, you may experience problems later. The remote connections will be terminated should your session disconnect.

Note that the remote connection persists even across transaction failures and other errors, so there is no need to reconnect.

The `postgres_fdw` extension can manage connections transparently and efficiently, so if your use case does not involve commands other than SELECT, INSERT, UPDATE, and DELETE then you should definitely go for it.

The `dblink()` module executes the remote query and will assemble the result set in the memory before the local reply begins to be sent. This means that very large queries might fail due to lack of memory, and everybody else will notice that. This isn't a problem; `dblink` is simply not designed to handle bulk data flows. Look at the *Loading data from flat files* recipe in *Chapter 5, Tables and Data*, if that's what you want to do.

Running slightly larger queries can be achieved using cursors. They allow us to bring the answer set back in smaller chunks. Conceptually, we need to open the cursor, loop while fetching rows until we are done, and then close the cursor. An example query for that is as follows:

```
postgres=# SELECT dblink_open('example',
       'SELECT generate_series(1,3)', true);
 dblink_open
-------------
 OK
(1 row)
postgres=# SELECT *
       FROM dblink_fetch('example', 10, true)
       AS link (col1 integer);
 col1
------
    1
    2
    3
(3 rows)
```

Notice that we didn't need to define the cursor when we opened it, though we do need to define the results from the cursor when we fetch from it, just as we did with a normal query. For instance, to fetch 10 rows at a time, we can do this:

```
postgres=# SELECT *
      FROM dblink_fetch('example', 10, true)
      AS link (col1 integer);
 col1
------
(0 rows)
postgres=# SELECT dblink_close('example');
 dblink_close
--------------
 OK
(1 row)
```

The `dblink` module also allows you to use more than one connection. Using just one connection is generally not good for modular programming. For more complex situations, it's good practice to assume that the connection you want is not the same as the connection that another part of the program might need. The `dblink` module allows named connections, so you don't need to hope that the default connection is still the right connection. There is also a function named `dblink_get_connections()` that will allow you to see which connections you have active.

There's more...

Remote data sources look as if they can be treated as tables, and in fact, they are represented as such by Foreign Data Wrappers. Unfortunately, in practice, this doesn't work in all the ways you might hope and expect.

However, by writing your queries and code in the standard way, you give the database usable context information about what you are trying to achieve; future PostgreSQL versions might achieve better optimization on the same SQL code. This is a general advantage over custom solutions, which are usually opaque to the server and thus cannot be optimized further.

Ideally, we would like to use foreign tables interchangeably with local tables, with minimum possible performance penalty and maintenance cost, so it is important to know what already works and what is still in the wish list.

First, here's the good news: from version 9.2 onwards, foreign tables can have statistics collected, just like ordinary tables, and they can be used as models to create local tables:

```
CREATE TABLE my_local_copy (LIKE my_foreign_table);
```

This is not supported by `dblink`, because it works on statements instead of managing tables. In general, there is no federated query optimizer. If we join a local table and a remote table with `dblink`, then data from the remote database is simply pulled through, even if it would have been quicker to send the data and then pull back matching rows. On the other hand, `postgres_fdw` can share information with the query planner, allowing some optimization, and more improvements are likely to come in the next years, now that the infrastructure has been built.

As of version 9.3, `postgres_fdw` transparently pushes WHERE clauses to the remote server. Suppose you issue this:

```
SELECT * FROM ft WHERE num = 2;
```

Then, only the matching rows will be fetched, using any remote index if available. This is a massive advantage in working with selective queries on large tables.

The `dblink` module cannot automatically send a local WHERE clause to the remote database, so a query like the following would perform poorly:

```
SELECT *
FROM dblink('otherdb',
    'SELECT * FROM bigtable') AS link ( … )
WHERE filtercolumn > 100;
```

We will need to explicitly add the WHERE clause to the remote query at the application level, like the following:

```
SELECT *
FROM dblink('otherdb',
    'SELECT * FROM bigtable' ||
    ' WHERE filtercolumn > 100') AS link ( … );
```

This means that, in general, setting up views of remote data this way isn't very helpful, as it encourages users to think that the table location doesn't matter, whereas from a performance perspective, it definitely does. This isn't really any different from other federated or remote access database products.

There are also a few performance considerations that you may wish to consider. The first is that when the remote query executes, the current session waits for it to complete. You can also execute queries without waiting for them to return, using the following functions:

- `dblink_send_query()`
- `dblink_is_busy()`
- `dblink_get_result()`

If you are concerned about the overhead of connection time, then you may want to consider using a session pool. This will reserve a number of database connections, which will allow you to reduce apparent connection time. For more information, look at the *Setting up a connection pool recipe* in *Chapter 4, Server Control*.

There's more...

Another—and sometimes easier—way of accessing other databases is with a tool named **PL/Proxy**, available as a PostgreSQL extension. PL/Proxy allows you to create a local database function that is a proxy for a remote database function. PL/Proxy works only for functions, and some people regard this as a restriction, in a way similar to `postgres_fdw`, which operates only on rows in tables. That is why these solutions complement `dblink`, rather than replacing it.

Creating a local proxy function is simple:

```
CREATE FUNCTION my_task(VOID)
RETURNS SETOF text AS $$
    CONNECT 'dbname=myremoteserver';
    SELECT my_task();
$$ LANGUAGE plproxy;
```

You need a local function, but you don't need to call a remote function; you can use SQL statements directly. The following example shows a parameterized function:

```
CREATE FUNCTION get_cust_email(p_username text)
RETURNS SETOF text AS $$
    CONNECT 'dbname=myremoteserver';
    SELECT email FROM users WHERE username = p_username;
$$ LANGUAGE plproxy;
```

PL/Proxy is specifically designed to allow more complex architecture for sharding and load balancing. The RUN ON command allows us to dynamically specify the remote database on which we will run the SQL statement. So, the preceding example becomes like the following:

```
CREATE FUNCTION get_cust_email(p_username text)
RETURNS SETOF text AS $$
    CLUSTER 'mycluster';
    RUN ON hashtext(p_username);
    SELECT email FROM users WHERE username = p_username;
$$ LANGUAGE plproxy;
```

You'll likely need to read *Chapter 12, Replication and Upgrades*, before you begin designing application architecture using these concepts.

Accessing objects in other foreign databases

In the previous recipe, you saw how to use objects from a different PostgreSQL database, either with `dblink` or by using the newer Foreign Data Wrapper infrastructure. Here we will explore another variant of the latter—using Foreign Data Wrappers to access databases other than PostgreSQL.

There are many Foreign Data Wrappers for other database systems, all of which are maintained as extensions independently from the PostgreSQL project. PGXN, the PostgreSQL Extension Network mentioned in *Chapter 3, Configuration*, is a good place where you can see which extensions are available.

Just note this so that you don't get confused: while you can find Foreign Data Wrappers to access several database systems, there are also other wrappers for different types of data sources, such as text files, web services, and so on. There is even `postgres_fdw`, a backport of the 9.3 contrib module, which we covered in the previous recipe for PostgreSQL 9.2 users. Its main limitation is that it is read-only, as writable Foreign Data Wrappers are only supported by 9.3 and later versions.

 When evaluating external extensions, I advise you to carefully examine the `README` file in each extension before making stable choices, as the code maturity varies a lot. Some extensions are still development experiments, while others are production-ready extensions, such as `oracle_fdw`.

Getting ready

For this example, we will use the Oracle Foreign Data Wrapper, `oracle_fdw`, whose version is 1.0.0.

You need PostgreSQL version 9.1 or later, and you must have obtained and installed the required Oracle software as specified in the `oracle_fdw` documentation at `https://github.com/laurenz/oracle_fdw/blob/ORACLE_FDW_1_0_0/README.oracle_fdw#L395`.

The `oracle_fdw` wrapper is available in the PostgreSQL Extension Network, so you can follow the straightforward installation procedure described in the *Installing modules from PGXN* section of the *Adding an external module to PostgreSQL* recipe in *Chapter 3, Configuration*.

Obviously, you must have access to an Oracle database server.

How to do it...

Here, we provide stepwise instructions on how to connect to an Oracle server using `oracle_fdw`:

1. First, we ensure that the extension is loaded:

   ```
   CREATE EXTENSION IF NOT EXISTS oracle_fdw;
   ```

2. Then, we configure the server and the user mapping:

   ```
   CREATE SERVER myserv
   FOREIGN DATA WRAPPER oracle_fdw
   OPTIONS (dbserver '//myhost/MYDB');
   CREATE USER MAPPING FOR myuser
   SERVER myserv;
   ```

3. Then, we create a PostgreSQL foreign table with the same column names as the source table in Oracle, and with compatible column types:

   ```
   CREATE FOREIGN TABLE mytab(id bigint, descr text)
   SERVER myserv
   OPTIONS (user 'oracleuser', password 'oraclepass');
   ```

4. Now, we can try to write to the table:

   ```
   INSERT INTO mytab VALUES (-1, 'Minus One');
   ```

5. Finally, we are able to read the values we have inserted:

   ```
   SELECT * FROM mytab WHERE id = -1;
   ```

   This should result in the following output:

   ```
    id |   descr
   ----+-----------
    -1 | Minus One
   (1 row)
   ```

How it works...

Our query has a `WHERE` condition that filters the rows we select from the foreign table. As in the `postgres_fdw` example from the previous recipe, Foreign Data Wrappers do the clever thing: the `WHERE` condition is pushed to the remote server, and only the matching rows are retrieved.

This is good in two ways: firstly, we delegate some work to another system, and secondly, we reduce the overall network traffic by not transferring unnecessary data.

We also notice that the `WHERE` condition is expressed in the PostgreSQL syntax; the Foreign Data Wrapper is able to translate it into whatever form required by the remote system.

There's more...

Starting from version 9.2, PostgreSQL provides the infrastructure for collecting statistics on foreign tables, so the planner will be able to consider such information, provided that the feature is implemented in the specific Foreign Data Wrapper you are using. For example, statistics are supported by `oracle_fdw`.

The latest improvement for foreign tables comes in version 9.4, which allows us to create triggers on foreign tables. This case is very similar to regular tables, except for `TRUNCATE` triggers, which are not allowed on foreign tables.

Another interesting extension is Multicorn (`http://multicorn.org`). It helps Python programmers create Foreign Data Wrappers by providing a dedicated interface. Multicorn reduces the creation of a basic Foreign Data Wrapper to the implementation of one Python method. Additional features, such as write access, are available through further optional methods.

Updatable views

PostgreSQL supports the SQL standard `CREATE VIEW` command, which, starting from version 9.3, supports automatic `UPDATE`, `INSERT`, and `DELETE` commands, provided they are simple enough.

With older PostgreSQL versions or with more complex views, these operations can be simulated with suitable **query rewrite** rules, or more recently by `INSTEAD OF` triggers. Note that according to community support policies, at least until September 2017, there will be PostgreSQL versions prior to 9.3 that are still supported and do not support automatic updatable views. Therefore, if you are using version 9.3 or later, only the discussion in the *Getting ready* section of this recipe will be of interest; the rest is implemented automatically.

Note also that certain types of updates are forbidden just because it is either impossible or impractical to derive a corresponding list of modifications on the constituent tables. We'll discuss those issues here.

Getting ready

First, you need to consider that only simple views can be made to receive insertions, updates, and deletions easily. The SQL standard differentiates between views that are "simple updatable" and more complex views that cannot be expected to be updatable.

So, before we proceed, we need to understand what is a simply updatable view and what is not. Let's start from the `cust` table:

```
postgres=# SELECT * FROM cust;
 customerid | firstname | lastname | age
------------+-----------+----------+-----
          1 | Philip    | Marlowe  |  38
          2 | Richard   | Hannay   |  42
          3 | Holly     | Martins  |  25
          4 | Harry     | Palmer   |  36
          4 | Mark      | Hall     |  47
(5 rows)
```

We create a very simple view on top of it, like the following:

```
CREATE VIEW cust_view AS
SELECT customerid
      ,firstname
      ,lastname
      ,age
FROM cust;
```

Each row in our view corresponds to one row in a single-source table, and each column is referred to directly without a function call. Thus, we expect to be able to make INSERT, UPDATE, and DELETE commands pass through our view into the base table, which is what happens in PostgreSQL 9.3 or later.

The following examples are three views where INSERT, UPDATE, and DELETE commands cannot be made to flow to the base table easily:

```
CREATE VIEW cust_avg AS
SELECT avg(age)
FROM cust;
```

```
CREATE VIEW cust_above_avg_age AS
SELECT customerid
            ,substr(firstname, 1, 20) as fname
            ,substr(lastname, 1, 20) as lname
            ,age -
            (SELECT avg(age)::integer
            FROM cust) as years_above_avg
FROM cust
WHERE age >
     (SELECT avg(age)
      FROM cust);


CREATE VIEW  potential_spammers AS
SELECT customerid
FROM cust
ORDER BY spam_score(firstname, lastname) DESC
LIMIT 100;
```

So, before we proceed to the steps to allow any or all of insertions, updates, or deletions to flow from views to base tables, we need to be clear about whether this makes sense conceptually.

How to do it...

In PostgreSQL version 9.1, INSTEAD OF triggers were introduced. They provide an alternate mechanism to implement updatable views by creating trigger functions that execute arbitrary code every time a data-modification command is executed on the view.

The INSTEAD OF triggers are part of the SQL standard, and other database systems support them. Conversely, query rewrite rules are specific to PostgreSQL and cannot be found anywhere else in this exact form.

There is no clearly preferable method. On one hand, rules can be more efficient than triggers, but on the other hand, they can be more difficult to understand than triggers, and could result in inefficient execution if the code is badly written (although the latter is not an exclusive property of rules, unfortunately).

In the absence of a clear primacy of one method over another, in this section we shall describe a solution based on rules, which applies to all the current versions of PostgreSQL.

As mentioned before, this example does not apply to PostgreSQL version 9.3 or later versions, where simple views are automatically made updatable.

The steps are as follows:

1. Let's start from a very simple view that might exist purely for administrative purposes, as follows:

```
CREATE VIEW cust_view AS
SELECT customerid
        ,firstname
        ,lastname
        ,age
FROM cust;
```

2. At first, if we try an INSERT command on our view, we get the following error:

```
postgres=# INSERT INTO cust_view
postgres-# VALUES (5, 'simon', 'riggs', 133);
ERROR:  cannot insert into a view
HINT:  You need an unconditional ON INSERT DO INSTEAD rule.
```

3. So, let's try the following query:

```
CREATE RULE cust_view_insert AS
ON insert TO cust_view
DO INSTEAD
INSERT INTO cust
VALUES (new.customerid, new.firstname, new.lastname, new.age);
```

4. Now, we can retry our INSERT command, as follows:

```
postgres=# INSERT INTO cust_view
postgres-# VALUES (5, 'simon', 'riggs', 133);
INSERT 0 1
```

5. This now works. Let's add rules for UPDATE and DELETE also, by running the following query:

```
CREATE RULE cust_view_update AS
ON  update TO cust_view
DO INSTEAD
```

```
UPDATE cust SET
  firstname = new.firstname
,lastname = new.lastname
,age = new.age
WHERE customerid = old.customerid;
CREATE RULE cust_view_delete AS
ON  delete TO cust_view
DO INSTEAD
DELETE FROM cust
WHERE customerid = old.customerid;
```

How it works...

We've just scratched the surface of what you can achieve with rules, though personally I find them too complex for widespread use.

You can do a lot of things with rules; you just need to be sure that everything you do makes sense and has a practical purpose. There are some other important points that I should mention about rules before you dive in and start using them everywhere.

Rules are applied by PostgreSQL after the SQL has been received by the server and parsed for syntax errors, but before the planner tries to optimize the SQL statement.

In the rules in the preceding recipe, we referenced the values of the old or the new row, just as we do within trigger functions, using the old and new keywords. Similarly, there are only new values in an INSERT command and only old values in a DELETE command.

One of the major downsides of using rules is that we cannot bulk load data into the table using the COPY command. Also, we cannot transform a stream of inserts into a single COPY command, nor can we do a COPY operation against the view. Bulk loading requires direct access to the table.

Suppose we have a view like the following:

```
CREATE VIEW cust_minor AS
SELECT customerid
      ,firstname
      ,lastname
      ,age
FROM cust
WHERE age < 18;
```

Then, we have some more difficulties. If we wish to update this view, then you might read the manual and understand that we can use a conditional rule by adding a WHERE clause to match the WHERE clause in the view, as follows:

```
CREATE RULE cust_minor_update AS
ON  update TO cust_minor
WHERE new.age < 18
DO INSTEAD
UPDATE cust SET
 firstname = new.firstname
,lastname = new.lastname
,age = new.age
WHERE customerid = old.customerid;
```

This fails, however, as you can see if you try to update cust_minor. The fix is to add two rules, one as an unconditional rule that does nothing (literally) and needs to exist for internal reasons, and the other to do the work we want:

```
CREATE RULE cust_minor_update_dummy AS
ON  update TO cust_minor
DO INSTEAD NOTHING;
CREATE RULE cust_minor_update_conditional AS
ON  update TO cust_minor
WHERE new.age < 18
DO INSTEAD
UPDATE cust SET
 firstname = new.firstname
,lastname = new.lastname
,age = new.age
WHERE customerid = old.customerid;
```

There's more...

There is yet another question posed by updatable views.

As an example, we shall use the cust_minor view we just defined, which does not allow performing insertions or updates such that the affected rows fall out of the view itself. For instance, consider this query:

```
UPDATE cust_minor SET age = 19 WHERE customerid = 123;
```

The preceding query will not affect any row because of the WHERE age < 18 condition in the rule definition.

Automatically updatable views do not place such a restriction, unless the CREATE VIEW statement uses the WITH CHECK OPTION clause, introduced in version 9.4.

In version 9.3, if a view includes a non-updatable column (for example, an expression, a literal, and so on), then no updates are allowed at all, even if they apply only to other updatable columns. In 9.4, we did the right thing by allowing updates on updatable columns.

Finally, it should be noted that some, or perhaps many, DBAs have found rules to be a serious annoyance. Here's one more reason for that: let's try running our main example in a different way, mixing rules with triggers. We'd like to make that view updatable so that it behaves like the following view:

```
CREATE VIEW cust_view AS
SELECT customerid
        ,firstname
        ,lastname
        ,age
FROM cust;
```

Before version 9.3, we couldn't create triggers on views, so let's try to create a table instead, as follows:

```
CREATE TABLE cust_view AS SELECT * FROM cust WHERE false;
```

We emulate the view by first creating a SELECT rule on the dummy table, and then try to create triggers on the table for the INSERT, UPDATE, and DELETE actions. The rule works only if it is named _RETURN and the table is completely empty:

```
postgres # CREATE RULE "_RETURN" AS
                ON SELECT TO cust_view
                DO INSTEAD
                SELECT * FROM cust;

CREATE RULE

postgres # CREATE TRIGGER cust_view_modify_after_trig
                AFTER INSERT OR UPDATE OR DELETE ON cust_view
                FOR EACH ROW

                EXECUTE PROCEDURE cust_view_modify_trig_proc();
ERROR:  "cust_view" is not a table
```

Huh? So what is it if it's not a table?

```
postgres # DROP TABLE cust_view;
ERROR:  "cust_view" is not a table
HINT:  Use DROP VIEW to remove a view
postgres # DROP VIEW cust_view;
DROP VIEW
```

Wow! That works! Yes, we created a table and then added a rule to it. This turned the table into a view. Now, we realize that we can't put triggers on a view and we can't put a SELECT rule on a table without it becoming a view. Since triggers are not fired by SELECT, this route won't work at all. It is probably best to accept that if you want to load data into a table, then you have to refer to the table directly, rather than use a view.

Using materialized views

Every time we select rows from a view, we actually select from the result of the underlying query. If that query is slow and we need to use it more than once, then it makes sense to run the query once, save its output as a table, and then select the rows from the latter.

This procedure has been available for a long time, and version 9.3 saw the addition of the dedicated syntax, CREATE MATERIALIZED VIEW, which we will describe in this recipe.

Getting ready

Let's create two "randomly" populated tables, of which one is large:

```
CREATE TABLE dish
( dish_id SERIAL PRIMARY KEY
, dish_description text
);


CREATE TABLE eater
( eater_id SERIAL
, eating_date date
, dish_id int REFERENCES dish (dish_id)
);
```

```
INSERT INTO dish (dish_description)
VALUES ('Lentils'), ('Mango'), ('Plantain'), ('Rice'), ('Tea');

INSERT INTO eater(eating_date, dish_id)
SELECT floor(abs(sin(n)) * 365) :: int + date '2014-01-01'
, ceil(abs(sin(n :: float * n))*5) :: int
FROM generate_series(1,500000) AS rand(n);
```

Notice that the data is not truly random. It is generated by a deterministic procedure, so you get exactly the same result if you copy the preceding code.

How to do it...

Let's create the following view:

```
CREATE VIEW v_dish AS
SELECT dish_description, count(*)
FROM dish JOIN eater USING (dish_id)
GROUP BY dish_description
ORDER BY 1;
```

Then, we'll query it:

```
SELECT * FROM v_dish;
```

We obtain the following output:

```
dish_description | count
-----------------+--------
 Lentils         |  64236
 Mango           |  66512
 Plantain        |  74058
 Rice            |  90222
 Tea             | 204972
(5 rows)
```

With a very similar syntax, we create a materialized view with the same underlying query:

```
CREATE MATERIALIZED VIEW m_dish AS
SELECT dish_description, count(*)
FROM dish JOIN eater USING (dish_id)
GROUP BY dish_description
ORDER BY 1;
```

The corresponding query yields the same output as before:

```
SELECT * FROM v_dish;
```

The materialized version is much faster than the non-materialized version. On my laptop, their execution times are 0.2 ms versus 300 ms.

How it works...

Creating a non-materialized view is exactly the same as creating an empty table with a `SELECT` rule, as we discovered from the previous recipe. No data is extracted until the view is actually used.

When creating a materialized view, the default is to run the query immediately and then store its results, like we do for table content.

In short, creating a materialized view is slow, but using it is fast. This is the opposite of standard views, which are created instantly and recomputed at every use.

There's more...

The output of a materialized view is physically stored like a regular table, and the analogy doesn't stop here. In both cases, it is possible to create indexes to speed up queries.

A materialized view will not automatically change when its constituent tables change. For that to happen, you must issue the following:

```
REFRESH MATERIALIZED VIEW m_dish;
```

As of 9.4, this replaces all the contents of the view with newly computed ones.

It is possible to quickly create an empty materialized view and populate it later. Just add `WITH NO DATA` at the end of the `CREATE MATERIALIZED VIEW` statement. Obviously, the view cannot be used before being populated, which you can do with `REFRESH MATERIALIZED VIEW`, as you just saw.

A materialized view cannot be read while it is being refreshed. For that, you need to use the `CONCURRENTLY` clause (introduced in 9.4) at the expense of a somewhat slower refresh.

As you can understand from these paragraphs, currently there is only a partial advantage in using materialized views, compared to previous solutions such as this:

```
CREATE UNLOGGED TABLE m_dish AS SELECT * FROM v_dish;
```

However, when using a declarative language, such as SQL, the same syntax may automatically result in a more efficient algorithm in case of future improvements of PostgreSQL. For instance, one day PostgreSQL will be able to perform a faster refresh by simply replacing those rows that changed, instead of recomputing the entire content.

8
Monitoring and Diagnosis

In this chapter, we will cover the following recipes:

- Checking whether a user is connected
- Checking which queries are running
- Checking which queries are active or blocked
- Knowing who is blocking a query
- Killing a specific session
- Detecting an in-doubt prepared transaction
- Knowing whether anybody is using a specific table
- Knowing when a table was last used
- Usage of disk space by temporary data
- Understanding why queries slow down
- Investigating and reporting a bug
- Producing a daily summary of log file errors
- Analyzing the real-time performance of your queries

Introduction

In this chapter, you will find recipes for some common monitoring and diagnosis actions you would want to do inside your database. They are meant to answer specific questions that you often face when using PostgreSQL.

Databases are not isolated entities. They live on computer hardware using CPUs, RAM, and disk subsystems. Users access databases using networks. Depending on the setup, databases themselves may need network resources to function in any of the following ways: performing some authentication checks when users log in, using disks that are mounted over the network (not generally recommended), or making remote function calls to other databases.

This means that *monitoring only the database is not enough*. As a minimum, one should also monitor everything directly involved in using the database. This means knowing the following:

▶ Is the database host available? Does it accept connections?

▶ How much of the network bandwidth is in use? Have there been network interruptions and dropped connections?

▶ Is there enough RAM available for the most common tasks? How much of it is left?

▶ Is there enough disk space available? When will it run out of disk space?

▶ Is the disk subsystem keeping up? How much more load can it take?

▶ Can the CPU keep up with the load? How many spare idle cycles do the CPUs have?

▶ Are other network services the database access depends on (if any) available? For example, if you use Kerberos for authentication, you need to monitor it as well.

▶ How many context switches are happening when the database is running?

▶ For most of these things, you are interested in history; that is, how have things evolved? Was everything mostly the same yesterday or last week?

▶ When did the disk usage start changing rapidly?

▶ For any larger installation, you probably have something already in place to monitor the health of your hosts and network.

The two aspects of monitoring are collecting historical data to see how things have evolved and getting alerts when things go seriously wrong. Tools based on **Round Robin Database Tool** (**RRDtool**) such as **Cacti** and **Munin** are quite popular for collecting the historical information on all aspects of the servers and presenting this information in an easy-to-follow graphical form. Seeing several statistics on the same timescale can really help when trying to figure out why the system is behaving the way it is.

Another popular open source solution is **Ganglia**, a distributed monitoring solution particularly suitable for environments with several servers and in multiple locations.

Another aspect of monitoring is getting **alerts** when something goes really wrong and needs (immediate) attention.

For alerting, one of the most widely used tools is **Nagios**, with its fork (**Icinga**) being an emerging solution. The aforementioned trending tools can integrate with Nagios.

However, if you need a solution for both the alerting and trending aspects of a monitoring tool, you might want to look into **Zabbix**.

Then, of course, there is **Simple Network Management Protocol** (**SNMP**), which is supported by a wide array of commercial monitoring solutions. Basic support for monitoring PostgreSQL through SNMP is found in **pgsnmpd**. This project does not seem very active though. However, you can find more information about pgsnmpd and download it from `http://pgsnmpd.projects.postgresql.org/`.

Providing PostgreSQL information to monitoring tools

Historical monitoring information is best to use when all of it is available from the same place and at the same timescale. Most monitoring systems are designed for generic purposes, while allowing application and system developers to integrate their specific checks with the monitoring infrastructure. This is possible through a plugin architecture. Adding new kinds of data inputs to them means installing a plugin. Sometimes, you may need to write or develop this plugin, but writing a plugin for something such as Cacti is easy. You just have to write a script that outputs monitored values in simple text format.

In most common scenarios, the monitoring system is centralized and data is collected directly (and remotely) by the system itself or through some distributed components that are responsible for sending the observed metrics back to the main node.

As far as PostgreSQL is concerned, some useful things to include in graphs are the number of connections, disk usage, number of queries, number of WAL files, most numbers from `pg_stat_user_tables` and `pg_stat_user_indexes`, and so on, as shown here:

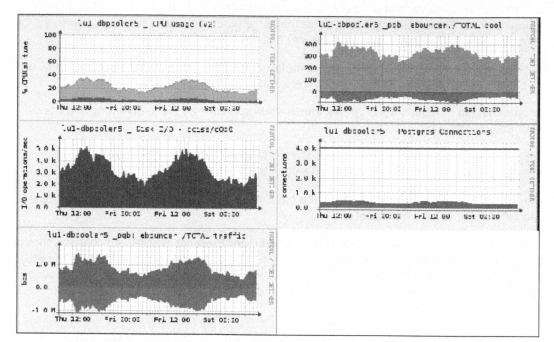

An example of a dashboard in Cacti

The preceding Cacti screenshot includes data for CPU, disk, and network usage; pgbouncer connection pooler; and the number of PostgreSQL client connections. As you can see, they are nicely correlated.

One *Swiss Army knife* script, which can be used from both Cacti and Nagios/Icinga, is `check_postgres`. It is available at `http://bucardo.org/wiki/Check_postgres`. It has ready-made reporting actions for a large array of things worth monitoring in PostgreSQL.

For Munin, there are some PostgreSQL plugins available at the Munin plugin repository at `https://github.com/munin-monitoring/contrib/tree/master/plugins/postgresql`.

The following screenshot shows a Munin graph about PostgreSQL buffer cache hits for a specific database, where cache hits (blue line) dominate reads from the disk (green line):

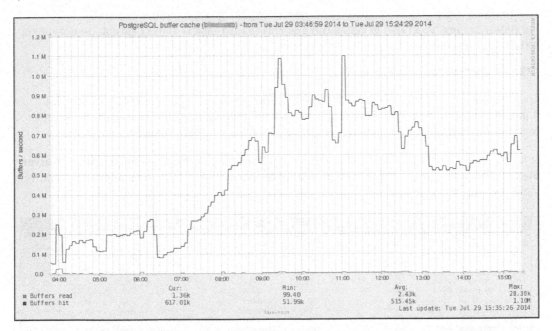

Finding more information about generic monitoring tools

Setting up the tools themselves is a larger topic, and it is beyond the scope of this book. In fact, each of these tools has more than one book written about them. The basic setup information and the tools themselves can be found at the following URLs:

- RRDtool: http://www.mrtg.org/rrdtool/
- Cacti: http://www.cacti.net/
- Ganglia: http://ganglia.sourceforge.net/
- Icinga: http://www.icinga.org
- Munin: http://munin-monitoring.org/
- Nagios: http://www.nagios.org/
- Zabbix: http://www.zabbix.org/

Real-time viewing using pgAdmin

You can also use pgAdmin to get a quick view of what is going on in the database. For better control, you need to install the `adminpack` extension in the destination database, by issuing this command:

```
CREATE EXTENSION adminpack;
```

This extension is a part of the additionally supplied modules of PostgreSQL (aka contrib). It provides several administration functions that PgAdmin (and other tools) can use in order to manage, control, and monitor a Postgres server from a remote location.

Once you have installed `adminpack`, connect to the database and then go to **Tools | Server Status**. This will open a window similar to what is shown in the following screenshot, reporting locks and running transactions:

Checking whether a user is connected

Here, we will show you how to learn whether a certain database user is currently connected to the database.

Getting ready

Make sure that you are logged in as a superuser.

How to do it...

Issue the following query to see whether the bob user is connected:

```
SELECT datname FROM pg_stat_activity WHERE usename = 'bob';
```

If this query returns any rows, then it means bob is connected to the database. The returned value is the name of the database to which the user is connected.

How it works...

PostgreSQL's pg_stat_activity system view keeps track of all running PostgreSQL backends. This includes information such as the query that is being currently executed (or the last query that was executed by a backend—available from 9.2); who is connected; when the connection, the transaction, and/or the query were started; and so on.

There's more...

If you've managed different versions of PostgreSQL, you may be aware that the pg_stat_activity view has undergone some important changes in PostgreSQL 9, especially from version 9.2 onwards.

I hereby include a list of all the relevant changes that have occurred since 9.0:

- ▶ PostgreSQL 9.1 has introduced the client_hostname column (reporting the reverse DNS lookup of client_addr for connections over the IP)
- ▶ In PostgreSQL 9.2, the procpid column was renamed pid (identifier of the backend process)
- ▶ In PostgreSQL 9.2, the current_query field was renamed query, and now reports the statement that is being executed or the statement that was last executed by that backend

- ▸ PostgreSQL 9.2 introduced the `state` and `state_change` columns, reporting the state of the backend (for example `active`, `idle`, or `idle in transaction`) and when the change of state occurred, respectively.

- ▸ The `state` column allows PostgreSQL database administrators to analyze queries that are being executed at that very moment (where state is `active`), as well as the most recent query executed by a backend, which is `idle` or `idle in transaction`

- ▸ In PostgreSQL 9.4, there are two more columns: `backend_xid` and `backend_xmin`, reporting the top-level transaction identifier and the `xmin` horizon of the current backend, respectively

I strongly advise you to spend a few minutes reading the PostgreSQL documentation that contains more detailed information about `pg_stat_activity`, available at `http://www.postgresql.org/docs/current/static/monitoring-stats.html#PG-STAT-ACTIVITY-VIEW`.

You can find answers to many administration-related questions by analyzing the `pg_stat_activity` view. One common example is outlined in the following section.

What if I want to know whether that computer is connected?

Often, several different processes may connect as the same database user. In that case, you may actually want to know whether there is a connection from a specific computer.

You still can get this information from the `pg_stat_activity` view, as it includes the connected clients' IP address, port, and hostname (where applicable). The port is only needed if you have more than one connection from the same client computer and you need to do further digging to see which process there connects to which database. Run the following command:

```
SELECT datname, usename, client_addr, client_port,
       application_name FROM pg_stat_activity;
```

The `client_addr` and `client_port` parameters help you look up the exact computer and even the process on that computer that has connected to the specific database. From version 9.1 onwards, you can also retrieve the hostname of the remote computer through the `client_hostname` option (this requires `log_hostname` to be set to on).

Finally, I would always recommend including `application_name` in your reports. This field has been introduced in PostgreSQL 9.0, and it is becoming widely recognized and honored by third-party application developers (I advise you to do the same with your own applications).

For information on how to set the application name for your connections, refer to *Database Connection Control Functions* in the PostgreSQL documentation at `http://www.postgresql.org/docs/current/static/libpq-connect.html`.

What if I want to repeatedly execute a query in psql?

PostgreSQL 9.3 introduces the \watch meta-command, which allows psql users to automatically (and continuously) re-execute a query.

This behavior is similar to the watch utility of some Linux and Unix environments.

In the following example, we run a simple query on pg_stat_activity and ask psql to repeat it every 5 seconds. You can exit at any time by pressing *Ctrl + C*:

```
gabriele=> SELECT count(*) FROM pg_stat_activity;
 count
-------
     1
(1 row)


gabriele=> \watch 5
Watch every 5s      Tue Aug 27 21:47:24 2013

 count
-------
     1
(1 row)
… <snip> …
```

For further information about the psql utility, refer to the PostgreSQL documentation at http://www.postgresql.org/docs/current/static/app-psql.html.

Checking which queries are running

Here, we will show you how to check which query is currently running.

Getting ready

You have to make sure that you are logged in as a superuser or as the same database user you want to check. Also, ensure that the parameter track_activities = on is set (default behavior).

This can be done either in the `postgresql.conf` file or by the superuser, using the following SQL statement:

```
SET track_activities = on
```

The way PostgreSQL allows a user to change configuration parameters at runtime is very powerful. You are advised to look at the reference page at `http://www.postgresql.org/docs/current/static/sql-set.html`.

How to do it...

To see which connected users are running at this moment, just run the following:

```
SELECT datname, usename, state, query
       FROM pg_stat_activity;
```

On systems with a lot of users, you may notice that the majority of backends have `state` set to `idle`. This denotes that no query is actually running, and PostgreSQL is waiting for new commands from the user. The `query` field shows the statement that was last executed by that particular backend.

Users of PostgreSQL 9.0 and 9.1 must use a different SQL statement, due to the aforementioned changes to the `pg_stat_activity` view:

```
SELECT datname, usename, current_query
       FROM pg_stat_activity;
```

In this case, idle backends are identified by the special query value of `<IDLE>` for `current_query`.

If, on the other hand, you are interested in active queries only, limit your selection to only those records that have `state` set to `active`:

```
SELECT datname, usename, state, query
       FROM pg_stat_activity WHERE state = 'active';
```

Again, PostgreSQL 9.0 and 9.1 users must use a different SQL statement and exclude the idle backends from their result set:

```
SELECT datname, usename, current_query
       FROM pg_stat_activity
       WHERE current_query != '<IDLE>';
```

How it works...

When `track_activities = on` is set, PostgreSQL collects data about all running queries. Users with sufficient rights can then view this data using the `pg_stat_activity` system view.

The `pg_stat_activity` view uses a system function named `pg_stat_get_activity (procpid int)`. You can use this function directly to watch for the activity of a specific backend by supplying the process ID as an argument. Giving `NULL` as an argument returns information for all backends.

There's more...

Sometimes, you wouldn't care about getting all queries that are currently running. You may be only interested in seeing some of these, or you may not like to connect to the database just to see what is running.

Catching queries which only run for a few milliseconds

As most queries on modern **online transaction processing** (**OLTP**) systems take only a few milliseconds to run, it is often hard to catch the active ones when simply probing the `pg_stat_activity` table.

Most likely, you will be able to see only the last executed query for those backends that have `state` different from `active`. In some cases, this can be enough.

Remember that if you are using PostgreSQL 9.0 or 9.1, you cannot benefit from the information regarding the last executed query of a backend through the `pg_stat_activity` view.

In general, if you need to perform a deeper analysis, I strongly recommend installing and configuring the `pg_stat_statements` module, which is described in the *Analyzing the real-time performance of your queries* recipe of this chapter. Another option is to run a post analysis of log files using pgBadger. Depending on the workload of your system, you may want to limit the production of highly granular log files (that is, log all queries) to a short period of time. For further information on PgBadger, refer to the *Producing a daily summary of log file errors* recipe of this chapter.

Watching the longest queries

Another thing of interest that you may want to look for is long-running queries. To get a list of running queries ordered by how long they have been executing, use the following:

```
SELECT
    current_timestamp - query_start AS runtime,
```

```
    datname, usename, query
FROM pg_stat_activity
WHERE state = 'active'
ORDER BY 1 DESC;
```

This will return currently running queries, with the longest running queries in the front.

If the version is older than PostgreSQL 9.2, users will have to use a slightly different query:

```
SELECT
    current_timestamp - query_start AS runtime,
    datname, usename, current_query
FROM pg_stat_activity
WHERE current_query != '<IDLE>'
ORDER BY 1 DESC;
```

On busy systems, you may want to limit the set of queries returned to only the first few queries (add LIMIT 10 at the end) or only the queries that have been running over a certain period of time. For example, to get the list of queries that have been running for more than a minute, use this query:

```
SELECT
    current_timestamp - query_start AS runtime,
    datname, usename, query
FROM pg_stat_activity
WHERE state = 'active'
    AND current_timestamp - query_start > '1 min'
ORDER BY 1 DESC;
```

Watching queries from ps

If you want, you can also make the queries being run show up in process titles by setting the following in the postgresql.conf file:

```
update_process_title = on
```

Although the ps and top output are not the best places for watching the database queries, they may make sense in some circumstances.

See also

The page in PostgreSQL's online documentation, which covers the related settings, is available at `http://www.postgresql.org/docs/current/static/runtime-config-statistics.html`.

Checking which queries are active or blocked

Here, we will show you how to know whether a query is actually running or it is waiting for another query.

Getting ready

Again, log in as a superuser.

How to do it...

Run this query:

```
SELECT datname, usename, query
      FROM pg_stat_activity
      WHERE waiting = true;
```

You will get a list of queries that are waiting on other backends. The following query will run on PostgreSQL versions older than 9.2:

```
SELECT datname, usename, current_query
      FROM pg_stat_activity
      WHERE waiting = true;
```

How it works...

The `pg_stat_activity` system view has a Boolean field named `waiting`. This field indicates that a certain backend is waiting on a system lock.

The preceding query uses it to filter out only those queries that are waiting.

There's more...

Some more explanations about the preceding queries are appropriate here.

No need for the = true part

As the `waiting` column is already Boolean, you can safely omit the `= true` part from the query and simply write the following:

```
SELECT datname, usename, query
     FROM pg_stat_activity
     WHERE waiting;
```

This catches only queries waiting on locks

The `pg_stat_activity.waiting` field shows only whether the query is waiting on a PostgreSQL internal lock.

Although this is the main cause of waiting when using pure SQL, it is possible to write some query in any of PostgreSQL's embedded languages that can wait on other system resources, such as waiting for an HTTP response, a file write to get completed, or just waiting on a timer.

As an example, you can make your backend "sleep" for a certain number of seconds using `pg_sleep(seconds)`. While you are monitoring `pg_stat_activity`, open a new terminal session with psql and run the following statement in it:

```
db=# SELECT pg_sleep(10);
<it "stops" for 10 seconds here>
pg_sleep
----------


(1 row)
```

It will show up as *not waiting* in the `pg_stat_activity` view, even though the query is, in fact, "blocked" in the timer.

Knowing who is blocking a query

Once you have found out that a query is blocked, you need to know who or what is blocking them.

Getting ready

Just get a superuser account to run the queries.

How to do it...

Run the following query on PostgreSQL 9.2 or later versions:

```
SELECT
    w.query AS waiting_query,
    w.pid AS waiting_pid,
    w.usename AS waiting_user,
    l.query AS locking_query,
    l.pid AS locking_pid,
    l.usename AS locking_user,
    t.schemaname || '.' || t.relname AS tablename
 FROM pg_stat_activity w
        JOIN pg_locks l1 ON w.pid = l1.pid AND NOT l1.granted
        JOIN pg_locks l2 ON l1.relation = l2.relation AND l2.granted
        JOIN pg_stat_activity l ON l2.pid = l.pid
        JOIN pg_stat_user_tables t ON l1.relation = t.relid
 WHERE w.waiting;
```

This returns the process ID, user, current query about both blocked and blocking backends, and the fully qualified name of the table that causes the blocking.

The equivalent query for PostgreSQL 9.0 and 9.1 is as follows:

```
SELECT
    w.current_query AS waiting_query,
    w.procpid AS waiting_pid,
    w.usename AS waiting_user,
    l.current_query AS locking_query,
    l.procpid AS locking_pid,
    l.usename AS locking_user,
    t.schemaname || '.' || t.relname AS tablename
FROM pg_stat_activity w
        JOIN pg_locks l1 ON w.procpid = l1.pid AND NOT l1.granted
        JOIN pg_locks l2 ON l1.relation = l2.relation AND l2.granted
        JOIN pg_stat_activity l ON l2.pid = l.procpid
        JOIN pg_stat_user_tables t ON l1.relation = t.relid
WHERE w.waiting;
```

How it works...

This query first selects all waiting queries (`WHERE w.waiting`), then gets the locks on those queries which are waiting (`JOIN pg_locks l1 ON w.pid = l1.pid AND NOT l1.granted`), and then looks up the lock that is granted on the same table (`JOIN pg_locks l2 ON l1.relation = l2.relation AND l2.granted`). Finally, it looks up a row in `pg_stat_activity` corresponding to the granted lock. It also resolves the relation identifier (`relid`) of the table to its full name using the `pg_stat_user_tables` system view.

Killing a specific session

Sometimes, the only way to let the system continue as a whole is by *surgically* terminating some offending database sessions. Yes, you read it right—surgically. You might indeed be tempted to *reboot* the server, but you should think of that as a last resort in a business continuity scenario.

In this recipe, you will be learning how to intervene, from gracefully canceling a query to brutally killing the actual process from the command line.

How to do it...

You can either run this function as a superuser or, when using PostgreSQL 9.2 or newer versions, with the same user as that of the offending backend (look for the `usename` field in the `pg_stat_activity` view).

Once you have figured out the backend you need to kill, use the function named `pg_terminate_backend(pid)` to kill it.

How it works...

When a backend executes the `pg_terminate_backend(pid)` function, it sends a signal, `SIGTERM`, to the backend as an argument after verifying that the process identified by the argument `pid` is actually a PostgreSQL backend.

The backend receiving this signal stops whatever it is doing, and terminates it in a controlled way.

The client using that backend loses the connection to the database. Depending on how the client application is written, it may silently reconnect, or it may show an error to the user.

There's more...

Killing the session may not always be what you really want, so consider other options as well.

It might also be a good idea to look at the *Server Signaling Functions* section in the PostgreSQL documentation at `http://www.postgresql.org/docs/current/static/functions-admin.html#FUNCTIONS-ADMIN-SIGNAL`.

Trying to cancel the query first

First, you may want to try `pg_cancel_backend(pid)`, a milder version of `pg_terminate_backend(pid)`.

The difference between these two is that `pg_cancel_backend()` just cancels the current query, whereas `pg_terminate_backend()` really kills the backend (therefore, this can be used for `idle` or `idle in transaction` backends).

What if the backend won't terminate?

If `pg_terminate_backend(pid)` fails to kill the backend and you really need to reset the database state to make it continue processing requests, then you have yet another option— sending `SIGKILL` to the offending backend.

This can be done only from the command line—as the `root` or the `postgres` system user—and on the same host the database is running, by executing the following code:

```
kill -9 <backend_pid>
```

This command kills that backend immediately, without giving it a chance to clean up. Consequently, the postmaster is forced to kill all the other backends as well and restart the whole cluster.

Therefore, it actually does not matter which of the PostgreSQL backends you kill.

You must be extremely careful if you have set the `synchronous_commit` parameter to `off`. You may end up losing some supposedly committed transactions if you use `kill -9` on a backend.

Thus, `kill -9` is the last resort, but only if nothing else helps, and not on a regular basis.

Using statement timeout to clean up queries that take too long to run

Often, you know that you don't have any use of queries running longer than a given time. Maybe, your web frontend just refuses to wait for more than 10 seconds for a query to complete and returns a default answer to users if it takes longer, abandoning the query.

In such a case, it might be a good idea to `set statement_timeout = 10 sec`, either in `postgresql.conf` or as a per user or per database setting. Once you do so, queries running too long won't consume precious resources and make others' queries fail.

The queries terminated by a statement timeout show up in the log, as follows:

```
hannu=# SET statement_timeout TO '3 s';
SET
hannu=# SELECT pg_sleep(10);
ERROR:  canceling statement due to statement timeout
```

For the older versions of PostgreSQL, they show up as a more confusing message—`query canceled due to user request`.

Killing Idle in transaction queries

Sometimes, people start a transaction, run some queries, and then just leave, without ending the transaction. This can leave some system resources in a state where some housekeeping processes can't be run. They may even have done something more serious, such as locking a table, thereby causing immediate *denial of service* for other users who need that table.

You can use the following query to kill all backends that have an open transaction but have been doing nothing for the last 10 minutes:

```
SELECT pg_terminate_backend(pid)
  FROM pg_stat_activity
WHERE state = 'idle in transaction'
    AND current_timestamp - query_start > '10 min';
```

For PostgreSQL 8.4, 9.0, or 9.1, you need to use this slightly different query:

```
SELECT pg_terminate_backend(procpid)
  FROM pg_stat_activity
WHERE current_query = '<IDLE> in transaction'
    AND current_timestamp - query_start > '10 min';
```

You can even schedule this to run every minute while you are trying to find the specific frontend application that ignores open transactions, or you have a lazy administration that leaves a psql connection open, or a flaky network that drops clients without the server noticing it.

Killing the backend from the command line

Another possibility to terminate a backend is by using a Unix/Linux command named `kill N`. This command orders the `SIGTERM` signal to process N on the system where it is running. You have to be either the `root` user or the user running the database backends (usually `postgres`) to be able to send signals to processes.

You can cancel a backend (and simulate the `pg_cancel_backend(pid)` function) by sending a `SIGINT` signal:

```
kill -SIGINT <backend_pid>
```

For more detailed information and the exact syntax, type `man kill` from your favorite shell environment.

Detecting an in-doubt prepared transaction

While using **two-phase commit** (**2PC**), you may end up in a situation where you have something locked but cannot find a backend that holds the locks. This recipe describes how to detect such a case.

How to do it...

You need to look up the `pg_locks` table for those entries with an empty `pid` value. Run this query:

```
SELECT t.schemaname || '.' || t.relname AS tablename,
       l.pid, l.granted
       FROM pg_locks l JOIN pg_stat_user_tables t
       ON l.relation = t.relid;
```

The output will be something similar to the following:

```
 tablename |  pid  | granted
-----------+-------+---------
    db.x   |       | t
    db.x   | 27289 | f
(2 rows)
```

The preceding example shows a lock on the `db.x` table, which has no process associated with it.

If you need to remove a particular prepared transaction, you can refer to the *Removing old prepared transactions* recipe in *Chapter 9, Regular Maintenance*.

Knowing whether anybody is using a specific table

This recipe helps you when you are in doubt whether some obscure table is used any more or it is left over from old times and just takes up space.

Getting ready

Make sure that you are a superuser, or at least have full rights to the table in question.

How to do it...

To see whether a table is currently in active use (that is, whether anyone is using it while you are watching it), run the following query on the database you plan to inspect:

```
CREATE TEMPORARY TABLE tmp_stat_user_tables AS
      SELECT * FROM pg_stat_user_tables;
```

Then wait a little, and see what has changed:

```
SELECT * FROM pg_stat_user_tables n
  JOIN tmp_stat_user_tables t
    ON n.relid=t.relid
   AND (n.seq_scan,n.idx_scan,n.n_tup_ins,n.n_tup_upd,n.n_tup_del)
    <> (t.seq_scan,t.idx_scan,t.n_tup_ins,t.n_tup_upd,t.n_tup_del);
```

How it works...

The `pg_stat_user_tables` view shows the current statistics for table usage.

To see whether a table is used, you check for changes in its usage counts.

The previous query selects all the tables where any of the usage counts for selector data manipulation have changed.

There's more...

You can use one of the following approaches to detect usage changes.

The quick and dirty way

If you are sure that you have no use of the cumulative statistics gathered by PostgreSQL, you can just reset all table statistics by executing the following command:

```
SELECT pg_stat_reset();
```

This sets all statistics to zero, and you can detect table use by just looking for tables where any usage count is not zero.

Of course, you can make a backup copy of the statistics table first, as follows:

```
CREATE TABLE backup_stat_user_tables AS
      SELECT current_timestamp AS snaptime,
             *
 FROM pg_stat_user_tables;
```

Collecting daily usage statistics

It is often useful to have historical usage statistics of tables when trying to solve performance problems or understand the usage patterns.

For this purpose, you can collect the usage data in a regular manner—daily or even more often—using either a cron or a PostgreSQL-specific scheduler such as `pg_agent`. Advanced users of PostgreSQL 9.3 can take advantage of background workers to schedule such an activity. For more information on background worker processes, go to `http://www. postgresql.org/docs/current/static/bgworker.html`.

The following query adds a snapshot of current usage statistics with a timestamp to the table created earlier:

```
INSERT INTO backup_stat_user_tables
      SELECT current_timestamp AS snaptime,
             *
 FROM pg_stat_user_tables;
```

Knowing when a table was last used

Once you come to know that a table is not used currently, the next question is "when was it last used?"

Getting ready

Get access to the database as a superuser or to the database host computer as a `postgres` system user.

How to do it...

PostgreSQL does not have any built-in "last used" information about tables, so you have to use other means to figure it out.

If you have set up a cron job to collect usage statistics, as described in the previous chapter, then it is relatively easy to find out the last date of change using a SQL query.

Other than this, there are basically two possibilities, neither of which gives you absolutely reliable answers.

You can either look at actual timestamps of the files in which the data is stored, or you can use the xmin and xmax system columns to find out the latest transaction ID that changed the table data.

In this recipe, we cover the first case and focus on the date information of the table's files.

The following PL/pgSQL function looks for the table's data files to get the value of their last access and modification times:

```
CREATE OR REPLACE FUNCTION table_file_access_info(
    IN schemaname text, IN tablename text,
    OUT last_access timestamp with time zone,
    OUT last_change timestamp with time zone
) LANGUAGE plpgsql AS $func$
DECLARE
    tabledir text;
    filenode text;
BEGIN
    SELECT regexp_replace(
        current_setting('data_directory') || '/' || pg_relation_
filepath(c.oid),
        pg_relation_filenode(c.oid) || '$', ''),
      pg_relation_filenode(c.oid)
    INTO tabledir, filenode
    FROM pg_class c
    JOIN pg_namespace ns
      ON c.relnamespace = ns.oid
      AND c.relname = tablename
      AND ns.nspname = schemaname;
    RAISE NOTICE 'tabledir: % - filenode: %', tabledir, filenode;
    -- find latest access and modification times over all segments
    SELECT max((pg_stat_file(tabledir || filename)).access),
           max((pg_stat_file(tabledir || filename)).modification)
      INTO last_access, last_change
```

```
        FROM pg_ls_dir(tabledir) AS filename
        -- only use files matching <basefilename>[.segmentnumber]
        WHERE filename ~ ('^' || filenode || '([.]?[0-9]+)?$');
END;
$func$;
```

How it works...

The `table_file_access_info(schemaname, tablename)` function returns the last access and modification times for a given table using the filesystem as a source of information.

The last query uses this data to get the latest time any of these files were modified or read by PostgreSQL. Beware that this is not a very reliable way to get information about the latest use of any table, but it gives you a rough upper-limit estimate about when it was last modified or read (for example, consider the autovacuum process accessing a table).

You can definitely improve and personalize the preceding function. I advise you to look at the PostgreSQL documentation and read about two built-in functions, `pg_ls_dir(dirname text)` and `pg_stat_file(filename text)`.

Another good source of information is the *Database File Layout* page on the PostgreSQL documentation at `http://www.postgresql.org/docs/current/static/storage-file-layout.html`.

There's more...

Recently, there have been discussions on adding last-used data to the information about tables that PostgreSQL keeps, so it is quite possible that answering the question "when did anybody last use this table?" will be much easier in the next version of PostgreSQL.

Usage of disk space by temporary data

In addition to ordinary stable tables, you can also create temporary tables.

Also, PostgreSQL may use temporary files for query processing if it can't fit all the necessary data into the memory.

So, how do you find out how much data is used by temporary tables and files? You can do this using any untrusted embedded language, or directly on the database host.

Getting ready

You have to use an untrusted language, because trusted languages run in a sandbox, which prohibits them from directly accessing the host filesystem.

How to do it...

Perform the following steps:

1. First, check whether your database defines special tablespaces for temporary files, as follows:

   ```
   SELECT current_setting('temp_tablespaces');
   ```

   As explained later on in this recipe, if the setting is empty, it means PostgreSQL is not using temporary tablespaces, and temporary objects will be located in the default tablespace for each database.

2. On the other hand, if `temp_tablespaces` has one or more tablespaces, then your task is easy because all temporary files—both of those used for temporary tables and those used for query processing—are inside the directories of these tablespaces. The following query (which uses `WITH` queries and string and array functions) demonstrates how to check the space used by temporary tablespaces:

   ```
   WITH temporary_tablespaces AS (
     SELECT unnest(string_to_array(
       current_setting('temp_tablespaces'), ',')
     ) AS temp_tablespace
   )
   SELECT tt.temp_tablespace,
     pg_tablespace_location(t.oid) AS location,
     -- t.spclocation AS location, -- for 9.0 and 9.1 users
     pg_tablespace_size(t.oid) AS size
   FROM temporary_tablespaces tt
   JOIN pg_tablespace t ON t.spcname = tt.temp_tablespace
     ORDER BY 1;
   ```

The output shows very limited use of temporary space (I ran the preceding query while I had two open transactions that had just created small, temporary tables using random data through `generate_series()`):

```
temp_tablespace |    location   |   size
----------------+---------------+---------
 pgtemp1        | /srv/pgtemp1  | 3633152
 pgtemp2        | /srv/pgtemp2  |  376832
(2 rows)
```

Even though you can obtain similar results using different queries, or just by checking the disk usage from the filesystem through `du` (once you know the location of tablespaces), I would like to focus on two functions here:

- `pg_tablespace_location(oid)`: Introduced in 9.2, this substitutes the previous `spclocation` field from the `pg_tablespace` catalogue view (9.0 and 9.1 users should change the preceding query accordingly)

- `pg_tablespace_size(oid)` or `pg_tablespace_size(name)`: This allows us to check the size used by a named tablespace directly within PostgreSQL

Because the amount of temporary disk space used can vary a lot in an active system, you may want to repeat the query several times to get a better picture of how the disk usage changes (with psql, use `\watch`, as explained in the *Checking whether a user is connected* recipe).

Further information on these functions can be found at `http://www.postgresql.org/docs/current/static/functions-admin.html`.

On the other hand, if the `temp_tablespaces` setting is empty, then the temporary tables are stored in the same directory as ordinary tables, and the temporary files used for query processing are stored in the `pgsql_tmp` directory inside the main database directory.

Look up the cluster's home directory using this query:

```
SELECT current_setting('data_directory') || '/base/pgsql_tmp'
```

The size of this directory gives the total size of current temporary files for query processing.

The total size of temporary files used by a database can be found in the `pg_stat_database` system view. PostgreSQL 9.2 introduced two fields, `temp_files` and `temp_bytes`. The following query returns the cumulative number of temporary files and the space used by every database since the last reset (`stats_reset`):

```
SELECT datname, temp_files, temp_bytes, stats_reset
  FROM pg_stat_database;
```

The `pg_stat_database` view holds very important statistics. I recommend that you look at the official documentation at `http://www.postgresql.org/docs/current/static/monitoring-stats.html#PG-STAT-DATABASE-VIEW` for detailed information and to get further ideas on how to improve your monitoring skills.

How it works...

Because all temporary tables and other temporary on-disk data are stored in files, you can use PostgreSQL's internal tables to find the locations of these files, and then determine the total size of these files.

There's more...

While the preceding information about temporary tables is correct, it is not the entire story.

Finding out whether a temporary file is in use any more

Because temporary files are not as carefully preserved as ordinary tables (this is actually one of the benefits of temporary tables, as less bookkeeping makes them faster), it may sometimes happen that a system crash leaves a few temporary files, which can (in the worst cases) take up a significant amount of disk space.

As a rule, you can clean up such files by shutting down the PostgreSQL server and then deleting all files from the `pgsql_tmp` directory.

Logging temporary file usage

If you set `log_temp_files = 0` or a larger value, then the creation of all temporary files that are larger than this value in kilobytes is logged to the standard PostgreSQL log.

If, while monitoring the log and the `pg_stat_database` view, you notice an increase in temporary file activity, you should consider increasing `work_mem`, either globally or (preferably) on a query/session basis.

Understanding why queries slow down

In production environments with large databases and high concurrent access, it might happen that queries that used to run in tens of milliseconds suddenly take several seconds.

Likewise, a summary query for a report that used to run in a few seconds might take half an hour to complete.

Here are some ways to find out what is slowing them down.

Getting ready

Any questions of the type "why is this different today from what it was last week?" are much easier to answer if you have some kind of historical data collection setup.

Tools such as Cacti or Munin (for monitoring general server characteristics such as CPU and RAM usage, disk I/O, network traffic, and load average) are very useful to see what has changed recently, and to try to correlate these changes with the observed performance of some database operations.

Also, collecting historical statistics data from `pg_stat_*` tables—be that daily, hourly, or even every five minutes if you have enough disk space—is also very useful for detecting possible causes for sudden changes or gradual degradation in performance.

If you are gathering both of these, then that's even better. If you have none, then the question is actually "Why is this query slow?"

But don't despair! There are a few things you can do to try to restore performance.

How to do it...

First, analyze your database using this code:

```
db_01=# analyse;
ANALYZE
Time: 6231.313 ms
db_01=#
```

This is the first thing to try, as it is usually cheap and is meant to be done quite often anyway.

If this restores the query's performance or at least improves the current performance considerably, then it means that autovacuum is not doing its task well, and the next thing to do is to find out why.

You must ensure that the performance improvement is not due to caching of the pages required by the requested query. Make sure that you repeat your query several times before classifying it as slow. Looking at `pg_stat_statements` (which is covered later in this chapter) can help you analyze the impact of a particular query in terms of caching, by inspecting two fields: `shared_blks_hit` and `shared_blks_read`.

How it works...

The `ANALYZE` command updates statistics about data size and data distribution in all tables. If a table size has changed significantly without its statistics being updated, then PostgreSQL's statistics-based optimizer may choose a bad plan. Manually running the `ANALYZE` command updates the statistics for all tables.

There's more...

There are a few other common problems.

Do the queries return significantly more data than they did earlier?

If you've initially tested your queries on almost empty tables, it is entirely possible that you are querying much more data than you need.

As an example, if you select all users' items and then show the first 10 items, this query runs very fast when the user has 10 or even 50 items, but not so well when they have 50,000.

Ensure that you don't ask for more data than you need. Use the `LIMIT` clause to return less data to your application (and to give the optimizer at least a chance to select a plan that processes less data when selecting and it may also have a lower startup cost). In some cases, you can evaluate the use of cursors for your applications.

Do the queries also run slowly when they are run alone?

If you can, then try to run the same slow query when the database has no (or very few) other queries running concurrently. If it runs well in this situation, then it may be that the database host is just overloaded (CPU, memory, or disk I/O) or other applications are interfering with Postgres on the same server. Consequently, a plan that works well under a light load is not so good any more. It may even be that this is not a very good query plan with which to begin, and you were fooled by modern computers being really fast:

```
db=# select count(*) from t;
  count
---------
 1000000
(1 row)
Time: 329.743 ms
```

As you can see, scanning 1 million rows takes just 0.3 seconds on a laptop that is a few years old if these rows are already cached.

However, if you have a few of such queries running in parallel, and also other queries competing for memory, this query is likely to slow down an order of magnitude or two.

See *Chapter 10, Performance and Concurrency*, for general advice on performance tuning.

Is the second run of the same query also slow?

This test is related to the previous test, and it checks whether the slowdown is caused by some of the necessary data not fitting into the memory or being pushed out of the memory by other queries.

If the second run of the query is fast, then you are probably facing a problem of not enough memory. Again, see *Chapter 10, Performance and Concurrency*, for the details about this.

Table and index bloat

A table bloat is something that can develop over time if some maintenance processes can't be run properly. In other words, due to the way **Multiversion Concurrency Control** (**MVCC**) works, your table will contain a lot of older versions of rows, if these versions can't be removed in a timely manner.

There are several ways this can develop, but all involve lots of updates or deletes and inserts, while the autovacuum is prevented from doing its job of getting rid of old tuples. It is possible that even after the old versions are deleted, the table stays at its newly acquired large size, thanks to visible rows being located at the end of the table and preventing PostgreSQL from shrinking the file. There have been cases where a one-row table has grown to several gigabytes in size.

If you suspect that some tables may contain bloat, then run the following query:

```
SELECT pg_relation_size(relid) AS tablesize,schemaname,relname,n_live_tup
FROM pg_stat_user_tables
WHERE relname = <tablename>;
```

Then, see whether the relation of `tablesize` to `n_live_tup` makes sense.

For example, if the table size is tens of megabytes, and there are only a small number of rows, then you have bloat, and proper VACUUM strategies are necessary (as explained in *Chapter 9, Regular Maintenance*).

It is important to check that the statistics are up to date. You might indeed need to run ANALYSE on the table and run the query again.

See also

- The *Collecting daily usage statistics* section shows one way to collect info on table changes

- *Chapter 9, Regular Maintenance*

- *Chapter 10, Performance and Concurrency*

- The *How many rows in a table?* recipe in *Chapter 2, Exploring the Database*, for an introduction to MVCC

- The `auto_explain` contrib module at `http://www.postgresql.org/docs/current/static/auto-explain.html`

- The `pg_stat_plans` extension at `https://github.com/2ndQuadrant/pg_stat_plans`

Investigating and reporting a bug

When you find out that PostgreSQL is not doing what it should, then it's time to investigate.

Getting ready

It is a good idea to make a full copy of your PostgreSQL installation before you start investigating. This will help you restart several times and be sure that you are actually investigating the results of the bug, and not chasing your own tail by looking at changes introduced by your last investigation and debugging attempt.

Do not forget to include your tablespaces too in the full copy.

How to do it...

Try to make a minimal repeatable test scenario that exhibits this bug. Sometimes, the bug disappears while doing this, but mostly it is needed for making the process easy. It is almost impossible to fix a bug that you can't observe and repeat at will.

If it is about query processing, then you can usually provide a minimal dump file (the result of running `pg_dump`) of your database together with a SQL script that exhibits the error.

If you have corrupt data, then you may want to make a subset of the corrupted data files available for people who have knowledge and time to look at it. Sometimes, you can find such people on the PostgreSQL hackers' list, and sometimes, you have to hire someone or even fix it yourself. The more preparatory work you do yourself and the better you formulate your questions, the higher the chance you have of finding help quickly.

If you suspect a data corruption bug and feel adventurous, then you can read about the data formats at `http://www.postgresql.org/docs/current/static/storage.html`, and investigate your data tables using the `pageinspect` package from contrib.

When reporting a bug, always include at least the PostgreSQL version you are using and the operating system on which you are using it.

More detailed information on this process is available at the PostgreSQL Wiki. By following the official recommendations at `http://wiki.postgresql.org/wiki/Guide_to_reporting_problems` and `http://wiki.postgresql.org/wiki/SlowQueryQuestions`, you will have a higher chance of getting your questions answered.

How it works...

If everything works really well, then it goes like the following:

1. A user submits a well-researched bug report to the PostgreSQL hackers' list.
2. Some discussions follow on the list, and the user may be asked to provide some additional information.
3. Somebody finds out what is wrong and proposes a fix.
4. The fix is discussed on the hackers' list.
5. The bug is fixed. There is a patch for the current version, and the fix is sure to be included in the next version.
6. Sometimes, the fix is backported to older versions.

Unfortunately, any step may go wrong due to various reasons, such as nobody feeling that this is their area of expertise, the right people not having time and hoping for someone else to deal with it, and these other people not reading the list at the right moment.

If this happens, follow up your question in a day or two to try to understand why there was no reaction.

Producing a daily summary of log file errors

PostgreSQL can generate gigabytes of logs per day. Lots of data is good if you want to investigate some specific event, but it is not what you will use for daily monitoring of database health.

In this recipe, we'll see how to perform a post analysis of our log files and get reports (and insights) about what has happened in a given period of time.

PostgreSQL 9.2 enhances real-time analysis of queries through the `pg_stat_statements` extension, which will be covered in the next recipe.

Getting ready

Make sure that your PostgreSQL is set up to rotate the log files, for example, daily. I personally prefer to integrate PostgreSQL with `rsyslog` and `logrotate` for log management on Linux or Unix systems, but you can use any method that is allowed by PostgreSQL (CSV or standard error, for example).

A typical default setup will divert log messages to `stderr`, and you can set up log rotation directly in PostgreSQL through the `log_rotation_age` configuration option.

Once you have your logs ready, it is time to feed them to a PostgreSQL log-processing program. Here, we describe how to do it using **pgBadger**, a multiplatform application written in Perl that has recently become more popular than its famous predecessor, **pgFouine**.

Some of the cool features of pgBadger include: multifile processing, parallel processing, auto-detection of the input format, on-the-fly decompression, as well as very light HTML reports with Javascript-generated charts (that have zooming capabilities), as shown here:

Report of time-consuming queries with pgBadger

For most Linux systems, you should be able to use your default package manager to install pgBadger. Otherwise, you can simply download its sources.

Configure your PostgreSQL server to produce log files in a format that pgBadger understands. Everything is thoroughly described in the online documentation of pgBadger at `http://dalibo.github.io/pgbadger/`.

Suppose you are using syslog and you want to exclude queries that take less than a second to be executed. You can have a logging configuration of your PostgreSQL server similar to this:

```
log_destination = syslog
syslog_facility = LOCAL0
syslog_ident = 'postgres'
log_line_prefix = 'user=%u,db=%d,client=%h '
log_temp_files = 0
log_statement = ddl
log_min_duration_statement = 1000
log_min_messages = info
log_checkpoints = on
log_lock_waits = on
```

The documentation of pgBadger is a great source of information regarding the PostgreSQL configuration in terms of logging. You are advised to read that together with the *Error Reporting and Logging* section of the Postgres documentation available at `http://www.postgresql.org/docs/current/static/runtime-config-logging.html`.

How to do it...

Set up a cron job to run regularly (for example once every hour, day, or week) and let pgBadger analyze one or more log files. Here, you can find a very simple example that can be used to prepare daily reports every hour.

For the sake of simplicity, the script has been purged of any error check. Production usage requires the addition of some basic shell controls:

```
#!/bin/bash
outdir=/var/www/reports
begin=$(date +'%Y-%m-%d %H:00:00' -d '-1 day')
end=$(date +'%Y-%m-%d %H:00:00')
outfile="$outdir/daily-$(date +'%H').html"

pgbadger -q -b "$begin" -e "$end" -o "$outfile" \
   /var/log/postgres.log.1 /var/log/postgres.log
```

The preceding script informs pgBadger to analyze the current log file (`/var/log/postgresql.log`) and the previously rotated file (`/var/log/postgres.log.1`), limit the reporting activity to the last 24 hours (see how the `date` command was used to generate timestamps), and then write the output to the `$outfile` HTML file.

Once again, this is just a very simple use case for pgBadger. I strongly advise you to look at the documentation and investigate all the options and possibilities that pgBadger offers.

I want to end this recipe with a practical idea that you can explore with your system administrators. You might have noticed that the output directory has been set as a common default DocumentRoot for Apache servers (`/var/www`).

A very practical way to use pgBadger is to integrate it with a web server.

Production environments may benefit from SSL encryption, basic authentication, and the `mod_dir` module, which allows you to make your reports automatically available through the Internet (or your Intranet).

How it works...

PgBadger condenses and ranks error messages for easy viewing, and produces a nicely formatted report in HTML. From that report, you can find out the most frequent errors.

As a rule, it is good practice not to tolerate errors in database logs if you can avoid them. Once the errors start showing up in the log and report, you should find their cause and fix them.

While it is tempting to leave the errors there and consider them as just a small nuisance because *they do no harm*, simple errors are often an indication of other problems in the application. These problems, if not found and understood, may lead to all kinds of larger problems, such as security breaches or eventual data corruption at the logical level.

There's more...

If you have only a small number of errors in your log files, then it may be sufficient to run each log file through grep to find errors:

```
user@dbhost: $ egrep "FATAL|ERROR" /var/log/postgres.log
```

See also

- The home page of pgBadger, including documentation, is available at http://dalibo.github.io/pgbadger/.

Analyzing the real-time performance of your queries

This recipe is mainly for users of PostgreSQL 9.2 and above, and it is about the `pg_stat_statements` extension. Even though this extension is available in PostgreSQL 8.4, it lacks a crucial feature—**query normalization**.

The `pg_stat_statements` extension adds the capability to track execution statistics of queries that are run in a database, including the number of calls, total execution time, total number of returned rows, as well as internal information on memory and I/O access.

It is evident how this approach opens up new opportunities in PostgreSQL performance analysis—by allowing DBAs to get insights directly from the database, through SQL and in real time.

Getting ready

The `pg_stat_statements` module is available as a contrib module of PostgreSQL. The extension must be installed as a superuser in the desired databases. It also requires administrators to add the library in the `postgresql.conf` file, as follows:

```
shared_preload_libraries = 'pg_stat_statements'
```

This change requires restarting of the PostgreSQL server.

Finally, in order to use it, the extension must be installed in the desired database through the usual `CREATE EXTENSION` command (run as superuser):

```
gabriele=# CREATE EXTENSION pg_stat_statements;
CREATE EXTENSION
```

PostgreSQL 9.0 users should use the pre-extension method, that is, execute the `pg_stat_statements.sql` file contained in the `contrib` directory.

How to do it...

Connect to a database where you have installed the `pg_stat_statements` extension, preferably as a superuser.

You can start by retrieving the list of the most frequent queries:

```
SELECT query FROM pg_stat_statements ORDER BY calls DESC;
```

Alternatively, you can retrieve the queries with the highest average execution time:

```
SELECT query, total_time/calls AS avg, calls
       FROM pg_stat_statements ORDER BY 2 DESC;
```

These are just examples. I strongly recommend that you look at the PostgreSQL documentation at `http://www.postgresql.org/docs/current/static/pgstatstatements.html` for more detailed information on the structure of the `pg_stat_statements` view.

How it works...

Since the `pg_stat_statements` shared library has been loaded by the PostgreSQL server, Postgres starts collecting statistics for every database in the instance.

The extension simply installs the `pg_stat_statements` view and the `pg_stat_statements_reset()` function in the current database, allowing the DBA to inspect the available statistics.

By default, read access to the `pg_stat_statements` view is granted to every user who can access the database (even though standard users are allowed to see only the SQL statements of their queries).

The `pg_stat_statements_reset()` function can be used to discard the statistics collected by the server up to that moment, and set all the counters to 0. It requires a superuser to be run.

There's more...

As mentioned before, a very important feature that has been added with PostgreSQL 9.2 is the normalization of queries that can be planned (SELECT, INSERT, DELETE, and UPDATE). You might have indeed noticed some ? characters in the `query` field returned by the queries outlined in the previous section. The normalization process intercepts constants in SQL statements run by users and substitutes them with a placeholder (identified by a question mark).

Consider the following queries:

```
SELECT * FROM bands WHERE name = 'AC/DC';
SELECT * FROM bands WHERE name = 'Lynyrd Skynyrd';
```

After the normalization process, these two queries appear as one in `pg_stat_statements`:

```
gabriele=# SELECT query, calls FROM pg_stat_statements;
                 query                    | calls
------------------------------------------+-------
 SELECT * FROM bands WHERE name = ?;      |    2
… <snip> …
```

This is the expected behavior, isn't it?

The extension comes with a few configuration options, such as the maximum number of queries to be tracked.

9

Regular Maintenance

In this chapter, we will cover the following recipes:

- ▸ Controlling automatic database maintenance
- ▸ Avoiding auto-freezing and page corruptions
- ▸ Avoiding transaction wraparound
- ▸ Removing old prepared transactions
- ▸ Actions for heavy users of temporary tables
- ▸ Identifying and fixing bloated tables and indexes
- ▸ Maintaining indexes
- ▸ Adding a constraint without checking existing rows
- ▸ Finding unused indexes
- ▸ Carefully removing unwanted indexes
- ▸ Planning maintenance

Introduction

PostgreSQL prefers regular maintenance, and there is a recipe discussing planning maintenance (the last one).

We recognize that you're here for a reason and are looking for a quick solution to your needs. You're probably thinking, "fix me first, and I'll plan later." So off we go!

PostgreSQL provides a utility command named VACUUM, which is a jokey name for a garbage collector that sweeps up all the bad things and fixes them—or at least, most of them. That's the single most important thing you need to remember to do—I say "single" because closely connected to that is the ANALYZE command, which collects optimizer statistics. It's possible to run VACUUM and ANALYZE as a single joint command, VACUUM ANALYZE, and those actions are automatically executed for you when appropriate by autovacuum, a special background process that forms part of the PostgreSQL server.

VACUUM performs a range of cleanup activities, some of them too complex to describe without a whole sideline into their internals. VACUUM has been heavily optimized over a 10-year period to take the minimum required lock levels on tables and execute in the most efficient manner possible, skipping all the unnecessary work and using L2 cache CPU optimizations when work is required.

Many experienced PostgreSQL DBAs will prefer to execute their own VACUUM commands, though autovacuum now provides a fine degree of control, and that can save much of your time by enabling and controlling it. Using both manual and automatic vacuuming gives you both control and a safety net.

Controlling automatic database maintenance

Autovacuum is enabled by default in PostgreSQL 9.4, and mostly does a great job of maintaining your PostgreSQL database. We say "mostly" because it doesn't know everything you do about the database, such as the best time to perform maintenance actions.

Getting ready

Exercising control requires some thinking about what you actually want:

- Which are the best times of day to do things? When are system resources more available?
- Which days are quiet, and which are not?
- Which tables are critical to the application, and which are not?

How to do it...

The first thing to do is to make sure that autovacuum is switched on. You must have both of the following parameters enabled in your `postgresql.conf` file:

```
autovacuum = on
track_counts = on
```

PostgreSQL controls autovacuum with 42 individually tunable parameters. That provides a wide range of options, though it can be a little daunting.

The following are the parameters that can be set in `postgresql.conf`:

```
autovacuum
autovacuum_analyze_scale_factor
autovacuum_analyze_threshold
autovacuum_freeze_max_age
autovacuum_max_workers
autovacuum_naptime
autovacuum_vacuum_cost_delay
autovacuum_vacuum_cost_limit
autovacuum_vacuum_scale_factor
autovacuum_vacuum_threshold
vacuum_cost_page_dirty
vacuum_cost_page_hit
vacuum_cost_page_miss
autovacuum_work_mem
log_autovacuum_min_duration
vacuum_multixact_freeze_min_age
autovacuum_multixact_freeze_max_age
vacuum_multixact_freeze_table_age
```

Individual tables can be controlled by storage parameters, which are set using the following command:

`ALTER TABLE mytable SET (storage_parameter = value);`

The storage parameters that relate to maintenance are as follows:

```
autovacuum_enabled
autovacuum_vacuum_cost_delay
autovacuum_vacuum_cost_limit
autovacuum_vacuum_scale_factor
autovacuum_vacuum_threshold
autovacuum_freeze_min_age
autovacuum_freeze_max_age
autovacuum_freeze_table_age
autovacuum_multixact_freeze_min_age
autovacuum_multixact_freeze_max_age
autovacuum_multixact_freeze_table_age
autovacuum_analyze_scale_factor
autovacuum_analyze_threshold
```

The TOAST tables can be controlled with the following parameters:

```
toast.autovacuum_enabled
toast.autovacuum_vacuum_cost_delay
toast.autovacuum_vacuum_cost_limit
toast.autovacuum_vacuum_scale_factor
toast.autovacuum_vacuum_threshold
toast.autovacuum_freeze_min_age
toast.autovacuum_freeze_max_age
toast.autovacuum_freeze_table_age
toast.autovacuum_multixact_freeze_min_age
toast.autovacuum_multixact_freeze_max_age
toast.autovacuum_multixact_freeze_table_age
```

How it works...

If autovacuum is set, then it will wake up every `autovacuum_naptime` second, and decide whether to run VACUUM, ANALYZE, or both.

There will never be more than `autovacuum_max_workers` maintenance processes running at any time. As these autovacuum slaves perform I/O, they accumulate cost points until they hit the `autovacuum_vacuum_cost_limit` value, after which they sleep for an `autovacuum_vacuum_cost_delay` period of time. This is designed to throttle the resource utilization of autovacuum to prevent it from using all of the available disk performance, which it should never do. So, increasing `autovacuum_vacuum_cost_delay` will slow down each VACUUM to reduce the impact on user activity. Autovacuum will run ANALYZE when there have been at least `autovacuum_analyze_threshold` changes and a fraction of the table defined by `autovacuum_analyze_scale_factor` has been inserted, updated, or deleted.

Autovacuum will run VACUUM when there have been at least `autovacuum_vacuum_threshold` changes, and a fraction of the table defined by `autovacuum_vacuum_scale_factor` has been updated or deleted.

If you set `log_autovacuum_min_duration`, then any autovacuum process that runs for longer than this value will be logged to the server log, like the following:

```
2010-04-29 01:33:55 BST (13130) LOG:  automatic vacuum of table
"postgres.public.pgbench_accounts": index scans: 1
      pages: 0 removed, 3279 remain
      tuples: 100000 removed, 100000 remain
      system usage: CPU 0.19s/0.36u sec elapsed 19.01 sec
2010-04-29 01:33:59 BST (13130) LOG:  automatic analyze of table
"postgres.public.pgbench_accounts"
      system usage: CPU 0.06s/0.18u sec elapsed 3.66 sec
```

Most of the preceding global parameters can also be set at the table level. For example, if you think that you don't want a table to be autovacuumed, then you can set this:

```
ALTER TABLE big_table SET (autovacuum_enabled = off);
```

It's also possible to set parameters for TOAST tables. A TOAST table is the location where oversize column values get placed, which the documents refer to as "supplementary storage tables." If there are no oversize values, then the TOAST table will occupy little space. Tables with very wide values often have large TOAST tables. TOAST (short for **the oversize attribute storage technique**) is optimized for UPDATE. If you have a heavily updated table, the TOAST table is untouched, so it may make sense to turn off autovacuuming of the TOAST table, as follows:

```
ALTER TABLE pgbench_accounts
SET ( toast.autovacuum_enabled = off);
```

This will turn off autovacuuming of the TOAST table.

 Note that autovacuuming of the TOAST table is performed completely separately from the main table, even though you can't ask for an explicit include or exclude of the TOAST table yourself when running VACUUM.

Use the following query to display the reloptions for tables and their TOAST tables:

```
postgres=# SELECT n.nspname, c.relname,
                pg_catalog.array_to_string(c.reloptions || array(
                select 'toast.' ||
                x from pg_catalog.unnest(tc.reloptions) x),', ')
                as relopts
FROM pg_catalog.pg_class c
LEFT JOIN
 pg_catalog.pg_class tc ON (c.reltoastrelid = tc.oid)
JOIN
 pg_namespace n ON c.relnamespace = n.oid
WHERE c.relkind = 'r'
AND nspname NOT IN ('pg_catalog', 'information_schema');
```

This query gives the following output:

```
nspname  |     relname      |     relopts
---------+------------------+------------------------------
```

```
public   | pgbench_accounts | fillfactor=100,
                              autovacuum_enabled=on,
                              autovacuum_vacuum_cost_delay=20
public   | pgbench_tellers  | fillfactor=100
public   | pgbench_branches | fillfactor=100
public   | pgbench_history  |
public   | text_archive     | toast.autovacuum_enabled=off
```

VACUUM allows insertions, updates, and deletions while it runs, but it prevents actions such as ALTER TABLE and CREATE INDEX. Autovacuum can detect if a user has requested a conflicting lock on the table while it runs, and it will cancel itself if it is getting in the user's way.

Note that VACUUM does not shrink a table when it runs, unless there is a large run of space at the end of a table, and nobody is accessing the table when we try to shrink it. To shrink a table properly, you'll need VACUUM FULL, but it locks up the whole table for a long time and should be avoided if possible. The VACUUM FULL command will literally rewrite every row of the table and completely rebuild all indexes. This process is faster than it used to be, though it's still a long time for larger tables.

There's more...

The postgresql.conf file also allows include directives, which look like the following:

```
include 'autovacuum.conf'
```

These specify another file that will be read at that point, just as if those parameters had been included in the main file.

This can be used to maintain multiple sets of files for the autovacuum configuration. Let's say we have a website that is busy mainly during the daytime, with some occasional night-time use. We decide to have two profiles: one for daytime, when we want less aggressive autovacuuming, and another at night, where we can allow more aggressive vacuuming:

1. We add the following lines to postgresql.conf:

```
autovacuum = on
autovacuum_max_workers = 3
include 'autovacuum.conf'
```

We remove all other autovacuum parameters.

2. We then create a file named `autovacuum.conf.day`, containing the following parameters:

```
autovacuum_analyze_scale_factor = 0.1
autovacuum_analyze_threshold = 50
autovacuum_vacuum_cost_delay = 30
autovacuum_vacuum_cost_limit = -1
autovacuum_vacuum_scale_factor = 0.2
autovacuum_vacuum_threshold = 50
```

Then, we create another file, named `autovacuum.conf.night`, that contains the following parameters:

```
autovacuum_analyze_scale_factor = 0.05
autovacuum_analyze_threshold = 50
autovacuum_vacuum_cost_delay = 10
autovacuum_vacuum_cost_limit = -1
autovacuum_vacuum_scale_factor = 0.1
autovacuum_vacuum_threshold = 50
```

3. To swap profiles, we simply do this:

```
$ ln -sf autovacuum.conf.night autovacuum.conf
$ pg_ctl -D datadir reload
```

The latter is the command to reload the server configuration, and it must be customized depending on your platform.

This then allows us to switch profiles twice per day without needing to edit the configuration files. You can also tell easily which is the active profile simply by looking at the full details of the linked file (using `ls -l`). The exact details of the schedule are up to you. "Night and day" was just an example, which is unlikely to suit everybody.

See also

- The `autovacuum_freeze_max_age` parameter is explained in the next recipe, *Avoiding auto-freezing and page corruptions*, as are the more complex table-level parameters.

Avoiding auto-freezing and page corruptions

There are some aspects of VACUUM whose reason to exist is complex to explain, and occasionally they have negative behavior. Let's look more deeply at those and find some solutions.

Getting ready

PostgreSQL performs regular sweeps to clean out old transaction identifiers, which is known as "freezing". It does this to defer transaction wraparound, which is discussed in more detail in the next recipe.

There are two routes that a row can take in PostgreSQL: a row version dies and needs to be removed by VACUUM, or a row version gets old enough and needs to be frozen, which is also performed by the VACUUM process.

Why do we care? Say, we load a table with 100 million rows, and everything is fine. When those rows have been there long enough to begin being frozen, the next VACUUM operation on that table will rewrite all of them to freeze their transaction identifiers. Put that another way, autovacuum will wake up and start using lots of I/O to perform the freezing.

How to do it...

The most obvious way to forestall that exact problem is to explicitly vacuum a table after a major load. Of course, that doesn't remove the problem entirely, and you might not have time for that.

Many people's knee-jerk reaction is to turn off autovacuum because it keeps waking up at the most inconvenient times. My way is described in the *Controlling automatic database maintenance* recipe.

Freezing takes place when a transaction identifier on a row becomes more than vacuum_freeze_min_age transactions older than the current next value. Normal VACUUM operations will perform a small amount of freezing as you go, and in most cases you won't notice that at all. As explained in the earlier example, large transactions leave many rows with the same transaction identifiers, so those might cause problems at freezing time.

The VACUUM command is normally optimized to look only at chunks of a table that require cleaning. When a table reaches vacuum_freeze_table_age, we ignore that optimization and scan the whole table. While it does so, it's fairly likely to see rows that need freezing, which need to be rewritten. So, that is what causes the great increase in I/O.

If you fiddle with those parameters to try to forestall heavy VACUUM operations, then you'll notice that the autovacuum_freeze_max_age parameter controls when the table will be scanned by a forced VACUUM command. To put that another way, you can't turn off the need to freeze rows, but you can get to choose when this happens. My advice is to control autovacuum as described in the previous recipe, or perform explicit VACUUM operations at a time of your choosing.

The VACUUM command is also an efficient way to confirm the absence of page corruptions, so it is worth scanning the whole database block by block from time to time. To do this, you can run the following script on each of your databases:

```
SET vacuum_freeze_table_age = 0;

VACUUM;
```

You can do this table by table as well. There's nothing special about whole database VACUUM operations anymore; in earlier versions of PostgreSQL this was important, so you may read in random places on the web that this is a good idea.

If you've never had a corrupt block, then you may only need to scan every two to three months. If you start to get corrupt blocks, then you may want to increase the scan rate to confirm everything is OK. Corrupt blocks are usually hardware induced, though they show up as database errors. It's possible but rare that the corruption was from a PostgreSQL bug instead.

There's no easy way to fix page corruptions at present. There are, however, ways to investigate and extract data from corrupt blocks, for example, using the pageinspect contrib utility that Simon wrote.

There's more...

In PostgreSQL version 9.4 and later, the COPY command has the interesting FREEZE option, which essentially loads the tuples as "already frozen" so that they won't require any additional freezing. This is a significant saving, especially if the said rows are not going to be updated.

You may ask, "if it's that good, why not make it the default behavior?" The reason is that a frozen tuple is visible to all sessions, even before commit, which means that COPY FREEZE does not respect transactional behavior. For instance, if another session queries the table while it is being loaded, that session will see the already loaded rows, contrarily to what happens with the standard COPY command or with other SQL commands such as INSERT.

Transactions exist because of a reason, and doing without them can create problems and complicate the understanding of how a query works. However, in the special case of bulk data being loaded from an external file, it could be that such problems are under control, for instance, if you are able to prevent or avoid accessing that table until all data has been loaded, and you know that existing sessions are not actually using that table.

Avoiding transaction wraparound

To many users, transaction wraparound sounds like a disease from space. Mentioning transaction wraparound usually earns the speaker points for technical merit. Let's take a look at it and how to avoid it.

Getting ready

First of all, have you ever seen this message?

```
WARNING: database "postgres" must be vacuumed within XXX transactions.
HINT: To avoid a database shutdown, execute a database-wide VACUUM in that database.
You might also need to commit or roll back old prepared transactions.
```

Even worse is the following message:

```
ERROR: database is not accepting commands to avoid wraparound data loss in database "template0"
HINT:  Stop the postmaster and use a standalone backend to vacuum that database.
You might also need to commit or roll back old prepared transactions.
```

If not, then you don't need to do anything apart from normal planned maintenance. These messages are reported to users, and they are also written to the server log.

How to do it...

If you have a support provider, now is a good time to call them. Don't panic, But technical bravado can land you in worse situations than that in which you already are. Let's continue to describe how to get out of this:

1. If you've received the warning described earlier, then follow both hints. First, let's perform the suggested VACUUM operation on the appropriate database. It might not be postgres, so replace the appropriate database name.

    One option is to run this:

    ```
    $ vacuumdb postgres
    ```

    Alternatively, you can use the following:

    ```
    psql -c "VACUUM" postgres
    ```

Other than these, you can use your admin tool to initiate a VACUUM operation on the appropriate database.

2. Next, find and follow the *Removing old prepared transactions* recipe.

How it works...

PostgreSQL uses internal transaction identifiers that are 4 bytes long, so we only have 2^32 transaction IDs (about 4 billion). PostgreSQL wraps around and starts again from the beginning when that wraps around, allocating new identifiers in a circular manner. The reason we do this is that moving to an 8-byte identifier has various other negative effects and costs that we would rather not pay, so we keep the 4-byte transaction identifier, which also has costs.

PostgreSQL is designed to continue using IDs even after the system wraps around. If properly maintained, everything will keep working forever, and you'll never notice what happens on the inside. To allow that to happen, we need to run regular VACUUM operations.

There's more...

If you received the aforementioned error and the database is no longer accepting commands, you're probably wondering what the phrase use a standalone backend to vacuum that database means.

A "standalone backend" means running the database server from just a single executable process. This is the equivalent of *nix run-level 1, also known as single-user mode. We restrict access to the database to just a single user.

The command to do this is the following. Note that --single must be the very first command on the command line:

```
$ postgres --single -D  /full/path/to/datadir postgres
```

This command assumes that postgresql.conf is in the data directory; this is the default in most cases, but has been changed in Debian and Ubuntu, as mentioned in the *Locating the database server files* recipe in *Chapter 2, Exploring the Database*, so that you need to issue a command like the following in order for the configuration file to be found:

```
$ /usr/lib/postgresql/9.4/bin/postgres --single -D ~postgres/9.4/main -c
config_file=/etc/postgresql/9.4/main/postgresql.conf postgres
```

You don't need to worry about pg_hba.conf in this special mode.

The expected outcome is the following command-line prompt:

```
PostgreSQL stand-alone backend 9.4
backend>
```

You can then run the `VACUUM` command from there, as follows:

```
PostgreSQL stand-alone backend 9.4
backend> VACUUM
backend>
```

When you're finished, type *Ctrl + D* (or whatever you have set EOF to be for your terminal window) to exit.

 Note the absence of the semicolon. The standalone backend does not use psql, and statements are separated by new lines. This is inconvenient, except for short statements. You can add the `-j` option to change the separator to EOF, in which case you'll need two consecutive EOFs to exit the standalone backend.

You should also check for old prepared transactions, as described in the *Removing old prepared transactions* recipe.

See also

The *Avoiding auto-freezing and page corruptions* recipe may also be relevant, or at least be an interesting read in a related area.

Removing old prepared transactions

You may have been routed here from other recipes, so you might not even know what prepared transactions are, let alone what an old prepared transaction looks like.

The good news is that prepared transactions don't just happen; they happen in certain specific situations. If you don't know what I'm talking about, it's OK! You won't need to, and better still, you probably don't have any prepared transactions either.

Prepared transactions are part of the two-phase commit feature, also known as **2PC**. A transaction commits in two stages rather than one, allowing multiple databases to have synchronized commits. Its typical use is to combine multiple so-called resource managers using the **XA** protocol, usually provided by a **Transaction Manager** (**TM**), as used by the **Java Transaction API** (**JTA**) and others. If none of this meant anything to you, then you probably don't have any prepared transactions.

Getting ready

First, check the setting of `max_prepared_transactions`. If this is zero, then you don't have any pre-existing prepared transactions, and you can safely skip this recipe:

```
SHOW max_prepared_transactions;
```

If your setting is more than zero, then check whether you have any prepared transactions. As an example, you may find something like the following:

```
postgres=# SELECT * FROM pg_prepared_xacts;
-[ RECORD 1 ]-----------------------------
transaction | 121083
gid         | prep1
prepared    | 2010-03-28 15:47:57.637868+01
owner       | postgres
database    | postgres
```

Here, the `gid` (global identifier) will usually have been automatically generated.

How to do it...

Removing a prepared transaction is also referred to as "resolving in-doubt transactions". The transaction is literally stuck between committing and aborting. The database or transaction manager may have crashed, leaving the transaction midway through the two-phase commit process.

If you have a connection pool of 100 active connections and something crashes, you'll probably find 1 to 20 transactions stuck in the prepared state, depending on how long your average transaction is.

To resolve the transaction, we need to decide whether we want that change or not. The best way is to check what happened externally to PostgreSQL. That should help you decide.

If you do need further help, look at the *There's more...* section.

If you wish to commit the changes, then use this command:

```
COMMIT PREPARED 'prep1';
```

If you want to rollback the changes, then use the following command:

```
ROLLBACK PREPARED 'prep1';
```

How it works...

Prepared transactions are persistent across crashes, so you can't just do a fast restart to get rid of them. They have both an internal transaction identifier and an external "global identifier". Either of these can be used to locate locked resources and decide how to resolve the transactions.

There's more...

If you're not sure what the prepared transaction actually did, you can go and look, though that is time consuming. The `pg_locks` view shows locks that are held by prepared transactions. You can get a full report of what is being locked using the following query:

```
postgres=# SELECT l.locktype, x.database, l.relation, l.page,
                   l.tuple,l.classid, l.objid, l.objsubid,
                   l.mode, x.transaction, x.gid, x.prepared,
                   x.owner
             FROM pg_locks l JOIN pg_prepared_xacts x
             ON l.virtualtransaction = '-1/' ||
                   x.transaction::text;
```

The documents mention that you can join `pg_locks` to `pg_prepared_xacts`, but they don't mention that if you join directly on the transaction ID, all it tells you is that there is a transaction lock, unless there are some row-level locks. The table locks are listed as being held by a virtual transaction. A simpler query is the following:

```
postgres=# SELECT DISTINCT x.database, l.relation
             FROM pg_locks l JOIN pg_prepared_xacts x
             ON l.virtualtransaction = '-1/' ||
                x.transaction::text
             WHERE l.locktype != 'transactionid';
 database | relation
----------+----------
 postgres |    16390
 postgres |    16401
(2 rows)
```

This tells you which relations in which databases have been touched by the remaining prepared transactions. We can't tell the names because we'd need to connect to those databases to check.

Finally, we can inspect which rows have been changed by the transaction. We will use `xmin`, which is a hidden column in each table. For more details on that, refer to the *Identifying and fixing bloated tables and indexes* recipe in this chapter.

You can then fully scan each of those tables, looking for changes like the following:

```
SELECT * FROM table WHERE xmax = 121083;
```

This query will show you all the rows in that table that will be deleted or updated by transaction `121083`, taken from the transaction column of `pg_prepared_xacts`.

 Not all rows touched by the transaction can be displayed, however. Newly inserted rows and new versions of updated rows will not be accessible in this way, for the very good reason that they must be invisible before the transaction is committed.

As you might expect, the PostgreSQL developers did their homework properly. Say that you have some prepared transactions and you change `max_prepared_transactions` to zero, which requires a restart to come into effect. No prepared transaction will sneak into your database unnoticed. When starting, PostgreSQL will try to recover every prepared transaction, and refuse to start unless `max_prepared_transactions` is large enough.

Actions for heavy users of temporary tables

If you are a heavy user of temporary tables in your applications, then there are some additional actions you may need to perform.

How to do it...

There are four main things to check, which are as follows:

- Make sure you run `VACUUM` on system tables, or enable autovacuum to do this for you.
- Monitor running queries to see how many temporary files are active and how large they are.

- ▶ Tune the memory parameters. Think about increasing the `temp_buffers` parameter, but be careful not to overallocate memory by doing so.

- ▶ Separate the temp table's I/O. In a query-intensive system, you may find that reads/writes to temporary files exceed reads/writes on permanent data tables and indexes. In this case, you should create new tablespace(s) on separate disks, and ensure that the `temp_tablespaces` parameter is configured to use the additional tablespace (s).

How it works...

In PostgreSQL 9.4, when we create a temporary table, we insert entries into the `pg_class`, `pg_type`, and `pg_attribute` catalog tables. These catalog tables and their indexes begin to grow and bloat—an issue covered in later recipes. To control that growth, you can either vacuum those tables manually, or set `autovacuum = on` in `postgresql.conf`. You cannot run `ALTER TABLE` against system tables, so it is not possible to set specific autovacuum settings for any of these tables.

If you vacuum the system catalog tables manually, make sure you get all of the system tables. You can get the full list of tables to vacuum and a list of their indexes using the following query:

```
postgres=# SELECT relname, pg_relation_size(oid)
              FROM pg_class
              WHERE relkind in ('i','r') and relnamespace = 11
              ORDER BY 2 DESC;
```

This results in the following output:

```
             relname             | pg_relation_size
---------------------------------+------------------
 pg_proc                         |           450560
 pg_depend                       |           344064
 pg_attribute                    |           286720
 pg_depend_depender_index        |           204800
 pg_depend_reference_index       |           204800
 pg_proc_proname_args_nsp_index  |           180224
 pg_description                  |           172032
 pg_attribute_relid_attnam_index |           114688
 pg_operator                     |           106496
```

```
pg_statistic                      |          106496

pg_description_o_c_o_index        |           98304

pg_attribute_relid_attnum_index   |           81920

pg_proc_oid_index                 |           73728

pg_rewrite                        |           73728

pg_class                          |           57344

pg_type                           |           57344

pg_class_relname_nsp_index        |           40960
```
...(partial listing)

The preceding values are for a newly created database. These tables can get very large if not properly maintained, with values of 11 GB for one index being witnessed at one unlucky installation.

Identifying and fixing bloated tables and indexes

PostgreSQL implements **Multiversion Concurrency Control** (**MVCC**), which allows users to read data at the same time as writers make changes. This is an important feature for concurrency in database applications, as it can allow the following:

- Better performance because of fewer locks
- Greatly reduced deadlocking
- Simplified application design and management

MVCC is a core part of PostgreSQL and cannot be turned off; nor would you really want it to be. The internals of MVCC have some implications for the DBA that need to be understood: each row represents a row version, and therefore it has two system columns—xmin and xmax—indicating the identifiers of the two transactions when the version was created and deleted respectively. The value of xmax is NULL if that version has not been deleted yet.

The general idea is that, instead of actually removing row versions, we alter their visibility by changing their xmin and/or xmax values. Precisely, when a row is inserted, its xmin value is set to the number of the creating transaction, while xmax is emptied; when a row is deleted, xmax is set to the number of the deleting transaction, without actually removing the row. An UPDATE operation is treated exactly like a DELETE followed by an INSERT; the deleted row represents the older version, and the row inserted is the newer version. Finally, when rolling back a transaction, all its changes are made invisible by just marking that transaction ID as aborted.

In this way, we get faster DELETE, UPDATE, and ROLLBACK statements, but the price of these benefits is that the SQL UPDATE command can cause tables and indexes to grow in size because they leave behind dead row versions. The DELETE and aborted INSERT statements take up space, which must be reclaimed by garbage collection. VACUUM is the mechanism by which we reclaim space, though there is another internal feature named **Heap-only Tuples** (**HOT**), which does much of this work automatically for us.

Knowing this, many people become worried by, and spend much time trying to rid themselves of, dead row versions. Many users will be familiar with tools used to perform tasks such as defragmentation, shrinking, reorganization, and table optimization. These tasks are necessary, but you should not be unduly worried by the need for vacuuming in PostgreSQL. Many users execute VACUUM far too frequently, while at the same time complaining about the cost of doing so.

This recipe is all about understanding when you need to run VACUUM by estimating the amount of bloat in tables and indexes.

How to do it...

The best way to understand things is to look at things the same way that autovacuum does. Use the following query, derived by Greg Smith for his book *PostgreSQL 9.0 High Performance*, *Packt Publishing*. The calculations are derived directly from the autovacuum documentation:

```
CREATE OR REPLACE VIEW av_needed AS
SELECT *,
  n_dead_tup > av_threshold AS "av_needed",
  CASE WHEN reltuples > 0
    THEN round(100.0 * n_dead_tup / (reltuples))
    ELSE 0
    END AS pct_dead
FROM
(SELECT
  N.nspname, C.relname,
  pg_stat_get_tuples_inserted(C.oid) AS n_tup_ins,
  pg_stat_get_tuples_updated(C.oid) AS n_tup_upd,
  pg_stat_get_tuples_deleted(C.oid) AS n_tup_del,
  CASE WHEN pg_stat_get_tuples_updated(C.oid) > 0 THEN
  pg_stat_get_tuples_hot_updated(C.oid)::real /
```

```
  pg_stat_get_tuples_updated(C.oid) END AS HOT_update_ratio,
  pg_stat_get_live_tuples(C.oid) AS n_live_tup,
  pg_stat_get_dead_tuples(C.oid) AS n_dead_tup,
  C.reltuples AS reltuples,round(
    current_setting('autovacuum_vacuum_threshold')::integer
    +current_setting('autovacuum_vacuum_scale_factor')::numeric
    * C.reltuples)
    AS av_threshold,  date_trunc('minute',greatest(pg_stat_get_last_
vacuum_time(C.oid),pg_stat_get_last_autovacuum_time(C.oid))) AS last_
vacuum, date_trunc('minute',greatest(pg_stat_get_last_analyze_time(C.
oid),pg_stat_get_last_analyze_time(C.oid))) AS last_analyze
 FROM pg_class C LEFT JOIN
  pg_index I ON C.oid = I.indrelid
  LEFT JOIN pg_namespace N ON (N.oid = C.relnamespace)
  WHERE C.relkind IN ('r', 't')
    AND N.nspname NOT IN ('pg_catalog', 'information_schema') AND
    N.nspname !~ '^pg_toast'
) AS av
ORDER BY av_needed DESC,n_dead_tup DESC;
```

We can then use this to look at individual tables, as follows:

```
postgres=# \x
postgres=# SELECT * FROM av_needed
                  WHERE relname = 'public.pgbench_accounts';
```

Thus, we get this output:

```
-[ RECORD 1 ]----+------------------------
nspname          | public
relname          | pgbench_accounts
n_tup_ins        | 100001
n_tup_upd        | 117201
n_tup_del        | 1
hot_update_ratio | 0.123454578032611
n_live_tup       | 100000
n_dead_tup       | 0
reltuples        | 100000
av_threshold     | 20050
```

```
last_vacuum        | 2010-04-29 01:33:00+01
last_analyze       | 2010-04-28 15:21:00+01
av_needed          | f
pct_dead           | 0
```

How it works...

We can compare the number of dead row versions, shown as `n_dead_tup` against the required threshold, `av_threshold`.

The preceding query doesn't take into account table-specific autovacuum thresholds. It could do so if you really need it, but the main purpose of the query is to give us information to understand what is happening, and then set the parameters accordingly—not the other way around.

Notice that the table query shows insertions, updates and deletions, so you can understand your workload better. There is also something named the `hot_update_ratio`. This shows the fraction of updates that take advantage of the HOT feature, which allows a table to self-vacuum as the table changes. If that ratio is high, then you may avoid VACUUM activities altogether or at least for long periods. If the ratio is low, then you will need to execute VACUUM commands or autovacuums more frequently. Note that the ratio never reaches 1.0, so if you have it above 0.95, then that is very good and you need not think about it further.

HOT updates take place when the UPDATE statement does not change any of the column values that are indexed by any index, and there is enough free space in the disk page where the updated row is located. If you change even one column that is indexed by just one index, then it will be a non-HOT update, and there will be a performance hit. So, careful selection of indexes can improve update performance and reduce the need for maintenance. Also, if HOT updates do occur, though not often enough for your liking, you might want to try to decrease the `fillfactor` storage parameter for the table to make more space for them. Remember that this will be important only on your most active tables. Seldom touched tables don't need much tuning.

To recap, non-HOT updates cause indexes to bloat. The following query is useful in investigating the index size and how it changes over time. It runs fairly quickly, and can be used to monitor whether your indexes are changing in size over time:

```
SELECT
    nspname,relname,
    round(100 * pg_relation_size(indexrelid) /
```

```
              pg_relation_size(indrelid)) / 100
           AS index_ratio,
     pg_size_pretty(pg_relation_size(indexrelid))
           AS index_size,
     pg_size_pretty(pg_relation_size(indrelid))
           AS table_size
FROM pg_index I
LEFT JOIN pg_class C ON (C.oid = I.indexrelid)
LEFT JOIN pg_namespace N ON (N.oid = C.relnamespace)
WHERE
  nspname NOT IN ('pg_catalog', 'information_schema', 'pg_toast') AND
  C.relkind='i' AND
  pg_relation_size(indrelid) > 0;
```

Another route is to use the `pgstattuple` contrib module. This provides overkill statistics about what's happening in your tables and indexes, which it derives by scanning the whole table or index and literally counting everything. It's very good, and I am not dismissing it; just use it carefully. If you have time to scan the table, you may as well vacuum the whole table anyway.

You can scan tables using `pgstattuple()`, as follows:

```
test=> SELECT * FROM pgstattuple('pg_catalog.pg_proc');
```

The output will look like the following:

```
-[ RECORD 1 ]------+-------
table_len          | 458752
tuple_count        | 1470
tuple_len          | 438896
tuple_percent      | 95.67
dead_tuple_count   | 11
dead_tuple_len     | 3157
dead_tuple_percent | 0.69
free_space         | 8932
free_percent       | 1.95
```

You can also scan indexes using `pgstatindex()`, as follows:

```
postgres=> SELECT * FROM pgstatindex('pg_cast_oid_index');
-[ RECORD 1 ]------+------
version            | 2
tree_level         | 0
index_size         | 8192
root_block_no      | 1
internal_pages     | 0
leaf_pages         | 1
empty_pages        | 0
deleted_pages      | 0
avg_leaf_density   | 50.27
leaf_fragmentation | 0
```

There's more...

You may want this as a Nagios plugin.

Look at `check_postgres_bloat`, which is a part of the `check_postgres` plugins. That provides some flexible options to assess bloat. Unfortunately, it's not that well documented, but if you've read this, it should make sense. You'll need to play with it to get the thresholding correct anyway, so that shouldn't be a problem.

Note also that the only way to know for certain the exact bloat of a table or index is to scan the whole relation. Anything else is just an estimate, and might lead to you running maintenance either too early or too late.

Maintaining indexes

Indexes can become a problem in many database applications that involve a high proportion of INSERT/DELETE commands. Just as tables can become bloated, so can indexes.

In the previous recipe, you saw that non-HOT updates can cause bloated indexes. Non-primary-key indexes are also prone to some bloat from normal INSERT commands, as is common in most relational databases.

Autovacuum does not detect bloated indexes, nor does it do anything to rebuild indexes. So, we need to look at other ways to maintain indexes.

Getting ready

PostgreSQL supports commands that will rebuild indexes for you. The client utility, reindexdb, allows you to execute the REINDEX command in a convenient way from the operating system:

```
$ reindexdb
```

This executes the SQL REINDEX command on every table in the default database. If you want to reindex all databases, then use the following:

```
$ reindexdb -a
```

That's what the manual says anyway. My experience is that most indexes don't need rebuilding, and even if they do, REINDEX puts a full-table lock (AccessExclusiveLock) on the table while it runs. That locks your database for possibly hours, and I advise that you think about not doing that.

Try these steps instead:

1. First, let's create a test table with two indexes—a primary key and an additional index—as follows:

   ```
   DROP TABLE IF EXISTS test;
   CREATE TABLE test
   (id INTEGER PRIMARY KEY
   ,category TEXT
   , value TEXT);
   CREATE INDEX ON test (category);
   ```

2. Now, let's look at the internal identifier of the tables, oid, and the current file number (relfilenodes), as shown next:

   ```
   SELECT oid, relname, relfilenode
   FROM pg_class
   WHERE oid in (SELECT indexrelid
                 FROM pg_index
                 WHERE indrelid = 'test'::regclass);
     oid  |       relname       | relfilenode
   -------+---------------------+-------------
    16639 | test_pkey           |       16639
    16641 | test_category_idx   |       16641
   (2 rows)
   ```

How to do it...

PostgreSQL supports a command known as CREATE INDEX CONCURRENTLY, which builds an index without taking a full table lock. PostgreSQL also supports the ability to have two indexes, with different names, that have exactly the same definition. So, the trick is to build another index identical to the one you wish to rebuild, drop the old index, and then rename the new index to the same name as the old index. Et voilà, fresh index, and no locking! Let's see that in slow motion:

```
CREATE INDEX CONCURRENTLY new_index
ON test (category);

BEGIN;

DROP INDEX test_category_idx;

ALTER INDEX new_index RENAME TO test_category_idx;

COMMIT;
```

When we check our internal identifiers again, we get the following:

```
SELECT oid, relname, relfilenode
FROM pg_class
WHERE oid in (SELECT indexrelid
              FROM pg_index
              WHERE indrelid = 'test'::regclass);
  oid  |       relname       | relfilenode
-------+---------------------+-------------
 16639 | test_pkey           |       16639
 16642 | test_category_idx   |       16642
(2 rows)
```

So, we can see that `test_category_idx` is now a completely new index.

That seems pretty good, and works on primary keys too, provided that you are using version 9.1 or newer, albeit in a slightly complex way: you need to create a new index using UNIQUE and CONCURRENTLY, and then issue this to make it a primary key:

```
ALTER TABLE ... ADD PRIMARY KEY USING INDEX ...
```

This is not optimal yet, because a primary key could be the target of one or more foreign keys. In that case, we need to drop and recreate the foreign keys, which unfortunately has no CONCURRENTLY variant. The next recipe, *Adding a constraint without checking existing rows*, is a recommended reading.

On older versions, you can't add a primary index to a table concurrently, so we have another trick, slightly more complex than the previous one:

1. First, we create another index with the same definition as the primary key, as follows:

```
CREATE UNIQUE INDEX new_pkey ON test (id);
```

2. Then, we check the internal identifiers again, like this:

```
SELECT oid, relname, relfilenode
FROM pg_class
WHERE oid in (SELECT indexrelid
                FROM pg_index
                WHERE indrelid = 'test'::regclass);
   oid   |       relname      | relfilenode
---------+--------------------+-------------
  16639  | test_pkey          |       16639
  16642  | test_category_idx  |       16642
  16643  | new_pkey           |       16643
(3 rows)
```

3. Now, we're going to swap the two indexes so that all the primary key constraints stay active, and so do all of the foreign keys that depend on them. Thus, we need to swap the `relfilenode` values, as follows:

```
BEGIN;
LOCK TABLE test;
UPDATE pg_class SET relfilenode = 16643 WHERE oid = 16639;
UPDATE pg_class SET relfilenode = 16639 WHERE oid = 16643;
DROP INDEX new_pkey;
COMMIT;
```

We can confirm that this has succeeded using the following query:

```
SELECT oid, relname, relfilenode
FROM pg_class
WHERE oid in (SELECT indexrelid
                FROM pg_index
                WHERE indrelid = 'test'::regclass);
```

Here is the result of this query:

```
  oid  |      relname       | relfilenode
-------+--------------------+-------------
 16639 | test_pkey          |    16643
 16642 | test_category_idx  |    16642

 (2 rows)
```

Yes, that's right! We just updated the core internal catalog tables of PostgreSQL. So make a mistake here, and you're in a big world of hurt! Make sure your backups are nicely polished before doing this.

How it works...

The `CREATE INDEX CONCURRENTLY` statement allows `INSERT`, `UPDATE`, and `DELETE` commands while the index is being created. It cannot be executed inside another transaction, and only one index per table can be created concurrently at any time.

Swapping the indexes is easy and doesn't use any trickery.

Swapping the primary keys before version 9.1 used some knowledge about the internals. The indexes themselves don't know their numbers, so you can swap them without problems—as long as you swap the correct two indexes, and they really do have identical definitions. Be especially careful about creating the indexes in the same tablespace, as this will fail if they're in different tablespaces.

There's more...

If you are fairly new to database systems, you might think rebuilding indexes for performance is something that only PostgreSQL needs to do. Other DBMSes require this as well, they just maybe don't say so.

Indexes are designed for performance, and in all databases, deleting index entries causes contention and loss of performance. PostgreSQL does not remove index entries for a row when that row is deleted, so an index can be filled with dead entries. PostgreSQL does attempt to remove dead entries when a block becomes full, but that doesn't stop a small numbers of dead entries from accumulating in many data blocks.

See also

I'm writing this book right after PostgreSQL 9.4 has come out. No simple `REINDEX CONCURRENTLY` command has been added yet, but an implementation has already been discussed. While there are still some open issues, it's likely that we'll get it in the medium term.

Adding a constraint without checking existing rows

A table constraint is a guarantee that must be satisfied by all the rows in the table. Therefore, adding a constraint to a table is a two-phase procedure: first, the constraint is created, and then all the existing rows are checked. Both happen in the same transaction, and the table cannot be accessed in the meantime. The constraint becomes visible after the check, yielding perfect consistency—which is usually the desired behavior—at the expense of availability, which is not that great.

This recipe demonstrates another case—how to enforce a constraint on future transactions *only*, without checking existing rows. This may be desirable in some specific cases, such as the following two:

- Enabling the constraint on newer rows of a large table that cannot remain unavailable for a long time
- Enforcing the constraint on newer rows, while keeping older rows that are known to violate the constraint

The constraint is marked as NOT VALID to make it clear that it does not exclude violations, unlike ordinary constraints.

In the first of the two examples you just saw, it is possible to validate the constraint at a later time, for example, when allowed by the workload or business continuity requirements. All existing rows will be checked, and then the NOT VALID mark will be removed from the constraint. Conversely, in the other example, the constraint will never be validated, and its only purpose will be to prevent further violations by rejecting incompatible transactions.

> Note that this recipe requires a recent PostgreSQL version. The NOT VALID constraints were introduced in PostgreSQL 9.1 for foreign keys only, and extended to CHECK constraints in PostgreSQL 9.2.

Getting ready

We'll start this recipe by creating two tables with a few test rows:

```
gianni=# CREATE TABLE ft(fk int PRIMARY KEY, fs text);
CREATE TABLE
gianni=# CREATE TABLE pt(pk int, ps text);
```

```
CREATE TABLE
gianni=# INSERT INTO ft(fk,fs) VALUES (1,'one'), (2,'two');
INSERT 0 2
gianni=# INSERT INTO pt(pk,ps) VALUES (1,'I'), (2,'II'), (3,'III');
INSERT 0 3
```

How to do it...

We have inserted inconsistent data on purpose so that any attempt to check existing rows will be revealed by an error message.

If we attempt to create an ordinary foreign key, we get an error, since the number 3 does not appear in the ft table:

```
gianni=# ALTER TABLE pt ADD CONSTRAINT pc FOREIGN KEY (pk) REFERENCES
ft(fk);
ERROR:  insert or update on table "pt" violates foreign key constraint
"pc"
DETAIL:  Key (pk)=(3) is not present in table "ft".
```

However, the same constraint can be successfully created as NOT VALID:

```
gianni=# ALTER TABLE pt ADD CONSTRAINT pc FOREIGN KEY (pk) REFERENCES
ft(fk) NOT VALID;
ALTER TABLE
```

Note that the invalid state of the foreign key is mentioned by psql:

```
gianni=# \d pt
      Table "public.pt"
 Column |  Type   | Modifiers
--------+---------+-----------
 pk     | integer |
 ps     | text    |
Foreign-key constraints:
    "pc" FOREIGN KEY (pk) REFERENCES ft(fk) NOT VALID
```

The violation is detected when we try to transform the NOT VALID constraint into a valid one:

```
gianni=# ALTER TABLE pt VALIDATE CONSTRAINT pc;
ERROR:  insert or update on table "pt" violates foreign key constraint
"pc"
DETAIL:  Key (pk)=(3) is not present in table "ft".
```

Validation becomes possible after removing the inconsistency, and the foreign key is upgraded to an ordinary one:

```
gianni=# DELETE FROM pt WHERE pk = 3;
DELETE 1
gianni=# ALTER TABLE pt VALIDATE CONSTRAINT pc;
ALTER TABLE
gianni=# \d pt
      Table "public.pt"
 Column |  Type   | Modifiers
--------+---------+-----------
 pk     | integer |
 ps     | text    |
Foreign-key constraints:
    "pc" FOREIGN KEY (pk) REFERENCES ft(fk)
```

There's more...

The long-term plan is to increase the value of NOT VALID constraints by reducing the locking level required during validation. This would provide a fully concurrent version of ALTER TABLE ... ADD CONSTRAINT in the same spirit of existing high-availability commands such as CREATE INDEX CONCURRENTLY. This is a complex task, and it requires a significant amount of work. At the time of writing, PostgreSQL version 9.4 has already been released, and this feature is not available yet.

Finding unused indexes

Selecting the correct set of indexes for a workload is known to be a hard problem. It usually involves trial and error by developers and DBAs to get a good mix of indexes.

Tools for identifying slow queries exist, and many `SELECT` statements can be improved by the addition of an index.

What many people forget is to check whether the mix of indexes remains valuable over time, which is something for the DBA to investigate and optimize.

How to do it...

PostgreSQL keeps track of each access against an index. We can view that information and use it to see whether an index is unused, as follows:

```
postgres=# SELECT schemaname, relname, indexrelname, idx_scan FROM pg_
stat_user_indexes ORDER BY idx_scan;
 schemaname |         indexrelname        | idx_scan
------------+-----------------------------+----------
 public     | pgbench_accounts_bid_idx    |        0
 public     | pgbench_branches_pkey       |    14575
 public     | pgbench_tellers_pkey        |    15350
 public     | pgbench_accounts_pkey       |   114400
(4 rows)
```

As we can see in the preceding code, there is one index that is totally unused, alongside others that have some usage. You now need to decide whether "unused" means you should remove the index. That is a more complex question, and we first need to explain how it works.

How it works...

The PostgreSQL statistics accumulate various pieces of useful information. These statistics can be reset to `zero` using an administrator function. Also, as the data accumulates over time, we usually find that objects that have been there for longer periods of time have higher apparent usage. So, if we see a low number for `idx_scan`, then it might be that the index was newly created (as was the case in my preceding demonstration), or that the index is only used by a part of the application that runs only at certain times of a day, week, month, and so on.

Another important consideration is that the index may be a unique constraint index that exists specifically to safeguard against duplicate `INSERT` commands. An `INSERT` operation does not show up as an `idx_scan`, even if the index was actually used while checking the uniqueness of the newly inserted values, whereas an `UPDATE` or `DELETE` might show up, because they have to locate the row first. So, a table that only has `INSERT` commands against it will appear to have unused indexes.

Also, some indexes that show usage might be showing usage that was historical, and there is no further usage. Or it might be the case that some queries use an index where they could just as easily and almost as cheaply use an alternative index. Those things are for you to explore and understand before you take action. A very common approach is to regularly monitor such numbers in order to gain knowledge by examining their evolution over time.

In the end, you may decide from this that you want to remove an index. If only there was a way to try removing an index and then put it back again quickly, in case you cause problems! Rebuilding an index might take hours on a big table, so these decisions can be a little scary. No worries! Just follow the next recipe, *Carefully removing unwanted indexes*.

Carefully removing unwanted indexes

Carefully removing? You mean press *Enter* gently after typing `DROP INDEX`? Err, no!

The thinking is that it takes a long time to build an index, and a short time to drop it. What we want is a way of removing an index such that if we discover that removing it was a mistake, we can put the index back again quickly.

How to do it...

We will describe a procedure that allows us to deactivate an index without actually dropping it, so that we can appreciate what its contribution was and possibly reactivate it:

1. First, create the following function:

```
CREATE OR REPLACE FUNCTION trial_drop_index(iname TEXT)
RETURNS VOID
LANGUAGE SQL AS $$
UPDATE pg_index
SET indisvalid = false
WHERE indexrelid = $1::regclass;
$$;
```

2. Then, run it to do a trial of dropping the index.

3. If you experience performance issues after dropping the index, then use this function to "undrop" the index:

```
CREATE OR REPLACE FUNCTION trial_undrop_index(iname TEXT)
RETURNS VOID
LANGUAGE SQL AS $$
UPDATE pg_index
SET indisvalid = true
WHERE indexrelid = $1::regclass;
$$;
```

How it works...

This recipe also uses some inside knowledge. When we create an index using CREATE INDEX CONCURRENTLY, it is a two-stage process. The first phase builds the index and then marks it invalid. INSERT, UPDATE, and DELETE statements now begin maintaining the index, but we perform a further pass over the table to see if we missed anything, before declaring the index valid. User queries don't use the index until it says that it is valid.

Once the index is built and the "valid" flag is set, then if we set the flag to invalid, the index will still be maintained. It's just that it will not be used by queries. This allows us to turn off the index quickly, though with the option to turn it on again if we realize that we actually do need the index after all. This makes it practical to test whether dropping the index will alter the performance of any of your most important queries.

Planning maintenance

In these busy times, many people believe, "if it ain't broken, don't fix it." I believe that too, but it isn't an excuse for not taking action to maintain your database servers and be sure that nothing will break.

Database maintenance is about making your database run smoothly.

Monitoring systems are not a substitute for good planning. They alert you to unplanned situations that need attention. The more unplanned things you respond to, the greater the chance that you will need to respond to multiple emergencies at once. And when that happens, something will break. Ultimately, that is your fault. If you wish to take your responsibilities seriously, you should plan ahead.

How to do it...

This recipe is about planning, so we'll provide discussion points rather than portions of code. We'll cover the main points that should be addressed, and also provide a list of points as food for thought, around which the actual implementation should be built:

▶ **Let's break a rule**: If you don't have a backup, take one now. I mean now, go on, and off you go! Then, let's talk some more about planning maintenance. If you already do, well done! It's hard to keep your job as a DBA if you lose data because of missing backups, especially today, when everybody's grandmother knows to keep her photos backed up.

▶ **First, plan your time**: Decide a regular date on which to perform certain actions. Don't allow yourself to be a puppet of your monitoring system, running up and down every time the lights change. If you keep getting dragged off on other assignments, then you must understand that you need to get a good handle on the database maintenance to make sure that it doesn't bite you.

▶ **Don't be scared**: It's easy to worry about what you don't know, and either overreact or underreact to the situation. Your database probably doesn't need to be inspected daily, but never is definitely a bad practice.

How it works...

Build a regular cycle of activity around the following tasks:

▶ **Capacity planning**: Observe long-term trends in system performance and keep track of the growth of database volumes. Plan to schedule any new data feeds and new projects that increase the rates of change. This is best done monthly so that you monitor what has happened and what will happen.

▶ **Backups, recovery testing, and emergency planning**: Organize regular reviews of written plans, and test scripts. Check the tape rotation, confirm that you still have the password to the off-site backups, and so on. Some sysadmins run a test recovery every night so that they always know that a successful recovery is possible.

▶ **Vacuum and index maintenance**: To reduce bloat, as well as collecting optimizer statistics through `ANALYZE`. Also, regularly check index usage and drop unused indexes.

▶ Consider `VACUUM` again, with the need to manage the less frequent **freezing** process. This is listed as a separate task so that you don't ignore this and let it bite you later!

▶ **Server log file analysis**: How many times has the server restarted? Are you sure you know about each incident?

▸ **Security and intrusion detection**: Has your database already been hacked? What did they do?

▸ **Understanding usage patterns**: If you don't know much about what your database is used for, then I'll wager it is not very well tuned or maintained.

▸ **Long-term performance analysis**: It's a common occurrence for me to get asked to come and tune a system that is slow. Often, what happens is that a database server gets slower over a very long period. Nobody ever noticed any particular day when it got slow—it just got slower over time. Keeping records of response times over time can help confirm whether everything is as good now as it was months or years earlier. This activity is where you might reconsider current index choices.

Many of these activities are mentioned in this chapter or throughout the rest of the cookbook. Some are not because they aren't so much technical tasks but more about planning and understanding of your environment.

You might also find time to consider the following:

▸ **Data quality**: Are the contents of the database accurate and meaningful? Could the data be enhanced?

▸ **Business intelligence**: Is the data being used for everything that can bring value to the organization?

10
Performance and Concurrency

In this chapter, we will cover the following recipes:

- ▶ Finding slow SQL statements
- ▶ Collecting regular statistics from `pg_stat*` views
- ▶ Finding out what makes SQL slow
- ▶ Reducing the number of rows returned
- ▶ Simplifying complex SQL queries
- ▶ Speeding up queries without rewriting them
- ▶ Why a query is not using an index
- ▶ Forcing a query to use an index
- ▶ Using optimistic locking
- ▶ Reporting performance problems

Introduction

Performance and concurrency are two problems that are often tightly coupled—when concurrency grows, performance usually degrades, in some cases a lot. If you take care of performance problems, you can achieve better concurrency.

In this chapter, we will show you how to find slow queries and also how to find queries that make other queries slow.

Performance tuning, unfortunately, is still not an exact science, so you may also encounter a performance problem not covered by any of the given methods.

We will also show you how to get help in the final recipe, *Reporting performance problems*, in case none of the other recipes covered here work.

Finding slow SQL statements

There are two main kinds of slowness that can manifest themselves in a database.

The first kind is a single query that can be too slow to be really usable, such as a customer information query in a CRM running for minutes, a password check query running in tens of seconds, or a daily data aggregation query running for more than a day. These can be found by logging queries that take over a certain amount of time, either at the client end or in the database.

The second kind is a query that is run frequently (say a few thousand times a second) and used to run in single-digit milliseconds, but is now running in several tens or even hundreds of milliseconds, thus slowing down the system. This kind of slowness is much harder to find.

Here, we will show you several ways to find the statements that are either slow or cause the database as a whole to slow down (although they are not slow by themselves).

Getting ready

Connect to the database as the user whose statements you want to investigate, or as a superuser to investigate all users' queries.

Get access to the PostgreSQL log files. They are usually located together with other log files; for example, on Debian/Ubuntu Linux, they are in the `/var/log/postgresql/` directory.

You should also set up logging of queries taking over x seconds. If you are not swamped with thousands of small and fast queries, you can also temporarily log all queries—at least for some period of time. This allows you to get an overview of the entire database activity, and not just individual slow queries.

How to do it...

The easiest way of finding single, slow queries is to set up PostgreSQL to log them all. So, if you decide to monitor a query taking over 10 seconds, then set up logging queries over 10 seconds by defining the following in `postgresql.conf`:

```
log_min_duration_statement = 10000;
```

Remember that the duration is in milliseconds. After doing this, reload PostgreSQL. All slow queries are now logged.

Another possibility to spot long queries is to look them up in the `pg_stat_activity` system view by repeatedly running this query:

```
SELECT now() - query_start AS running_for, query
       FROM pg_stat_activity WHERE state = 'active'
       ORDER BY 1 DESC LIMIT 5;
```

On PostgreSQL 9.0 and 9.1, you should use the following:

```
SELECT now() - query_start AS running_for, current_query
       FROM pg_stat_activity
       WHERE current_query != '<IDLE>'
          ORDER BY 1 DESC LIMIT 5;
```

 Users of versions earlier than PostgreSQL 9.2 need to look at the *Checking whether a user is connected* recipe from *Chapter 8, Monitoring and Diagnosis*, as it contains detailed information about changes that have been introduced to the `pg_stat_activity` view.

This query looks up the top five currently running queries, ordered by how long they have been executing. You don't usually get the real runtime this way, but spotting something here hints that it may need optimizing.

PostgreSQL 9.3 introduces the `\watch` meta-command in psql, which allows us to repeatedly and automatically execute a query. More details can be found in the *Checking whether a user is connected* recipe from *Chapter 8, Monitoring and Diagnosis*.

Sometimes, a single query execution is not slow by itself, but the aggregate effect of running hundreds or even thousands of such queries per second has a net effect of making the server slow by increasing the CPU and I/O load.

These queries do not show up in logs with slow query logging turned on, but there are other ways by which they can be found.

You can start by watching the `pg_stat_activity` view by repeatedly running (the same preceding query, but without sort/limit):

```
SELECT now() - query_start AS running_for, query
       FROM pg_stat_activity WHERE state = 'active';
```

PostgreSQL 9.0 and 9.1 users should try the following statement:

```
SELECT now() - query_start AS running_for, current_query
    FROM pg_stat_activity WHERE current_query != '<IDLE>';
```

If the same query keeps coming up often but the `running_for` time remains slow, then there is a good chance that this is the query that consumes a lot of resources (and is at least partly responsible for generally slow performance).

You can gather such statistics in a semi-automated way, by continuously running the preceding query (or a different version containing fields that you require) in a shell command that takes advantage of the psql application. You can expand and elaborate the following idea (based on a one-line shell command):

```
while psql -qAt -c "COPY (SELECT query, now() - query_start AS running_
for FROM pg_stat_activity WHERE state = 'active' AND pid != pg_backend_
pid()) TO STDOUT" >> query_stats.txt; do sleep 1; done
```

On PostgreSQL 9.0 and 9.1, use this slightly different version:

```
while psql -qAt -c "COPY (SELECT current_query, now() - query_start AS
running_for FROM pg_stat_activity WHERE current_query != '<IDLE>' AND
procpid != pg_backend_pid()) TO STDOUT" >> query_stats.txt; do sleep 1;
done
```

The preceding shell line issues the `SELECT` query at 1-second intervals and collects the output via `COPY` in the `query_stats.txt` file. After running it for a few seconds, you can stop it by pressing *Ctrl + C* and then looking at the sorted output to find the repeating queries:

```
sort query_stats.txt | less
```

Feel free to use more columns from the `pg_stat_activity` table and/or refine your filter criteria.

However, in some cases, `pg_stat_activity` is not enough and you'll need finer statistics about the impact of a query on one or more tables. For this purpose, you can look at suspicious behavior in the `pg_stat_user_tables` and `pg_statio_user_tables` system views. Specific things to look out for are as follows:

- In `pg_stat_user_tables`, fast growth of `seq_tup_read` means that there are lots of sequential scans occurring. The ratio of `seq_tup_read` to `seq_scan` shows how many tuples each `seqscan` reads.

- In `pg_statio_user_tables`, watch the `heap_blks_hit` and `heap_blks_read` fields. They give you a fairly good idea on how much of your data is found in PostgreSQL's shared buffers (`heap_blks_hit`) and how much had to be fetched from the disk (`heap_blks_read`). If you see large numbers of blocks being read from the disk continuously, you may want to tune those queries, or if you determine that the disk reads were justified, you can make the configured `shared_buffers` value bigger.

Once you have found the query that you suspect is slowing you down, you can force that query to appear in the slow query log. The trick is to lock any table involved in this query for a slightly longer period than `log_min_duration_statement`, as configured in the `postgresql.conf` file.

A sample psql session for logging all queries accessing `my_suspect_table` is as follows:

```
gabriele=# BEGIN;
BEGIN
gabriele=# LOCK TABLE my_suspect_table;
LOCK TABLE
SELECT pg_sleep(12);
gabriele=# ROLLBACK;
ROLLBACK
```

This also works when you have not found a single suspect query, but have found a table that is accessed in a suspicious manner, and you want to find out which queries use that table. Beware that LOCK TABLE acquires an exclusive lock on the table and prevents users from accessing it, for both reads and writes.

If your slow query makes direct or indirect (through a database adapter) use of prepared statements, you need to be able to connect the PREPARE statement that is creating the prepared query plan with the actual invocation of the query, using EXECUTE.

This can be done by configuring PostgreSQL to log all queries. You are advised to set the configuration file parameter, `log_line_prefix`, so that it includes either process ID (`%p`) or session ID (`%c`). This will help you to trace back matching PREPARE statements in the log if you see a slow EXECUTE command. Further information on prepared statements can be found in the documentation of PostgreSQL at `http://www.postgresql.org/docs/current/static/sql-prepare.html`.

See also

- There is more information on tools for query analysis at the end of *Chapter 8, Monitoring and Diagnosis*.

Collecting regular statistics from pg_stat* views

This recipe describes how to collect the statistics needed to understand what is going on in the database system on a regular basis so that they can be used to further optimize the queries that are slow or are becoming slow as the database changes.

We have included an example of extension, called `pgstatslog`. It can be used to track these changes. The extension works on PostgreSQL 9.1, 9.2, 9.3 and 9.4.

Porting of this extension to PostgreSQL 9.0 is simple and can be performed as an exercise by you.

Look at the *Using an installed module* and *Managing installed extensions* recipes from *Chapter 3, Configuration*, for an overview of the extensions infrastructure in PostgreSQL.

Further information on extensions can be found in the PostgreSQL documentation at `http://www.postgresql.org/docs/current/static/sql-createextension.html`.

Chapter 10, Publishing Your Code as PostgreSQL Extensions, of *PostgreSQL Server Programming, Hannu Krosing, Jim Mlodgenski, and Kirk Roybal, Packt Publishing*, contains a detailed guide on writing and maintaining extensions.

Getting ready

Find the `pgstatslog` directory in the set of files distributed along with this book.

Then, copy that directory to the PostgreSQL server where you want to install the extension. Next, perform these steps:

1. As a root user, enter that directory and type the following:

   ```
   make install
   ```

2. You can execute the same operation as the `postgres` user through sudo:

   ```
   sudo make install
   ```

3. Now that the extension has been installed in your PostgreSQL server, it is time to install it in each database you want to monitor. As the `postgres` user, connect to the destination database (for example, `gabriele`) and execute the following `CREATE EXTENSION` statement:

```
gabriele=# CREATE EXTENSION pgstatslog;
CREATE EXTENSION
```

4. You can verify that the extension is installed by typing `\dx` in psql.

How to do it...

You can collect information by executing the following query for each database you intend to monitor:

```
SELECT collect_deltas();
```

This will collect the changes in the `pg_stat_user_*` and `pg_statio_user_*` tables that have occurred since the last invocation.

You should probably set up a cron job to run on a regular basis so that you have good coverage of what happens at what time of the day and week. Running it at an interval of 5 to 15 minutes should usually give you enough temporal resolution to understand what is going on with your tables.

For example, you can add this (or a similar variation) to the `postgres` user's cron table:

```
*/5 * * * * /usr/bin/psql -c 'SELECT collect_deltas()' gabriele
```

How it works...

The `collect_deltas()` function makes static copies of the `pg_stat_user_tables`, `pg_statio_user_tables`, `pg_stat_user_indexes`, and `pg_statio_user_indexes` tables at each run. It then compares the current copies with the copies saved at the last run, and saves the timestamped deltas in the `stat_user_tables_delta_log` and `stat_user_indexes_delta_log` log tables. These tables can then be analyzed later to get an insight into access and I/O patterns.

The latest set of deltas is also kept in the `stat_user_tables_delta` and `stat_user_indexes_delta` tables, which can be used for external monitoring systems, such as Cacti, to get a graphical representation of it.

There's more...

The `collect_deltas()` function simply appends data to the same tables. This should not cause performance problems, as the large log tables are without indexes. Thus, insertions in them are fast, but if you are low on disk space and have many tables, you may want to introduce a rotation scheme for these tables that throws away older data.

In case you experience performance issues with the proposed approach, you might want to either purge the old data from the `*_delta_log` tables (and keep a window of the last four weeks) or use horizontal partitioning.

In the first approach, you can set a weekly cron job that deletes all records that are older than 4 weeks from the tables. For this purpose, we have created the `rotate_deltas()` function in the `pgstatslog` extension.

In the second approach, you can keep longer series of data, by creating monthly tables for example, and let PostgreSQL manage partitioning using table inheritance. For further information about partitioning and inheritance, refer to `http://www.postgresql.org/docs/current/static/ddl-partitioning.html` and `http://www.postgresql.org/docs/current/static/tutorial-inheritance.html`.

As a final note, we suggest that you take some time and investigate the content of the extension, in particular the `pgstatslog--1.0.sql` file. It contains definitions for tables, views and functions, as well as usage instructions.

Another statistics collection package

If you are interested in a more powerful way of tracking database statistics over time, I suggest you to look at `pg_statsinfo`, an open source package available at `http://pgstatsinfo.projects.pgfoundry.org/` and developed by our friends from NTT.

Finding out what makes SQL slow

A SQL statement can be slow for a lot of reasons. Here, we will give a short list of these, with at least one way of recognizing each reason.

How to do it...

Perform the following steps:

1. Run the query with `EXPLAIN ANALYZE` to see how much data is processed in order to complete the query, as follows:

    ```
    mydb=# EXPLAIN ANALYZE SELECT count(*) FROM t;
                            QUERY PLAN
    ```

```
---------------------------------------------------------------
---- Aggregate  (cost=4427.27..4427.28 rows=1 width=0) \
            (actual time=32.953..32.954 rows=1 loops=1)
   ->  Seq Scan on t  (cost=0.00..4425.01 rows=901 width=0) \
            (actual time=30.350..31.646 rows=901 loops=1)
 Total runtime: 33.028 ms
(3 rows)
```

2. See how many rows are processed and how many blocks of data are accessed by comparing the output of the following query before and after the query is run on an idle system (the `pg_stat*` views are global and collect information from all parallel queries):

```
SELECT
    s.relid, s.schemaname, s.relname,
    seq_scan, seq_tup_read,
    idx_scan, idx_tup_fetch,
    heap_blks_read, heap_blks_hit,
    idx_blks_read, idx_blks_hit,
    toast_blks_read, toast_blks_hit
FROM pg_stat_user_tables s
JOIN pg_statio_user_tables sio ON s.relid = sio.relid
WHERE s.schemaname = 'public' AND s.relname = 't'
```

3. For example, if you want to get the three latest rows in a 1-million-row table. Then, run this query:

```
SELECT * FROM events ORDER BY id DESC LIMIT 3;
```

4. You can either read through just three rows using an index on the serial `id` column, or you can perform a sequential scan of all rows followed by a sort, as shown in the following snippet. Your choice depends on whether you have a usable index on the field on which you want to get the top three rows:

```
mydb=# CREATE TABLE events(id SERIAL);
NOTICE:  CREATE TABLE will create implicit sequence
   "events_id_seq" for serial column "events.id"
CREATE TABLE
mydb=# INSERT INTO events SELECT generate_series(1,1000000);
INSERT 0 1000000
mydb=# EXPLAIN ANALYZE SELECT * FROM events ORDER BY id DESC LIMIT
3;
```

```
                        QUERY PLAN
------------------------------------------------------------
---- Limit  (cost=25500.67..25500.68 rows=3 width=4) \
            (actual time=3143.493..3143.502 rows=3 loops=1)
     ->  Sort  (cost=25500.67..27853.87 rows=941280 width=4)
            (actual time=3143.488..3143.490 rows=3 loops=1)
         Sort Key: id
         Sort Method:  top-N heapsort  Memory: 17kB
     ->  Seq Scan on events
            (cost=0.00..13334.80 rows=941280 width=4)
            (actual time=0.105..1534.418 rows=1000000 loops=1)
 Total runtime: 3143.584 ms
(6 rows)


mydb=# CREATE INDEX events_id_ndx ON events(id);
CREATE INDEX
mydb=# EXPLAIN ANALYZE SELECT * FROM events ORDER BY id DESC LIMIT
3;
                        QUERY PLAN
------------------------------------------------------------------
----
 Limit  (cost=0.00..0.08 rows=3 width=4) (actual
  time=0.295..0.311 rows=3 loops=1)
    ->  Index Scan Backward using events_id_ndx on events
        (cost=0.00..27717.34 rows=1000000 width=4) (actual
        time=0.289..0.295 rows=3 loops=1)
 Total runtime: 0.364 ms
(3 rows)
```

This produces a 10,000-times difference in query runtime, even when all of the data is in the memory.

There's more...

If not enough of the data fits in shared buffers, lots of rereading of the same data happens, causing performance issues. This manifests as a big change in any of the `heap_blks_read`, `idx_blks_read`, or `toast_blks_read` fields in the `pg_stat*` view before and after the query is run.

It is somewhat normal to have a big difference before and after the first run of the query, as some of the data may just not be accessed recently, but if you run the query immediately for a second time and any of the `*_blks_read` fields still changes a lot, it means you have this problem for sure.

If your `shared_buffers` parameter is tuned properly and you can't rewrite the query to perform less block I/O, you probably need to get a beefier computer.

You can find a lot of resources on the web that explain how shared buffers work and how to set them based on your available hardware and your expected data access patterns. Our professional advice is to always test your database servers and perform benchmarks before you deploy them in production. Information on the `shared_buffers` configuration parameter can be found at `http://www.postgresql.org/docs/current/static/runtime-config-resource.html`.

The query returns too much data

Sometimes, lazy programmers write a query that returns a lot more rows than needed. This usually goes unnoticed when the data volumes are small, but can quickly become problematic once more data appears in the database. For example, you have a picture database and an application showing a list of pictures. If you are showing only 10 pictures at a time, you should not request more than 10 from the database (or maybe 11 if you want to display the next link). For thousands of pictures, it makes sense to have a separate `count(*)` query to determine the total number of pictures, and not select all pictures and count them in the client. For high-performance websites, you would want to replace even the count query with a separately maintained count in some table to further reduce the work done at display time. See the *Reducing the number of rows returned* recipe.

Locking problems

Thanks to its MVCC design, PostgreSQL does not suffer from most locking problems, such as writers locking out readers or readers locking out writers, but it still has to take locks when more than one process wants to update the same row. Also, it has to hold the write lock until the current writer's transaction finishes.

So, if you have a database design where many queries update the same record, you can have a locking problem.

The easiest way to find out if you do is to see if there are many backends waiting on locks by running the following query:

```
SELECT * FROM pg_locks WHERE NOT granted;
```

If this comes up empty, or with only one or two rows, then you probably don't have this problem.

To see which queries are waiting on which other queries, run the following:

```
SELECT
    a1.query AS blocking_query, a1.state AS blocking_query_state,
    a2.query AS waiting_query, a2.state AS waiting_query_state,
    t.schemaname || '.' || t.relname AS locked_table
 FROM pg_stat_activity a1
 JOIN pg_locks p1 ON a1.pid = p1.pid AND p1.granted
 JOIN pg_locks p2 ON p1.relation = p2.relation AND NOT p2.granted
 JOIN pg_stat_activity a2 ON a2.pid = p2.pid
 JOIN pg_stat_all_tables t ON p1.relation = t.relid;
```

PostgreSQL 9.0 and 9.1 administrators need to use a slightly different query, as the pg_stat_activity view does not contain the state field and both the pid and the query fields have a different name. Once again, refer to *Chapter 8, Monitoring and Diagnosis*, for detailed information about the changes in the pg_stat_activity view.

Users of PostgreSQL 9.2 and later versions should receive a result very similar to the following (I have enabled the expanded mode in psql using \x):

```
-[ RECORD 1 ]--------+------------------------
blocking_query       | lock t;
blocking_query_state | idle in transaction
waiting_query        | SELECT count(*) FROM t;
waiting_query_state  | active
locked_table         | public.t
-[ RECORD 2 ]--------+------------------------
blocking_query       | lock t;
blocking_query_state | idle in transaction
waiting_query        | SELECT * FROM t;
waiting_query_state  | active
locked_table         | public.t
```

Here, the idle in transaction state is caused by an open-console connection, which has issued only the following commands:

```
BEGIN;
LOCK t;
```

And then it is waiting for further input.

Refer to the *Knowing who is blocking a query* recipe of *Chapter 8, Monitoring and Diagnosis*, for more detailed information (including compatibility with PostgreSQL 9.0 and 9.1).

Not enough CPU power or disk I/O capacity for the current load

These issues are usually caused by suboptimal query plans, but sometimes, your computer is just not powerful enough.

In this case, `top` is your friend. For quick checks, run the following from the command line:

```
user@host:~$ top
```

First, watch the percentage of idle CPU from `top`. If this is in low single digits for most of the time, you probably have problems with the CPU's power.

If you have a high load average with a lot of CPU idle left, you are probably out of disk bandwidth. In this case, you should also have lots of `postgres` processes in the D status, meaning that the process is in an uninterruptible state (usually waiting for I/O).

EXPLAIN options

From version 9.0 of Postgres onwards, it is possible to specify a few more options in the `EXPLAIN` command using an alternative syntax:

```
EXPLAIN [(option[, …])] statement
```

The available options are `ANALYZE`, `VERBOSE`, `FORMAT`, `COSTS`, `BUFFERS`, and `TIMING` (the latter from 9.2).

Through the `FORMAT` option, it is possible to retrieve the output of `EXPLAIN` in a different format, such as JSON, XML, and YAML. The following command is an example of this:

```
EXPLAIN (ANALYZE, TIMING, COSTS, BUFFERS) SELECT count(*) FROM t;
```

See also

For further information on the syntax of the `EXPLAIN` SQL command, refer to the PostgreSQL documentation at `http://www.postgresql.org/docs/current/static/sql-explain.html`.

Reducing the number of rows returned

Although often the problem is producing many rows in the first place, it is made worse by returning all the unnecessary rows to the client. This is especially true if the client and server are not on the same host.

Here are some ways to reduce the traffic between the client and server.

How to do it...

Consider the following scenario: a full-text search returns 10,000 documents, but only the first 20 are displayed to users. In this case, order the documents by ranking on the server, and return only the top 20 that actually need to be displayed:

```
SELECT title, ts_rank_cd(body_tsv, query, 20) AS text_rank
  FROM articles, plainto_tsquery('spicy potatoes') AS query
  WHERE body_tsv @@ query
  ORDER BY rank DESC
  LIMIT 20
;
```

If you need the next 20 documents, don't just query with a limit of 40 and throw away the first 20. Instead, use OFFSET 20 LIMIT 20 to return the next 20 documents.

To gain some stability so that the documents with the same rank still come out in the same order when using OFFSET 20, add a unique field (like the id column of the articles table) to ORDER BY in both queries:

```
SELECT title, ts_rank_cd(body_tsv, query, 20) AS text_rank
  FROM articles, plainto_tsquery('spicy potatoes') AS query
  WHERE body_tsv @@ query
  ORDER BY rank DESC, articles.id
  OFFSET 20 LIMIT 20;
```

Another use case is an application that requests all products of branch office to run a complex calculation over them. In such a case, try to do as much data analysis as possible inside the database.

So, there is no need to run the following:

```
SELECT * FROM accounts WHERE branch_id = 7;
```

Also, instead of counting and summing the rows on the client side, you can run this:

```
SELECT count(*), sum(balance) FROM accounts WHERE branch_id = 7;
```

With some research on the SQL language, which is supported by PostgreSQL, you can carry out an amazingly large portion of your computation using plain SQL (for example, do not underestimate the power of window functions).

If SQL is not enough, you can use PL/pgSQL or any other embedded procedural languages supported by PostgreSQL for even more flexibility.

There's more...

Consider one more scenario: an application runs a huge number of small lookup queries. This can easily happen with modern **Object Relational Mappers** (**ORMs**) and other toolkits that do a lot of work for the programmer, but at the same time, hide a lot of what is happening.

For example, if you define an HTML report over a query in a templating language, and then define a lookup function to resolve an ID inside the template. You may end up with a form that performs a separate, small lookup for each row displayed, even when most of the values looked up are the same. This doesn't usually pose a big problem for the database, as queries of the `SELECT name FROM departments WHERE id = 7` form are really fast when the row for `id = 7` is in shared buffers. However, repeating this query thousands of times still takes seconds, due to network latency, process scheduling for each request, and other factors.

The two proposed solutions are as follows:

- ► Make sure that the value is cached by your ORM
- ► Perform the lookup inside the query that gets the main data so that it can be displayed directly

Exactly how to carry out these solutions depends on the toolkit, but they are both worth investigating, as they really can make a difference in speed and resource usage.

Simplifying complex SQL queries

There are two types of complexity that you can encounter in SQL queries.

First, the complexity can be directly visible in the query, if it has hundreds or even thousands of rows of SQL code in a single query code. This can cause both maintenance headaches and slow execution.

The complexity can also be hidden in subviews, so the SQL code of the query may seem simple, but it uses other views and/or functions to do part of the work, which in turn can use others. This is much better for maintenance, but it can still cause performance problems.

Both the types of queries can either be written manually by programmers or data analysts, or can emerge as a result of a query generator.

Getting ready

First, verify that you really have a complex query.

A query that simply returns lots of database fields is not complex by itself. In order to be complex, the query has to join lots of tables in complex ways.

The easiest way to find out whether the query is complex is to look at the output of EXPLAIN. If it has lots of rows, the query is complex, and it's not just that there is a lot of text.

All examples in this recipe have been written with a very typical use case in mind—sales.

Here follows a description of the fictitious model used in this recipe. The most important **fact** is the *sale event*, stored in the `sale` table (I specifically used the word "fact" as this would be the right term to be used in a *data warehousing* context). Every sale takes place at a point of sale (the `salespoint` table) at a specific time and involves an item. That item is stored in a warehouse (see the `item` and `warehouse` tables, as well as the `item_in_wh` link table).

Both the warehouse and the point of sale are located in a geographical area (the `location` table). This is important, for example, to study the provenance of a transaction.

Here is a simplified entity-relationship model, useful for understanding all the joins that occur in the following queries:

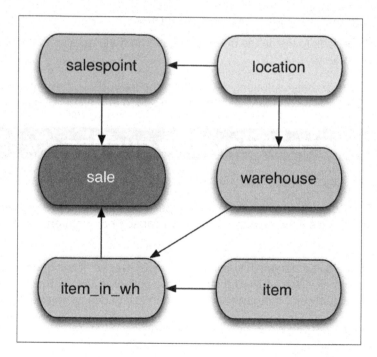

How to do it...

Simplifying a query usually means restructuring it so that parts of it can be defined separately and then used by other parts.

We'll illustrate the possibilities with rewriting the following query in several ways.

The complex query in our example case is a so-called **pivot** or **cross-tab** query. This query retrieves quarterly profit for nonlocal sales from all shops, as shown next:

```
SELECT shop.sp_name AS shop_name,
       q1_nloc_profit.profit AS q1_profit,
       q2_nloc_profit.profit AS q2_profit,
       q3_nloc_profit.profit AS q3_profit,
       q4_nloc_profit.profit AS q4_profit,
       year_nloc_profit.profit AS year_profit
  FROM (SELECT * FROM salespoint ORDER BY sp_name) AS shop
  LEFT JOIN (
      SELECT
         spoint_id,
         sum(sale_price) - sum(cost) AS profit,
         count(*) AS nr_of_sales
      FROM sale s
      JOIN item_in_wh iw ON s.item_in_wh_id=iw.id
      JOIN item i ON iw.item_id = i.id
      JOIN salespoint sp ON s.spoint_id = sp.id
      JOIN location sploc ON sp.loc_id = sploc.id
      JOIN warehouse wh ON iw.whouse_id = wh.id
      JOIN location whloc ON wh.loc_id = whloc.id
      WHERE sale_time >= '2013-01-01'
        AND sale_time <  '2013-04-01'
        AND sploc.id != whloc.id
      GROUP BY 1
     ) AS q1_nloc_profit
    ON shop.id = Q1_NLOC_PROFIT.spoint_id
  LEFT JOIN (
```

```
< similar subquery for 2nd quarter >
    ) AS q2_nloc_profit
    ON shop.id = q2_nloc_profit.spoint_id
  LEFT JOIN (
< similar subquery for 3rd quarter >
    ) AS q3_nloc_profit
    ON shop.id = q3_nloc_profit.spoint_id
  LEFT JOIN (
< similar subquery for 4th  quarter >
    ) AS q4_nloc_profit
    ON shop.id = q4_nloc_profit.spoint_id
  LEFT JOIN (
< similar subquery for full year >
    ) AS year_nloc_profit
    ON shop.id = year_nloc_profit.spoint_id
ORDER BY 1
;
```

As the preceding query has an almost identical repeating part for finding the sales for a period (the four quarters of 2013 in this case), it makes sense to move it to a separate view (for the whole year) and then use that view in the main reporting query, as follows:

```
CREATE VIEW non_local_quarterly_profit_2013 AS
    SELECT
        spoint_id,
        extract('quarter' from sale_time) as sale_quarter,
        sum(sale_price) - sum(cost) AS profit,
        count(*) AS nr_of_sales
    FROM sale s
    JOIN item_in_wh iw ON s.item_in_wh_id=iw.id
    JOIN item i ON iw.item_id = i.id
    JOIN salespoint sp ON s.spoint_id = sp.id
    JOIN location sploc ON sp.loc_id = sploc.id
    JOIN warehouse wh ON iw.whouse_id = wh.id
    JOIN location whloc ON wh.loc_id = whloc.id
    WHERE sale_time >= '2013-01-01'
    AND sale_time <  '2014-01-01'
```

```
            AND sploc.id != whloc.id
        GROUP BY 1,2;


SELECT shop.sp_name AS shop_name,
        q1_nloc_profit.profit as q1_profit,
        q2_nloc_profit.profit as q2_profit,
        q3_nloc_profit.profit as q3_profit,
        q4_nloc_profit.profit as q4_profit,
        year_nloc_profit.profit as year_profit
    FROM (SELECT * FROM salespoint ORDER BY sp_name) AS shop
    LEFT JOIN non_local_quarterly_profit_2013 AS q1_nloc_profit
        ON shop.id = Q1_NLOC_PROFIT.spoint_id
      AND q1_nloc_profit.sale_quarter = 1
    LEFT JOIN non_local_quarterly_profit_2013 AS q2_nloc_profit
        ON shop.id = Q2_NLOC_PROFIT.spoint_id
    AND q2_nloc_profit.sale_quarter = 2
    LEFT JOIN non_local_quarterly_profit_2013 AS q3_nloc_profit
        ON shop.id = Q3_NLOC_PROFIT.spoint_id
    AND q3_nloc_profit.sale_quarter = 3
    LEFT JOIN non_local_quarterly_profit_2013 AS q4_nloc_profit
        ON shop.id = Q4_NLOC_PROFIT.spoint_id
    AND q4_nloc_profit.sale_quarter = 4
    LEFT JOIN (
          SELECT spoint_id, sum(profit) AS profit
            FROM non_local_quarterly_profit_2013 GROUP BY 1
      ) AS year_nloc_profit
      ON shop.id = year_nloc_profit.spoint_id
ORDER BY 1;
```

Moving the subquery to a view has made the query not only shorter but also easier to understand and maintain.

If you are using PostgreSQL 9.3 or a later version, you might want to consider **materialized views**. Even though their support does not yet allow differential updates, you can still benefit from on-demand refreshing of the view results and, most importantly, indexes. Materialized views are described later in this recipe.

Before that, we will be using common table expressions (also known as WITH queries) instead of a separate view. Starting with PostgreSQL version 8.4, indeed, you can use the WITH statement to define the view inline, like the following:

```
WITH nlqp AS (
    SELECT
        spoint_id,
        extract('quarter' from sale_time) as sale_quarter,
        sum(sale_price) - sum(cost) AS profit,
        count(*) AS nr_of_sales
    FROM sale s
    JOIN item_in_wh iw ON s.item_in_wh_id=iw.id
    JOIN item i ON iw.item_id = i.id
    JOIN salespoint sp ON s.spoint_id = sp.id
    JOIN location sploc ON sp.loc_id = sploc.id
    JOIN warehouse wh ON iw.whouse_id = wh.id
    JOIN location whloc ON wh.loc_id = whloc.id
    WHERE sale_time >= '2013-01-01'
     AND sale_time <  '2014-01-01'
     AND sploc.id != whloc.id
    GROUP BY 1,2
)
SELECT shop.sp_name AS shop_name,
       q1_nloc_profit.profit as q1_profit,
       q2_nloc_profit.profit as q2_profit,
       q3_nloc_profit.profit as q3_profit,
       q4_nloc_profit.profit as q4_profit,
       year_nloc_profit.profit as year_profit
  FROM (SELECT * FROM salespoint ORDER BY sp_name) AS shop
  LEFT JOIN nlqp AS q1_nloc_profit
      ON shop.id = Q1_NLOC_PROFIT.spoint_id
   AND q1_nloc_profit.sale_quarter = 1
  LEFT JOIN nlqp AS q2_nloc_profit
      ON shop.id = Q2_NLOC_PROFIT.spoint_id
   AND q2_nloc_profit.sale_quarter = 2
  LEFT JOIN nlqp AS q3_nloc_profit
```

```
         ON shop.id = Q3_NLOC_PROFIT.spoint_id
  AND q3_nloc_profit.sale_quarter = 3
  LEFT JOIN nlqp AS q4_nloc_profit
         ON shop.id = Q4_NLOC_PROFIT.spoint_id
  AND q4_nloc_profit.sale_quarter = 4
  LEFT JOIN (
         SELECT spoint_id, sum(profit) AS profit
          FROM nlqp GROUP BY 1
       ) AS year_nloc_profit
       ON shop.id = year_nloc_profit.spoint_id
ORDER BY 1;
```

For more information on WITH queries (also known as **Common Table Expressions (CTEs)**),
read the official documentation at http://www.postgresql.org/docs/current/
static/queries-with.html.

There's more...

Another ace in the hole is represented by temporary tables to be used for parts of the query.
By default, a temporary table is dropped at the end of a Postgres session, but the behavior
can be changed at the time of creation.

PostgreSQL itself can choose to materialize parts of the query during the query optimization
phase, but sometimes, it fails to make the best choice for the query plan, either due to
insufficient statistics, or because—as it can happen for large query plans, where **genetic
query optimization (GEQO)** is used—it may have just overlooked some possible query plans.

If you think that materializing (separately preparing) some parts of the query is a good idea,
you can do it using a temporary table, simply by running CREATE TEMPORARY TABLE my_
temptable01 AS <the part of the query you want to materialize>, and then
using my_temptable01 in the main query instead of the materialized part.

You can even create indexes on the temporary table for PostgreSQL to use in the main query:

```
BEGIN;
CREATE TEMPORARY TABLE nlqp_temp ON COMMIT DROP
  AS
      SELECT
          spoint_id,
          extract('quarter' from sale_time) as sale_quarter,
          sum(sale_price) - sum(cost) AS profit,
```

```
        count(*) AS nr_of_sales
    FROM sale s
    JOIN item_in_wh iw ON s.item_in_wh_id=iw.id
    JOIN item i ON iw.item_id = i.id
    JOIN salespoint sp ON s.spoint_id = sp.id
    JOIN location sploc ON sp.loc_id = sploc.id
    JOIN warehouse wh ON iw.whouse_id = wh.id
    JOIN location whloc ON wh.loc_id = whloc.id
    WHERE sale_time >= '2013-01-01'
      AND sale_time <  '2014-01-01'
      AND sploc.id != whloc.id
    GROUP BY 1,2
;
```

You can create indexes on the table and analyze the temporary table here:

```
SELECT shop.sp_name AS shop_name,
       q1_NLP.profit as q1_profit,
       q2_NLP.profit as q2_profit,
       q3_NLP.profit as q3_profit,
       q4_NLP.profit as q4_profit,
       year_NLP.profit as year_profit
  FROM (SELECT * FROM salespoint ORDER BY sp_name) AS shop
  LEFT JOIN nlqp_temp AS q1_NLP
      ON shop.id = Q1_NLP.spoint_id AND q1_NLP.sale_quarter = 1
  LEFT JOIN nlqp_temp AS q2_NLP
      ON shop.id = Q2_NLP.spoint_id AND q2_NLP.sale_quarter = 2
  LEFT JOIN nlqp_temp AS q3_NLP
      ON shop.id = Q3_NLP.spoint_id AND q3_NLP.sale_quarter = 3
  LEFT JOIN nlqp_temp AS q4_NLP
      ON shop.id = Q4_NLP.spoint_id AND q4_NLP.sale_quarter = 4
  LEFT JOIN (
      select spoint_id, sum(profit) AS profit FROM nlqp_temp GROUP BY 1
      ) AS year_NLP
      ON shop.id = year_NLP.spoint_id
ORDER BY 1
;
COMMIT; -- here the temp table goes away
```

Using materialized views (long-living, temporary tables)

If the part you put in the temporary table is large, does not change very often, and/or is hard to compute, then you may be able to do it less often for each query using a technique named materialized views.

Materialized views are views that are prepared before they are used (similar to a cached table). They are either fully regenerated as underlying data changes or in some cases, can update only those rows that depend on the changed data.

Starting from version 9.3, PostgreSQL natively supports materialized views through the CREATE MATERIALIZED VIEW, ALTER MATERIALIZED VIEW, REFRESH MATERIALIZED VIEW, and DROP MATERIALIZED VIEW commands. At the time of writing this book, PostgreSQL supports full regeneration only of the "cached" tables. PostgreSQL 9.4 introduces concurrent REFRESH of the materialized view.

A fundamental aspect of materialized views is that they can have their own indexes, like any other table. See http://www.postgresql.org/docs/current/static/sql-creatematerializedview.html for more information on creating materialized views.

For instance, you can rewrite the example of the previous recipe in PostgreSQL 9.3 using a materialized view instead of a temporary table:

```
CREATE MATERIALIZED VIEW nlqp_temp AS
      SELECT spoint_id,
            extract('quarter' from sale_time) as sale_quarter,
            sum(sale_price) - sum(cost) AS profit,
            count(*) AS nr_of_sales
      FROM sale s
      JOIN item_in_wh iw ON s.item_in_wh_id=iw.id
      JOIN item i ON iw.item_id = i.id
      JOIN salespoint sp ON s.spoint_id = sp.id
      JOIN location sploc ON sp.loc_id = sploc.id
      JOIN warehouse wh ON iw.whouse_id = wh.id
      JOIN location whloc ON wh.loc_id = whloc.id
            WHERE sale_time >= '2013-01-01'
            AND sale_time <  '2014-01-01'
            AND sploc.id != whloc.id
            GROUP BY 1,2
```

Prior to version 9.3, there was no explicit support for materialized views in PostgreSQL. However, there are several sample implementations for achieving the same functionality. Visit `http://wiki.postgresql.org/wiki/Materialized_Views` for more discussion and examples.

Using set-returning functions for some parts of queries

Another possibility of achieving similar results to temporary tables and/or materialized views is by using a **set-returning function** for some parts of the query.

It is easy to have a materialized view freshness check inside a function. However, a detailed analysis and an overview of these techniques go beyond the goals of this book, as they require a deep understanding of the PL/pgSQL procedural language.

> More information on this topic can be found in *Chapter 4, Returning Structured Data*, of *PostgreSQL Server Programming, Hannu Krosing, Jim Mlodgenski, and Kirk Roybal, Packt Publishing*.

Speeding up queries without rewriting them

Often, you either can't or don't want to rewrite the query. However, you can still try and speed it up through any of the techniques discussed here.

How to do it...

As a first step, you can start providing better information to the optimizer.

If `EXPLAIN ANALYZE` reveals that the estimates in the database differ a lot from the metrics returned by the actual query execution, you need to instruct PostgreSQL to collect more fine-grained statistics.

The current default statistics target can be shown using this command:

```
SHOW default_statistics_target;
```

You can set it to a higher value in the `postgresql.conf` file. Alternatively, if you want to do this only for a single database, you can use `ALTER DATABASE`, as follows:

```
ALTER DATABASE mydb SET default_statistics_target = 200;
```

Usually, you wouldn't want to set it too high for all tables and fields, as it slows down the `ANALYZE` command. In fact, PostgreSQL gives you a more fine-grained way of doing this on a field-by-field basis:

```
ALTER TABLE mytable ALTER col_with_bad_stats SET statistics 500;
```

The new statistical values take effect the next time `ANALYZE` is run on the table. It makes sense then to run `ANALYZE` after changing these values. The maximum value is 10000, while the default is 100.

If you set the `default_statistics_target` parameter for a database, then it takes effect the next time anyone connects to the database. So, you should either reconnect or set it for your current session by issuing `SET default_statistics_target = 300` before `ANALYZE` if you want the new value to be used.

See `http://www.postgresql.org/docs/current/static/planner-stats.html` for detailed information on statistics used by the planner.

If you are not completely satisfied by this proposal, you can try and add a multicolumn index that is specifically tuned for that query.

If you have a query that, for example, selects rows from the `t1` table on the `a` column and sorts on the `b` column, then creating the following index enables PostgreSQL to do it all in one index scan:

`CREATE INDEX t1_a_b_ndx ON t1(a, b);`

Also, version 9.2 of PostgreSQL introduces a new plan type—**index-only scans**. This feature is also widely known as **covering indexes**.

If all the columns requested by the `SELECT` list of a query are available in an index, that particular index is a covering index for that query. This technique allows PostgreSQL to fetch valid rows directly from the index, without accessing the table (**heap**), as was done in the previous versions. In this way, performance improves significantly.

Another often underestimated (or unknown) feature of PostgreSQL is represented by **conditional indexes**. If you use `SELECT` on a condition—and especially if this condition only selects a small number of rows—you can use a conditional index on that expression, like this:

```
CREATE INDEX t1_proc_ndx ON t1(i1)
    WHERE needs_processing = TRUE;
```

It is used in a query like the following for finding rows that need some processing to be done:

`SELECT id, … WHERE needs_processing AND i1 = 5;`

Performance gains in Postgres can also be obtained with another technique: **clustering tables on specific indexes**. However, index access indeed may still not be very efficient if the values accessed by the index are distributed randomly all over the table. If you know that some fields are likely to be accessed together, then *cluster* the table on an index defined on those fields. For a multicolumn index, you can use the following command:

`CLUSTER t1_a_b_ndx ON t1;`

Clustering a table on an index rewrites the whole table in index order. This can lock the table for a long time, so don't do it on a busy system. Also, CLUSTER is a one-time command. New rows do not get inserted in cluster order, and to keep the performance gains, you may need to cluster the table every now and then.

Once a table is clustered on an index, you don't need to specify the index name in following cluster commands. It is enough to type this:

```
CLUSTER t1;
```

It still takes time to rewrite the entire table, though it is probably a little faster once most of the table is in index order.

There's more...

If you have a huge table and a query to select only a subset of that table, then you can partition that table and use constraint exclusion so that PostgreSQL knows which partitions it needs to access for a specific query. This technique is known as **horizontal partitioning** (a large table is horizontally split into distinct subsets based on the value of a field, which is usually a measure of time).

Table partitioning is still not directly supported in PostgreSQL 9, but PostgreSQL has the basic capabilities in place for you to define it yourself. Unfortunately, it needs a much longer explanation than we have here. You can check out the official documentation on partitioning at http://www.postgresql.org/docs/current/static/ddl-partitioning.html.

 There is a full chapter on table partitioning in another Packt Publishing book, which is *Chapter 15, Partitioning Data*, from *PostgreSQL 9.0 High Performance, Gregory Smith, Packt Publishing*. It goes well beyond what is covered by the standard PostgreSQL documentation.

In case of many updates, set fillfactor on the table

If you often update only some tables and can arrange your query/queries so that you don't change any indexed fields, then setting fillfactor to a lower value than the default of 100 for those tables enables PostgreSQL to use **Heap-only Tuples** (**HOT**) updates, which can be an order of magnitude faster than ordinary updates. HOT updates not only avoid creating new index entries but can also perform a fast mini-vacuum inside the page to make room for new rows:

```
ALTER TABLE t1 SET (fillfactor = 70);
```

This tells PostgreSQL to fill only 70 percent of each page in table t1 when performing insertions so that 30 percent is left for use by in-page (HOT) updates.

Rewriting the schema – a more radical approach

In some occasions, it may make sense to rewrite the database schema and provide an old view for unchanged queries using views, triggers, rules, and functions.

One such case occurs when refactoring the database, and you would want old queries to keep running while changes are made.

Another case is an external application that is unusable with the provided schema but can be made to perform OK with a different distribution of data between tables.

Why a query is not using an index

This recipe explains what to do if you think your query should use an index, but it does not.

There can be several reasons for this, but most often, the reason is that the optimizer believes that, based on the available distribution statistics, it is cheaper and faster to use a query plan that does not use an index.

How to do it...

Force index usage and compare plan costs with an index and without, like this:

```
mydb=# CREATE TABLE itable(id int PRIMARY KEY);
NOTICE:  CREATE TABLE / PRIMARY KEY will create implicit index
  "itable_pkey" for table "itable"
CREATE TABLE
mydb=# INSERT INTO itable SELECT generate_series(1,10000);
INSERT 0 10000
mydb=# ANALYZE;
ANALYZE
mydb=# EXPLAIN ANALYZE SELECT count(*) FROM itable WHERE id > 500;
                        QUERY PLAN
-----------------------------------------------------------------
 Aggregate   (cost=188.75..188.76 rows=1 width=0)
           (actual time=37.958..37.959 rows=1 loops=1)
     -> Seq Scan on itable   (cost=0.00..165.00 rows=9500 width=0)
           (actual time=0.290..18.792 rows=9500 loops=1)
         Filter: (id > 500)
 Total runtime: 38.027 ms
(4 rows)
```

```
mydb=# SET enable_seqscan TO false;
SET
mydb=# EXPLAIN ANALYZE SELECT count(*) FROM itable WHERE id > 500;
                        QUERY PLAN
--------------------------------------------------------------------
 Aggregate   (cost=323.25..323.26 rows=1 width=0)
             (actual time=44.467..44.469 rows=1 loops=1)
    ->  Index Scan using itable_pkey on itable
             (cost=0.00..299.50 rows=9500 width=0)
             (actual time=0.100..23.240 rows=9500 loops=1)
          Index Cond: (id > 500)
 Total runtime: 44.556 ms
(4 rows)
```

As you see, PostgreSQL estimates (rightly in this case) that this query is better served by performing a sequential scan.

Forcing a query to use an index

Here, we will show you how to force the database to use an index. In fact, it is not possible to tell PostgreSQL to use an index by submitting an access path hint, like other DBMS products do. However, you can trick it into using an index by telling the optimizer that all other options are prohibitively expensive.

Getting ready

First, you have to make sure that it is worth it to use the index. This is best done on a development or testing system, but if you are careful, it can also be done on the production server. Sometimes, it is very hard to generate a load similar to a live system in a test environment, and then your best option may be to carefully test it on the production server.

As the PostgreSQL optimizer does not take into account the parallel load caused by other backends, it may make sense to lie to PostgreSQL about some statistics in order to make it use indexes.

How to do it...

Try running this command:

```
SET enable_seqscan TO false;
```

Here, you tell PostgreSQL that it is really very expensive to do sequential scans. It still performs `seqscan` (instead of failing) if it is the only way to do the query:

```
mydb=# CREATE TABLE table_with_no_index(id int);
CREATE TABLE
mydb=# SET enable_seqscan TO false;
SET
mydb=# EXPLAIN SELECT * FROM table_with_no_index WHERE id > 10;
                         QUERY PLAN
------------------------------------------------------------------
- Seq Scan on table_with_no_index  (cost=10000000000.00..10000000040.00
rows=800 width=4)
    Filter: (id > 10)
(2 rows)
```

However, it is very likely that it selects some other way of doing the query, considering that as cheaper:

```
mydb=# CREATE INDEX table_with_no_index_now_has_one ON
table_with_no_index(id);
CREATE INDEX
mydb=# EXPLAIN SELECT * FROM table_with_no_index WHERE id > 10;
                         QUERY PLAN
------------------------------------------------------------------
- Bitmap Heap Scan on table_with_no_index  (cost=10.45..30.45
rows=800 width=4)
    Recheck Cond: (id > 10)
      -> Bitmap Index Scan on table_with_no_index_now_has_one
(cost=0.00..10.25 rows=800 width=0)
          Index Cond: (id > 10)
(4 rows)
```

Once you enable `seqscan` again, it will use a sequential scan instead of the more costly (in this case) bitmap index scan, as follows:

```
mydb=# SET enable_seqscan TO true;
SET
mydb=# EXPLAIN SELECT * FROM table_with_no_index WHERE id > 10;
                         QUERY PLAN
-----------------------------------------------------------------
 Seq Scan on table_with_no_index
    (cost=0.00..40.00 rows=800 width=4)
   Filter: (id > 10)
(2 rows)
```

Another technique you can use is to lower `random_page_cost`. For a softer nudge towards using indexes, you can indeed set `random_page_cost` to a lower value—maybe even equal to `seq_page_cost`. This makes PostgreSQL prefer index scans on more occasions, but it still does not produce entirely unreasonable plans, at least for cases where data is mostly cached in shared buffers, or systems disk cache or underlying disks are solid-state drives.

The default values for these parameters are as follows:

```
    random_page_cost = 4;
    seq_page_cost = 1;
```

Try setting this:

```
set random_page_cost = 2;
```

See if it helps; if not, you can try and set it to 1.

There's more...

You might find it useful to look at the `pg_hint_plan` extension. It is available for PostgreSQL 9.1and newer versions. For more information and to download, go to `http://pghintplan.sourceforge.jp/`.

Using optimistic locking

Suppose you are doing lots of transactions, like the following:

```
BEGIN;
SELECT * FROM accounts WHERE holder_name ='BOB' FOR UPDATE;
<do some calculations here>
UPDATE accounts SET balance = 42.00 WHERE holder_name ='BOB';
COMMIT;
```

Then, you may gain some performance by moving from explicit locking (SELECT ... FOR UPDATE) to optimistic locking.

Optimistic locking assumes that others don't update the same record, and checks this at update time instead of locking the record for the time it takes to process the information on the client side.

How to do it...

Rewrite your application so that the preceding transaction is transformed into something like the following (pay attention to the placeholders):

```
BEGIN;
SELECT A.*, (A.*::text) AS old_acc_info
  FROM accounts a WHERE holder_name ='BOB';
<do some calculations here>
UPDATE accounts SET balance = 42.00
 WHERE holder_name ='BOB'
 AND (A.*::text) = <old_acc_info from select above>;
COMMIT;
```

Then, check whether the UPDATE operation really did update one row in your application code. If it did not, then the account for Bob was modified between SELECT and UPDATE, and you probably need to rerun your entire transaction.

The default transaction isolation level in PostgreSQL is read committed, but you can choose from two more levels—repeatable read and serializable—if you require stricter control over transaction concurrency. PostgreSQL 9.0 has only two isolation levels, read committed and serializable (the equivalent of repeatable read from 9.1 onwards). For further information, refer to the official documentation at http://www.postgresql.org/docs/current/static/transaction-iso.html.

How it works...

Instead of locking Bob's row for the time the data from the first `SELECT` command is processed in the client, PostgreSQL queries the old state of Bob's account record in the `old_acc_info` variable, and then uses this value to check that the record has not changed.

You can also save all fields individually and then check them all in the `UPDATE` query, or if you have an automatic `last_change` field, then you can use it. Alternatively, if you actually care only about a few fields changing, such as `balance`, and can ignore others, such as `email`, then you only need to check the relevant fields in the `UPDATE` statement.

There's more...

In some cases, moving the entire computation to the database function can be a very good idea. If you can pass all of the necessary information to the database for processing as a database function, it will run even faster, as you save several round trips to the database. If you use a PL/pgSQL function, you also benefit from automatically saving query plans on the first call in a session, and using saved plans in subsequent calls.

Therefore, the preceding transaction is replaced by a function in the database that looks as follows:

```
CREATE OR REPLACE FUNCTION consume_balance (
    i_username text, i_amount numeric(10,2), max_credit numeric(10,2),
    OUT success boolean, OUT remaining_balance numeric(10,2)) AS
$$
BEGIN
    UPDATE accounts SET balance = balance - i_amount
    WHERE username = i_username
      AND balance - i_amount > - max_credit
 RETURNING balance
    INTO remaining_balance;
  IF NOT FOUND THEN
    success := FALSE;
    SELECT balance
      FROM accounts
     WHERE username = i_username
      INTO remaining_balance;
  ELSE
```

```
        success := TRUE;

    END IF;

END;

$$ LANGUAGE plpgsql;
```

You can call it simply by running this line from your client:

```
SELECT * FROM consume_balance ('bob', 7, 0);
```

The output will return the success variable. It tells you whether there was sufficient balance in Bob's account. The output will also return a number telling the balance Bob has left after this operation.

Reporting performance problems

Sometimes, you face performance issues and feel lost, but you should never feel alone when working with one of the most successful open source projects ever.

How to do it...

If you need to get some advice on your performance problems, then the right place to do so is the performance mailing list at `http://archives.postgresql.org/pgsql-performance/`.

You may want to first ensure that it is not a well-known problem by searching the mailing list archives.

A very good description of what to include in your performance problem report is available at `http://wiki.postgresql.org/wiki/Guide_to_reporting_problems`.

There's more...

More performance-related information can be found at `http://wiki.postgresql.org/wiki/Performance_Optimization`.

Another good reference for performance-related information is *PostgreSQL 9.0 High Performance, Packt Publishing*.

11
Backup and Recovery

In this chapter, we will cover the following recipes:

- Understanding and controlling crash recovery
- Planning backups
- Hot logical backup of one database
- Hot logical backup of all databases
- Hot logical backup of all tables in a tablespace
- Backup of database object definitions
- Standalone hot physical database backup
- Hot physical backup and continuous archiving
- Recovery of all databases
- Recovery to a point in time
- Recovery of a dropped/damaged table
- Recovery of a dropped/damaged tablespace
- Recovery of a dropped/damaged database
- Improving performance of backup/recovery
- Incremental/differential backup and restore
- Hot physical backups with Barman
- Recovery with Barman

Introduction

Most people admit that backups are essential, though they also devote a very small amount of time to thinking about the topic.

The first recipe is about understanding and controlling crash recovery. You need to understand what happens if the database server crashes so that you can understand when you might need to recover.

The next recipe is all about planning. That's really the best place to start before you go charging ahead to do backups.

The physical backup mechanisms here were initially written by me (Simon Riggs) for PostgreSQL in release 8.0 in 2004, and have been supported by me ever since then, now with increasing help from the community as its popularity grows. 2ndQuadrant has also been providing database recovery services since 2004, and regrettably many people have needed them as a result of missing or damaged backups.

Understanding and controlling crash recovery

Crash recovery is the PostgreSQL subsystem that saves us, should the server crash or fail as part of a system crash.

It's good to understand a little about it and to do what we can to control it in our favor.

How to do it...

If PostgreSQL crashes, there will be a message in the server log with the severity level of `PANIC`. PostgreSQL will immediately restart and attempt to recover using the transaction log or **Write-Ahead Log (WAL)**.

The WAL consists of a series of files written to the `pg_xlog` subdirectory of the PostgreSQL `data` directory. Each change made to the database is recorded first in WAL, hence the name "write-ahead" log, as a synonym of "transaction log". When a transaction commits, the default—and safe—behavior is to force the WAL records to disk. Should PostgreSQL crash, the WAL will be replayed, which returns the database to the point of the last committed transaction, and thus ensures the durability of any database changes.

 Database changes themselves aren't written to disk at transaction commit. Those changes are written to disk sometime later by the background writer on a well-tuned server.

Crash recovery replays the WAL, but from what point does it start to recover? Recovery starts from points in the WAL known as **checkpoints**. The duration of crash recovery depends on the number of changes in the transaction log since the last checkpoint. A checkpoint is a known safe starting point for recovery, since it guarantees that all the previous changes to the database have already been written to disk.

A checkpoint can become a performance bottleneck on busy database servers because of the number of writes required. We will see a number of ways of tuning that, but you must also understand the effect that those tuning options may cause on crash recovery.

A checkpoint can be either immediate or scheduled. Immediate checkpoints are triggered by some action of a superuser, such as the `CHECKPOINT` command or other; scheduled checkpoints are decided automatically by PostgreSQL.

Two parameters control the occurrence of scheduled checkpoints. The first is `checkpoint_segments`, which controls the number of 16 MB WAL files that will be written before a checkpoint is triggered. While this parameter considers the amount of WAL written, the second parameter is time-based instead; it is known as `checkpoint_timeout`, and is the number of seconds until the next checkpoint. A checkpoint is called whenever either of these two limits is reached.

It's tempting to banish checkpoints as much as possible by setting the following parameters:

```
checkpoint_segments = 1000
checkpoint_timeout = 3600
```

However, if you do this, you should give some thought to how long the crash recovery will be if you do and whether you want that.

Also, you should make sure that the `pg_xlog` directory is mounted on disks with enough disk space for at least 3 x 16 MB x `checkpoint_segments` or 16 MB x `wal_keep_segments`, whichever is bigger. Put another way, you normally need 48 GB of disk space in `pg_xlog` for `checkpoint_segments` equal to 1000, assuming that `wal_keep_segments` is less than 3000.

> This formula is a rough estimate, not an absolute limit. It is based on the assumption that the workload has not changed in the recent past. The actual amount of WAL files can be bigger, because PostgreSQL will produce as many WAL files as needed, and they will be removed from `pg_xlog` based on the completion of later checkpoints.
>
> In PostgreSQL 9.5 and beyond, this complex formula is replaced by the `max_wal_size` parameter, which is easier to understand and set correctly, and uses the same formula internally.

How it works...

Recovery continues until the end of the transaction log. WAL is being written continually, so there is no defined end point; it is literally the last correct record. Each WAL record is individually CRC-checked so that we know whether a record is complete and valid before trying to process it. Each record contains a pointer to the previous record, so we can tell that the record forms a valid link in the chain of actions recorded in WAL. As a result of that, recovery always ends with some kind of error in reading the next WAL record. That is normal and means "the next record does not exist (yet)".

Recovery performance can be very fast, though its speed does depend on the actions being recovered. The best way to test recovery performance is to set up a standby replication server, described in *Chapter 12, Replication and Upgrades*, because it is actually implemented as a variant of crash recovery.

There's more...

It's possible for a problem to be caused by replaying the transaction log, so that the database server will fail to start.

Some people's response to this is to use a utility named `pg_resetxlog`, which removes the current transaction log files and tidies up after that surgery has taken place.

The `pg_resetxlog` utility destroys data changes, and that means data loss. If you do decide to run that utility, make sure you take a backup of the `pg_xlog` directory first. Our advice is to seek immediate assistance rather than do this. You don't know for certain that doing this will fix a problem, though once you've done it, you will have difficulty going backwards.

Planning backups

This recipe is all about thinking ahead and planning. If you're reading this recipe before you take a backup, well done!

The key thing to understand is that you should plan your recovery, not your backup. The type of backup you take influences the type of recovery that is possible, so you must give some thought to what you are trying to achieve beforehand.

If you want to plan your recovery, then you need to consider the different types of failures that can occur. What type of recovery do you wish to perform?

You need to consider the following main aspects:

- ► Full or partial database?
- ► Everything or just object definitions only?

- ▸ Point-in-Time Recovery
- ▸ Restore performance

We need to look at the characteristics of the utilities to understand what our backup and recovery options are. It's often beneficial to have multiple types of backup to cover the different types of failure possible.

Your main backup options are the following:

- ▸ Logical backup, using `pg_dump`
- ▸ Physical backup, which is a filesystem backup

The `pg_dump` utility comes in two main flavors: `pg_dump` and `pg_dumpall`. `pg_dump` has a `-F` option for producing backups in various file formats. The file format is very important when it comes to restoring from backup, so you need to pay close attention to it.

How to do it...

The following table shows the features available, depending on the backup technique selected. The details of these techniques are covered in the remaining recipes in this chapter.

	SQL dump to an archive file: `pg_dump -F c`	SQL dump to a script file: `pg_dump -F p` **or** `pg_dumpall`	Filesystem backup using `pg_start_backup`
Backup type	Logical	Logical	Physical
Recover to point in time?	No	No	Yes
Back up all databases?	One at a time	Yes (`pg_dumpall`)	Yes
All databases backed up at same time?	No	No	Yes
Selective backup	Yes	Yes	No (see note 3)
Incremental backup	No	No	Possible (see note 4)
Selective restore	Yes	Possible (see note 1)	No (see note 5)
`DROP TABLE` recovery	Yes	Yes	Possible (see note 6)
`DROP TABLESPACE` recovery	Possible (see note 2)	Possible (see note 6)	Possible (see note 6)
Compressed backup files	Yes	Yes	Yes
Backup in multiple files	No	No	Yes

	SQL dump to an archive file: `pg_dump -F c`	SQL dump to a script file: `pg_dump -F p` **or** `pg_dumpall`	Filesystem backup using `pg_start_backup`
Parallel backup possible?	No	No	Yes
Parallel restore possible?	Yes	No	Yes
Restore to later release?	Yes	Yes	No
Standalone backup	Yes	Yes	Yes (see note 7)
Allows DDL during backup	No	No	Yes

Here follow the notes referenced in the preceding table:

1. If you've generated a script with `pg_dump` or `pg_dumpall` and need to restore just a single object, then you will to need to go deep. You will need to write a Perl script (or similar) to read the file and extract the parts you want. This is messy and time-consuming, but probably faster than restoring the whole thing to a second server, and then extracting just the parts you need with another `pg_dump`.

2. See the *Recovery of a dropped/damaged tablespace* recipe.

3. Selective backup with a physical backup is possible, but will cause problems later when you try to restore.

4. See the *Incremental/differential backup and restore* recipe.

5. Selective restore with a physical backup isn't possible with the currently supplied utilities.

6. See the *Recovery of a dropped/damaged tablespace* recipe.

7. See the *Standalone hot physical database backup* recipe.

Hot logical backup of one database

Logical backup makes a copy of the data in the database by dumping the content of each table.

How to do it...

The command to do this is simple, as follows:

```
pg_dump -F c > dumpfile
```

Or, you can use the following command:

```
pg_dump -F c -f dumpfile
```

You can also do this through pgAdmin3, as shown in the following screenshot:

How it works...

The `pg_dump` utility produces a single output file. This output file can use the `split` command to separate the file into multiple pieces, if required.

The `pg_dump` archive file, also known as **custom format**, is lightly compressed by default. Compression can be removed or made more aggressive.

`pg_dump` runs by executing SQL statements against the database to unload data. When PostgreSQL runs an SQL statement, we take a "snapshot" of currently running transactions, which freezes our viewpoint of the database. From version 9.3 onwards, `pg_dump` can take a parallel dump of a single database using the **snapshot export** feature, introduced in the previous version.

We can't (yet) share that snapshot across sessions connected to more than one database, so we cannot run an exactly consistent pg_dump in parallel across many databases.

The time of the snapshot is the only time we can recover to—we can't recover to a time either before or after that time. Note that the snapshot time is the start of the backup, not the end.

When pg_dump runs, it holds the very lowest kind of lock on the tables being dumped. Those are designed to prevent DDL from running against the tables while the dump takes place. If a dump is run at the point at which other DDL are already running, then the dump will sit and wait. If you want to limit the waiting time, you can do that by setting the --lock-wait-timeout option.

Since pg_dump runs SQL queries to extract data, it will have some performance impact, which must be taken into account on a live server in view of the available capacity.

The pg_dump utility allows you to take a selective backup of tables. The -t option also allows you to specify views and sequences. There's no way to dump other object types individually using pg_dump. You can use some supplied functions to extract individual snippets of information. These functions are available at http://www.postgresql.org/docs/9.4/static/functions-info.html#FUNCTIONS-INFO-CATALOG-TABLE.

The pg_dump utility works against earlier releases of PostgreSQL, so it can be used to migrate data between releases.

Before extension support was introduced in version 9.1, pg_dump didn't generally handle included modules very well. More specifically, objects created as parts of these modules (for example, functions and configuration tables) were treated in the same way as objects belonging to the database, so the backup included a copy of all the objects in each module. This causes an unnecessary increase in backup complexity and size, plus possible module upgrade activities on each restore. One main feature of extension support is to make pg_dump aware of additional tables and functions that have been installed as part of an additional package, such as PostGIS or Slony, so that they are recreated by issuing appropriate CREATE EXTENSION commands, instead of dumping and restoring them together with the other database objects. Extension support removes such difficulties when restoring from a logical backup, maintaining the list of additional tables that have been created as part of the software installation process. Look at the *Managing installed extensions* recipe in *Chapter 3, Configuration*, for more details.

There's more...

What time was the pg_dump taken? The snapshot for a pg_dump is taken at the beginning of a run. The file modification time will tell you when the dump finished. The dump is consistent at the time of the snapshot, so you may want to know that time.

If you are making a script dump, you can do a dump verbose, as follows:

```
pg_dump -v
```

This then adds the time to the top of the script. Custom dumps store the start time as well, and that can be accessed using the following:

```
pg_restore --schema-only -v dumpfile | head | grep Started
-- Started on 2010-06-03 09:05:46 BST
```

See also

 ▸ Note that pg_dump does not dump roles (such as users and groups) and tablespaces. Those two are only dumped by pg_dumpall; see the next recipes for more detailed descriptions.

Hot logical backup of all databases

If you have more than one database in your PostgreSQL server, you may want to back up all the databases together.

How to do it...

My recommendation is that you do exactly what you did for one database to each database in your cluster.

You can run those individual dumps in parallel if you want to speed things up.

Once this is complete, dump the global information also using the following:

```
pg_dumpall -g
```

How it works...

To back up all databases, you may be told you need to use the pg_dumpall utility. I have four reasons why you shouldn't do that, which are as follows:

 ▸ If you use pg_dumpall, then the only output produced is in a script file. Script files can't use the parallel restore feature of pg_restore, so by taking your backup in this way, you will be forcing the restore to be slower than it needs to be.

 ▸ The pg_dumpall utility produces dumps of each database one after another. This means that pg_dumpall is slower than running multiple pg_dump tasks in parallel, one against each database.

▶ The dumps of individual databases are not consistent to a particular point in time. As we pointed out in a previous recipe, if you start the dump at 04:00 and it ends at 07:00, then you cannot be sure exactly what time the dump relates to; it could be anytime between 04:00 and 07:00.

▶ Options for `pg_dumpall` are similar in many ways to `pg_dump`, though not all of them exist, so some things aren't possible.

See also

▶ Also, look at the Hot physical backup options.

Hot logical backup of all tables in a tablespace

Sometimes, we may wish to make a dump of tables and data in a tablespace. Unfortunately, there isn't a simple command to do this, so we need to write some reusable scripts.

How to do it...

It is possible for a tablespace to contain objects from more than one database, so run the following query to see from which databases you need to dump:

```
SELECT datname
FROM pg_database
WHERE oid IN (
    SELECT pg_tablespace_databases(ts.oid)
    FROM pg_tablespace ts
    WHERE spcname = 'mytablespacename');
```

The following procedure allows you to dump all tables that reside on a given tablespace and within *one* database only:

1. Create a file named `onets.sql` that contains the following SQL. This query extracts the list of tables in a tablespace:

```
SELECT 'pg_dump '
|| array_to_string(
    array_agg('-t ' || n.nspname || '.' || t.relname)
  , ' ')
|| ' -F c ' || :'DBNAME'
|| ' > dumpfile_' || :'DBNAME' -- name of the output file
FROM pg_class t
```

```
JOIN pg_tablespace ts
  ON ts.oid = t.reltablespace
JOIN pg_namespace n
  ON n.oid = t.relnamespace
WHERE ts.spcname = :'TSNAME'
  AND t.relkind = 'r';
```

2. Execute the query on the chosen database to build the corresponding pg_dump script:

    ```
    psql -Aqt -v TSNAME=mytablespace -f onets.sql mydb > get_my_ts_
    mydb
    ```

3. From the recovered database server, dump the tables in the tablespace, including data and definitions. The output file is named dumpfile_mydb from the last line in the first step:

    ```
    chmod 755 get_my_ts_mydb
    ./get_my_ts_mydb
    ```

How it works...

The pg_dump utility allows you to specify more than one table on the command line, so it's possible to generate a list of tables directly from the database.

We use the named parameter in psql to create a parameterized script, which we then execute to create a dump.

The script name includes the database name to reduce the chances of making mistakes in multidatabase installations.

Backup of database object definitions

Sometimes, it's useful to get a dump of the object definitions that make up a database. This is useful for comparing what's in the database against the definitions in a data- or object-modeling tool. It's also useful to make sure you can recreate objects in the correct schema, tablespace, and database with the correct ownership and permissions.

How to do it...

The basic command to dump the definitions only is the following:

```
pg_dumpall --schema-only > myscriptdump.sql
```

This includes all objects, including roles, tablespaces, databases, schemas, tables, indexes, triggers, constraints, views, functions, ownerships, and privileges.

If you want to dump PostgreSQL role definitions, you can use this command:

```
pg_dumpall --roles-only > myroles.sql
```

If you want to dump PostgreSQL tablespace definitions, you can use the following:

```
pg_dumpall --tablespaces-only > mytablespaces.sql
```

If you want to dump both roles and tablespaces, then you can use this:

```
pg_dumpall --globals-only > myglobals.sql
```

The output is a human-readable script file that can be re-executed to recreate each of the databases.

 The short form for the `--globals-only` option is `-g`, which we have already seen in a previous recipe, *Hot logical backup of all databases*. Similar abbreviations exist for `--schema-only` (`-s`), `--tablespaces-only` (`-t`), and `--roles-only` (`-r`).

There's more...

In PostgreSQL, the word "schema" is also used to describe a set of related database objects similar to a directory, also known as a "namespace". Be careful that you don't confuse what is happening here. The `--schema-only` option makes a backup of the "database schema", that is, the definitions of all objects in the database (and in all namespaces). To make a backup of the data and definitions in just one namespace and one database, use `pg_dump` with the `-n` option. To make a backup of only the definitions, in just one namespace and one database, use `pg_dump` with both `-n` and `--schema-only` together.

Standalone hot physical database backup

Hot physical backup is an important capability for databases.

Physical backup allows us to get a completely consistent view of the changes to all databases at once. Physical backup also allows us to back up even while DDL changes are being executed on the database. Apart from resource constraints, there is no additional overhead or locking with this approach.

Physical backup procedures are slightly more complex than logical backup procedures. So, let's start with a simple procedure to produce a standalone backup.

How to do it...

The following steps assume that a number of environment variables have been set, which are as follows:

- ▶ $PGDATA is the path to the PostgreSQL `data` directory, ending with /
- ▶ $BACKUPNAME is the filename of a backup file, that is, `mybackup.tar`
- ▶ All required PostgreSQL connection parameters have been set

 The initial procedure is step 1 onwards. If you are running subsequent backups, start from step 6.

The steps are as follows:

1. Create a new archive directory, if it is not already present, as follows:

   ```
   cd $PGDATA
   mkdir ../standalone
   ```

2. Set an `archive_command`. In `postgresql.conf` you will need to add the following lines and restart the server, or just confirm that they are present:

   ```
   archive_mode = on
   archive_command = 'test ! ../standalone/archiving_active ||
                      cp -i %p ../standalone/archive/%f'
   ```

   The last setting is split into two lines only for typesetting reasons; in `postgresql.conf`, you must keep it in a single line.

   You must also ensure that `wal_level` is set to a value different from minimal, for instance:

   ```
   wal_level = archive
   ```

3. Start archiving, as follows:

   ```
   mkdir ../standalone/archive
   touch ../standalone/archiving_active
   ```

4. Start the backup, as follows:

   ```
   psql -c "select pg_start_backup('standalone')"
   ```

5. Take a base backup—copy the data files (excluding the content of the `pg_xlog` directory), using this command:

   ```
   tar -cv --exclude="pg_xlog/*" \
   -f ../standalone/$BACKUPNAME $PGDATA
   ```

6. Stop the backup, as follows:

```
psql -c "select pg_stop_backup(), current_timestamp"
```

7. Stop archiving, as follows:

```
rm ../standalone/archiving_active
```

8. Move the files to the `archive` subdirectory, ready for recovery, as follows:

```
mv ../standalone/archive/ archive/
```

9. Add the archived files to the standalone backup, like this:

```
tar -rf  ../standalone/$BACKUPNAME  archive/
```

10. Write a `recovery.conf` file with which to recover. Note that the archive directory mentioned here must match the location to which files are moved in step 8:

```
echo "restore_command = 'cp archive/%f %p'" > recovery.conf
echo "recovery_end_command = 'rm -R archive' " >> recovery.conf
```

11. Add the `recovery.conf` to the archive, as follows:

```
tar -rf  ../standalone/$BACKUPNAME  recovery.conf
```

12. Store `../standalone/$BACKUPNAME` somewhere safe. A safe place is definitely not on the same server.

This procedure ends with a file named $BACKUPNAME in the standalone directory. So, you need to remember to copy it somewhere safe. This file contains everything that you need to recover, including a recovery parameter file.

How it works...

The backup produced by the preceding procedure allows you to restore only to a single point in time. That point is the time of the `pg_stop_backup()` function.

A physical backup takes a copy of all files in the database (step 5: the "base backup"). That alone is not sufficient as a backup, and you need the other steps as well. A simple copy of the database produces a time-inconsistent copy of the database files. To make the backup time consistent, we need to add to it all the changes that took place from the start to the end of the backup. That's why we have steps 4 and 6 to bracket our backup step.

The changes made are put in the standalone/archive directory as a set of archived transaction log or Write-Ahead log (WAL) files. Step 1 creates the archive directory. Step 2 sets the parameters that copy the files to the archive. Changing `archive_mode` requires us to restart the database server, so we use a well-known trick to avoid restarting while switching archiving on and off: `archive_command` is conditional upon the existence of a file named `archiving_active`, whose presence enables or disables the archiving process.

Note that this is just one of the possible ways to configure archiving, so PostgreSQL doesn't always need to work this way. Steps 3 and 7 enable and disable archiving respectively, so we only store copies of the WAL files created during the period of the backup. Thus, steps 1 and 2 are about setup, and steps 3 to 9 are where the backup happens. Step 10 onwards is gift wrapping, so that the backup script ends with everything in one neat file.

Step 8 moves the archived files under the `data` directory, a more convenient location from which to restore. Step 9 appends the WAL files to the backup file so that it is just one file.

Steps 10 and 11 add a `recovery.conf` file with its parameters set up so that there are no manual steps when we recover from this backup. This isn't explained here; to know more, refer to the *Recovery of all databases* recipe.

The key to understanding this is that we need both the base backup and the appropriate archived WAL files to allow us to recover. Without both of these, we have nothing. Most of the steps are designed to ensure that we really will have the appropriate WAL files in all cases.

There's more...

From version 9.1 onwards, PostgreSQL ships a command-line utility called `pg_basebackup`. This uses the streaming replication infrastructure to carry out steps 4 to 6, which you just saw. As an alternative, it is simpler than using `rsync` and issuing `pg_start_backup()` and `pg_stop_backup()` manually, but it requires configuration of streaming replication (as covered in the *Setting up streaming replication* recipe in *Chapter 12, Replication and Upgrades*). Another alternative is to use the Barman software, which we will describe in two recipes: *Hot physical backups with Barman* and *Recovery with Barman*.

See also

> ▶ It's common to use continuous archiving when using the physical backup technique because that allows you to recover to any point in time, should you need that.

Hot physical backup and continuous archiving

This recipe describes how to set up a hot physical backup with a continuous archiving mechanism. The purpose of continuous archiving is to allow us to recover to any point in time from the time of the backup.

Manually performing each step of this procedure is a great way to gain a clear understanding of PostgreSQL's backup and restore infrastructure. However, to reduce the chances of human errors, it is best practice to avoid reliance on complex activities that must be performed by a human operator. Procedures such as taking a hot physical backup or restoring it up to a given point in time are at least automated with custom scripts, and normally it is preferable to use a third-party, specialized tool because independent inspection and exposure to many users help prevent subtle bugs, which could even lead to data loss.

My (Gianni's) favorite tool is Barman, an open source command-line utility in Python written by my colleagues; you can see its use in two upcoming recipes: *Hot physical backups with Barman* and *Recovery with Barman*.

Other open source tools include **pg-rman** and **OmniPITR**, all with different sets of features. You can find more information on these on their respective websites:

- **Barman**: http://www.pgbarman.org/
- **pg-rman**: http://code.google.com/p/pg-rman/
- **OmniPITR**: http://github.com/omniti-labs/omnipitr/

Getting ready

This recipe builds upon the previous recipe, *Standalone hot physical database backup*. You should read that before following this recipe.

You need to decide a few things, which are as follows:

- Where will you store the WAL files (known as the archive)?
- How will you send WAL files to the archive?
- Where will you store your base backups?
- How will you take base backups?
- How many backups will you keep? What is your policy for maintaining the archive?

These are hard questions to answer immediately. So, we give a practical example as a way of explaining how this works, and then let the user decide how they would like it to operate.

How to do it...

The rest of this recipe assumes the following answers to the key questions:

- The archive is a directory on a remote server named $OTHERNODE
- We send WAL files to the archive using scp

- ▸ Base backups are also stored on $OTHERNODE
- ▸ Base backups are made using rsync
- ▸ We'll keep two backups, overwriting alternate backups as we take new backups, and backups are taken every Sunday

The following steps assume that a number of environment variables have been set, which are as follows:

- ▸ $PGDATA is the path to the PostgreSQL data directory, ending with /.
- ▸ $OTHERNODE is the name of the remote server.
- ▸ $BACKUPNAME is either b1/ or b2/, and we alternate this each time we take a backup. Two backups are the minimum; you may wish to use more copies.
- ▸ All the required PostgreSQL connection parameters have been set.

We also assume that the postgres user can connect via SSH to the backup server from the server where PostgreSQL is running, without having to type a passphrase. This is a standard procedure, which is described in detail in several places, including Barman's documentation at http://docs.pgbarman.org/.

The procedure is as follows:

1. Create the archive and backup directories on a backup server.
2. Set an archive_command. In postgresql.conf, you will need to add the following lines and restart the server, or just confirm that they are present.

   ```
   archive_mode = on
   archive_command = 'scp %p $OTHERNODE:/archive/%f'
   ```

3. Start the backup, as follows:

   ```
   psql -c "select pg_start_backup('my backup')"
   ```

4. Copy the data files (excluding the content of the pg_xlog directory), like this:

   ```
   rsync -cva --inplace -exclude='pg_xlog/*' \
   ${PGDATA}/   $OTHERNODE:$BACKUPNAME/$PGDATA
   ```

5. Stop the backup, as follows:

   ```
   psql -c "select pg_stop_backup(), current_timestamp"
   ```

It's also good practice to put a README.backup file in the data directory prior to the backup so that it forms a part of the set of files that make up the base backup. This should say something intelligent about the location of the archive, including any identification numbers, names, and so on.

Notice that we didn't put a `recovery.conf` in the backup this time. That's because we're assuming we want flexibility at the time of recovery, rather than a gift-wrapped solution. The reason for that is we don't know when, where, or how we will be recovering, nor do we need to make a decision on that yet.

How it works...

The key point here is that we must have both the base backup and the archive in order to recover. Where you put them is entirely up to you. You can use any filesystem backup technology and/or filesystem backup management system to do this.

Many backup management systems have claimed that they have a PostgreSQL interface or plugin, but this most often means they support logical backup. However, there's no need for them to officially support PostgreSQL; there isn't any "Runs on PostgreSQL" badge or certification required. If you can copy files, then you can run the preceding processes to keep your database safe.

The preceding procedure uses a simple secure file copy, though it could've also used `rsync`. In case the network or backup server goes down, then the command will begin to fail. When the `archive_command` fails, it will repeatedly retry until it succeeds. PostgreSQL does not remove WAL files from `pg_xlog` until they have been successfully archived, so the end result is that your `pg_xlog` directory fills up. It's a good idea to have an `archive_command` that reacts better to that condition, though that is left as an improvement for the sysadmin. A typical action is to make it an emergency call-out so that we can resolve the problem manually. Automatic resolution is difficult to get right, as this condition is one for which it is hard to test.

While continuously archiving, we will generate a considerable number of WAL files. If `archive_timeout` is set to 30 seconds, we will generate a minimum of 2*60*24 = 2880 files per day, each 16 MB in size. This amounts to a total volume of 46 GB per day (minimum). With a reasonable transaction rate, a database server might generate 100 GB of archive data per day, so you should use that as a rough figure for calculations before you get better measurements. Of course, the rate could be much higher, with rates of 1 TB per day or higher being possible. Clearly, we would only want to store WAL files that are useful for backup, so when we decide that we no longer wish to keep a backup, we will also want to remove files from the archive. In each base backup, you will find a file called `backup_label`. The earliest WAL file required by a physical backup is the filename mentioned in the first line of the `backup_label` file. We can use a contrib module called `pg_archivecleanup` to remove any WAL files created earlier than the earliest file.

If you compress WAL files regularly, you may have noticed that files produced by PostgreSQL 9.4 can be compressed better than those produced by earlier versions. This is a positive side effect of the new WAL insertion mechanism, which improves performance on concurrent workloads.

Recovery of all databases

Recovery of a complete database server, including all of its databases, is an important feature. This recipe covers how to do that in the simplest way possible.

Some complexities are discussed here, though most are covered in later recipes.

Getting ready

Find a suitable server on which to perform the restore.

Before you recover onto a live server, always take another backup. Whatever problem you thought you had could just be about to get worse.

How to do it...

Here, we'll provide three distinct examples, depending on what type of backup was taken.

Logical – from the custom dump taken with pg_dump -F c

The procedure is as follows:

1. Restore of all databases means simply restoring each individual database from each dump you took. Confirm that you have the correct backup before you restore:

   ```
   pg_restore --schema-only -v dumpfile | head | grep Started
   ```

2. Reload global objects from the script file, as follows:

   ```
   psql -f myglobals.sql
   ```

3. Reload all databases. Create the databases using parallel tasks to speed things up. This can be executed remotely without the need to transfer a dumpfile between systems. Note that there is a separate dumpfile for each database:

   ```
   pg_restore -d postgres -j 4 dumpfile
   ```

Logical – from the script dump created by pg_dump –F p

As earlier, though with this command to execute the script, this can be executed remotely without needing to transfer the dumpfile between systems:

1. Confirm that you have the correct backup before you restore. If the following command returns nothing, then it means the file is not timestamped, and you'll have to identify it in a different way:

   ```
   head myscriptdump.sql | grep Started
   ```

2. Reload globals from the script file, as follows:

```
psql -f myglobals.sql
```

3. Reload all scripts like the following:

```
psql -f myscriptdump.sql
```

Logical – from the script dump created by pg_dumpall

We need to follow the procedure that is shown next:

1. Confirm that you have the correct backup before you restore. If the following command returns nothing, then it means the file is not timestamped, and you'll have to identify it in a different way:

```
head myscriptdump.sql | grep Started
```

2. Find a suitable server, or create a new virtual server.

3. Reload the script in full:

```
psql -f myscriptdump.sql
```

Physical

The steps are as follows:

1. If you've used the *Standalone hot physical database backup* recipe, then recovery is very easy. Restore the backup file in the target server.

2. Extract the backup file to the new `data` directory.

3. Confirm that you have the correct backup before you restore:

```
$ cat backup_label
START WAL LOCATION: 0/12000020 (file 000000010000000000000012)
CHECKPOINT LOCATION: 0/12000058
START TIME: 2010-06-03 19:53:23 BST
LABEL: standalone
```

4. Verify that all file permissions and ownerships are correct and links are valid. This should already be the case if you are using the `postgres` user ID everywhere, which is recommended.

5. Start the server.

This procedure is so simple because in the *Standalone hot physical database backup* recipe we gift-wrapped everything for you. That also helped you understand that you need both a base backup and the appropriate WAL files.

If you've used other techniques, then you need to step through the tasks to make sure you cover everything required, as follows:

1. Shut down any server running in the `data` directory.

2. Restore the backup so that any files in the `data` directory that have matching names are replaced with the version from the backup. (The manual says, "delete all files and then restore the backup". That might be a lot slower than running an `rsync` between your backup and the destination without the `--update` option.) Remember that this step can be performed in parallel to speed things up, though it is up to you to script that.

3. Ensure that all file permissions and ownerships are correct and links are valid. This should already be the case if you are using the `postgres` user ID everywhere, which is recommended.

4. Remove any files that are in `pg_xlog/`. If you've been following my recipes, you'll be able to skip this step because we never backed them up in the first place.

5. Add a `recovery.conf` and set its file permissions correctly.

6. Copy in `pg_xlog/` the latest WAL files from a running server, if there are any.

7. Start the server.

The only part that requires some thought and checking is which parameters you select for the `recovery.conf` file. There's only one that matters here, and that is the `restore_command`.

The `restore_command` tells us how to restore archived WAL files. It needs to be the command that will be executed to bring back WAL files from the archive.

The reason we copy additional WAL files in step 5 is to ensure that PostgreSQL can restore the most recent WAL records, even from the WAL file that is currently written (and therefore, not archived yet).

If you are thinking ahead, there'll be a `README.backup` file for you to read and find out how to set the `restore_command`. If it is not there, then presumably, you've got the location of the WAL files you've been saving written down somewhere. Say, for example, that your files are being saved to a directory named `/backups/pg/servername/archive`, owned by the `postgres` user.

On a remote server named `backup1`, we would then write all this on one line of the `recovery.conf` file, as follows:

```
restore_command = 'scp backup1:/backups/pg/servername/archive/%f
    %p'
```

How it works...

PostgreSQL is designed to require very minimal information to perform a recovery. We'll try hard to wrap all the details up for you:

- **Logical recovery:** This executes SQL to recreate the database objects. If performance is an issue, look at the *Improving performance of backup/recovery* recipe.

- **Physical recovery:** This reapplies data changes at the block level, and so, tends to be much faster than logical recovery. It requires both a base backup and a set of archived WAL files.

There is a file named `backup_label` in the `data` directory of the base backup. This tells us to retrieve a `.backup` file from the archive that contains the start and stop WAL locations of the base backup. Recovery then starts to apply changes from the starting WAL location, and it must proceed as far as the stop address for the backup to be valid.

After the recovery is complete, the `recovery.conf` file is renamed to `recovery.done` to prevent the server from re-entering recovery.

The server log records each WAL file restored from the archive, so you can check the progress and rate of recovery. You can query the archive to find the name of the latest restored WAL file to allow you to calculate how many files are left to recover.

The `restore_command` should return 0 if a file has been restored and non-zero for cases of failure. Recovery will proceed until there is no next WAL file, so eventually there will be an error recorded in the logs.

If you have lost some of the WAL files, or they are damaged, then recovery will stop at that point. No further changes after that will be applied, and you will likely lose those changes. That will be the time to call your support vendor.

There's more...

You can start and stop the server once recovery has started without any problem. It will not interfere with the recovery.

You can connect to the database server while it is recovering and run queries, if that is useful. This is known as **Hot Standby mode**, and is discussed in *Chapter 12, Replication and Upgrades*.

See also

- Once the recovery reaches the stop address, you can stop it at any point, as discussed in the *Recovery to a point in time* recipe.

- The procedure described in this recipe is covered by the command-line utility, Barman, mentioned in the *Hot physical backup and continuous archiving recipe*.

Recovery to a point in time

If your database suffers a problem at 3:22 p.m. and your backup was taken at 4:00 a.m., you're probably hoping there is a way to recover the changes made between those two times. What you need is known as **Point-in-Time Recovery (PITR)**.

Regrettably, if you've made a backup with `pg_dump` at 4:00 a.m. then you won't be able to recover to any other time. As a result, the term PITR has become synonymous with the physical backup and restore technique in PostgreSQL.

Getting ready

If you have a backup made with `pg_dump`, then give up all hope of using that as a starting point for a PITR. It's a frequently asked question, but the answer is still *no*. The reason it gets asked is exactly why I'm pleading with you to plan your backups ahead of time.

First, you need to decide what the point of time is to which you would like to recover. If the answer is "as late as possible", then you don't need to do a PITR at all, just recover until end of logs.

How to do it...

How do you decide to what point to recover? The point where we stop recovery is known as the **recovery target**. The most straightforward way is to do this based on a timestamp.

In `recovery.conf`, you can add (or uncomment) a line that says the following, or something similar:

```
recovery_target_time = '2010-06-01 16:59:14.27452+01'
```

Note that you need to be careful to specify the time zone of the target so that it matches the time zone of the server that wrote the log. That might differ from the time zone of the current server, so check them.

After that, you can check the progress during a recovery by running queries in Hot Standby mode.

How it works...

Recovery works by applying individual WAL records. These correspond to individual block changes, so there are many WAL records for each transaction. The final part of any successful transaction is a commit WAL record, though there are abort records as well. Each transaction completion record has a timestamp that allows us to decide whether to stop at that point or not.

You can also define a recovery target using a **transaction ID (xid)**, though finding out which xid to use is somewhat difficult, and you may need to refer to external records, if they exist.

The recovery target is specified in `recovery.conf` and cannot change while the server is running. If you want to change the recovery target, you can shut down the server, edit the `recovery.conf`, and then restart the server. Be careful, however; if you change the recovery target and recovery is already past the new point, it can lead to errors. If you define a `recovery_target_timestamp` that has already been passed, then the recovery will stop almost immediately, though this will be after the correct stopping point. If you define a `recovery_target_xid` that has already been passed, then the recovery will just continue until the end of the logs. Restarting a recovery from the beginning using a fresh restore of the base backup is always safe.

Once a server completes the recovery, it will assign a new timeline. Once a server is fully available, we can write new changes to the database. Those changes might differ from the changes we made in a previous "future history" of the database. So, we differentiate between alternate futures using different timelines. If we need to go back and run the recovery again, we can create a new server history using the original or subsequent timelines. The best way to think about this is that it is exactly like a Sci-fi novel—you can't change the past, but you can return to an earlier time and take a different action instead. However, you'll need to be careful not to get confused.

There's more...

The `pg_dump` utility cannot be used as a base backup for a PITR. The reason is that a log replay contains the physical changes to data blocks, not the logical changes based on primary keys. If you reload `pg_dump`, the data will likely go back into different data blocks, so the changes wouldn't correctly reference the data.

WAL doesn't contain enough information to fully reconstruct all SQL that produced those changes. Later feature additions to PostgreSQL may add the required information to WAL.

See also

PostgreSQL 9.1 introduces the ability to pause, resume, and stop recovery while the server is up dynamically. This allows you to use the Hot Standby facility to locate the correct stopping point more easily. You can trick Hot Standby into stopping recovery, which may help. See the *Delaying, pausing, and synchronizing replication* recipe in *Chapter 12, Replication and Upgrades*, on managing Hot Standby. This procedure is also covered by the command-line utility Barman, mentioned in the *Hot physical backup and continuous archiving* recipe.

Recovery of a dropped/damaged table

You may drop or even damage a table in some way. Tables could be damaged for physical reasons, such as disk corruption, or they could also be damaged by running poorly specified UPDATE or DELETE commands, which update too many rows or overwrite critical data.

It's a common request to recover from this situation from a backup.

How to do it...

The methods differ, depending on the type of backup you have available. If you have multiple types of backup, you have a choice.

Logical – from the custom dump taken with pg_dump -F c

If you've taken a logical backup using pg_dump in a custom file, then you can simply extract the table you want from the dumpfile, like the following:

```
pg_restore -t mydroppedtable dumpfile | psql
```

Alternatively, you can directly connect to the database using -d.

The preceding command tries to recreate the table and then load data into it. Note that the pg_restore -t option does not dump any of the indexes on the selected table. This means we need a slightly more complex procedure than it would first appear, and the procedure needs to vary depending on whether we are repairing a damaged table or putting back a dropped table.

To repair a damaged table we would want to replace the data in the table in a single transaction. There isn't a specific option to do this, so we need to do the following:

1. Dump the table to a script file, as follows:

   ```
   pg_restore -t mydamagedtable dumpfile > mydamagedtable.sql
   ```

2. Edit a script named repair_mydamagedtable.sql with the following code:

   ```
   BEGIN;
   TRUNCATE mydamagedtable;
   \i mydamagedtable.sql
   COMMIT;
   ```

3. Then, run it using the following command:

   ```
   psql -f repair_mydamagedtable.sql
   ```

If you've dropped a table then you need to perform these steps:

1. Create a new database in which to work, and name it `restorework`, as follows:

   ```
   CREATE DATABASE restorework;
   ```

2. Restore the complete schema to the new database, like this:

   ```
   pg_restore --schema-only -d restorework dumpfile
   ```

3. Now, dump only the definitions of the dropped table in a new file. It will contain `CREATE TABLE`, indexes, and other constraints and grants. Note that this database has no data in it, so specifying `--schema-only` is optional, as follows:

   ```
   pg_dump -t mydroppedtable --schema-only restorework >
   mydroppedtable.sql
   ```

4. Now, recreate the table on the main database:

   ```
   psql -f mydroppedtable.sql
   ```

5. Now, reload only the data into the `maindb` database, like this:

   ```
   pg_restore -t mydroppedtable --data-only -d maindb dumpfile
   ```

If you've got a very large table, then the fourth step can be a problem because it builds indexes as well. If you want, you can manually edit the script in two pieces, one before the load ("preload") and one after the load ("postload"). There are some ideas for that at the end of this recipe.

Logical – from the script dump

An easy way to restore a single table from a script is as follows:

1. Find a suitable server, or create a new virtual server.

2. Reload the script in full, as follows:

   ```
   psql -f myscriptdump.sql
   ```

3. From the recovered database server, dump the table, its data, and all the definitions of the dropped table into a new file:

   ```
   pg_dump -t mydroppedtable -F c mydatabase > dumpfile
   ```

4. Now, recreate the table in the original server and database, using parallel tasks to speed things up:

   ```
   pg_restore -d mydatabase -j 2 dumpfile
   ```

The last step can be executed remotely without having to transfer the dumpfile between systems. Just add connection parameters to `pg_restore`, as in the following example:

```
pg_restore -h remotehost -U remoteuser ...
```

The only way to extract a single table from a script dump without doing all the preceding steps is to write a custom script to read and extract only those parts of the file that you want. This can be complicated because you may need certain SET commands at the top of the file, the table, and data in the middle of the file, and the indexes and constraints on the table are near the end of the file. It's complex; the safer route is what we just mentioned.

Physical

To recover a single table from a physical backup, we need to perform these steps:

1. Find a suitable server, or create a new virtual server.

2. Recover the database server in full, as described in previous recipes on physical recovery, including all databases and all tables. You may wish to stop at a useful point in time, in which case you can look at the *Recovery to a point in time* recipe later in the chapter.

3. From the recovered database server, dump the table, its data, and all the definitions of the dropped table into a new file, as follows:

```
pg_dump -t mydroppedtable -F c mydatabase > dumpfile
```

4. Now, recreate the table in the original server and database using parallel tasks to speed things up. This can be executed remotely without needing to transfer the dumpfile between systems:

```
pg_restore -d mydatabase -j 2 dumpfile
```

How it works...

At present, there's no way to restore a single table from a physical restore in just a single step.

See also

Starting from PostgreSQL version 9.2, `pg_dump` and `pg_restore` are able to split the dump into three parts: pre-data, data, and post-data. Both commands support a `--section` option used to specify which section (s) should be dumped or reloaded.

Recovery of a dropped/damaged tablespace

Recovering a complete tablespace is also required sometimes. It's actually a lot easier than recovering a single table.

How to do it...

The methods differ, depending on the type of backup you have available. If you have multiple types of backup, you have a choice.

Logical – from the custom dump taken with pg_dump -F c

If you've taken a logical backup using `pg_dump` in a custom file, then you can simply extract the tables you want from the dumpfile, like the following:

```
pg_restore -t mytab1 -t mytab2 …  dumpfile | psql
```

Alternatively, you can directly connect to the database using `-d`.

Of course, you may have difficulty remembering exactly which tables were there. So, you may need to proceed like this:

1. Find a suitable server, or create a new virtual server.
2. Reload the dump in full, using four parallel tasks, as follows:

   ```
   pg_restore -d mydatabase -j 4 dumpfile
   ```

3. Once the restore is complete, you can dump the tables in the tablespace by following the *Hot logical backup of all tables in a tablespace* recipe.
4. Now, recreate the tables in the original server and database, using parallel tasks to speed things along. This can be executed remotely without needing to transfer the dumpfile between systems, as follows:

   ```
   pg_restore -d mydatabase -j 2 dumpfile
   ```

Logical – from the script dump

There's no easy way to extract the required tables from a script dump. We need to follow this procedure:

1. Find a suitable server, or create a new virtual server.
2. Reload the script in full:

   ```
   psql -f myscriptdump.sql
   ```

3. Once the restore is complete, you can dump the tables in the tablespace by following the *Hot logical backup of all tables in a tablespace* recipe.

4. Now, recreate the tables in the original server and database, using parallel tasks to speed things along. This can be executed remotely without needing to transfer the dumpfile between systems, like the following:

```
pg_restore -d mydatabase -j 2 dumpfile
```

Physical

To recover a single tablespace from a physical backup, we need to follow these steps:

1. Find a suitable server, or create a new virtual server, with a dedicated directory for each nondefault tablespace.

2. Recover the database server in full, as described in the previous recipes on physical recovery, including all databases and all tables. You may wish to stop at a useful point in time, in which case you can look at the *Recovery to a point in time* recipe later in the chapter.

3. Once the restore is complete, you can dump the tables in the tablespace by following the *Hot logical backup of all tables in a tablespace* recipe.

4. Now, recreate the tables in the original server and database, using parallel tasks to speed things along. This can be executed remotely without needing to transfer the dumpfile between systems, like the following:

```
pg_restore -d mydatabase -j 2 dumpfile
```

There's more...

When recovering from a custom backup file (-F c), you can also use the -l option to list the contents of the archive. You can then edit that file to remove, comment out, or reorder the actions. The pg_restore can then reuse the list file as an input, using the -L option.

Recovery of a dropped/damaged database

Recovering a complete database is also required sometimes. It's actually a lot easier than recovering a single table. Many users choose to place all their tables in a single database; in that case, this recipe isn't relevant.

How to do it...

The methods differ, depending on the type of backup you have available. If you have multiple types of backup, you have a choice.

Logical – from the custom dump -F c

Recreate the database in the original server using parallel tasks to speed things along. This can be executed remotely without needing to transfer the dumpfile between systems, as shown in the following example, where we use the `-j` option to specify four parallel processes:

```
pg_restore -h myhost -d postgres --create -j 4 dumpfile
```

Logical – from the script dump created by pg_dump

Recreate the database in the original server. This can be executed remotely without needing to transfer the dumpfile between systems, as shown here, where we must create the empty database first:

```
createdb myfreshdb

psql -h myhost -f myscriptdump.sql myfreshdb
```

Logical – from the script dump created by pg_dumpall

There's no easy way to extract the required tables from a script dump. We need to follow this procedure:

1. Find a suitable server, or create a new virtual server.
2. Reload the script in full, as follows:

   ```
   psql -f myscriptdump.sql
   ```

3. Once the restore is complete, you can dump the tables in the tablespace by following the *Hot logical backup of one database* recipe.
4. Now, recreate the database as described for logical dumps earlier in this recipe.

Physical

To recover a single database from a physical backup, we need to do the following:

1. Find a suitable server, or create a new virtual server.
2. Recover the database server in full, as described in the previous recipes on physical recovery, including all databases and all tables. You may wish to stop at a useful point in time, in which case you can look at the recipe on that topic later in the chapter.
3. Once the restore is complete, you can dump the tables in the database by following the *Hot logical backup of one database* recipe.
4. Now, recreate the database as described for logical dumps earlier in this recipe.

Improving performance of backup/recovery

Performance is often a concern in any medium or large database.

Backup performance is often a delicate issue, because resource usage may need to be limited to within certain boundaries. There may also be a restriction on the maximum runtime for the backup, for example, if the backup runs every Sunday.

Again, restore performance may be more important than backup performance, even if backup is the more obvious concern.

Getting ready

If performance is a concern or is likely to be, then you should read the *Planning backups* recipe first.

How to do it...

Backup and restore performance can be improved in different ways, depending on the backup type:

- **Physical backup**: Improving the performance of a physical backup can be done by taking the backup in parallel, that is, copying the files using more than one task. The more tasks you use, the more it will impact on the current system. When backing up, you can skip certain files. You won't need the following:

  - Any files placed in the data directory by DBA that shouldn't actually be there
  - Any files in `pg_xlog`
  - Any old server log files in `pg_log` (even the current one)

  Remember, it's safer not to try to exclude files at all because if you miss something critical, you may end up with data loss. Also remember that your backup speed may be bottlenecked by your disks or your network. Some larger systems have dedicated networks in place, solely for backups.

- **Logical backup**: As explained in a previous recipe, if you want to back up all databases in a database server, then you should use multiple `pg_dump` tasks running in parallel. You may want to increase the dump speed of a `pg_dump` task, but there really isn't an easy way of doing that right now. If you're using compression, look at the *There's more...* at the end of this recipe.

- ▸ **Physical restore**: Just as with physical backup, it's possible for us to put everything back quicker if we use parallel restore, as well as a file copy utility such as `rsync`, which is able to speed things up by automatically reusing existing files.

- ▸ **Logical restore**: Whether you use psql or `pg_restore`, you can speed up the program by assigning `maintenance_work_mem = 128MB` or more, either in `postgresql.conf` or on the user that will run the restore. If neither of those ways is easily possible, you can specify the option using the `PGOPTIONS` environment variable, as follows:

  ```
  export PGOPTIONS ="-c work_mem = 128000"
  ```

  This will then be used to set that option value for subsequent connections.

If you are running archiving or streaming replication, then transaction log writes may become a problem. This can be mitigated by increasing the size of the WAL buffer and making checkpoints less frequent. Set `wal_buffers` between 16 MB and 64 MB, and set `checkpoint_segments` to 1024 so that it has room to breathe.

If you aren't running archiving or streaming replication, or you've turned it off during the restore, then you'll be able to minimize the amount of transaction log writes. In that case, you may wish to use the `--single-transaction` option, as that will also help improve performance.

If a `pg_dump` was made using `-F c` (custom format), then we can restore in parallel, as follows:

```
pg_restore -j NumJobs
```

You'll have to be careful about how you select the degree of parallelism to use. A good starting point is the number of CPUs. Be very careful that you don't overflow the available memory when using parallel restore. Each job will use memory up to the value of `maintenance_work_mem`, so the whole restore could begin swapping when it hits larger indexes later in the restore. Plan the size of `shared_buffers` and `maintenance_work_mem` according to the number of jobs specified.

Whatever you do, make sure you run `ANALYZE` afterwards on every object created. This will happen automatically if autovacuum is enabled. It often helps to disable autovacuum completely while running a large restore, so double-check that you have it switched on again after the restore. The consequence of skipping this step will be extremely poor performance when you start your application again, which can easily set everybody off in a panic.

How it works...

Physical backup and restore is completely up to you. Copy those files as fast as you like, and in any way you like. Put them back in the same way or a different way.

Logical backup and restore involve moving data out of and into the database. That's typically going to be slower than physical backup and restore. Particularly with a restore, rebuilding indexes and constraints takes time, even when run in parallel. Plan ahead and measure the performance of your backup and restore techniques so that you have a chance when you need your database back in a hurry.

There's more...

Compressing backups is often considered as a way to reduce the size of the backup for storage. Even mild compression can use large amounts of CPU. In some cases, this might offset network transfer costs, so there isn't any hard rule as to whether compression is always good.

Compression for WAL files from physical backups is a common practice and is more efficient from version 9.4, as noted in the *Hot physical backup and continuous archiving* recipe. Physical backups can be compressed in various ways, depending on the exact backup mechanism used. By default, the custom dump format for logical backups will be compressed. Even when compressed, the objects can be accessed individually if required.

Using - -compress with script dumps will result in a compressed text file, just as if you had dumped the file and then compressed it. Access to individual tables is not possible.

PostgreSQL utilities do have a compress/decompress option, though this isn't always that efficient. Consider this code:

```
pg_dump --compress=0
```

It will typically be slower than the following:

```
pg_dump | gzip
```

Of course, feel free to use your favorite fast-compression tool instead, which is likely to vary, depending on the type of data in use.

Using multiple processes is known as pipeline parallelism. If you're using physical backup, then you can copy the data in multiple streams, which also allows you to take advantage of parallel compression/decompression.

See also

If taking a backup is an expensive operation, then a way around that is to take the backup from a replica instead, which offloads the cost of the backup operation away from the master. Look at the recipes in *Chapter 12, Replication and Upgrades*, to see how to set up a replica.

Incremental/differential backup and restore

If you have performance problems with backup of a large PostgreSQL database, then you may consider incremental or differential backup.

An incremental backup is a backup of all files that have changed since the last full backup. In order to perform a restore, you must restore the full backup and then each set of incremental changes.

A differential backup is a backup of all individual changes since the last full backup. Again, restore requires you to restore the full backup and then apply any changes since then.

How to do it...

To perform a differential physical backup, you can use `rsync` to compare the existing files against the previous full backup, and then overwrite only the changed data blocks. It's a bad plan to overwrite your last backup because if the new backup fails, you are left without backups. Therefore, keep two or more copies. An example backup schedule can be as follows:

Day of the week	Backup set 1	Backup set 2
Sunday	New full backup to set 1	New full backup to Set 2
Monday	Differential to set 1	Differential to Set 2
Tuesday	Differential to set 1	Differential to Set 2
Wednesday	Differential to set 1	Differential to Set 2
Thursday	Differential to set 1	Differential to Set 2
Friday	Differential to set 1	Differential to Set 2
Saturday	Differential to set 1	Differential to set 2

You should keep at least two full backup sets.

Many large databases have tables that are insert-only. In that case, it's easy to store parts of those tables. If the tables are partitioned by insertion date, creation date, or a similar field, it makes our task much simpler. Either way, you're still going to need a good way of recording which data is where in your backup.

In general, there's no easy way to run a differential backup using `pg_dump`.

How it works...

PostgreSQL doesn't explicitly keep track of the last changed date or similar information for a file or table. PostgreSQL tables are held as files, so you should be able to rely on the modification time (`mtime`) of the files on the filesystem. If, for some reason, you don't trust it or it has been disabled, then incremental backup is not for you.

The `pg_dump` doesn't allow `WHERE` clauses to be specified, so even if you add your own columns to track `last_changed_date`, you'll still need to manually perform that somehow.

There's more...

The article at `http://en.wikipedia.org/wiki/Backup_rotation_scheme` gives further useful information.

When thinking about incremental backup, you should note that replication techniques work by continually applying changes to a full backup. This could be considered a technique for an incremental updated backup, also known as an "incremental forever" backup strategy. The changes are applied ahead of time so that you can restore easily and quickly. You should still take a backup, but you can take it from the replication standby instead.

It's possible to write a utility that takes a differential backup of data blocks. You can read each data block and check the block's **Log Sequence Number** (**LSN**) to see whether it has changed in comparison to a previous copy. In fact, at the time of writing this book a patch that does exactly this using `pg_basebackup` is being discussed for PostgreSQL 9.5, meaning that this feature could be committed by the time you read this sentence.

In the *Hot physical backup and continuous archiving* recipe, we discussed using third-party backup and recovery software. All the tools we mentioned support compression of WAL files by invoking popular general-purpose compression utilities such as bzip2, gzip and lzh directly on WAL files. This is safe and does not increase the actual risk of data loss. Such utilities have been extensively used for many years, and all serious bugs have been ironed out.

`pg_rman` can also read changed data blocks and compress them using detailed knowledge of the internals of PostgreSQL's data blocks. Any bugs that exist there could cause data loss in your backups, and issues with third-party tools aren't resolved by the main PostgreSQL project. Therefore, I personally wouldn't advise using this utility without a formal support contract. Various companies support this; ask them.

Hot physical backups with Barman

The main reason I (Gabriele) came up with the idea of starting a new open source project for disaster recovery of PostgreSQL databases was the lack of a simple and standard procedure for managing backups and, most importantly, recovery. Disasters and failures in ICT will happen.

As a database administrator, your duty is to plan for backups and recovery of PostgreSQL databases and perform regular tests in order to sweep away stress and fear, which typically follow those unexpected events. **Barman**, which stands for Backup and Recovery Manager, is definitely a tool that you can evaluate for these purposes.

Before you dive into this recipe and the next one, which will introduce you to Barman, I recommend that you read the following recipes from earlier in this chapter: *Understanding and controlling crash recovery, Planning backups, Hot physical backup and continuous archiving*, and *Recovery to a point in time*. Although Barman hides the complexity of the underlying concepts, it is important that you be aware of them, as it will make you more resilient to installation and configuration issues of Barman.

Barman is currently available only for Linux systems and is written in Python. It supports PostgreSQL versions from 8.3 onwards. Among its main features, worth citing are remote backup, remote recovery, multiple server management, backup catalogs, incremental backups, retention policies, compression of WAL files, and backup from standby (for 9.2 and later versions).

For the sake of simplicity, in this recipe we will assume the following architecture:

▶ One Linux server named `angus`, running your PostgreSQL production database server

▶ One Linux server named `malcolm`, running Barman for disaster recovery of your PostgreSQL database server

▶ Both the servers are in the same LAN, and for better business continuity objectives, the only resource they share is the network

Later on, we will see how easy it is with Barman to add more Postgres servers (such as `bon`) to our disaster recovery solution on `malcolm`.

Getting ready

Although Barman can be installed via sources or through pip—Python's main package manager—the easiest way to install Barman is by using the software package manager of your Linux distribution.

Currently, 2ndQuadrant maintains packages for RHEL, CentOS 5/6/7, Debian, and Ubuntu systems. If you are using a different distribution or another Unix system, you can follow the instructions written in the official documentation of Barman, available at `http://docs.pgbarman.org/`.

In this book, I will cover the installation of Barman on CentOS 6 and Ubuntu 12.04 LTS Linux servers.

If you are using RHEL or CentOS 6 on the `malcolm` server, you need to install the following repositories:

- Fedora **Extra Packages Enterprise Linux** (**EPEL**), available at `http://fedoraproject.org/wiki/EPEL`
- PostgreSQL Global Development Group RPM repository, available at `http://yum.postgresql.org/`

Then, as `root`, type this:

`yum install barman`

If you are using Ubuntu on `malcolm`, you need to install the APT repository of PostgreSQL, available at `http://apt.postgresql.org/`. Then, as `root`, type this:

`apt-get install barman`

From now on, we will assume the following:

- PostgreSQL is running on `angus` as the `postgres` system user and listening to the default port (`5432`). Its configuration is such that the `barman` system user on `malcolm` can connect as the `postgres` database user without having to type a password.
- Barman is installed on `malcolm` and runs as the `barman` system user.
- TCP connections for SSH and PostgreSQL are allowed between the two servers (check your firewall settings).
- Two-way automated communication via SSH is properly set up between these users.

The last operation requires "exchanging" a public SSH key without passphrase between the `postgres` user on `angus` and the `barman` user on `malcolm`. If you are not familiar with this topic, which goes beyond the scope of this book, you are advised to follow Barman's documentation or surf on the Internet for more information.

How to do it...

We will start by looking at Barman's main configuration file:

1. As `root` on `malcolm`, open the `/etc/barman.conf` file for editing. This file contains global options for Barman. Once you are familiar with the main configuration options, I recommend that you set the default compression method and the directory for configuration files by uncommenting the following lines:

   ```
   compression = gzip
   configuration_files_directory = /etc/barman.d
   ```

2. Then, create the `/etc/barman.d` directory:

```
mkdir /etc/barman.d
```

3. Add the configuration file for the `angus` server. Drop the `angus.conf` file, containing the following lines, into the `/etc/barman.d` directory:

```
[angus]
description =  "PostgreSQL Database on angus"
ssh_command = ssh postgres@angus
conninfo = host=angus user=postgres port=5432
```

4. You have just added the `angus` server to the list of Postgres servers managed by Barman. You can verify this by typing `barman list-server`, as follows:

```
[root@malcolm]# barman list-server

angus - PostgreSQL Database on angus
```

5. In this recipe, I will be executing commands as `root` user. Be aware, however, that every command will be executed by the `barman` system user (or, more generally, as specified in the configuration file by the `barman_user` option).

   Anyway, it is now time to set up continuous archiving of WAL files between Postgres and Barman. Execute the `barman show-server angus` command and write down the directory for incoming WALs (`incoming_wals_directory`):

```
[root@malcolm]# barman show-server angus

Server angus:

        active: true

        description: PostgreSQL Database on angus

        ssh_command: ssh postgres@angus

        conninfo: host=angus user=postgres port=5432

        ...

        incoming_wals_directory: /var/lib/barman/angus/incoming

        ...
```

6. The next task is to initialize the directory layout for the `angus` server, through the `check` command. You are advised to add this command to your monitoring infrastructure as, among other things, it ensures that connection to the Postgres server via SSH and libpq is working properly, as well as continuous archiving. It returns `0` if everything is fine:

```
[root@malcolm]# barman check angus

Server angus:

        ssh: OK

        PostgreSQL: OK

        archive_mode: FAILED (please set it to 'on')
```

```
        archive_command: FAILED (please set it accordingly to
documentation)

        directories: OK

        retention policy settings: OK

        compression settings: OK

        minimum redundancy requirements: OK (have 0 backups,
expected at least 0)


[root@malcolm]# echo $?

1
```

7. As you can see, the returned value is 1, meaning that the angus server is not yet ready for backup. The output suggests that archive_mode and archive_command in Postgres are not set for continuous archiving. Connect to angus and modify the postgresql.conf file by adding this:

    archive_mode = on

    archive_command = 'scp %p barman@malcolm:/var/lib/barman/angus/ incoming/%f'

    # Set wal_level to archive or hot_standby (in case you are using Hot Standby)

    wal_level = archive

8. Restart the PostgreSQL server, run the check command on malcolm (suppressing the output with -q) again, and compare the results with what you got earlier:

    [root@malcolm]# barman -q check angus

    [root@malcolm]# echo $?

    0

    All good! PostgreSQL on angus should now be regularly shipping WAL files to Barman on malcolm, depending on the write workload of your database. I recommend that you check both the PostgreSQL and Barman log files and verify that WALs are correctly shipped. Continuous archiving is indeed the main requirement for physical backups in Postgres.

9. Once you have set up continuous archiving, in order to add the disaster recovery capability to your Postgres server, you need to have at least one full base backup. Taking a full base backup in Barman is as easy as typing one single command. It should not be hard for you to guess that the command to execute is barman backup angus.

    Barman initiates the physical backup procedure and waits for the checkpoint to happen, before copying the data files from angus to malcom using rsync:

    [root@malcolm]# barman backup angus

```
Starting backup for server angus in /var/lib/barman/angus/
base/20131228T180640

Backup start at xlog location: 0/5000028
(000000010000000000000005, 00000028)

Copying files.

Copy done.

Asking PostgreSQL server to finalize the backup.

Backup end at xlog location: 0/50000B8 (000000010000000000000005,
000000B8)

Backup completed
```

> It is worth noting that, during the backup procedure, your PostgreSQL server is available for both read and write operations. This is because PostgreSQL natively implements **hot backup**, a feature that other DBMS vendors might make you pay for.

From now on, your `angus` PostgreSQL server is continuously backed up on `malcolm`. You can now schedule weekly backups (using the `barman` user's cron) and manage retention policies so that you can build a catalog of backups covering you for weeks, months, or years of data and allowing you to perform recovery operations at any point in time between the first available backup and the last successfully archived WAL file.

How it works...

Barman is a Python application that wraps PostgreSQL core technology for continuous backup and PITR. It also adds some practical functionality focused on helping the database administrator manage disaster recovery of one or more PostgreSQL servers.

When devising Barman, we decided to keep the design simple and not to use any daemon or client/server architecture. Maintenance operations are simply delegated to the `barman cron` command, which is mainly responsible for archiving WAL files (moving them from the incoming directory to the WAL file and compressing them) and managing retention policies.

If you have installed Barman through RPM or APT packages, you will notice that maintenance is run every minute through cron:

```
[root@malcolm ~]# cat /etc/cron.d/barman
# m h  dom mon dow   user       command
  * *    *   *   *    barman    [ -x /usr/bin/barman ] && /usr/bin/barman
-q cron
```

Barman follows the "convention over configuration" paradigm and uses an INI format configuration file with options operating at two different levels:

- ▶ **Global options**: These are options specified in the `[barman]` section, used by any Barman command and for every server. Several global options can be overridden at the server level.

- ▶ **Server options**: These are options specified in the `[SERVER_ID]` section, used by server commands. These options can be customized at the server level (including overriding general settings).

The `SERVER_ID` placeholder (such as `angus`) is fundamental, as it identifies the server in the catalogue (therefore, it must be unique).

Similarly, commands in Barman are of two types:

- ▶ **Global commands**: These are general commands, not tied with any server in particular, such as a list of the servers managed by the Barman installation (`list -server`) and maintenance (`cron`)

- ▶ **Server commands**: These are commands executed on a specific server, such as diagnostics (`check` and `status`), backup control (`backup`, `list-backup`, `delete`, and `show-backup`) and recovery control (`recover`, which is discussed in the next recipe, *Recovery with Barman*)

The previous sections of this recipe showed you how to add a server (`angus`) to a Barman installation on the `malcolm` server. You can easily add a second server (`bon`) to the Barman server on `malcolm`. All you have to do is create the `bon.conf` file in the `/etc/barman.d` directory and repeat the steps outlined in the *How it works...* section, as you have done for `angus`.

There's more...

Every time you execute the `barman backup` command for a given server, you take a full base backup (a more generic term for this is **periodical full backup**). Once completed, this backup can be used as a base for any recovery operation from the start time of the backup to the last available WAL file for that server (provided there is continuity among all the WAL segments).

As mentioned earlier, by scheduling daily or weekly automated backups, you end up having several periodic backups for a server. In Barman's jargon, this is known as the **backup catalogue** and it is one of my favorite features of this tool.

At any time, you can get the list of available backups for a given server through the `list -backup` command:

```
[root@malcolm ~]# barman list-backup angus
angus 20131228T180640 - Sat Dec 28 18:06:42 2013 - Size: XX - WAL Size: XX
```

The last informative command you might want to get familiar with is `show-backup`, which gives you detailed information on a specific backup regarding the server, base backup time, WAL archive, and context within the catalog (for example, the last available backup):

```
[root@malcolm ~]# barman show-backup angus 20131228T180640
```

Rather than the full backup ID (`20131228T180640`), you can use a few synonyms, such as these:

> ▶ **Last** or **latest**: This refers to the latest available backup (the last in the catalog)

> ▶ **First** or **oldest**: This refers to the oldest available backup (the first in the catalog)

For the `show-backup` command, however, I will use a real and concrete example, taken directly from one of our customers' installation of Barman on a 12.4 TB Postgres 8.4 database:

```
Backup 20140725T130001:
  Server Name           : skynyrd
  Status                : DONE
  PostgreSQL Version    : 80417
  PGDATA directory      : /srv/pgdata
  Tablespaces:
    tb_data: /srv/tb_data (oid: 16385)
    tb_temp: /srv/tb_temp (oid: 19812)


  Base backup information:
    Disk usage          : 12.4 TiB
    Timeline            : 1
    Begin WAL           : 0000000100008C0500000094
    End WAL             : 0000000100008C54000000BD
    WAL number          : 20187
    WAL compression ratio: 73.89%
    Begin time          : 2014-07-25 13:00:02.303786+00:00
    End time            : 2014-07-28 14:49:59.169349+00:00
    Begin Offset        : 32
    End Offset          : 1410632
    Begin XLOG          : 8C05/94000020
    End XLOG            : 8C54/BD158648
```

```
WAL information:
   No of files          : 7253
   Disk usage           : 26.8 GiB
   Compression ratio    : 76.33%
   Last available       : 0000000100008C710000002F


Catalog information:
   Retention Policy     : not enforced
   Previous Backup      : 20140718T130001
   Next Backup          : - (this is the latest base backup)
```

As you can see, Barman is a production-ready tool that can be used in large, business-critical contexts, as well as in basic Postgres installations. It provides good **Recovery Point Objective (RPO)** outcomes, allowing you to limit potential data loss to a single WAL file.

Barman is distributed under GNU GPL 3 terms and is available for download at `http://www.pgbarman.org/`.

There is also a module for Puppet available at `https://github.com/2ndquadrant-it/puppet-barman`.

For further and more detailed information, refer to the following:

▸ The `man barman` command, which gives the man page for the Barman application

▸ The `man 5 barman` command, which gives the man page for the configuration file

▸ The `barman help` command, which gives a list of the available commands

▸ The official documentation of Barman, publicly available at `http://docs.pgbarman.org/`

▸ The mailing list for community support at `http://www.pgbarman.org/support/`

Recovery with Barman

This recipe assumes that you have read the previous recipe, *Hot physical backups with Barman*, and successfully installed Barman on the `malcolm` server, backing up the Postgres databases running on `angus` and `bon`. We will use the same nomenclature in the examples of this recipe.

A recovery procedure is a reaction to a failure. In database terms, this could be related to an unintentional human error (for example, `DROP` operation of a table), an attack (think of *Little Bobby Tables*), a hardware failure (for example, a broken hard drive), or—less likely—a natural disaster.

Even though you might be tempted to think that you are immune to disasters or failures (I wish you were), you are advised to perform regular tests and simulations of recovery. If you have a team of engineers, I suggest that you schedule a simulation every 6 months (at least) and regularly test your backups through the safest way of checking their content—performing a recovery.

You don't want to be somebody who has been taking backups for years and, in the moment of need, suddenly discovers that they have not been working for the last 3 months.

Barman allows you to perform two types of recovery:

- **Local recovery**: This involves restoring a PostgreSQL instance on the same server where Barman resides
- **Remote recovery**: This involves restoring a PostgreSQL instance directly from the Barman server to another server, through the network

It is important to note that the terms "local" and "remote" are defined from Barman's standpoint, as every recovery command is executed where Barman is installed.

In this recipe, we will cover a single use case: total failure of one of the servers where PostgreSQL is running (fortunately, it is backed up by Barman) and full remote recovery on a third server.

Getting ready

Even though Barman can centrally manage backups of several servers that have different versions of PostgreSQL, when it comes to recovery, the same requirements of PostgreSQL's PITR technology apply. In particular, the following:

- You must recover on a server with the same hardware architecture and PostgreSQL version
- Recovery is full, meaning the entire Postgres cluster will be restored (and not a single database)

The use case of this recipe is the following:

- The bon server has been lost forever, due to a permanent hardware failure
- The brian server, having similar characteristics to bon, has been selected for recovery
- The same Linux distribution and PostgreSQL packages have been installed on brian
- Barman will be used to perform remote recovery of the latest backup available for bon on the brian server

In order to proceed, you need to add the public SSH key of the `barman` user on `malcolm` in the `~/.ssh/authorized_keys` file of the `postgres` user on `brian`. If you are not familiar with the process of exchanging a public SSH key, which goes beyond the scope of this book, you are advised to follow Barman's documentation or surf on the Internet for more information.

The first preparatory step is to make sure that the `PGDATA` directory, as specified in the `bon` backup, exists on `brian` and can be written by the `postgres` user.

Ask Barman for the location of `PGDATA` by querying the latest available backup metadata:

barman show-backup bon last

Write down the content of the `PGDATA directory` entry:

PGDATA directory : /var/lib/pgsql/9.4/data

You might have noticed that we are using the default `PGDATA` directory for a RHEL/CentOS cluster based on packages maintained by the PostgreSQL community. On Ubuntu, you will probably have `/var/lib/postgresql/9.4/main`.

As the second step, make sure also that PostgreSQL is not running on `brian`, using either the `service` command or `pg_ctl`.

> Executing a recovery operation on a target directory used by a running PostgreSQL instance will permanently damage that instance. Be extremely careful when you perform such an operation.

How to do it...

Connect as the `barman` user on `malcolm` and type the following:

barman recover --remote-ssh-command 'ssh postgres@brian' bon last /var/lib/pgsql/9.4/data

The preceding command will use the latest available backup for the `bon` server and prepare everything you need to restore your server in the PostgreSQL destination directory (`/var/lib/pgsql/9.4/data`), as shown in the output:

```
Starting remote restore for server bon using backup 20140101T141550
Destination directory: /var/lib/pgsql/9.4/data
Copying the base backup.
Copying required wal segments.
The archive_command was set to 'false' to prevent data losses.
```

Your PostgreSQL server has been successfully prepared for recovery!

Please review network and archive related settings in the PostgreSQL configuration file before starting the just recovered instance.

Once again, Ubuntu users will have to use a different destination directory, such as `/var/lib/postgresql/9.4/main`.

Before you start the server, you are advised to connect to `brian` as `postgres` and inspect the content of the Postgres destination directory. You should notice that its content should be very similar to what was in the `bon` server before the crash.

You are also strongly encouraged to review the content of the `postgresql.conf` file before starting the server, even though Barman takes care of disabling or removing some potentially dangerous options. The most critical option is `archive_command`, which is pre-emptively set to `false`, forcing you to deliberately analyze and consider new continuous archiving strategies (for example, you might want to add the new `brian` server to Barman by repeating the steps outlined in the previous recipe).

When you are ready, you can start Postgres as a standard service. On CentOS 6, for example, you can execute as `root`, as follows:

service postgresql-9.4 start

On Ubuntu, use this command:

service postgresql start

Look at the logs to verify that you do not have any problem, and then at `ps -axf`.

Your PostgreSQL databases that were hosted on `bon` have been successfully restored on `brian`, using all the WAL files that had been shipped to the backup server.

How it works...

When executed with the `--remote-ssh-command` option, the recover command will activate remote recovery and will be using those credentials to connect to the remote server (similar to what the `ssh-command` configuration option does in the backup phase—see the *Hot physical backups with Barman* recipe—but in the other direction). Internally, Barman relies on `rsync` for this operation.

When performing a full recovery (that is, up to the latest available archived WAL file), Barman recreates the structure of the `PGDATA` according to the backup. It will then deposit all the needed WAL files in the `pg_xlog` directory.

A careful analysis of the content of the restored `PGDATA` directory shows that no `recovery.conf` file is generated by Barman in the case of a full recovery.

It will just simulate a standard crash recovery of PostgreSQL and start replaying the WAL files from the `REDO` point, contrary to the *Recovery of all databases* recipe, where `recovery.conf` was used.

We decided to adopt this strategy in Barman so that we could maintain the same timeline (as a `recovery.conf` file would start a new era in the cluster's existence), and avoid setting `restore_command`.

There's more...

If you are using tablespaces, you may be wondering if and how Barman manages them. Barman fully supports tablespaces, including their relocation at recovery time, through the `--tablespace` runtime option. For information on the syntax of the relocation rules, type any of the following commands:

- ▶ `barman help recover`
- ▶ `man barman`

In this recipe, we have seen only one use case, which covers remote recover. As mentioned before, however, Barman allows DBAs to recover instances of PostgreSQL on the same server as Barman.

This is called local recovery. For local recovery, you will need to have installed the binaries and libraries of the same version of PostgreSQL on the Barman server as the backup file you want to restore.

You can dedicate a directory in Barman for local recovery, to be used as the destination directory of your recover commands.

A typical use case for local recovery is to restore the situation of a PostgreSQL server at a specific point in time, usually before an unintentional action such as the `DROP` of a table.

Barman supports Point-in-Time Recovery, as explained in the *Recovery to a point in time* recipe, through three options that define the recovery target:

- ▶ `--target-time TARGET_TIME`: The target is a timestamp.
- ▶ `--target-xid TARGET_XID`: The target is a transaction ID.
- ▶ `--target-name TARGET_NAME`: The target is a named restore point, previously created with the `pg_create_restore_point(name)` function. This is only available for Postgres 9.1 and later versions.

When executed with one of these options, Barman will generate the `recovery.conf` file for you. Advanced users might want to activate the Hot Standby facility and take advantage of the `pause_at_recovery_target` option (by default set to `true`, and effective only if `hot_standby` is enabled in the `postgresql.conf` file).

This will allow you to check whether the database is in the desired state. If not, you can stop the server, change the recovery target time, and start it again. Repeat this operation until you reach your goal, keeping in mind that PostgreSQL can only roll forward WAL files (they are called REDO operations for a reason).

You can then follow the instructions outlined in the *Recovery of a dropped/damaged table* recipe to restore the objects in the primary database.

At the end of any recovery operation, remember to stop the running of local servers and remove recovered instances (even though this is not mandatory, as Barman uses rsync and will be able to perform an incremental copy of the files where applicable).

As a final note for this recipe, another important use case for Barman is to regularly create copies of the server to be used for **business intelligence** purposes or even **staging/development**. These environments normally do not require a strictly up-to-date situation and are very often happy to work on a snapshot of the previous day. A typical workflow for this use case can be like this:

1. Stop the PostgreSQL server on the BI/staging server.
2. Issue a full remote recovery operation of the desired backup from Barman to the BI server (rsync will use the existing data directory for incremental copy).
3. Start the PostgreSQL server on the BI/staging server.

This recipe has covered only a few aspects of the recovery process in Barman. For further and more detailed information, refer to:

► The official documentation of Barman, publicly available at http://docs.pgbarman.org/

► The mailing list for community support at http://www.pgbarman.org/support/

12
Replication and Upgrades

In this chapter, we will cover the following recipes:

- ► Replication best practices
- ► Setting up file-based replication – deprecated
- ► Setting up streaming replication
- ► Setting up streaming replication security
- ► Hot Standby and read scalability
- ► Managing streaming replication
- ► Using repmgr
- ► Using Replication Slots
- ► Monitoring replication
- ► Performance and Synchronous Replication
- ► Delaying, pausing, and synchronizing replication
- ► Logical Replication
- ► Bi-Directional Replication
- ► Archiving transaction log data
- ► Upgrading – minor releases
- ► Major upgrades in-place
- ► Major upgrades online

Introduction

The software described in this chapter is evolving quickly each year. It is important to understand the release levels of the database servers you are targeting so that you don't just assume that all required features are available.

Replication isn't magic, though it can be pretty cool! It's even cooler when it works, and that's what this chapter is all about.

Replication requires understanding, effort, and patience. There are a significant number of points to get right. My emphasis here is on providing simple approaches to get you started, and some clear best practices on operational robustness.

PostgreSQL has included some form of native or "in-core" replication since version 8.2, though that support has steadily improved over time. External projects and tools have always been a significant part of the PostgreSQL landscape, with most of them being written and supported by very skilled PostgreSQL technical developers. Some people with a negative viewpoint have observed that this weakens PostgreSQL or emphasizes shortcomings. My view would be that PostgreSQL has been lucky enough to be supported by a huge range of replication tools, together offering a wide set of supported use cases from which to build practical solutions. This view extends throughout this chapter on replication, with many recipes using tools that are not part of the core PostgreSQL project yet.

All the tools mentioned in this chapter are actively enhanced by current core PostgreSQL developers. The pace of change in this area is high, and it is likely that some of the restrictions mentioned here could well be removed by the time you read this book. Double-check the documentation for each tool or project.

"Which technique is best?" is a question that gets asked many times. The answer varies depending on the exact circumstances. In many cases, people use one technique on one server and a different technique to protect other servers. Even the developers of particular tools use other tools when it is appropriate. Use the right tools for the job. All the tools and techniques listed in this chapter have been recommended by me at some time, in relevant circumstances. If something isn't mentioned here by me, that does probably imply that it is less favorable for various reasons, and there are some tools and techniques that I would personally avoid altogether in their present form or level of maturity.

I (Simon Riggs) must also confess to being the developer or designer of many parts of the basic technology presented here. That gives me some advantages and disadvantages over other authors. It means I understand some things better than others, which hopefully translates into better descriptions and comparisons. It may also hamper me by providing too narrow a focus, though the world is big and this book is already long enough!

This book, and especially this chapter, cover technology in depth. As a result, we face the risk of minor errors. We've gone to a lot of trouble to test all of our recommendations, but just as with software, I learn that books can be buggy too. I hope our efforts to present actual commands rather than just words will be appreciated by you.

Replication concepts

Replication technology can be confusing. You might be forgiven for thinking that people have a reason to keep it that way. My observation is that there are many techniques, each with their own advocates, and the strengths and weaknesses are often hotly debated.

There are some simple underlying concepts that can help you understand the various options available. The terms used here are designed to avoid favoring any particular technique, and we've used standard industry terms whenever available.

Topics

Database replication is the term we use to describe the technology used to maintain a copy of a set of data on a remote system.

There are usually two main reasons for you wanting to do this, and those reasons are often combined:

- **High availability**: Reducing the chances of data unavailability by having multiple systems, each holding a full copy of the data.
- **Data movement**: Allowing data to be used by additional applications or workload on additional hardware. Examples of this are **Reference Data Management**, where a single central server might provide information to many other applications, and **Business Intelligence/Reporting Systems**.

Of course, both of those topics are complex areas, and there are many architectures and possibilities for implementing each of them.

What we will talk about here is High Availability, where there is *no transformation* of the data. We simply copy the data from one PostgreSQL database server to another. So, we are specifically avoiding all discussion on ETL tools, EAI tools, inter-database migration, data warehousing strategies, and so on. Those are valid topics in IT architecture; it's just that we don't cover them in this book.

Basic concepts

Let's look at the basic architecture. Typically, individual database servers are referred to as nodes. The whole group of database servers involved in replication is known as a cluster. That is the common usage of the term, but be careful; the term "cluster" is also used for two other quite separate meanings elsewhere in PostgreSQL. Firstly, cluster is sometimes used to refer to the entire database instance, though I prefer the term "database server". Secondly, there is a command named CLUSTER. It is designed to sort data in a specific order within a table.

A database server that allows a user to make changes is known as a **master** or **primary**, or may be described as a **source** of changes.

A database server that only allows read-only access is known as a Hot Standby, or sometimes, a slave server.

The key aspect of replication is that data changes are captured on a master, and then transferred to other nodes. In some cases, a node may send data changes to other nodes, which is a process known as **cascading** or **relay**. Thus, the master is a sending node but not all sending nodes need to be masters.

Replication is often categorized by whether more than one master node is allowed, in which case it will be known as multimaster replication. There is a significant difference between how single-master and multimaster systems work, so we'll discuss that aspect in more detail later. Each has its advantages and disadvantages.

History and scope

PostgreSQL didn't always have in-core replication. For many years, PostgreSQL users needed to use one of many external packages to provide this important feature.

Slony was the first package to provide useful replication features. Londiste was a variant system that was somewhat easier to use. Both of those systems provided single-master replication based around triggers. Another variant of this idea was the Bucardo package, which offered multimaster replication using triggers.

Trigger-based replication has now been superseded by transaction-log-based replication, which provides considerable performance improvements. There is some discussion on exactly how much difference that makes, but log-based replication is approximately twice as fast, though many users have reported much higher gains. Trigger-based systems also have considerably higher replication lag. Lastly, triggers need to be added to each table involved in replication, making these systems more time-consuming to manage and sensitive to production problems. These factors taken together mean that trigger-based systems will likely be avoided for new developments, and I'm taking the decision not to cover them at all in the latest edition of this book. Having said that, Slony is being updated to utilize newer logical replication techniques, so there may be some life in future versions.

Outside the world of PostgreSQL, there are many competing concepts and much recent research. This is a practical book, so we've mostly avoided comments on research or topics on computer science.

The focus of this chapter is replication technologies that are part of the core software of PostgreSQL, or will be so in the reasonably near future. The first of these is known as Streaming Replication, introduced in PostgreSQL 9.0, but based on earlier file-based mechanisms for physical transaction log replication. In this book, we refer to this as **Physical Streaming Replication** (**PSR**) because we take the transaction log (often known as the Write-Ahead log or WAL) and ship that data to the remote node. WAL contains an exact physical copy of the changes made to a data block, so the remote node is an exact copy of the master. Therefore, it cannot execute transactions that write to the database; this type of node is known as a standby.

Starting in PostgreSQL 9.4, we introduced an efficient mechanism for reading the transaction log (WAL) and transforming it into a stream of changes, a process known as logical decoding. This is then the basis for the later, even more useful mechanism, known as **Logical Streaming Replication** (**LSR**). This allows a receiver to replicate data without needing to keep an exact copy of the data blocks, as we do with PSR. This has significant advantages, which we will discuss later.

PSR requires us to have only a single master node, though it allows multiple standbys. LSR can be used for all the same purposes as PSR. It just has fewer restrictions and allows a great range of additional use cases. Crucially, LSR can be used as the basis of multimaster clusters.

PSR and LSR are sometimes known as **Physical Log Streaming Replication** (**PLSR**) and **Logical Log Streaming Replication** (**LLSR**). Those terms are sometimes used to explain differences between transaction-log-based and trigger-based replication.

Practical aspects

Since we refer to the transfer of replicated data as "streaming", it becomes natural to talk about the flow of data between nodes as if it were a river or stream. Cascaded data can flow through a series of nodes to create complex architectures. From the perspective of any node, it may have downstream nodes that receive replicated data from it and/or upstream nodes that send data to it. Practical limits need to be understood to allow us to understand and design replication architectures.

After a transaction commits on the master, the time taken to transfer data changes to a remote node is usually referred to as the **latency**, or **replication delay**. Once the remote node has received the data, changes must then be applied to the remote node, which takes an amount of time known as the **apply delay**. The total time a record takes from the master to a downstream node is the replication delay plus the apply delay. Be careful to note that some authors describe those terms differently, and sometimes confuse the two, which is easy to do. Also, be careful to note that these delays will be different for any two nodes.

Replication delay is best expressed as an interval (in seconds), but that is much harder to measure than it first appears. In most cases, you will see the apply delay expressed in terms of the total volume of changes currently outstanding, expressed in bytes (usually MB). Note that the throughput, or rate of data transfer (measured in MB), is interesting, but it is not the same thing as the latency or replication delay; however, the former may drive the latter.

All forms of replication are initialized in roughly the same way. First, you enable change capture, and then make a full replica of the data set on the remote node, which we refer to as the **base backup**. After that, we begin applying the changes, starting from the point immediately before the base backup started and continuing with any changes that occurred while the base backup was taking place. As a result, the replication delay immediately following the initial copy task will be equal to the duration of the initial copy task. The remote node will then begin to catch up with the master, and the replication delay will begin to reduce. The time taken to get the lowest replication delay possible is known as the catch-up interval. If the master is busy generating new changes, which can increase the time it takes for the new node to catch up, you should try to generate new nodes during quieter periods, if any exist. Note that in some cases, the catch-up period will be too long to be acceptable. Be sure to include this understanding in your planning and monitoring. The faster and more efficient your replication system, the easier it will be to operate in the real world. *Performance matters!*

Either replication will copy all tables, or in some cases, we can copy a subset of tables, in which case we call it **selective replication**. If you choose selective replication, you should note that the management overhead increases roughly as the number of objects managed increases. Replicated objects are often manipulated in groups known as **replication sets** to help minimize the administrative overhead.

Data loss

By default, PostgreSQL implements **asynchronous replication**, where data is streamed out whenever convenient for the server. If replicated data is acknowledged back to the user prior to commit, we refer to that as **synchronous replication**.

With synchronous replication, the replication delay *directly* affects the elapsed time of transactions on the master. With asynchronous replication, the master may continue at full speed, though this opens up a possible risk that the standby may not be able to keep pace with the master. All replication must be monitored to ensure that a significant lag does not develop, which is why we must be careful to monitor the replication delay.

Synchronous replication guarantees that data is written to at least two nodes before the user or application is told that a transaction has committed. More advanced specifications with $N > 2$ are theoretically possible and will be added in later releases.

Single-master replication

In single-master replication, if the master dies, one of the standbys must take its place. Otherwise, we will not be able to accept new write transactions. Thus, the term designations, master and standby, are just roles that any node can take at some point. To move the master role to another node, we perform a procedure named **Switchover**. If the master dies and does not recover, then the more severe role change is known as a **Failover**. In many ways, these can be similar, but it helps to use different terms for each event.

We use the term clusterware for software that manages the cluster. Clusterware may provide features such as automatic failover, and in some cases, load balancing.

The complexity of failover makes single-master replication harder to configure correctly than many people would like it to be. The good news is that from an application perspective it is safe and easy to retrofit this style of replication to an existing system. Or put another way, since application developers frequently don't worry about high availability and replication until the very end of the project, single-master replication is frequently the best solution, be it PSR or LSR.

Multinode architectures

Multinode architectures allow users to write data to multiple nodes concurrently. There are two main categories: tightly coupled and loosely coupled.

- **Tightly coupled database clusters**: These allow a single image of the database, so there is less perception that you're even connected to a cluster at all. This consistency comes at a price—the nodes of the cluster cannot be geographically separated, which means if you need to protect against site disasters, then you'll need additional technology to allow disaster recovery. Clustering requires replication as well.

  Tightly coupled systems are discussed later in the *Clustered or massively parallel databases* section.

- **Loosely coupled database clusters**: These have greater independence for each node, allowing us to spread out nodes across wide areas, such as across multiple continents. You can connect to each node individually. There are two benefits of this. The first is that all data access can be performed quickly against local copies of the data. The second benefit is that we don't need to work out how to route read-only transactions to (a) standby node (s) and read-write transactions to the master node.

  Loosely coupled systems are discussed later in the *Multimaster replication* section.

Clustered or massively parallel databases

An example of a tightly coupled system is the open source Postgres-XL. This supersedes the earlier Postgres-XC clustering software. These systems introduced the concept of a **Global Transaction Manager** (**GTM**), which allows nodes in a tightly coupled system to work together.

Postgres-XL spreads data across multiple nodes. Larger tables can be distributed evenly, using a hash-based distribution scheme. This feature allows Postgres-XL to scale well for both high-transaction-rate (OLTP) and business intelligence (OLAP) systems.

On Postgres-XL, smaller tables can be duplicated on all nodes. Changes to smaller tables are coordinated, so there is no possibility of the multiple copies diverging from one another. The synchronization cost is high, and XL is not suitable for geographically distributed databases.

Postgres-XL is not covered in this book, simply because of lack of time and space.

Multimaster replication

An example of a loosely coupled system would be **Bi-Directional Replication** (**BDR**). BDR does not utilize a Global Transaction Manager, so the nodes contain data that is eventually consistent. Without the GTM, we can remove a single point of failure and a multimaster configuration can be very robust.

In its simplest multimaster configuration, each node has a copy of similar data. You can update data on any node and the changes will flow to other nodes. This makes it ideal for databases that have users in many different locations, which is probably the case with most websites. Each location can have its own copy of the application code and database, giving fast response times for all your users, wherever they are located.

It is *possible* to make changes to the same data at the same time on different nodes, causing update conflicts. These could become a problem, but the reality is that it is also *easily possible* to design applications that do not generate conflicts in normal running, especially if each user is modifying their own data (for example, in social media, retail, and so on).

We need to understand where conflicts might arise so that we can resolve them. On a single node, any application that allows concurrent updates to the same data will experience poor performance because of contention. The negative effect of contention will get much worse on multimaster clusters. In addition, multiple nodes require us to allow for the possibility that the updated data differs, so must implement conflict-handling logic to resolve data differences between nodes. *With some thought and planning, we can use multimaster technologies very effectively in the real world.*

Visit `http://en.wikipedia.org/wiki/Replication_(computer_science)` for more information on this.

Scalability tools

Many PostgreSQL users have designed applications that scale naturally by routing database requests based on the client number or a similar natural sharding key. This is what we call manual sharding at the application level.

For PostgreSQL 9.5 and earlier versions, PostgreSQL does not directly support features for automatic write scalability, such as sharding. This is an active area of work, and much will change in this area.

Postgres-XL provides automatic hash sharding and is currently the most complete open source implementation that allows automatic write scalability at the database level.

A number of toolkits that provide sharding exist:

▶ PL/Proxy provides a mature mechanism for database scalability. It was originally designed for Skype, but is also in use at a number of high-volume sites. It provides most of the things you'll need to create a scalable cluster. PL/Proxy requires that you define your main database accesses as functions, which requires early architectural decisions about your application architecture.

▶ pg_shard is a recently released tool that provides an optimizer plugin that can route simple SQL to specific shards. This is more basic than the features of Postgres-XL, since multishard queries are not supported at this time.

Other approaches to replication

This book covers in-database replication only. Replication is also possible in the application layer (that is, above the database) or in the operating system (OS) layers (that is, below the database):

▶ **Application-level replication**: For example, HA-JDBC and rubyrep

▶ **OS-level replication**: For example, DRBD

None of these approaches are very satisfying, since core database features cannot easily integrate with them in ways that truly work. From a sysadmin's perspective, they work, but not very well from the perspective of a database architect.

Replication best practices

Some general best practices for running replication systems are described in this recipe.

How to do it...

- Use the latest release of PostgreSQL. Replication features are changing fast, with each new release improving on the previous in major ways based on our real-world experience. The idea that earlier releases are somehow more stable, and thus more easily usable, is definitely not the case for replication.

- Use similar hardware and OS on all systems. Replication allows nodes to switch roles. If we switchover or failover to different hardware, we may get performance issues and it will be hard to maintain a smoothly running application.

- Configure all systems identically as far as possible. Use the same mount points, directory names, and users; keep everything possible the same. Don't be tempted to make one system more important than others in some way. It's just a single point of failure and gets confusing.

- Give systems/servers good names to reduce confusion. Never, ever call one of your systems master and the other slave. When you do a switchover, you will get very confused! Try to pick system names that have nothing to do whatsoever with their role. Replication roles will inevitably change; system names should not. If one system fails, and you add a new system, never reuse the name of the old system: pick another name, or it will be too confusing. Don't pick names that relate to something in the business. Colors are also a bad choice, because if you have two servers named yellow and red, you then end up saying things like "there is a red alert on server yellow", which can easily be confusing. Don't pick place names either. Otherwise, you'll be confused trying to remember that London is in Edinburgh and Paris is in Rome. Make sure you use names, rather than IP addresses.

- Set the `application_name` parameter to be the server name in the replication connection string.

- Keep the system clocks synchronized. This helps you keep sane when looking at log files produced by multiple servers. You should automate this, rather than do it manually, but however you do it, make sure it works.

- Use a single, unambiguous time zone. Use **Coordinated Universal Time** (**UTC**) or something similar. Don't pick a time zone that has **Daylight Saving Time**, especially in regions that have complex DST rules. This just leads to (human) confusion with replication, as servers are often in different countries and time zone differences vary throughout the year. Do this even if you start with all servers in one country, because over the lifetime of the application, you may need to add new servers in different locations. Think ahead.

- ▶ Monitor each of the database servers. If you want high availability, then you'll need to regularly check that your servers are operational. I speak to many people who would like to regard replication as a one-shot deal. Think of it more as a marriage, and plan for it to be a happy one!

- ▶ Monitor the replication delay between servers. All forms of replication are only useful if the data is flowing correctly between the servers. Monitoring the time it takes for the data to go from one server to another is essential to understanding whether replication is working for you or not. Replication can be bursty, so you'll need to watch to make sure it stays within sensible limits. You may be able to set tuning parameters to keep things low, or you may need to look at other factors.

The important point is that your replication delay is directly related to the amount of data you're likely to lose when running asynchronous replication. Be careful here because it is the replication delay, not the apply delay, that affects data loss. A long apply delay may be more acceptable as a result.

As described previously, your initial replication delay will be high, and it should reduce to a lower and more stable value over a period of time. For large databases, this could take days, so be careful to monitor during the catch-up period.

There's more...

The preceding list doesn't actually say this explicitly, but you should use the same major version of PostgreSQL for all systems. With PSR, you are required to do that, so it doesn't even need to be said.

I've heard people argue that it's OK to have dissimilar systems and even that it's a good idea because if you get a bug, it only affects one node. I'd say that the massive increase in complexity is much more likely to cause problems.

Setting up file-based replication – deprecated

The technique is mostly superseded by streaming replication (PSR), so if you are a novice, you probably wouldn't want this recipe yet. Nonetheless, this is relevant and useful as part of a comprehensive backup strategy. It is also worth understanding how this works, as this technique can also be used as the starting phase for a large streaming replication setup. Look at the next recipes for some further details on that.

Log shipping is a replication technique used by many database management systems. The master records database changes in its transaction log, and then the log files are shipped from the master to the standby, where the log is replayed.

File-based log shipping has been available for PostgreSQL for many years now. It is simple, has very low overhead, and is a trustworthy form of replication.

Getting ready

If you haven't read the *Replication concepts* section and the *Replication best practices* recipe at the start of this chapter, go and read them now. Replication is complex, and even if you think like "no problem, I know that", it's worth just checking out the basic concepts and names that I'll be using here. Note that log shipping replication refers to the master node as the primary node, and these two terms are used interchangeably.

How to do it...

Follow these steps for initial configuration of file-based log shipping:

1. Identify your archive location and ensure that it has sufficient space. This recipe assumes that the archive is a directory on the standby node, identified by the $PGARCHIVE environment variable. This is set on both the master and standby nodes, as the master must write to the archive and the standby must read from it. The standby node is identified on the master using $STANDBYNODE.

2. Configure replication security. Perform a key exchange to allow the master and the standby to run the rsync command in either direction.

3. Adjust the master's parameters in postgresql.conf, as follows:

    ```
    wal_level = 'archive'
    archive_mode = on
    archive_command = 'scp %p $STANDBYNODE:$PGARCHIVE/%f'
    archive_timeout = 30
    ```

4. Adjust Hot Standby parameters if required (see the *Hot Standby and read scalability* recipe).

5. Take a base backup, very similar to the process for taking a physical backup described in *Chapter 11, Backup and Recovery*.

6. Start the backup by running the following command:

    ```
    psql -c "select pg_start_backup('base backup for log shipping')"
    ```

7. Copy the data files (excluding the pg_xlog directory). Note that this requires some security configuration to ensure that rsync can be executed without needing to provide a password when it executes. If you skipped step 2, do this now, as follows:

    ```
    rsync -cva --inplace --exclude=*pg_xlog* \
    ${PGDATA}/ $STANDBYNODE:$PGDATA
    ```

8. Stop the backup by running the following command:

    ```
    psql -c "select pg_stop_backup(), current_timestamp"
    ```

9. Set the `recovery.conf` parameters in the `data` directory on the standby server, as follows:

```
standby_mode = 'on'
restore_command = 'cp $PGARCHIVE/%f %p'
archive_cleanup_command = 'pg_archivecleanup $PGARCHIVE %r'
trigger_file = '/tmp/postgresql.trigger.5432'
```

10. Start the standby server.

11. Carefully monitor the replication delay until the catch-up period is over. During the initial catch-up period, the replication delay will be much higher than we would normally expect it to be. You are advised to set `hot_standby` to `off` for the initial period only.

Use a script; don't do this by hand, even when testing or just exploring the capabilities. If you make a mistake, you'd want to rerun things from the start again, and doing things manually is both laborious and an extra source of error.

How it works...

Transaction log (WAL) files will be written on the master. Setting `wal_level` to `archive` ensures that we collect all of the changed data, and that WAL is never optimized away. WAL is sent from the master to the archive using `archive_command`, and from there, the standby reads WAL files using `restore_command`. Then, it replays the changes.

The `archive_command` is executed when a file becomes full, or an `archive_timeout` number of seconds have passed since any user inserted change data into the transaction log. If the server does not write any new transaction log data for an extended period, then files will switch every `checkpoint_timeout` seconds. This is normal, and not a problem.

The preceding configuration assumes that the archive is on the standby, so the `restore_command` shown is a simple copy command (`cp`). If the archive was on a third system, then we would need to either mount the filesystem remotely or use a network copy command.

The `archive_cleanup_command` ensures that the archive only holds the files that the standby needs for restarting, in case it stops for any reason. Files older than the last file required are deleted regularly to ensure that the archive does not overflow. Note that if the standby is down for an extended period, then the number of files in the archive will continue to accumulate, and eventually they will overflow. The number of files in the archive should also be monitored.

In the configuration shown in this recipe, a contrib module named `pg_archivecleanup` is used to remove files from the archive. This is a module supplied with PostgreSQL 9.0. The `pg_archivecleanup` module is designed to work with one standby node at a time. Note that `pg_archivecleanup` requires two parameters: the archive directory and `%r`, with a space between them. PostgreSQL transforms `%r` into the cut-off filename.

If you wish to have multiple standby nodes, then a shared archive would be a single point of failure and should be avoided, so each standby should maintain its own archive. We must modify the `archive_command` to be a script, rather than execute the command directly. This allows us to handle archiving to multiple destinations:

```
archive_command = 'myarchivescript %p %f'
```

Then, we can write `myarchivescript` so that it looks somewhat like the following, though you'll need to add suitable error checking for your environment:

```
scp $1 $STANDBYNODE1:$PGARCHIVE/$2
scp $1 $STANDBYNODE2:$PGARCHIVE/$2
scp $1 $STANDBYNODE3:$PGARCHIVE/$2
```

The initial copy, or base backup, is performed using the `rsync` utility, which may require you to have direct security authorization, for example, using SSH and key exchange. You may also choose to perform the base backup a different way. If so, feel free to substitute your preferred method.

There's more...

Monitoring file-based log shipping can be performed in a number of ways. You can look at the current files on both the master and standby, as follows:

```
ps -ef | grep archiver          on master
postgres: archiver process  last was   000000010000000000000040
ps -ef | grep startup           on standby
postgres: startup process  waiting for   000000010000000000000041
```

This allows you to see the replication delay in terms of the number of WAL files by which the standby is behind the master. Prior to PostgreSQL 9.0, it was difficult to measure the replication delay as a time interval with any accuracy, and some "hackish" methods were needed. Those aren't presented here. The latest ways of monitoring replication are covered in more detail in the *Monitoring replication* recipe.

See also

If you have configuration instructions written for versions ranging from PostgreSQL 8.2 to 8.4, then they will work almost exactly the same from PostgreSQL 9.0 onwards. The only difference is that you will also need to specify `wal_level`, as just shown. Note that the procedures covered here are not the default configuration, and they do differ from earlier releases. In PostgreSQL 9.0, the `pg_standby` utility is no longer required, as many of its features are now performed directly by the server. If you prefer to continue using `pg_standby` with PostgreSQL 9.0, then you do not need to use the `archive_cleanup_command`, `standby_mode`, or `trigger_file` parameters at all.

Setting up streaming replication

Log shipping is a replication technique used by many database management systems. The master records change in its transaction log (WAL), and then the log data is shipped from the master to the standby, where the log is replayed.

In PostgreSQL, streaming replication transfers WAL data directly from the master to the standby, giving us integrated security and reduced replication delay.

There are two main ways to set up streaming replication: with or without an additional archive. Setting it up without an external archive is presented here, as it is the more simple and efficient way. However, there is one downside that suggests that the simple approach may not be appropriate for larger databases, which is explained later in the recipe.

Getting ready

If you haven't read the *Replication concepts* section and the *Replication best practices* recipes at the start of this chapter, go and read them now. Note that streaming replication refers to the master node as the primary node, and the two terms can be used interchangeably.

How to do it...

As of PostgreSQL 9.1, there are two procedures for setting up streaming replication. Both are presented here. The first works with 9.0 and later versions.

Carry out the following steps:

1. Identify your master and standby nodes, and ensure that they have been configured according to the *Replication best practices* recipe.
2. Configure replication security. Create or confirm the existence of the replication user on the master node:

```
CREATE USER repuser
        SUPERUSER
        LOGIN
        CONNECTION LIMIT 1
        ENCRYPTED PASSWORD 'changeme';
```

3. Allow the replication user to authenticate. The following example allows access from any IP address using MD5-encrypted password authentication; you may wish to consider other options. Add the following line to `pg_hba.conf`:

```
Host    replication    repuser    127.0.0.1/0    md5
```

4. Set the logging options in `postgresql.conf` on both the master and the standby so that you can get more information regarding replication connection attempts and associated failures:

```
log_connections = on
```

5. Set `max_wal_senders` on the master in `postgresql.conf`, or increase it if the value is already nonzero:

```
max_wal_senders = 2
wal_level = 'archive'
archive_mode = on
archive_command = 'cd .'
```

6. Adjust `wal_keep_segments` on the master in `postgresql.conf`. Set this to a value no higher than the amount of free space on the drive on which the `pg_xlog` directory is mounted, divided by 16 MB. If `pg_xlog` isn't mounted on a separate drive, then don't assume that all of the current free space is available for transaction log files.

```
wal_keep_segments = 10000    # e.g. 160 GB
```

7. Adjust the Hot Standby parameters if required (see the *Hot Standby and read scalability* recipe).

8. Take a base backup, very similar to the process for taking a physical backup, as described in *Chapter 11, Backup and Recovery*:

   1. Start the backup:

      ```
      psql -c "select pg_start_backup('base backup for streaming rep')"
      ```

   2. Copy the data files (excluding the `pg_xlog` directory):

      ```
      rsync -cva --inplace --exclude=*pg_xlog* \
      ${PGDATA}/ $STANDBYNODE:$PGDATA
      ```

   3. Stop the backup:

      ```
      psql -c "select pg_stop_backup(), current_timestamp"
      ```

9. Set the `recovery.conf` parameters on the standby. Note that `primary_conninfo` must not specify a database name, though it can contain any other PostgreSQL connection option. Note also that all options in `recovery.conf` are enclosed in quotes, whereas the `postgresql.conf` parameters need not be:

```
standby_mode = 'on'
primary_conninfo = 'host=alpha user=repuser'
trigger_file = '/tmp/postgresql.trigger.5432'
```

10. Start the standby server.

11. Carefully monitor the replication delay until the catch-up period is over. During the initial catch-up period, the replication delay will be much higher than we would normally expect it to be.

Here is the alternative procedure, which works with PostgreSQL 9.1 using a tool called `pg_basebackup`. From PostgreSQL 9.2 onwards, you can run this procedure on a standby node rather than the master:

1. First, perform steps 1 to 5 of the preceding procedure.

2. Use `wal_keep_segments`, as shown in step 6 of the previous procedure, or in PostgreSQL 9.4 or later, use Replication Slots (see later recipe).

3. Adjust the Hot Standby parameters if required (see later recipe).

4. Take a base backup:

```
pg_basebackup -d 'connection string' -D /path/to_data_dir
```

For PostgreSQL 9.2 and later versions, you are advised to use the following additional option on the `pg_basebackup` command line. This option allows the required WAL files to be streamed alongside the base backup on a second session, greatly improving the startup time on larger databases, without the need to fuss over large settings of `wal_keep_segments` (as seen in step 6 of the previous procedure):

```
--xlog-method=stream
```

For PostgreSQL 9.4 and later versions, if the backup uses too many server resources (CPU, memory, disk, or bandwidth), you can throttle down the speed for the backup using the following additional option on the `pg_basebackup` command line. The `RATE` value is specified in kB/s by default:

```
--max-rate=RATE
```

5. Set the `recovery.conf` parameters on the standby. Note that `primary_conninfo` must not specify a database name, though it can contain any other PostgreSQL connection option. Note also that all options in `recovery.conf` are enclosed in quotes, whereas the `postgresql.conf` parameters need not be. For PostgreSQL 9.4 and later versions, you can skip this step if you wish by specifying the `--write-recovery-conf` option on `pg_basebackup`:

```
standby_mode = 'on'
primary_conninfo = 'host=192.168.0.1 user=repuser'
# trigger_file = ''  # no need for trigger file 9.1+
```

6. Start the standby server.

7. Carefully monitor the replication delay until the catch-up period is over. During the initial catch-up period, the replication delay will be much higher than we would normally expect it to be.

The `pg_basebackup` utility also allows you to produce a compressed tar file, using this command:

```
pg_basebackup -F -z
```

How it works...

Multiple standby nodes can connect to a single master. Set `max_wal_senders` to the number of standby nodes, plus at least one. If you are planning to use `pg_basebackup --xlog-method=stream`, then allow for an additional connection per concurrent backup you plan for. You may wish to set up an individual user for each standby node, though it may be sufficient just to set the `application_name` parameter in `primary_conninfo`.

The architecture for streaming replication is this: on the master, one WALSender process is created for each standby that connects for streaming replication. On the standby node, a WALReceiver process is created to work cooperatively with the master. Data transfer has been designed and measured to be very efficient—data is typically sent in 8,192-byte chunks, without additional buffering at the network layer.

Both WALSender and WALReceiver will work continuously on any outstanding data to be replicated until the queue is empty. If there is a quiet period, then WALReceiver will sleep for 100 ms at a time, and WALSender will sleep for `wal_sender_delay`. Typically, the value of `wal_sender_delay` need not be altered because it only affects the behavior during momentary quiet periods. The default value is a good balance between efficiency and data protection. If the master and standby are connected by a low-bandwidth network and the write rate on the master is high, you may wish to lower this value to perhaps 20 ms or 50 ms. Reducing this value will reduce the amount of data loss if the master becomes permanently unavailable, but will also marginally increase the cost of streaming the transaction log data to the standby.

The standby connects to the master using native PostgreSQL libpq connections. This means that all forms of authentication and security work for replication just as they do for normal connections. Note that, for replication sessions, the standby is the "client" and the master is the "server", if any parameters need to be configured. Using standard PostgreSQL libpq connections also means that normal network port numbers are used, so no additional firewall rules are required. You should also note that if the connections use SSL, then encryption costs will slightly increase the replication delay and the CPU resources required.

There's more...

If the connection between the master and standby drops, it will take some time for that to be noticed across an indirect network. To ensure that a dropped connection is noticed as soon as possible, you may wish to adjust the timeout settings.

If you want a standby to notice that the connection to the master has dropped, you need to set the `wal_receiver_timeout` value in the `postgresql.conf` file on the standby.

If you want the master to notice that a streaming standby connection has dropped, you can set the `wal_sender_timeout` parameter in the `postgresql.conf` file on the master.

You may also wish to increase `max_wal_senders` to one or two more than the current number of nodes so that it will be possible to reconnect even before a dropped connection is noted. This allows a manual restart to re-establish connections more easily. If you do this, then also increase the connection limit for the replication user. Changing that setting requires a restart.

Data transfer may stop if the connection drops or the standby server or the standby system is shut down. If replication data transfer stops for any reason, it will attempt to restart from the point of the last transfer. Will that data still be available? Let's see.

For streaming replication, the master keeps a number of files that is at least equal to `wal_keep_segments`. If the standby database server has been down for long enough, the master will have moved on and will no longer have the data for the last point of transfer. If that should occur, then the standby needs to be reconfigured using the same procedure with which we started.

For PostgreSQL 9.2 and later versions, you should plan to use `pg_basebackup -xlog-method=stream`. If you choose not to, you should note that the standby database server will not be streaming during the initial base backup. So, if the base backup is long enough, we might end up with a situation where replication will never start because the desired starting point is no longer available on the master. This is the error that you'll get:

```
FATAL:   requested WAL segment 000000010000000000000002 has already been
removed
```

It's very annoying, and there's no way out of it—you need to start over. So, start with a very high value of `wal_keep_segments`. Don't guess this randomly; set it to the available disk space on `pg_xlog` divided by 16 MB, or less if it is a shared disk. If you still get that error, then you need to increase `wal_keep_segments` and try again, possibly also using techniques to speed up the base backup, which are discussed in *Chapter 11, Backup and Recovery*.

If you can't set `wal_keep_segments` high enough, there is an alternative. You must configure a third server or storage pool with increased disk storage capacity, which you can use as an archive. The master will need to have an `archive_command` that places files on the archive server, rather than the dummy command shown in the preceding procedure, in addition to parameter settings to allow streaming to take place. The standby will need to retrieve files from the archive using `restore_command`, as well as streaming using `primary_conninfo`. Thus, both the master and standby have two modes for sending and receiving, and they can switch between them should failures occur. This is the typical configuration for large databases. Note that this means that the WAL data will be copied twice, once to the archive and once directly to the standby. Two copies are more expensive, but also more robust.

The reason for setting `archive_mode = on` in the preceding procedure is that altering that parameter requires a restart, so you may as well set it on just in case you need it later. All we need to do is use a dummy `archive_command` to ensure that everything still works OK. By "dummy command", I mean a command that will do nothing and then provide a return code of zero, for example, `cd` or `true`.

One thing that is a possibility is to set `archive_command` only until the end of the catch-up period. After that, you can reset it to a dummy value and then continue with only streaming replication. Data is transferred from the master to the standby only once it has been written (or more precisely, fsynced) to the disk. So, setting `synchronous_commit = off` will not improve the replication delay, even if it improves performance on the master. Once WAL data is received by the standby, the WAL data is fsynced to disk on the standby to ensure that it is not lost when the standby system restarts.

Setting up streaming replication security

Streaming replication is at least as secure as normal user connections to PostgreSQL.

Replication uses standard libpq connections, so we have all the normal mechanisms for authentication and SSL support, and all the firewall rules are similar.

Replication must be specifically enabled on both the sender and standby sides. Cascading replication does not require any additional security.

When performing a base backup, the pg_basebackup, pg_receivexlog, and pg_recvlogical utilities will use the same type of libpq connections as a running streaming standby. You can use other forms of base backup, such as rsync, though you'll need to manually set up the security configuration.

 Standbys are identical copies of the master, so all users exist on all nodes with identical passwords. All of the data is identical (eventually) and all the permissions are the same too. If you wish to control access more closely, then you'll need different pg_hba.conf rules on each server to control this. Obviously, if your config files differ between nodes, then Failover will be slightly more dramatic, unless you've given that some prior thought.

Getting ready

Identify or create a user/role to be used solely for replication. Decide what form of authentication will be used. If you are going across data centers or the wider Internet, take this very seriously.

How to do it...

On the master, perform these steps:

1. Enable replication by setting a specific host access rule in pg_hba.conf.

2. Give the selected replication user/role the REPLICATION attribute:

   ALTER ROLE replogin REPLICATION;

   Alternatively, create it using this command:

   CREATE ROLE replogin WITH REPLICATION;

On the standby, perform these steps:

1. Request replication by setting primary_conninfo.

2. If you are using SSL connections, use sslmode=verify-full.

3. Enable per-server rules, if any, for this server in pg_hba.conf.

How it works...

Streaming replication connects to a virtual database called `replication`. We do this because the WAL data contains changes to objects in *all* databases, so in a way, we aren't just connecting to one database—we are connecting to all of them.

Streaming replication connects similar to a normal user, except that instead of a normal user process, we are given a WALSender process.

You can set a connection limit on the number of replication connections in two ways:

▶ At the role level by issuing the following command:

   `ALTER ROLE replogin CONNECTION LIMIT 2;`

▶ By limiting the overall number of WALSender processes via the `max_wal_senders` parameter

Always allow one more connection than you think is required, to allow for disconnections and reconnections.

There's more...

You may notice that the WALSender process may hit 100 percent CPU if you use SSL with compression enabled and write lots of data, or generate a large WAL volume from things such as DDL or vacuuming. You can disable compression on fast networks when you aren't paying per bandwidth charges, using `sslcompression=0` in the connection string specified for `primary_conninfo`.

Hot Standby and read scalability

Hot Standby is the name for the PostgreSQL feature that allows us to connect to a standby node and execute read-only queries. Most importantly, Hot Standby allows us to run queries while the standby is being continuously updated through either file-based or streaming replication.

Hot Standby allows you to offload large or long running queries or parts of your read-only workload to the standby nodes. Should you need to switch over or fail over to the standby node, your queries will keep executing during the promotion process to avoid any interruption of service.

You can add additional Hot Standby nodes to scale the read-only workload. There is no hard limit on the number of standby nodes, as you ensure enough server resources are available and parameters are set correctly. 10, 20, or more nodes are easily possible.

There are two main capabilities provided by a Hot Standby node. The first is that the standby node provides a secondary node in case the primary node fails. The second capability is that we can run queries on that node. In some cases, those two aspects can come into conflict with each other and can result in queries being cancelled. We need to decide ahead of time the importance we attach to each capability so that we can prioritize between them.

In most cases, the role of standby will take priority. Queries are good, but it's OK to cancel them to ensure that we have a viable standby. If we have more than one Hot Standby node, it may be possible to have one node nominated as standby and others dedicated to serving queries, without any regard for their need to act as standbys.

Standby nodes are started and stopped using the same server commands as master servers, which were covered in earlier chapters.

Getting ready

Hot Standby is usable with the following:

- File-based replication
- Streaming replication
- While performing a point-in-time recovery
- When using a permanently frozen standby

For the first two replication mechanisms, you will need to configure replication as described in earlier recipes. In addition, you will need to configure the following parameters:

On the master, set the following in `postgresql.conf`:

```
wal_level = 'hot_standby'
```

On the standby, set the following in `postgresql.conf`:

```
hot_standby = on
```

Neither of those settings are the default, so you will need to make the changes. You will need to do a clean restart of the database server on the master. Then, wait a few seconds and restart the standby for these changes to take effect. If you restart the standby too quickly, it will still keep reading the older transaction log data and fail to start. It will give a log message saying `you need to enable Hot Standby`, so be patient. You only need to configure this once, not every time you restart. See the *Delaying, pausing, and synchronizing replication* recipe to work out how to wait for actions on the master to arrive on the standby.

A permanently frozen standby can be created by specific settings in the `recovery.conf` file. Neither `restore_command` nor `primary_conninfo` should be set, in the case of `standby_mode = on`. In this mode, the server will start but will always remain at the exact state of the database as it was when the `pg_stop_backup()` function completed.

Another point to note is that during the initial catch-up period, the replication delay will be much higher than we would normally expect it to be. You are advised to set `hot_standby = off` for the initial period immediately following the creation of the standby only. User connections during that initial period may use system resources or cause conflicts that could extend the catch-up delay. When the standby is fully caught up with the primary, then we can set `hot_standby = on` and restart, or simply prevent user access via `pg_hba.conf` until the standby catches up.

How to do it...

On the standby, node changes from the master are read from the transaction log and applied to the standby database. Hot Standby works by emulating running transactions from the master so that queries on the standby have the visibility information they need to fully respect MVCC. This makes the Hot Standby mode particularly suitable for serving a large workload of short or fast `SELECT` queries. If the workload is consistently short, then few conflicts will delay the standby, and the server will run smoothly.

Queries that run on the standby node see a version of the database that is slightly behind the primary node. We describe this as eventually consistent. How long is "eventually"? That time is exactly the replication delay plus the apply delay, as discussed in the *Replication concepts* section. In PostgreSQL 9.4 and later versions, you may also request that standby servers delay applying changes. See the *Delaying, pausing, and synchronizing replication* recipe later on this topic.

Resource contention (CPU, I/O, and so on) may increase apply delay. If the server is busy applying changes from the master, then you will have fewer resources to use for queries. This means that if there are no changes arriving, then you'll get more query throughput. If there are predictable changes in the write workload on the master, then you may need to throttle back your query workload on the standby when they occur.

Replication apply may also generate conflicts with running queries. Conflict may cause the replay to pause, and eventually queries on the standby may be cancelled or disconnected. There are three main types of conflicts that can occur between the master and queries on the standby, which are as follows:

- Locks such as `Access Exclusive` locks
- Cleanup records
- Other special cases

If cancellations do occur, they will throw either an error or fatal-level errors. These will be marked with `SQLSTATE 40001 SERIALIZATION FAILURE`. This could be trapped by an application, and the SQL can be resubmitted.

You can monitor the number of conflicts that occur in two places. The total number of conflicts in each database can be seen using this query:

```
SELECT datname, conflicts FROM pg_stat_database;
```

You can drill down further to look at the types of conflict seen using the following query:

```
SELECT
 datname
,confl_tablespace
,confl_lock
,confl_snapshot
,confl_bufferpin
,confl_deadlock
FROM pg_stat_database_conflicts;
```

Tablespace conflicts are the easiest to understand. If you try to drop a tablespace that someone is still using, then you're going to get a conflict. Don't do that!

Lock conflicts are also easy to understand. If you wish to run a command on the master, such as `ALTER TABLE … DROP COLUMN`, then you must lock the table first to prevent all types of access. The lock request is sent to the standby server as well, which will then cancel standby queries that are currently accessing that table after a configurable delay.

On high-availability systems, making DDL changes to tables that cause long periods of locking on the master can be difficult. You may want the tables on the standby to stay available for reads during the period in which the changes are being made on the master. To do that, temporarily set these parameters on the standby: `max_standby_streaming delay = -1` and `max_standby_archive_delay = -1`. Then, reload the server. As soon as the first lock record is seen on the standby, all further changes will be held. Once the locks on the master are released, you can reset the original parameter values on the standby, which will then allow the changes to be made there.

Setting the `max_standby_streaming_delay` and `max_standby_archive_delay` parameters to -1 is very timid and may not be useful for normal running if the standby is intended to provide high availability. No user query will ever be cancelled if it conflicts with applying changes. It will cause the apply process to wait indefinitely. As a result, the apply delay can increase significantly over time, depending on the frequency and duration of queries and the frequency of conflicts. To work out an appropriate setting for these parameters, you need to understand more about the other types of conflict, though there is also a simple way to avoid this problem entirely.

Snapshot conflicts require some understanding of the internal workings of MVCC, which many people find confusing. To avoid snapshot conflicts, you should set `hot_standby_feedback = on` in the standby's `postgresql.conf` file.

In some cases, this could cause table bloat on the master, so it is not set by default. If you don't wish to set `hot_standby_feedback = on`, then you have further options to consider. You can set an upper limit on the acceptable apply delay caused by conflicts by controlling two similar parameters: `max_standby_streaming_delay` and `max_standby_archive_delay`. As a last resort, you can also provide some protection against cancelled queries by setting `vacuum_defer_cleanup_age` to a value higher than `0`. This parameter is fairly hard to set accurately, though I would suggest starting with a value of `1000` and then tune upwards. A vague and inaccurate assumption would be to say that each `1000` will be approximately 1 second of additional delay. This is probably helpful more often than it is wrong. Other conflict types (bufferpin, deadlocks) are possible, but they are rare.

If you want a completely *static* standby database with no further changes applied, then you can do this by stopping the server, modifying `recovery.conf` such that neither `restore_command` nor `primary_conninfo` are set but `standby_mode` is on, and then restarting the server. You can come back out of this mode, but only if the archive contains the required WAL files to catch up. Otherwise, you will need to reconfigure the standby from a base backup again.

If you attempt to run a non-read-only query, then you will receive an error marked with `SQLSTATE 25006 READ ONLY TRANSACTION`. That could be used to redirect SQL to the master, where it can execute successfully.

How it works...

Changes made by a transaction on the master will not be visible until the commit is applied onto the standby. So, for example, we have a master and a standby with a replication delay of 4 seconds between them. A long-running transaction may write changes to the master for 1 hour. How long does it take before those changes are visible on the standby? With Hot Standby, the answer is four seconds after the commit on the master. This is because the changes made during the transaction on the master are streamed while the transaction is still in progress, and in most cases, they are already applied on the standby when the commit record arrives. Note that this is a very different situation for trigger-based replication, such as Slony and Londiste, where the data does not start transferring until after a transaction has committed on the master. So, with trigger-based replication, the data would likely become visible many minutes after the commit on the master. With trigger-based replication, the effective apply delay also depends on the transaction duration on the master.

Hot Standby can also be used when running a Point-in-Time recovery, so the WAL records applied to the database need not arrive immediately from a live database server. We can just use file-based recovery in that case, not streaming replication.

Finally, query performance has been dramatically improved in Hot Standby from PostgreSQL 9.4 onwards, so it's a good idea to upgrade for that reason alone.

Managing streaming replication

Replication is great provided it works. Replication works well if it's understood and works even better if it's tested.

Getting ready

You need to have a plan for the objectives for each individual server in the cluster. Which standby server will be the failover target?

How to do it...

Switchover is a controlled switch from the master to the standby. If performed correctly, there will be no data loss. To be safe, simply shut down the master node cleanly, using either the `smart` or `fast` shutdown modes. Do not use the `immediate` mode shutdown because you will almost certainly lose data that way.

Failover is a forced switch from the master node to a standby because of the loss of the master. So, in that case, there is no action to perform on the master; we presume it is not there anymore.

Next, we need to promote one of the standby nodes to be the new master. A standby node can be triggered into becoming a master node in one of two ways:

- `pg_ctl promote`
- Suppose you originally specified a `trigger_file` parameter like this:

  ```
  trigger_file = '/tmp/postgresql.trigger.5432'
  ```

  Then, you can create the trigger file by executing this:

  ```
  touch /tmp/postgresql.trigger.5432
  ```

The trigger file will be deleted when the transition is complete.

Note that the **trigger file** has nothing to do whatsoever with trigger-based replication. The trigger file name can be anything you like. We use a suffix of 5432 to ensure that we trigger only one server if there are multiple PostgreSQL servers operating on the same system.

The standby will become the master only once it has fully caught up. If you haven't been monitoring replication, this could take some time.

In versions before PostgreSQL 9.3, switching from standby to master may take some time while the database performs an immediate checkpoint, at least with database servers with large caches and high rate of changes being replicated from the master. From PostgreSQL 9.3 onwards, we can switch from the standby to the master very quickly, and then perform a smooth background checkpoint. There may still be significant I/O as writes begin on the new master.

Once the ex-standby becomes a master, it will begin to operate all normal functions, including starting to archive files if configured. Be careful to verify that you have all the correct settings for when this node begins to operate as a master. It is likely that the settings will be different from those on the original master from which they were copied.

Note that I refer to this new server as "a Master", not "the Master". It is up to you to ensure that the previous master doesn't continue to operate—a situation known as a **split-brain situation**. You must be careful to ensure that the previous master stays down.

Management of complex failover situations is not provided with PostgreSQL, nor is automated failover. Situations can be quite complex with multiple nodes, and clusterware is used in many cases to manage this.

The role of the `recovery_end_command` is to clean up at the end of the switchover or failover process. You do not need to explicitly remove the trigger file, as was recommended in previous releases.

There's more...

Following a switchover from one node to another, it is common to think of performing a switchover back to the old master server, which is sometimes called failback or switchback.

Once a standby has become a master, it cannot go back to being a standby again. So, with log replication, there is no explicit switchback operation. This is a surprising situation for many people and is a repeated question, but it is quick to work around. Once you have performed a switchover, all you need to do is the following:

1. Reconfigure the old master node again, repeating the same process as before to set up a standby node.

2. Switchover from the current to the old master node.

The important part here is that if we perform the first step without deleting the files on the old master, it allows `rsync` to go much faster. When no files are present on the destination, `rsync` just performs a copy. When similarly named files are present on the destination, then `rsync` will compare the files and send only the changes. So, the `rsync` we perform on a switchback operation performs much less data transfer than in the original copy. It is likely that this will be enhanced in later releases of PostgreSQL. There are also ways to avoid this, as shown in the repmgr utility, which will be discussed later.

The `pg_rewind` utility has been developed as a way to perform an automated switchback operation. It also performs a faster switchback when there is a large database with few changes to apply. To allow correct operation, this program must run using the `wal_log_hints = on` parameter, which is available only in PostgreSQL 9.4 and later versions. Using that parameter can cause more I/O on large databases.

See also

Clusterware may provide additional features, such as automated failover, monitoring, or ease of management of replication.

 ▶ repmgr is designed to manage PostgreSQL replication and failover. This is discussed in more detail in the *Using repmgr* recipe.

 ▶ pgpool is designed to allow session pooling and routing of requests to standby nodes.

Using repmgr

As said before, replication is great provided it works. It works well if it's understood and works even better if it's tested. This is a great reason to use repmgr.

repmgr is an open source tool designed specifically for PostgreSQL replication. To get additional information about repmgr, visit `http://projects.2ndQuadrant.com/repmgr/`.

repmgr provides a command-line interface and a management process (daemon) used to monitor and manage PostgreSQL servers involved in replication. repmgr easily supports more than two nodes, with automatic failover detection.

Getting ready

Install repmgr from binary packages on each PostgreSQL node.

Set up replication security and network access between nodes according to the *Setting up streaming replication security* recipe.

How to do it...

repmgr provides a set of single command-line actions that perform all the required activities on one node:

- To register the current master with repmgr, use the following command:

  ```
  repmgr master register
  ```

- To register an existing standby with repmgr, use the following command:

  ```
  repmgr standby register
  ```

- Use the next command to request repmgr to create a new standby for you by copying node1. This will fail if you specify an existing data directory:

  ```
  repmgr standby clone node1 -D /path/of_new_data_directory
  ```

- To switch back to an old master, first force it to become a standby, and then promote it back again to a master:

  ```
  repmgr standby clone --force
  repmgr standby promote
  ```

- To promote a standby to be the new master, use the following command:

  ```
  repmgr standby promote
  ```

- To request a standby to follow a new master, use the following command:

  ```
  repmgr standby follow
  ```

- Check the status of each registered node in the cluster, like this:

  ```
  repmgr cluster show
  ```

- Request cleanup of monitoring data, as follows. This is relevant only if --monitoring-history is used:

  ```
  repmgr cluster cleanup
  ```

- Create a witness server for use with auto-failover voting, like this:

  ```
  repmgr witness create
  ```

The preceding commands are presented in a simplified form. Each command also takes one of these options:

- --verbose: This is useful when exploring new features
- -f: This specifies the path to the repmgr.conf file

For each node, create a `repmgr.conf` file containing at least the following parameters. Note that the `node` and `node_name` parameters need to be different on each node:

```
cluster=demo
node=2
node_name=beta
conninfo='host=node2 user=repmgr'
```

Once all the nodes are registered, you can start the repmgr daemon on each node, like this:

`repmgrd -d -f /var/lib/pgsql/repmgr/repmgr.conf &`

If you would like the daemon to generate monitoring information for that node, you should also add the `--monitoring-history` option.

Monitoring data can be accessed using this:

```
$ psql -x -c "SELECT * FROM repmgr.repl_status"
-[ RECORD 1 ]-------------+----------------------------
primary_node              | 1
standby_node              | 2
last_monitor_time         | 2015-02-23 08:19:39.791974-05
last_wal_primary_location | 0/1902D5E0
last_wal_standby_location | 0/1902D5E0
replication_lag           | 0 bytes
apply_lag                 | 0 bytes
time_lag                  | 00:26:13.30293
```

How it works...

repmgr 2 works with PostgreSQL 9.0 and newer versions. repmgr 3 supports newer features of PostgreSQL, such as cascading, synchronous replication, and replication slots. It uses `pg_basebackup`, allowing you to clone from a standby. The use of `pg_basebackup` also removes the need for `rsync` and key exchange between servers. Also, cascaded standby nodes no longer need to re-follow.

There's more...

The default behavior for repmgr is manual failover.

repmgr also supports automatic failover capabilities. It can automatically detect failures of other nodes and then decide which server should become the new master by voting among all of the still available standby nodes. repmgr supports a witness server to ensure that there are an odd number of voters in order to get a clear winner in any decision.

Using Replication Slots

Replication Slots are a new feature in PostgreSQL 9.4. They allow you to define your replication architecture explicitly. They also allow you to track details of nodes even when they are disconnected. Replication Slots work with both PSR and LSR.

Replication Slots make data persist about the downstream node. They are crash-safe, so if a connection is lost, the slot still continues to exist. By tracking data on downstream nodes, we avoid these problems:

> ▶ When a standby disconnects, the feedback data provided by `hot_standby_feedback` is lost. When the standby reconnects, it may be sent cleanup records that result in query conflicts. Replication Slots remember the standby's `xmin` value even when disconnected, ensuring that cleanup conflicts can be avoided.

> ▶ When a standby disconnects, the knowledge of which WAL files were required is lost. When the standby reconnects, we may have discarded the required WAL files, requiring us to completely regenerate the downstream node (assuming that this is possible). Replication Slots ensure that nodes retain the WAL files needed by all downstream nodes.

Replication Slots are required by Logical Streaming Replication and for any other use of Logical Decoding. Replication Slots are optional with Physical Streaming Replication.

Getting ready

This recipe assumes you have already set up replication according to the earlier recipes so that `wal_level`, `max_wal_senders`, and other parameters are set.

A replication slot represents one link between two nodes. At any time, each slot can support one connection. If you draw a diagram of your replication architecture, then each connecting line is one slot. Each slot must have a unique name. The slot name must contain only lowercase letters, numbers, and underscores.

As discussed previously, each node should have a unique name. So, a suggestion would be to construct the slot name from the two node names that it links. For various reasons, there may be a need for multiple slots between two nodes, so additional information is also required for uniqueness. For two servers called `alpha` and `beta`, an example of a slot name would be `alpha_beta_1`.

For Logical Streaming Replication, each slot refers to a single database rather than the whole server. In that case, slot names could also include database names.

How to do it...

1. Set `max_replication_slots > 0` on each sending node. This change requires a restart. Set the value to one more than the number of planned slots:

   ```
   max_replication_slots = 2
   ```

2. For Physical Streaming Replication slots, you have to first create the slot on the sending node, like this:

   ```
   SELECT pg_create_physical_replication_slot('alpha_beta_1');
   pg_create_physical_replication_slot

   ------------------------------------

   (nodea_nodeb_1,)
   ```

3. Confirm it has been created:

   ```
   SELECT * FROM pg_replication_slots;
   ```

4. In the `recovery.conf` file in the `data` directory on the standby, set the `primary_slot_name` parameter using the unique name you assigned earlier:

   ```
   primary_slot_name = 'alpha_beta_1'
   ```

Slots can be removed using the following query:

```
SELECT pg_drop_physical_replication_slot('alpha_beta_1');
```

There's more...

Replication Slots can be used to support applications where downstream nodes are disconnected for extended periods of time. Replication Slots prevent removal of WAL files, which are needed by disconnected nodes. Therefore, it is important to be careful that WAL files don't build up, causing "out of disk space" errors due to physical replication slots created with no currently connected standby.

See also

▸ See the *Logical Replication* recipe for more details on using slots with LSR.

Monitoring replication

Monitoring the status and progress of your replication is essential. We'll start by looking at the server status and then query the progress of replication.

Getting ready

You'll need to start by checking the state of your server (s).

Check whether a server is up using `pg_isready` or another program that uses the `PQping()` API call. You'll get one of the following responses:

- ▶ `PQPING_OK (return code 0)`: The server is running and appears to be accepting connections.

- ▶ `PQPING_REJECT (return code 1)`: The server is running but is in a state that disallows connections (startup, shutdown, or crash recovery) or a standby that is not enabled with Hot Standby.

- ▶ `PQPING_NO_RESPONSE (return code 2)`: The server could not be contacted. This might indicate that the server is not running, there is something wrong with the given connection parameters (for example, wrong port number), or there is a network connectivity problem (for example, a firewall blocking the connection request).

- ▶ `PQPING_NO_ATTEMPT (return code 3)`: No attempt was made to contact the server, for example, invalid parameters.

 We don't differentiate between a master and a standby, though this may change in later releases. Neither do we say whether a server is accepting write transactions or only read-only transactions (a standby or a master connection in read-only mode).

You can know whether a server is a master or a standby by connecting and executing this query:

```
SELECT pg_is_in_recovery();
```

There are also two other states that may be important for backup and replication: paused and in-exclusive-backup. The paused state doesn't affect user queries, but replication will not progress at all when paused. Only one exclusive backup may occur at any one time.

You can also check whether replay is paused by executing this query:

```
SELECT pg_is_xlog_replay_paused();
```

If you want to check whether a server is in-exclusive-backup mode, execute the following query:

```
SELECT pg_is_in_backup();
```

There is no supported function that shows whether a non-exclusive backup is in progress, though there isn't as much to worry about if there is. If you care about that, make sure you set the application_name of the backup program so that it shows up in the session status output of pg_stat_activity, as discussed in an *Chapter 8, Monitoring and Diagnosis*.

How to do it...

The rest of this recipe assumes that you have enabled hot_standby. This is not an absolute requirement but it makes things much, much easier.

Both repmgr and pgpool provide replication monitoring facilities. Munin plugins are available for graphing replication and apply delay.

Replication works by processing the WAL transaction log on other servers. You can think of WAL as a single, serialized stream of messages. Each message in the WAL is identified by an 8-byte integer known as a **Log Sequence Number** (**LSN**). For historical reasons, we show this as two separate hex numbers; for example, the LSN value X is shown as XXXX/YYYY. Various points in the log are referred to as locations, so each location has an LSN. You can compare any two LSNs using pg_xlog_location_diff().

To understand how to monitor progress, you need to understand a little more about replication as a transport mechanism. The stream of messages flows through the system like water through a pipe. You can work out how much progress has been made by measuring the LSN at different points in the pipe. You can also check for blockages in the pipe by measuring the relative progress between points.

New WAL records are inserted into the WAL files on the master. The current insert location can be found using this query:

```
SELECT pg_current_xlog_insert_location();
```

However, WAL records are not replicated until they have been written and synced to the WAL files on the master. The location of the most recent WAL write is given by this query on the master:

```
SELECT pg_current_xlog_location();
```

Once written, WAL records are then sent to the standby. The recent status can be found by running this query on the standby (this and the later functions return NULL on a master):

```
SELECT pg_last_xlog_receive_location();
```

Once WAL records have been received, they are written to WAL files on the standby. When the standby has written those records, they can then be applied to it. The location of the most recent apply is found using this standby query:

```
SELECT pg_last_xlog_replay_location();
```

Remember that there will always be timing differences if you run status queries on multiple nodes. What we really need is to see all of the information on one node. A view called `pg_stat_replication` provides the information we need:

```
SELECT
 pid
,application_name                       /* or other unique key */
,pg_current_xlog_insert_location()      /* WAL Insert location */
,sent_location                         /* WALSender location */
,write_location                        /* WALReceiver write loc */
,flush_location                        /* WALReceiver flush loc */
,replay_location                       /* Standby apply location */
FROM pg_stat_replication;
```

Each row in this view represents one connected standby node. The standby sends regular status messages to let the sender know how far it has progressed. If you run this query on the master, you'll be able to see all the directly connected standbys. If you run this query on a standby, you'll see values representing any cascaded standbys, but nothing about the master. Note that because the data has been sent from a remote node, it is very likely that processing will have progressed beyond the point being reported, but we don't know that for certain. That's just physics. Welcome to the world of distributed systems!

You can also ask a standby what the timestamp of the last committed transaction was:

```
SELECT pg_last_xact_replay_timestamp();
```

This sounds useful, but there is no corresponding last-committed timestamp on the master to compare it with yet (wait for 9.5!). So, we can't run a simple query on each and then compare; we need to do something more complex than that.

There's more...

The `pg_stat_replication` view shows only the currently connected nodes. If a node is supposed to be connected but it isn't, then there is no record of it at all, anywhere. If you don't have a list of the nodes that are supposed to be connected, then you'll just miss it.

Replication Slots give you a way to define which connections are supposed to be present. If you have defined a slot and it is currently connected, then you will get one row in `pg_stat_replication` for the connection and one row in `pg_replication_slots` for the corresponding slot. To find out which slots don't have current connections, you can run this query:

```
SELECT slot_name, database, age(xmin), age(catalog_xmin)
FROM pg_replication_slots
WHERE NOT active;
```

Regrettably, in 9.4, there is no `pid` column in `pg_replication_slots`, nor `slotname` in `pg_stat_replication`, so you have no direct way of telling which slots match against which connections. The only way to do this is by matching the `slot_name` against the `application_name` of the connection; luckily, we set things up that way earlier. To find the details of the currently connected slots, run something like this query:

```
SELECT slot_name
FROM pg_replication_slots
JOIN pg_stat_replication ON
  application_name LIKE slot_name || '%';
```

However, the exact query depends completely on what you choose your naming conventions to be and how many slots you expect per node.

Performance and Synchronous Replication

We usually refer to Synchronous Replication as simply "sync rep". Sync rep allows us to offer a confirmation to the user that a transaction has been committed and fully replicated on at least one standby server. To do that, we must wait for the transaction changes to be sent to at least one standby, and then have that feedback returned to the master. The additional time taken for the message's round trip will add elapsed time for write transactions, which increases in proportion to the distance between servers. PostgreSQL offers a choice to the user as to what balance they would like between durability and response time.

Getting ready

The user application must be connected to a master to issue transactions that write data. The default level of durability is defined by the `synchronous_commit` parameter. That parameter is user settable, so it can be set for different applications, sessions, or even individual transactions.

We must decide which standbys should take over from the master in the event of a failover. We do this by setting a parameter called `synchronous_standby_names`.

> You will need to configure at least three nodes to use sync rep correctly.

How to do it...

Make sure you have set the `application_name` on each standby node. Decide the order of servers to be listed in the `synchronous_standby_names` parameter. Note that the standbys named must be directly attached standby nodes or else their names will be ignored. Synchronous replication is not possible for cascaded nodes, though cascaded standbys may be connected downstream.

Set `synchronous_standby_names` on all of the nodes, not just the master.

You can see the sync state of connected standbys using this query on the master:

```
SELECT
 application_name
,state                    /* startup, backup, catchup or streaming */
,sync_priority            /* 0, 1 or more */
,sync_state               /* async, sync or potential */
FROM pg_stat_replication
ORDER BY sync_priority;
```

There are a few columns here with similar names, so be careful not to confuse them.

The `sync_state` column is just a human-readable form of `sync_priority`. When `sync_state` is `async`, the `sync_priority` value will be zero (`0`). Standby nodes mentioned in the `synchronous_standby_names` parameter will have a nonzero priority that corresponds to the order in which they are listed. The standby node with a priority of one (`1`) will be listed as having a `sync_state` value of `sync`. We refer to this node as the "sync standby". Other standby nodes configured to provide feedback are shown with a `sync_state` value of `potential` and a `sync_priority` value more than `1`.

If a server is listed in the `synchronous_standby_names` parameter but is not currently connected, then it will not be shown at all by the preceding query, so it is possible that the node is shown with a lower actual priority value than the stated ordering in the parameter. Setting `wal_receiver_status_interval` to `0` on the standby will disable status messages completely, and the node will show as an `async` node, even if it is named in the `synchronous_standby_names` parameter. You may wish to do this when you are completely certain that a standby will never need to be a failover target, such as a test server.

The state for each server is shown as one of `startup`, `catchup`, or `streaming`. When another node connects, it will first show as `startup`, though only briefly before it moves to `catchup`. Once the node has caught up with the master, it will move to `streaming`, and only then will `sync_priority` be set to a nonzero value.

Catch-up typically occurs quickly after a disconnection or reconnection, such as when a standby node is restarted. When performing an initial base backup, the server will show as `backup`. After this, it will stay for an extended period at `catchup`. The delay at this point will vary according to the size of the database, so it could be a long period. Bear this in mind when configuring sync rep.

When a new standby node moves to the `streaming` mode, you'll see a message like this in the master node log:

```
LOG standby $APPLICATION_NAME is now the synchronous standby with
priority N
```

How it works...

Standby servers send feedback messages that describe the LSN of the latest transaction they have processed. Transactions committing on the master will wait until they receive feedback saying that their transaction has been processed. If there are no standbys available for sending feedback, then the transactions on the master will wait for standbys, possibly for a very long time. That is why we say that you must have at least three servers to sensibly use sync rep. It probably occurs to you that you could run with just two servers. You can, but such a configuration does not offer any transaction guarantees; it just appears to. Many people are confused on that point, but please don't listen to them!

Sync rep increases the elapsed time of write transactions (on the master). This can reduce performance of applications from a user perspective. The server itself will spend more time waiting than before, so it's possible to run with more sessions active when using sync rep.

Remember that when using sync rep, the overall system is still **eventually consistent**. Transactions committing on the master are visible first on the standby, and a brief moment later those changes will be visible on the master (yes, standby, and then master). This means that an application that issues a write transaction on the master followed by a read transaction on the sync standby will be guaranteed to see its own changes.

There's more...

There is a small window of uncertainty for any transaction that is in progress just at the point the master goes down. This can be handled within the application by checking the return code following a `COMMIT` operation, rather than just assuming that it has completed successfully, as developers often do.

If the commit fails, it is possible that the server committed the transaction successfully but was unable to communicate that to the client, but we don't know for certain. We can resolve that uncertainty by rechecking a unique aspect of the transaction, such as re-confirming the existence of an object identifier that was inserted.

If such an object identifier doesn't exist, we can create a table for this purpose:

```
CREATE TABLE TransactionCheck
(TxnId      SERIAL PRIMARY KEY);
```

During the transaction, we insert a row into that table using this query:

```
INSERT INTO TransactionCheck DEFAULT VALUES RETURNING TxnId;
```

Then, if the commit appears to fail, we can later reread this value to confirm the transaction state as committed or aborted.

Delaying, pausing, and synchronizing replication

Some advanced features and thoughts for replication are covered here.

Getting ready

If you have multiple standby servers, you may want to have one or more servers operating in a delayed apply state, for example, 1 hour behind the master. This can be useful to help recover from user errors such as mistaken transactions or dropped tables.

How to do it...

Normally, a standby will apply changes as soon as possible. When you set the `recovery_min_apply_delay` parameter in `recovery.conf`, the application of commit records will be delayed by the specified duration. Note that only commit records are delayed, so you may receive Hot Standby cancellations using this feature. You can prevent that by setting `hot_standby_feedback` to `on`, but use this with caution, since it can cause significant bloat on a busy master if `recovery_min_apply_delay` is large.

If something bad happens, then hit the pause button.

Hot Standby allows you to pause and resume replay of changes.

To pause the replay, issue this query:

```
SELECT pg_xlog_replay_pause();
```

Once paused, all queries will receive the same snapshot, allowing lengthy repeated analyses of the database, or retrieval of a dropped table.

To resume (un-pause) processing, use this query:

```
SELECT pg_xlog_replay_resume();
```

Be careful not to promote a delayed standby. If your delayed standby is the last server available, you should reset `recovery_min_apply_delay`, then restart the server, and allow it to catch up before issuing a **promote** action.

There's more...

A standby is an exact copy of the master. But how do you synchronize things so that the query results you get from a standby are the same as you'd get from the master? Well, that in itself is not possible. It's just the physics of an eventually consistent system. We need it to be eventually consistent because otherwise, the synchronization would become a performance bottleneck.

What we can do is synchronize two requests on different servers, for example, if we wish to issue a write on the master and then later issue a read from a standby. Such a case is automatically handled by synchronous replication. If we aren't using sync rep, then we can wait for the standby to catch up with an action on the master, remembering that the master will have moved on by the time we've done this. To perform the wait you need to do the following:

1. On the master, perform an action that writes WAL. Just for testing purposes—not for real usage—we can issue a request like this:

    ```
    SELECT pg_create_restore_point('my action name');
    ```

2. On the master, commit the transaction using COMMIT; with any setting other than `synchronous_commit = off`.

3. On the master, find the current write location using this query:

    ```
    SELECT pg_current_xlog_write_location();
    ```

4. On the standby, execute the following query repeatedly until the LSN value returned is equal to or higher than the LSN from the master:

    ```
    SELECT pg_last_xlog_replay_location();
    ```

The following function performs such a wait (for PostgreSQL 9.4 and higher versions). Similar code can be used on earlier releases:

```
CREATE OR REPLACE FUNCTION wait_for_lsn(loc pg_lsn)
RETURNS VOID
LANGUAGE plpgsql
```

```
AS $$
DECLARE
    currloc pg_lsn;
BEGIN
/*  IF NOT pg_is_in_recovery() THEN
        RETURN;
    END IF;  */


    LOOP
        IF pg_last_xlog_replay_location() >= loc THEN
            RETURN;
        END IF;
        PERFORM pg_sleep(0.1);   /* 100ms */
    END LOOP;
END $$;
```

Logical Replication

Logical Replication allows us to stream logical data changes between two nodes. By logical, we mean streaming changes without referring to specific physical attributes such as block number and row ID.

The main benefits of Logical Replication are as follows:

▸ Performance is roughly two times better than that of the best trigger-based mechanisms

▸ Selective replication is supported, so we don't need to replicate the entire database

▸ Replication can occur between different major releases (PostgreSQL 9.4 onwards), which can allow a zero-downtime upgrade

PostgreSQL 9.4 provides a feature called Logical Decoding. This allows you to stream a set of changes out of a master server. This allows a master to become a sending node in Logical Replication. The receiving node requires the logical replication plugin to allow replication between two nodes.

Previously, we referred to physical replication as "streaming replication". Now, we have to modify our descriptions so that we can refer to **Physical Streaming Replication** (**PSR**) and **Logical Streaming Replication** (**LSR**). In terms of security, network data transfer, and general management, the two modes are very similar. Concepts used to monitor PSR can also be used to monitor LSR.

Since the target systems are fully writable masters in their own right, we can use the full power of PostgreSQL without restrictions. We can use temporary tables, triggers, different user accounts, and GRANT permissions differently. We can also define indexes differently, collect statistics differently, and run VACUUM on different schedules.

As a result, calling nodes just as "sending" and "receiving" nodes isn't enough. We refer to them as upstream and downstream masters.

Getting ready

Logical Replication is possible only when the master uses a wal_level value of logical.

All nodes involved in logical replication must have the extension installed:

CREATE EXTENSION btree_gist;

CREATE EXTENSION bdr;

shared_preload_libraries = 'bdr'

Any user-installed data types must exist on both the sending and receiving nodes.

Identify all the nodes that will work together as parts of your replication architecture:

- Each LSR link can replicate changes from a single database. If you have multiple databases in your PostgreSQL server, you will need one LSR link per database (not counting template0 and template1).
- Each LSR link will use one connection and one slot. Set the max_replication_ slots and max_connections parameters to match those requirements.
- Each LSR link requires one WAL sender on the master. Set max_wal_senders to match this requirement.
- Each LSR link requires one apply process on the downstream master, which is one background worker process. Set max_worker_processes to match this requirement.

An example of a postgresql.conf file on the source node for the preceding steps looks like this:

```
# Record data for logical replication
wal_level = 'logical'
# Load the BDR extension
shared_preload_libraries = 'bdr'
 # Allow replication slot creation (we need just one but it does not
hurt to have more)
max_replication_slots = 10
```

```
# Allow streaming replication (we need one for slot and one for
basebackup but again, it does not hurt to have more)
max_wal_senders = 10
```

Logical Replication supports selective replication, which means that you don't need to specify all the tables in the database. Identify the tables to be replicated. Define Replication Sets that correspond to groups of tables that should be replicated together. Ensure that all the transactions that touch any table in the set touch only a subset of the set, or the whole set.

Tables that will be replicated may need some preparatory steps as well. To allow logical replication to apply UPDATE and DELETE commands correctly on the target node, we need to define how we search for unique rows. This is known as the replica identity. By default, the replica identity will be the primary key of a table, so you need not take any action if you have already defined primary keys on your tables. In some cases, you may need to define the replica identity explicitly, using a command like this:

`ALTER TABLE mytable REPLICA IDENTITY USING INDEX myuniquecol_idx;`

Logical Replication also supports filtered replication, which means that only certain actions are replicated on the target node; for example, we can specify that INSERT commands are replicated while DELETE commands are filtered away. This allows Logical Replication to support a greater range of data movement applications than was previously possible with Slony or Londiste.

How to do it...

Commands for Logical Replication are simple, but the software is planned to undergo rapid development, and the command specifications are subject to change. Check out http://www.2ndQuadrant.com/BDR/ for the latest details.

How it works...

Logical Decoding is very efficient because it reuses the transaction log data (WAL) that was already being written for crash safety. Triggers are not used at all for this form of replication. Physical WAL records are translated into logical changes, which are then sent to the receiving node. Only real data changes are sent; no records are generated from changes to indexes, cleanup records from VACUUM, and so on. So, bandwidth requirements are somewhat reduced, depending on the exact application.

Changes are discarded if the top-level transaction aborts (save points and other subtransactions are supported normally). Changes are applied in the order of the transactions committed, so replication never breaks because it sees an inconsistent sequence of activities, as can occur with other cruder replication techniques such as statement-based replication.

On the receiving side, changes are applied using direct database calls, leading to a very efficient mechanism. SQL is not re-executed, so volatile functions in the original SQL don't produce any surprises. For example, suppose you make an update like this:

```
UPDATE table
SET
 col1 = col1 + random()
,col2 = col2 + random()
WHERE key = value
```

Then, the final calculated values of `col1` and `col2` are sent, instead of repeating the functions when we apply the changes. Triggers are not fired on the apply node.

Logical Replication will work even if you update one or more columns of the key (or any other replica identity), since it will detect that situation and send the old values of the columns with the changed row values. Statements that write many rows get turned into a stream of single row changes.

Locks taken at table-level (`LOCK`) or row-level (`SELECT ... FOR...`) are not replicated, nor are `SET` or `NOTIFY` commands.

Logical replication doesn't suffer from cancellations of queries on the apply node in the way Hot Standby does. There isn't any need for a feature such as `hot_standby_feedback`.

Both the sending and receiving nodes are masters, so it would be technically possible for writes (`INSERT`, `UPDATE`, and `DELETE`) and/or row-level locks (`SELECT ... FOR...`) to be made on the apply-side database. As a result, it is possible that local changes could lock out, slow down, or interfere with the application of changes from the source node. It is up to the user to enforce restrictions to ensure that this does not occur. You can do this by having a user role defined specifically for replication and then using `REVOKE` on all access apart from the `SELECT` privilege to replicated tables, rather than the user role applying the changes.

Data can be read on the apply side while changes are being made. That is just normal, and it's the beautiful power of PostgreSQL's MVCC feature.

The use of Replication Slots means that if the network drops, or if one of the nodes is offline, we can pick up the replication again from the precise point we stopped.

There's more...

LSR can work alongside PSR. There are no conflicting parameters; just ensure that all requirements are met for both PSR and LSR.

In PostgreSQL 9.4, neither DDL nor sequences are replicated; only the data changes (DML) are sent. Only the full version of BDR provides these features at present.

Logical Replication is one-way only, so if you want multimaster replication, see the *Bi-Directional Replication* recipe. Logical Replication provides cascaded replication.

See also

Logical Replication is part of the BDR project; you can get further details about it in the *Bi-Directional Replication* recipe and at `http://www.2ndQuadrant.com/BDR/`.

Bi-Directional Replication

Bi-Directional Replication (**BDR**) is a project used to allow multimaster replication with PostgreSQL. There is a range of possible architectures. The first use case we support is "all-nodes-to-all-nodes". BDR will eventually support a range of complex architectures, which is discussed later.

BDR is a fully open source project owned by the PostgreSQL Global Development Group. BDR aims for eventual inclusion within core PostgreSQL, though knowing that is a long and rigorous process, it also aims to provide working software solutions, now!

BDR aims to allow the nodes of the cluster to be physically distributed, allowing worldwide access to data and allowing for disaster recovery. Each BDR master node runs individual transactions; there is no globally distributed transaction manager.

BDR includes replication of data changes and data definition (DDL) changes. New tables are added automatically, ensuring that managing BDR is a low-maintenance overhead for applications.

BDR also provides global sequences, if you wish to have a sequence that works across a distributed system. Normal "local" sequences are not replicated.

The key advantage of BDR is that you can segregate your write workload across multiple nodes by application, user group, or geographical proximity. Each node can be configured differently, yet all work together to provide access to the same data. Some examples of use cases for this are as follows:

- Social media applications, where users need fast access to their local server, yet the whole database needs a single database view to cater for links and interconnections.
- Distributed businesses, where orders are taken by phone in one location and by websites in another location. Then, they are fulfilled via several other locations.
- Multinational companies that need fast access to data from many locations, yet wish to see a single, common view of their data.

BDR builds upon the basic technology of Logical Replication, enhancing it in various ways. We refer heavily to the previous recipe, *Logical Replication*.

Getting ready

Currently, BDR can be deployed in the all-to-all architecture, which has been tested on clusters of up to 99 master nodes. Each of those nodes is a normal, fully functioning PostgreSQL server that can perform both reads and writes.

BDR connects directly between each node, forming a mesh or plex of connections. Changes flow directly to other nodes in constant time, no matter how many nodes are in use. This is quite different from circular replication used by other database systems.

All BDR nodes should have `pg_hba.conf` definitions to allow paths between each node. It would be easier to have these settings the same on all nodes, but that is not required.

Each node requires one LSR link to all other nodes for each replicated database. So, a 32-node BDR cluster will require 31 LSR links per node. Ensure that the parameters are configured to allow for this and any possible future expansion. The parameters should be the same on all nodes to avoid confusion. Remember that changes require restarting.

BDR nodes also require configuring the mechanism for conflict detection:

```
track_commit_timestamps = on
```

BDR requires a modified version of PostgreSQL 9.4. The modifications are in the process of being merged into future versions of PostgreSQL, so this functionality should eventually become available as a part of the core PostgreSQL. Binary versions are available. Check out `http://www.2ndQuadrant.com/BDR/`.

How to do it...

To create a new node, we take a copy of one of the databases on the source nodes. This can be accomplished using either a physical base backup or a logical base backup. A physical copy includes all databases on the source node, so this mechanism is most suitable where there is only one active database on that node.

Command specifications are subject to change. Check out `http://www.2ndQuadrant.com/BDR/` for the latest details on them.

How it works...

BDR optimistically assumes that changes on one node do not conflict with changes on other nodes. Any conflicts are detected and then resolved automatically using a predictable "last update wins" strategy, though custom conflict handlers are supported to allow more precise definition for particular applications.

Applications that regularly cause conflicts won't run very well on BDR. Having said that, such applications would also suffer from lock waits and resource contention on a normal database; the effects will be somewhat amplified by the distributed nature of BDR, but only the existing problems are amplified. Applications that are properly designed to be scalable and contention free will work well on BDR.

BDR replicates changes at the row level. This has some implications for applications:

> ▶ Suppose we perform two simultaneous updates on different nodes like this:
>
> `UPDATE foo SET col1 = col1 + 1 WHERE key = value;`
>
> Then, in the event of a conflict, we will keep only one of the changes (the last change). What we might like in this case is to make the changes additive. This requires a custom conflict handler.

> ▶ Two updates that change different columns on different nodes will still cause replication conflicts.

Theoretically, you can resolve those conflicts before commit ("pre-commit") or after commit ("post-commit"). At the time of writing this book, BDR supports only post-commit conflict resolution, though there is work to provide both mechanisms in future.

BDR provides tools to diagnose and correct contention problems. Conflicts are logged so that they can be identified and removed at the application level. You can log either the conflicting statement or the entire conflicting transaction. Optionally, they can be also saved in a table for easier analysis.

There's more...

If a node fails, there is no requirement for failover, so other nodes continue processing normally—there is no wait for failover, nor is there the need for complex voting algorithms to identify the best new master. Failed servers will need to rejoin the cluster. It is possible to have each master protected by one or more physical standbys as well to provide a second layer of high availability.

Each of the master nodes supports normal physical streaming replication, so each master can be protected by one or more standby nodes to ensure that it stays up. Thus, BDR supports a two-level cluster architecture, where each master has its own private standbys.

BDR will eventually support a range of complex architectures:

> ▶ **Cascading**: BDR doesn't support cascading yet

> ▶ **Circular replication**: This reduces overhead of connections but is brittle, and the delay for changes to propagate through the cluster increases as the number of nodes increases

- **Group to group**: This involves more complex regional or geographically disparate systems
- **Central rollup**: This involves central servers sending changes from remote nodes
- **Central broadcast**: This involves central servers sending changes out to remote nodes

Archiving transaction log data

Starting with PostgreSQL 9.2, streaming replication can send transaction log data to a remote node even if the node is not a full PostgreSQL server. This can be useful for archiving copies of transaction log data for various purposes.

PostgreSQL includes two client tools to stream data from the server to the client. The tools are designed using a "pull" model; that is, you run the tools on the node you wish the data to be saved on:

- pg_receivexlog: This is available from PostgreSQL 9.2 onwards. It archives physical transaction log data (WAL files). This utility produces a straight copy of the original WAL files. Replication Slots are recommended when using this tool from 9.4 onwards.
- pg_recvlogical: This is available from PostgreSQL 9.4 onwards. It archives the results of logical decoding of transaction log data. This utility produces a copy of the transformed data rather than physical WAL. Replication slots are required for this tool. You will need to use that with a logical decoding plugin.

Getting ready

This recipe assumes you have already set up replication according to the earlier recipes so that wal_level, max_wal_senders and other parameters are set. Remember that for pg_recvlogical, you must set wal_level to logical.

This recipe is a different way of archiving WAL files than using archive_command, so you will likely want to unset that parameter if you use this recipe.

You will need to configure security just as you did for replication. So, you will need a PostgreSQL connection string, just as before.

Decide where you want to put the data on the client. Remember that WAL files look the same for each server, so you need to put them in a directory with a useful name so that you don't confuse files from different servers. You don't need to do this step for normal replication because streaming replication normally copies the files to the downstream node's pg_xlog directory.

How to do it...

To archive a physical WAL from a server called alpha, follow these steps:

1. If you decide to use Replication Slots, then create a slot using steps 1 to 3 of the *Using Replication Slots* recipe.

2. Execute the tool on the client:

   pg_receivexlog -D /pgarchive/alpha -d $MYCONNECTIONSTRING &

   If using slots, also use the --slot=slotname parameter on the command line.

If the connection from the client tool to the server is lost, the default behavior is to loop indefinitely while trying to re-establish a connection. If you want the client tool to exit if the connection is lost, then specify the –n or --no-loop options.

The pg_recvlogical utility requires some form of logical decoding plugin, so look at the instructions for the plugin you are using to describe exactly how to use that.

There's more...

While playing with this feature for the first time, try the --verbose option.

Replication monitoring will show pg_receivexlog and pg_recvlogical in exactly the same way as it shows other connected nodes, so there is no additional monitoring required. The default application_name is the same as the name of the tool, so you may want to set that parameter to something more meaningful to you.

With pg_recvlogical, you can use the --create-slot and --drop-slot options to control replication slots. From PostgreSQL 9.5 onwards, you can also use those options with pg_receivexlog.

From PostgreSQL 9.5 onwards, you can archive WAL files using synchronous replication by specifying pg_receivexlog --synchronous. This causes a disk flush (fsync) on the client so that WAL data is robustly saved to the disk, it then passes status information back to the server to acknowledge that the data is safe (whatever the setting of the -s parameter).

See also

If you want to browse the content of the WAL files, you'll need the pg_xlogdump program, which is an additional server-side utility. Regrettably, that doesn't yet allow you to make a remote connection to use it.

Upgrading – minor releases

Minor release upgrades are released regularly by all software developers, and PostgreSQL has its share of corrections. When a minor release occurs, we bump the last number, usually by one. So, the first release of a major release 9.4 is 9.4.0. The first set of bug fixes is 9.4.1, then 9.4.2, and so on.

This recipe is about moving from a minor release to minor release.

Getting ready

First, get hold of the new release, by downloading either the source or fresh binaries.

How to do it...

In most cases, PostgreSQL aims for minor releases to be simple upgrades. We make great efforts to keep the on-disk format the same for both data/index files and transaction log (WAL) files, but this isn't always the case. Some temporary files can change sometimes.

The upgrade process is as follows:

1. Read the release notes to see whether there are any special actions that need to be taken for this particular release.

2. If you have professional support, talk to your support vendor to see whether additional safety checks over and above the upgrade instructions are required or recommended. Also, verify that the target release is fully supported by your vendor on your hardware, OS, and OS release level; it may not be, yet.

3. Apply any special actions or checks; for example, if the WAL format has changed, then you may need to reconfigure log-based replication following the upgrade. You may need to scan tables, rebuild indexes, or perform some other actions. Not every release has such actions, but watch closely for them, because if they exist, then they are important.

4. If you are using replication, test the upgrade by disconnecting one of your standby servers from the master.

5. Follow the instructions for your OS distribution and binary packager to complete the upgrade. These can vary considerably.

6. Start up the database server being used for a test, apply any post-upgrade special actions, and check that things are working for you.

7. Repeat steps 4 to 6 for other standby servers.

8. Repeat steps 4 to 6 for the primary server.

How it works...

Minor upgrades mostly affect the binary files, so it should be a simple matter of replacing those files and restarting. But check.

Major upgrades in-place

PostgreSQL provides an Additional Supplied Program, called `pg_upgrade`, that allows you to migrate between major releases, such as from 9.1 to 9.2; or you can upgrade straight to the latest server version. These upgrades are performed in-place, meaning that we upgrade your database without moving to a new system. That does sound good, but `pg_upgrade` has a few things that you may wish to consider as potential negatives, which are as follows:

- The database server must be shut down while the upgrade takes place.

- Your system must be large enough to hold two copies of the database server: old and new copies. If it's not, then you have to use the link option of `pg_upgrade`, or use the *Major upgrades online* recipe later. If you use the link option on `pg_upgrade`, then there is no `pg_downgrade` utility. The only option in that case is a restore from backup, and that means extended unavailability while you restore.

- If you copy the database, then the upgrade time will be proportional to the size of the database.

- The `pg_upgrade` utility does not validate all your additional add-in modules, so you will need to set up a test server and confirm that these work, ahead of performing the main upgrade.

The `pg_upgrade` utility supports versions from PostgreSQL 8.3 onwards and allows you to go straight from your current release to the latest release in one hop.

Getting ready

Find out the size of your database (using the *How much disk space does a database use?* recipe in *Chapter 2, Exploring the Database*). If the database is large or you have an important requirement for availability, you should consider doing the major upgrade using replication tools as well. Then, check out the next recipe.

How to do it...

1. Read the release notes for the new server version to which you are migrating. Pay attention to the incompatibilities section carefully; PostgreSQL does change from release to release.

2. Set up a test server with the old software release on it. Restore one of your backups in it. Upgrade that system to the new release to verify that there are no conflicts from software dependencies. Test your application. Make sure you identify and test each add-in PostgreSQL module you were using to confirm that it still works at the new release level.

3. Back up your production server. Prepare for the worst; hope for the best!

4. Most importantly, work out who you will call if things go badly, and exactly how to restore from that backup you just took.

5. Install new versions of all the required software on the production server, and create a new database server.

6. Don't disable security during the upgrade. Your security team will do backflips if they hear about this. Keep your job!

7. Now, go and do that backup. Don't skip this step; it isn't optional. Check whether the backup is actually readable, accessible, and complete.

8. Shut down the database servers.

9. Run `pg_upgrade` and then run any required post-upgrade scripts. Make sure you check whether any were required.

10. Start up the new database server and immediately run a server-wide `ANALYZE` operation.

11. Run through your tests to check whether it worked or you need to start performing the contingency plan.

12. If all is OK, re-enable wide access to the database server. Restart the applications.

13. Don't delete your old server directory if you used the link method. The old `data` directory still contains the data for the new database server. Confusing! So, don't get caught by this.

How it works...

The `pg_upgrade` utility works by creating a new set of database catalog tables, and then creating the old objects again in the new tables using the same identifiers as before.

The `pg_upgrade` utility works easily because the data block format hasn't changed between some releases. That won't always be the case; specifically, we expect the upgrade from PostgreSQL 9.x to 10.x to require an online upgrade via replication. Since we can't (always) see the future, make sure you read the release notes.

Major upgrades online

Upgrading between major releases is hard, and it should be deferred until you have some good reasons and sufficient time to get it right.

You can use replication tools to minimize the downtime required for an upgrade, so we refer to this recipe as **online upgrade**.

How to do it...

The following general steps should be followed, allowing at least a month for the complete process to ensure that everything is tested and everybody understands the implications:

1. Set up a new release of the software on a new test system.
2. Take a standalone backup from the main system and copy it to the test system. Test the applications extensively against the new release on the test system.
3. When everything works and performs correctly, then do the following:
   1. Set up a connection pooler to the main database (it may be there already).
   2. Set up replication using Londiste or Slony on the new system, if upgrading to 9.4. If upgrading to PostgreSQL 9.5 or a later release, use Logical Replication.
   3. Retest the application extensively against the new release on live data, then when ready for the final cut-over, we can do the following:
      1. Prepare a new connection pool config to point to the new system.
      2. Pause the connection pool.
      3. Switch over to the new system.
      4. Point the connection pool to the new system, and reload.

How it works...

Both Slony and Londiste work against multiple releases of PostgreSQL, so you can be sure that cross-release replication works and works well. The preceding recipe allows online upgrades with zero data loss because of the use of the clean switchover process. There's no need for lengthy downtime during the upgrade, and there's much reduced risk in comparison with an in-place upgrade. It works best with new hardware, and is a good way to upgrade the hardware or change the disk layout at the same time. This is also very useful for changing server encoding.

Logical Replication (BDR) allows you to upgrade from PostgreSQL 9.4 to 9.5 and beyond. That capability was one of the original design objectives of the BDR project.

Index

S

PostgreSQL Replication

ISBN: 978-1-84951-672-3   Paperback: 250 pages

Understand basic replication concepts and efficiently replicate PostgreSQL using high-end techniques to protect your data and run your server without interruptions

1. Explains the new replication features introduced in PostgreSQL 9.

2. Contains easy to understand explanations and lots of screenshots that simplify an advanced topic like replication.

3. Teaches PostgreSQL administrators how to maintain consistency between redundant resources and to improve reliability, fault-tolerance, and accessibility.

PostgreSQL 9 High Availability Cookbook

ISBN: 978-1-84951-696-9   Paperback: 398 pages

Over 100 recipes to design and implement a highly available server with the advanced features of PostgreSQL

1. Create a PostgreSQL cluster that stays online even when disaster strikes.

2. Avoid costly downtime and data loss that can ruin your business.

3. Perform data replication and monitor your data with hands-on industry-driven recipes and detailed step-by-step explanations.

Please check **www.PacktPub.com** for information on our titles